PUNK REVOLUTION!

PUNK REVOLUTION!

An Oral History of Punk Rock Politics and Activism

JOHN MALKIN
FOREWORD BY **KLEE BENALLY**

ROWMAN & LITTLEFIELD
Lanham • Boulder • New York • London

Published by Rowman & Littlefield
An imprint of The Rowman & Littlefield Publishing Group, Inc.
4501 Forbes Boulevard, Suite 200, Lanham, Maryland 20706
www.rowman.com

86-90 Paul Street, London EC2A 4NE

Copyright © 2023 by The Rowman & Littlefield Publishing Group, Inc.

Cover photos by John Malkin. Clockwise from upper left: Keith Morris (Black Flag, Circle Jerks, Off!), Greg Graffin (Bad Religion), Masha [Maria] Alyokhina and Kiryl Kanstantsinau (Pussy Riot), Jeff Ott (Fifteen), Andy Gill (Gang of Four), Jello Biafra and Kimo Ball (Dead Kennedys, Jello Biafra & The Guantanamo School of Medicine), Lenny Kaye (Patti Smith Band)

All rights reserved. No part of this book may be reproduced in any form or by any electronic or mechanical means, including information storage and retrieval systems, without written permission from the publisher, except by a reviewer who may quote passages in a review.

British Library Cataloguing in Publication Information Available

Library of Congress Cataloging-in-Publication Data
Names: Malkin, John, editor.
Title: Punk revolution! : an oral history of punk rock politics and activism / [edited by] John Malkin.
Description: Lanham : Rowman & Littlefield, 2023. | Includes bibliographical references and index.
Identifiers: LCCN 2022056447 (print) | LCCN 2022056448 (ebook) | ISBN 9781538171721 (cloth) | ISBN 9781538171738 (ebook)
Subjects: LCSH: Punk rock music—Political aspects—History. | Punk rock musicians—Interviews. | LCGFT: Oral histories.
Classification: LCC ML3918.R63 P86 2023 (print) | LCC ML3918.R63 (ebook) | DDC 781.66—dc23/eng/20221129
LC record available at https://lccn.loc.gov/2022056447
LC ebook record available at https://lccn.loc.gov/2022056448

Dedicated to Bodhi
and the next generation

John Malkin interviews Dick Lucas after 2008 Subhumans concert in Santa Cruz, California. Photo by Matt Fitt

CONTENTS

FOREWORD ix

ACKNOWLEDGMENTS AND GRATITUDE xi

INTRODUCTION "What You Think Changes How You Act" xiii

1   **MIXING PUNK AND POLITICS** Common Ground for the Revolution   1

2   **DO IT YOURSELF** DIY Together   19

3   **WE ARE ALL PUSSY RIOT** Punk on the Front Lines, Russia to Myanmar, China to Mexico   37

4   **EAST BERLIN PUNK** Clandestine Concerts behind the Berlin Wall   51

5   **MUSIC IS THAT POWERFUL TOOL** Blackfire Navajo Punks   69

6   **TIJUANA NO!** Latin Punk Rock from Peru to Mexico to East LA   85

7   **PANSY DIVISION** Out of the Closet, into the Slampit   95

8   **POSITIVE FORCE** Mark Andersen and Fugazi in Washington, DC   111

9   **"FIGHT WAR NOT WARS"** Punk Rock, Militarism, and War   125

10	**JUST ANOTHER GULF WAR** Punk, US Wars in Iraq and Afghanistan, and 9/11	147
11	**"AMERICA! FUCK YEAH!"** Punks Perform for US Soldiers	165
12	**"NAZI TRUMPS FUCK OFF!"** Punk in the Trump Era	175
13	**"I AM AN ANARCHIST"** Anti-authoritarian Soundtrack	189
14	**"TO HELL WITH POVERTY"** Capitalism and Class in Punk Rock	209
15	**"WHITE RIOT"** Race and Anti-racism in Punk	223
16	**"EQUAL BUT DIFFERENT"** Gender and Feminism in Punk	239
17	**THE REVOLUTION IS PERSONAL** Politics with a Small "P"	255
18	**THE REVOLUTION WILL BE COMMODIFIED**	271
19	**BURN PUNK LONDON** Joe Corré and Extinction Rebellion	293
20	**HOW REVOLUTIONARY HAS PUNK ROCK BEEN?**	303
21	**WHERE IS THE REVOLUTION NOW?**	315

NOTES 331
LIST OF INTERVIEWS 335
INDEX 341
ABOUT THE AUTHOR 357

FOREWORD

Punk is undead.

I came into punk in the '80s when it still had a pulse. I found refuge in the electric signals reproduced by magnets in the Side A and Side B of tape deck riots. I found affinity against existential traumas in the circle pit. Angsty diatribes at 180 beats per minute shaped and defined my rejection of authority. The blunt "fuck you" manifesto of punk rock was readily cut and pasted onto the Indigenous resistance struggles I was born into. I still adorn myself with turquoise and spikes while preparing for a protest, "Hey Ho, Let's Go!"

The killing of punk was mostly in its domestication, in the shaping of it as a commodified artifact. As it initially was an expression of class warfare, the threat it once posed had been bled out into shopping malls and superficial songs steeped in its own consumption. It had been rendered a perpetual lifestylist rebellion—never quite critical enough to personify the revolution it is attributed and never quite "revolutionary" enough to finish the job and do itself in while taking the society it initially rejected along with it.

Is punk's history of antagonisms against the dominant social order what makes it "revolutionary"? Do "fuck you's" etched deep into wax grooves count for dramatic social transformation? Do patches and spikes on covers of glossy magazines herald the change of social order? Is it in the freedom from authoritarian control that is celebrated in squatted buildings? Is it in insurrectionary riots with burning garbage bins and a G.L.O.S.S. song buzzing in your head? Is it dumpster diving for Food Not Bombs? Or is it that punk deviance was simply a rock smashing the spectacle of mainstream society's moral aesthetics into irreparable pieces?

FOREWORD

Punk was a going against—an affinity of rages—a self and collective destruction of the imposed identity of the social order that those who identified as "punks" were subordinate to. Punk embraced and celebrated that its deviance was so vilified. It was first an implicit expression of social war: a direct threat to the ruling class. The fervor against punk was mostly due to the matter that the elite class's own children were rejecting the world they had built for them. It's no surprise that punk would proliferate in Britain considering their genocidal and ecocidal project of spreading "civilization." The cacophony of colonial capitalist society turning against itself gave birth to punk. In its most spectacular dramatic form, punk embodied raw antisocial expression. At its worst, punk reveled in its white dominance, casual privilege, and the profitability of its aesthetics. While it exists as a sub- and countercultural antagonism, it also exists as a reactionary working-class fetish reinforcing the very institutions it professes to rebel against. But punk's initial appeal—its spirit—is a living dead force of social transformation. Punk is undead.

John Malkin is an adept necromancer. There are few who would be willing and capable of digging so deeply into the undead corpse of punk to reanimate and interpret its multitude of contradictions. As part historian and part subcultural archaeologist, Malkin conducts an ontological summoning of the spirit (or essence) of punk. In a grotesque and beautiful process, the living dead words of aged and aging punks (and some, like Lydon, who are just lifeless caricatures of their former selves) are topographically arranged in raw interviews the way that you'd imagine Gee Vaucher would be wrestling Banksy in the twisted trash-pile-wreckage aftermath of a Van's Warped Tour show.

Malkin stage dives right in and pulls us into the swirling mosh pit of the open conflicts that punk will always be. When you turn these pages, hear the sleeve come off the seven-inch and the drop of the needle. The raw buzz of an ungrounded amp at max volume with a broken speaker cone. There is something uncomplicated and mysterious in the discordant power of this undead force that was unleashed decades ago with just three chords and distorted amplification, this antagonistic spirit we call "punk."

—Klee Benally, January 2023

ACKNOWLEDGMENTS AND GRATITUDE

I know this book has taken twenty years to create because I've got a marker: the September 19, 2004, *Boston Sunday Globe* mentioned I was working on this book in an article titled "Zen and the Art of Slam Dancing" by David F. Smydra Jr.

I'm grateful to all who have supported my two-decade effort, especially my wife, Alison, and son, Bodhi. Early on in 2003, Noah Levine told me, "I'm glad you're writing this book—now I don't have to." Gary Gach reminded me to keep doing what I love. Lori Wilde and John Stockberger offered optimism that I'd find a publisher. Bridget Lyons, Erin Cusick, Bryan Ray Turcotte, Rachel Neumann, David Ensminger, and Jana Anderson offered feedback and encouragement. Thoughtful conversations with friends and relatives helped propel my ideas, including Ed Colver, Gabriel Constans, Scott Clements, Petra Serafim, Dave the gardener, Jason Arredondo, Matthew Embry, Trey Donovan, Natalya Bruner, Antonino D'Ambrosio, Keith McHenry, Chris Krohn, Ron Pomerantz, Grant Wilson, Tim Fitzmaurice, Meris Walton, Susan Rockrise, Rene Netter, Paula Lykins, Scott Smyers, Chris Cutri, Bart Abicht, Erich Holden, and Paula Feuer. Thanks to Matt Fitt for the great photos and Lawrence Rachleff for technical support! Special thanks to Justin Cooper at Revelation Records, who encouraged me for many years, and David Zeltser, who told me to edit it down. Thanks to Beth Nauman-Montana for creating a great index for *Punk Revolution!*. It all started with my punk rock friends in H. B.—Chandler Haun, Tim Sharp, Wolfe Wilder, April Partin, Clare O'Regan, Jeff Cowart, David M., Ken Needham, Paul Dambski, Lynel and Stacey Murray, Linelle Lamson, and Matt Cox. Gratitude also to my punk friends in Berlin—Holger Roessler, Lutz

ACKNOWLEDGMENTS AND GRATITUDE

Helmke, Olaf Schreiber, Angela Bachfeld, and Christian Kesten. I'm grateful to Michael Tan at Rowman & Littlefield for providing valuable feedback and editing essential for completing this project. Many thanks to those who contributed images and photos for this project and to all the tour managers, publicists, producers, oracles, and friends of friends who helped me make contact with a multitude of talented, thoughtful musicians and activists. I'm deeply grateful to everyone I've been able to interview. It's been exhilarating to share ideas with so many creative, courageous people.

I have made considerable effort to find and contact the copyright owners of images and seek permission from interviewees. Should the rights owners come forth, I shall obtain permissions and include the appropriate permissions wording in future printings of this book. My interviews with Henry Rollins (Black Flag) are not included in this book and are available online.

INTRODUCTION
"WHAT YOU THINK CHANGES HOW YOU ACT"

Punk is what brought back the spirit of rock 'n' roll.

—Jello Biafra (Dead Kennedys)

Punk rock is dead. Punk is profitable. Punk rock created a great ethos for living. Punk is changing the world. No matter what you think about punk rock, it's now heard all over the planet. It could be argued that punk is now bigger than ever. New bands continue springing up while some of punk's legends—Iggy Pop, Patti Smith, and John Lydon—continue to record and tour. During 2020 and 2021 you could've seen live shows by Gang of Four, X, Charged GBH, Social Distortion, TSOL, Sonic Youth, Good Riddance, Swans, Pussy Riot, Peter Murphy, Billy Idol, Shelter, Cro-Mags, Blondie, Public Image Limited, The Damned, The Mekons, Dead Kennedys, Joan Jett, The Dickies, Jello Biafra and The Guantanamo School of Medicine, Pennywise, Adolescents, Circle Jerks, The Vandals, Agent Orange, Bad Religion, and on and on. In 2019 Subhumans released *Crisis Point*, their first album in twelve years. In early 2023, Iggy Pop, now 75 years young, released a new album titled *Every Loser*. The year 2022 saw the release of memoirs by Kid Congo Powers (*Some New Kind of Kick*), Greg Graffin (*Punk Paradox*), and James Spooner (*The High Desert: Black. Punk. Nowhere*). Steve Ignorant toured Britain in 2020 performing Crass songs and Anti-Flag's 2023 album is titled *Lies They Tell Our Children*.

Like all performing arts, punk rock tours ended at the beginning of the pandemic and continue to be affected even now. On August 11, 2022, Blondie tweeted, "While we work to overcome recent positive COVID tests, we regret to announce this Sunday's Blondie performance at LB Pavilion (Boston) will

INTRODUCTION

need to be rescheduled." Recent years have also seen the death of some of punk's greatest including Ian Dury (March 27, 2000), Joey Ramone (April 15, 2001), Lux Interior (2009), Ari Up (2010), Poly Styrene (2011), Lou Reed (2013), Mark E. Smith (2018), Glenn Branca (2018), Andy Gill (2020), Sylvain Mizrahi (2021), Keith Levene (2022), and D. H. Peligro (2022).

Meanwhile the energized sounds, ideas, and fashion of punk rock continue to find their way into literature, films, ads, and political philosophy. The female character in the 2014 Swedish film *The Girl Who Kicked the Hornet's Nest* is invariably referred to as "punk" in movie reviews because of a tough attitude, Mohawk haircut, and sexually alluring leather clothes. The 2017 young adult novel *The First Rule of Punk* by Celia C. Perez presents "a classic tale of friendship, identity, and punk rock!"

A musical play based on Green Day's *American Idiot* album was performed 422 times on Broadway during 2010 and 2011. Children's TV cartoons like "Phineas and Ferb" and "Johnny Test" have theme songs that sound like Green Day and Buzzcocks. And Rick Riordan's bestselling young adult novels are filled with references to punk rock like "she wore jeans and a black leather jacket that was held together with safety pins and had patches for the Ramones and Dead Kennedys."[1]

Marjane Satrapi's autobiographical graphic novel and film *Persepolis* (2007) illustrates the distance that punk traveled, inspiring youth rebellion in 1970s Iran. Meanwhile, the British-based Punk Scholars Network was founded in 2012 to organize "conferences, symposiums, publications, talks and exhibitions, whilst seeking to maintain its original aim as an international forum for scholarly debate."[2] The Las Vegas Punk Rock Museum opened in January 2023 and is also "a bar, a tattoo parlor, a wedding chapel, a punk shop and more."[3] Meanwhile *Punk Science: Inside the Mind of God* by Dr. Manjir Samanta-Laughton "outlines a new vision of the cosmos."[4]

PUNK REVOLUTION!

The punk revolution arrived on the heels of the 1960s hippie peace movement that had encompassed a variety of perspectives: anti-war, civil rights, free speech, feminism, and Black, Chicano, and Native American power. The year 1968 marked a year of extreme backlash against the 1960s revolution with police/military riots and massacres in Mexico City, Tokyo, London, and Berkeley, to name a few. Both Martin Luther King Jr. and US senator Robert Kennedy were assassinated in 1968 and in 1969 the FBI assassinated two Black Panthers in Chicago: Mark Clark and Fred Hampton. Earlier, in 1965, Malcolm X was assassinated. In 1970, state violence responded to anti-war demonstrators, leaving four students dead and nine wounded at Kent State University (Ohio) and two killed and twelve wounded at Jackson State College (Mississippi).

In the mid-1970s and early 1980s punk rock was a blast of fresh revolutionary energy that called for a wider perspective on politics and society. Punks channeled their anger about racism, poverty, and war into energy that aimed to destroy harmful social institutions and construct new DIY communities built on music and cooperation. Punk rock has often provided the soundtrack for direct actions against corporate globalization and militarism. Fugazi performed in 1991 in Washington, DC, concerts to address poverty and oppose the initial US war on Iraq. Jello Biafra performed at the "Battle of Seattle" to disrupt the World Trade Organization in 1999 and Tom Morello (Rage Against the Machine) sang out against capitalism during the Occupy movement of 2011. Positive Force in Washington, DC, was created in 1985 as a hub for punk-infused activism and communal living and Crass, the band, was one project among many from a group of British activists and artists living outside of the established society. Today, Positive Force DC and Dial House continue as thriving experiments in living free.

Punk bands and activists continue to sing out and protest against unjust economic/social/political systems and build communities based on mutual aid. Klee Benally of Navajo punk band Blackfire provided masks, food, water, and hand-washing stations for the hardest hit during the early days and months of isolation in the ongoing COVID-19 pandemic. Mark Andersen, cofounder of the Washington, DC, Positive Force activist collective, is still meeting people's needs by delivering groceries to low-income residents. Masha Alyokhina continues her activism with Pussy Riot after her 2022 escape from Russia following arrests in 2021 for attending protests and posting on social media. Kyaw Thu Win and his punk band Rebel Riot continue to serve food to hungry and unhoused people in Myanmar as a local branch of the international organization Food Not Bombs and in early 2022 participated in a traveling exhibition to Manchester, England, called "A New Burma" to build resistance against the current military regime in Myanmar. Also in 2022, Dave Dictor (Millions of Dead Cops) and Grimace Records released the first three of six compilations titled "Punk for Ukraine" to oppose the ongoing Russian invasion of Ukraine and raise funds for Doctors Without Borders.

Not all punk is political or revolutionary. The wild "anything goes" sensibility of punk quickly split into myriad expressions and has been combined with anything and everything: Buddhism; living drug and alcohol free; Celtic, country, and electronic music; humor; hip-hop; Christianity; feminism; Islam; and white power. Some manifestations became violent, authoritarian, and macho, demanding that punk's free expression be confined to a particular sound and style: fast and furious with cropped haircuts. Corporate record labels and musicians have teamed up to package the punk revolution as another source for profit.

Punk Revolution! is partly a self-reflection by the players on how well punk has fared through the hurdles of creativity and social change while grappling with the day-to-day challenges of life within capitalism. *Punk Revolution!* is also a celebration of the first forty-five years of punk rock. Some of the voices within these pages say plainly, "Punk rock saved my life." These discussions are best read like a documentary film that flows among diverse voices around the world and across decades offering ideas, critiques, and insights that can be applied to contemporary revolutionary movements for justice, peace, and living free.

FORTY-FIVE YEARS YOUNG

The *New York Times* celebrated the fortieth birthday of punk rock with two stories on August 14, 2016, by Christopher D. Shea, "Forty Years On, What Does Punk Rock Mean?" and "Hey Ho, It's Old: England Embraces Punk Rock 40 Years Later." In the latter article, Steve Diggles of The Buzzocks says of an early Sex Pistols gig at Lesser Free Trade Hall in Manchester on June 4, 1976, "If Jesus was born in Bethlehem, British punk was born in Manchester at that gig."

In 2016 the London establishment also celebrated punk rock's birthday with exhibits and shows and by curating something of a Sex Pistols museum in the house where bandmembers had lived back in the day. John Lydon's magic marker graffiti from the 1970s still adorns the walls of the building now "preserved" by the Department of Culture. Heritage Minister David Evennett was quoted in the British press: "These 17th-century townhouses not only exhibit well-preserved architectural detail but helped nurture Soho's influence on the global music industry during the 1960s and 1970s. As we celebrate 40 years of punk, I'm delighted to be granting further protection to these buildings, which acted as a home and studio to the Sex Pistols."[5]

In March 2022, when lawyer Stella Moris married imprisoned WikiLeaks founder Julian Assange, she wore a graffiti-filled wedding dress designed by Vivienne Westwood. Back in the 1970s Westwood partnered with Malcolm McLaren to design early punk fashion while McLaren was manager for the Sex Pistols. Their son Joe Corré, born in 1967, also became a fashion designer. In a dramatic winter 2016 protest against the commodification of punk called

INTRODUCTION

Burn Punk London, Corré burned £5 million worth of Sex Pistols memorabilia including T-shirts, vinyl, and Sid Vicious dolls handmade by his parents.

MUSIC OF NO MUSIC

Punk rock has sometimes been an attempt to take music beyond the confines of music, thereby manifesting the *music of no music*. This sentiment easily coalesces with Alan Watts's 1951 book, *The Wisdom of Insecurity*, where he describes Buddhism as *"the religion of no religion."* These negations point to the reality that living free requires no intermediary between you and your life. In practice, many punk artists have removed the middleman/authority from performance, recording, touring, and record distribution. This autonomous force draws on the great history of social-political activists who have connected with life directly. Today, punk rock continues forward as a DIY way of life.

> *Everything is connected with everything else.*
> —Sign on studio wall at end of video for
> "Failed Imagineer" by Propagandhi (2017)

How will rock and roll evolve next? Will it be a catalyst for rebellion, compassion, and living free? What kinds of sound and noise will young (and middle-aged and old) people combine and invent to subvert domination cultures and create self-designed social systems? The revolutionary movements that swept Northern Africa and the Middle East in 2010 (the Arab Spring) were propelled by political idealism, hip-hop, and DIY sensibilities. Uprisings in Tunisia, Egypt, Yemen, Libya, Kuwait, and elsewhere helped to inspire the Occupy movements of Europe and the United States. How will youth of 2030 or 2060 express anger and creativity through music, art, and action? In times of authoritarian control artists often become frontline activists in the struggle to fan the flames of radical and compassionate action. *What you think changes how you act.* Don't believe everything you think. Question authority. Do it together.

LISTEN TO THIS!

The interviews within *Punk Revolution!* span twenty-five years and were originally broadcast on Free Radio Santa Cruz (1997 to 2017), San Francisco

INTRODUCTION

Liberation Radio (1999–2000), and KZSC at the University of California Santa Cruz (2016 to the present). Sections of some interviews were previously published in *Z Magazine*, *Razorcake*, *Punk Planet*, *Spirituality & Health*, *Lion's Roar*, *Adbusters*, *Alternet*, *Indymedia*, *In These Times*, the *Santa Cruz Sentinel*, and *Santa Cruz Good Times*.

Punk Revolution! is the first book in a set of three based on 250 interviews. *Punk Spirit* focuses on spirituality and punk rock and *Punk Roots* dives into the origins of punk and how it has rippled out to invigorate other musical genres and social-political landscapes. I'm personally grateful that punk rock came along when I was a teenager and that it has supported my own creativity and activism for forty years, including efforts to end militarism and the CIA, free political prisoners, support Indigenous cultures, and defund/abolish police and prisons.

MIXING PUNK AND POLITICS
COMMON GROUND FOR THE REVOLUTION

The original aim of rock and roll when it first came out was to establish an alternative media.

—David Bowie (Anthony O'Grady, *New Music Express*, August 1975)

Should we be assimilationists as gay people and try to placate the mainstream? Or are we more liberationists?

—Jon Ginoli (Pansy Division)

Talk Minus Action Equals Zero.

—Slogan of D.O.A. (Vancouver, BC, Canada)

I've often reflected on the fact that it was from the 1979 film *Apocalypse Now* and a punk rock band that I first learned that the US war in Vietnam (1968–1975) included egregious bombing and murder in the neighboring countries of Cambodia and Laos. The 1979 song "Holiday in Cambodia" by Dead Kennedys also made a significant political-philosophical connection; these US acts of state-sanctioned terrorism contributed to the rise of Pol Pot in Cambodia and the subsequent genocidal rampage. A parallel can be drawn to the more recent birth of terrorist groups in the Middle East like Al Qaida and the self-proclaimed Islamic State in response to long-running US wars and militarism in Iraq, Afghanistan, Libya, Lebanon, Palestine, and elsewhere before and after the September 11, 2001, attacks on the United States.

CHAPTER 1

In opposing capitalism, militarism, and racial patriarchy, activists choose either actions that attempt to reform current systems or they engage in building new, self-designed social systems based on collaboration instead of coercion. That's revolution. Punk rock artists have engaged in a wide spectrum of activism ranging from establishment politics to anarchist anti-politics.

Jello Biafra of Dead Kennedys came in fourth place in 1979 when he ran for mayor of San Francisco. At the massive 1999 "Battle of Seattle" protests against the World Trade Organization, Biafra and former members of Nirvana and Soundgarden performed together on December 1 as the No WTO Combo. The live album of that performance was released by Biafra's Alternative Tentacles Records, and Biafra told MTV News, "The protests in Seattle were important not because it was any sort of revolution, but because it may be the shot heard 'round the world that finally starts the long-term revolution against corporate feudalist dictatorship."[1] This impulse to create a kind of punk rock journalism was reflected in Biafra's sixth spoken word album, *Become the Media* (2000).

During the 2011 Occupy movement Anti-Flag performed at Zuccotti Park and Patti Smith donated a tent to house the People's Library at Occupy Wall Street. Canadian punks D.O.A. played for Houston Occupy and a year later recorded the song "We Occupy" with Jello Biafra for their album *We Come in Peace*. Tom Morello (Rage Against the Machine) and Biafra took the stage to refuel the revolution on the one-year anniversary of Occupy at a series of shows in New York City.

Punk musicians have put time, energy, and music into myriad socio-political movements. They've supported activist campaigns to increase voter turnout, release political prisoners like Mumia Abu Jamal, end mass incarceration and police brutality, support miners and unions, fund women's health centers, and enhance immigrant rights. Organizations like PETA, Greenpeace, Earth First!, Animal Liberation Front, Amnesty International, and Democracy Now! have been supported by punk musicians. Back in 1984 Dave Dictor (Millions of Dead Cops) and R Radical Records produced the *P.E.A.C.E.* compilation album and raised over $10,000 for grassroots anti-nuclear groups like Seeds of Peace, Seabrook Alliance, and Big Mountain–Navajo Group. The double album featured Dead Kennedys, Crass, Subhumans, Anti-Flag, and dozens of other international punk bands. In 2020 *P.E.A.C.E.* was re-released by Dictor and Grimace Records, with all streaming revenues benefiting COVID-19 relief by the anarchist organization Mutual Aid Disaster Relief. In 2020 Rebel Riot from Myanmar recorded a single with UK punks Throwing Stuff to benefit Black Lives Matter called "ACIYHAB" (All Cops Inside Your Head Are

Bastards). And Positive Force in Washington, DC has served as a center for radical organizing and punk music since the 1980s.

CHANGING THE WORLD

MARK ANDERSEN (Positive Force cofounder, author of *Dance of Days: Two Decades of Punk in the Nation's Capital*): The story for me begins with punk rock in the mid to late 1970s: Patti Smith, Sex Pistols, Clash, Avengers, Dils, and Stiff Little Fingers. That's what helped me be aware of my own critique of the world. And then helped me believe in the power I have to help change the world.

I was struggling as a lost and lonely teenage misfit in a very rural part of this country: Sheraton County, Montana. Searching for personal meaning and purpose helped bring me to activism. Punk rock was the bridge from the struggle for personal identity and purpose to seeing how that required me to step out of simply being concerned with myself to a broader engagement. Underneath it all, I now see that I was on a spiritual journey before punk, and punk became the vehicle to expand and fulfill that journey for the last thirty years. Punk is still part of that spiritual journey today.

When I refer to myself as "revolutionary" it goes in quotes. I also say "would-be revolutionary." This is an aspiration; this is what we're aiming towards. We're not there yet. I believe people have power to change the world and themselves. I think Karl Marx dealt with this when saying that people make history, but they don't make it just as they will. We're dealing with something that is beyond our comprehension, beyond the tools that we have at hand.

THURSTON MOORE (Sonic Youth): Punk came out of the gate as a political cry. It was political by its very nature by saying, "We're separating ourselves from these ideas of what success is." Punk rock was not, at first, at all having to do with money equating success. It was somewhat anti-money and anti-materialistic with no ambition towards that as far as success was concerned. It was really important music especially for people our age. It struck a chord. Of course, all of the bands were very young. They were all in their early twenties. You don't have sophisticated political thought. But then you started having groups like The Pop Group, who did "We Are All Prostitutes" and "She Is Beyond Good and Evil," which is one of the greatest post-punk political love songs of all time. They took the music of punk, funk, and reggae—all musics of the people—and mashed them together and made this wonderful sound.

CHAPTER 1

JELLO BIAFRA (Dead Kennedys / Guantanamo School of Medicine): Is it important that music be political? Anybody who is famous in this day and age, we all have a responsibility to speak up for people who don't have the avenues to speak up for themselves.

JM: I agree. You've said something pretty clear about that regarding Green Day. There's nothing wrong with them getting to be well known, but it would be nice if they used that for some positive social messaging.

JELLO BIAFRA: I may have said that before *American Idiot* came out.

JM: Yes, there are parts of that album that are pretty powerful.

JELLO BIAFRA: Overall, for somebody that big they've done a pretty good job of trying to figure out, and hang onto, who they are as people and where their souls are at. They had to deal with, first, the crab-in-the-bucket underground punk scene attitude that they're getting too big, and "We don't want to hear love songs," and stuff like that. Then they get *way*, way bigger and some people in the underground actually kind of declared war on them. To the point where Billy Joe told me that he had to glue a fake beard on himself to go to Gilman shows! To make sure people didn't give him a bunch of shit! It never should have come to that. That's in very stark contrast to hip-hop, for example. After my knee got smashed by thugs calling me, "Sell out! Sell out!" I asked, "Gee, why doesn't this happen to you?" They said, "It's different. We come from the hood where people don't grow up with a lot of money and our whole attitude is: if one of us actually makes it, it's a victory for the hood!"

EAST BAY RAY (Dead Kennedys): There were a lot of political bands back in the day, but some of that has gone out of date. There's a difference between journalism and poetry. Journalism comes and goes really quick, and poetry is more artistic and appeals at different times to different people. That's what I think of our music. We were so creative as a band together at the time and the music lasts. I notice that on tour, the response to the songs is just amazing.

THE POWER OF WORDS

JM: Punk rock took on a caricature in mainstream media of being violent. And some punk rock did become violent.

JOHN LYDON (Sex Pistols / Public Image Limited): There was politics behind that because we raised too many issues they didn't want to be answered. One of the major things in the early days was the royal family. Should that be openly discussed? I thought so. And that wasn't quite acceptable by British society then. I don't know if it is to this day. I followed that up with my fellow Sex Pistols with "Anarchy in the UK" and that got us into an open debate in the Houses of Parliament on the Traitors and Treason Act which carried a death penalty. So, there you go—the power of words. I have to dance the light fantastic sometimes.

LYDIA LUNCH (Teenage Jesus & The Jerks): The words are always the most important thing to me. The music is just a machine gun or a soft velvet caress, an irritant to back up the words. Oral tradition is one of the oldest forms of communication, the oldest art form. Even photographs come down to the titles. I never thought of myself as a performance artist. I'm not performing. I'm merely channeling parts of myself that need to come out. That's strictly what I do.

I've never been censored, and I've never felt I've been followed (by the FBI) because I'm just a small woman with a big mouth. I don't make enough money for them to care. They have bigger fish to fry. I'm on TSA approval and I didn't even apply—go figure that one out! But I've talked about tracking and surveillance for over a decade. I think I was one of the first artists to talk about RFID chips, which is just the latest way to track you.

Historically, artists like this have always been under the gun. Look at the Black Panthers or Angela Davis or the anti-Commie movement. Dead Kennedys had a lot of hassle because of the name Dead Kennedys. They were accosted for using Geiger's artwork, which is ridiculous. I debated Jack Thompson, who with Tipper Gore started the record labeling bullshit (Parents Music Resource Center), which also was part of Biafra's downfall. He was very vociferous against Tipper Gore. And now we have Al Gore, supposedly pro-environment (2015). And we have his wife, who is anti-art. Whatever, go figure.

My statement against Jack Thompson, it was the Two Live Crew controversy. I said, "What you don't get is that art is a reflection of society's problems. It is not the *creator* of society's problems. You're worried about violence being stimulated by pornography or rap or heavy metal music? Let's go back to the Bible, which has been responsible for more murder than any other book ever written." Once you say that, they have very little recourse. It's just the truth. The image of a nude and bloodied man, who happens to be your son, nailed to a cross bleeding, is one of the most pornographic images ever created. I did not create that. Although I wish I did.

JORDAN PUNDIK (New Found Glory): Politics is really important. I tend to get obsessive and I'm always on NPR, BBC, and CNN and I'm always reading. The Middle East crisis and ISIS—I kind of obsess about it. On the other hand, with the type of music that we do as a band, we don't have many political songs. There's so much of that going on that I feel our band is more of an escape where people can relate to reality in a personal way. All of that stuff is going on overseas and it's not something we should forget about, but I don't think it's that personal for people. When people listen to our records, they can forget about all of that stuff. We want to be a positive force in people's lives. There are a lot of different pathways in punk and our way is about feeling better about what's going on.

JM: The Social Distortion song "1945" is an example of the power of punk because it unveils a history that's become hidden. It's about the nuclear bombing of Japan by the United States government. Punk opened up the possibility of discussing in music some of the hidden histories of genocide, slavery, and war.

JONNY WICKERSHAM (Social Distortion): These bands have been talking about these things the whole time. It's true. Some older people from the punk rock scene may be laughing at these hardcore or thrash bands, but these kids were tackling subjects that nobody else was.

THE CLASH IS A NEWS BAND: CREATIVE RESPONSE

"The Clash is a news band." This is how Mick Jones described his band during a 1981 TV interview with a visibly nervous Tom Snyder. The band's only triple album—*Sandinista*—stands out as a uniquely political album offering analysis of socio-political realms including covert US wars, coups, and assassinations ("Washington Bullets"); the so-called Cold War ("Ivan Meets GI Joe"); resisting the draft ("The Call Up"); the US war on Vietnam ("Charlie Don't Surf"); and police brutality ("Police on My Back").

ANTONINO D'AMBROSIO (*Let Fury Have the Hour: Joe Strummer, Punk, and the Movement that Shook the World*): The Clash were the starting point of a cultural, political, social, spiritual, and emotional awakening for me. They were writing songs from the perspective of working people, about ideas of world citizenship and speaking truth to power through creativity. That is what I now call *creative response* and it's always been a core element in all my work. I'm always exploring that creative response whether it's in my film about Johnny Cash's sole protest album on behalf of Native Americans (*Bitter Tears: Ballads of the American Indian*, 1964) or Frank Serpico's efforts to expose abuse of police power.

Another thing I learned from The Clash and during my time with Strummer is: you're not going to find the answers in the political system. The political system is occupied with maintaining and pursuing power and the power is based in an ideology that doesn't bind us together. It depends on cynicism and living in the past. We've seen its awful effects with "Make America Great Again." We have this alternative idea from The Clash, and it goes back to Picasso painting *Guernica*. We find it throughout history and later with Woody Guthrie and Pete Seeger; this idea of collective action and solidarity with people who are suffering.

When I met with Joe Strummer in New York in 2001, I spent four days with him. He was very reflective about his history including some things he regretted that happened within the band, like firing their drummer, Topper Headon. Strummer told me that we have to have regrets. To me that was a rejection of the idea that we're indoctrinated with here that you can never be wrong, and everything has to be easy and comfortable. And that a person who has regrets is not successful. Strummer said, "It isn't about succeeding or failing. It's about trying." Perhaps the greatest creative response that we possess as human beings is that we survive. And that survival is this ultimate creative response, and it comes from never relenting and having will.

I got the sense from my conversation with Strummer that he felt he'd lived a life where he'd tried to do something positive, particularly with *Sandinista*. It was a very bold move to name a record after a guerrilla movement in Central America! He said the record label was extremely angry about it. Now, that record is starting to get its due as one of the great records of the last three or four decades.

JM: Your music has had political elements and yet I know you have ideas about how your music has been different than, for example, The Clash.

JOHN LYDON (Sex Pistols / Public Image Limited): I don't believe in sloganeering.

JM: At the same time, you've confronted racism and corporate power and tried to cultivate community. Why is that important to you?

JOHN LYDON: To be honest and direct is one of the gifts you're given in nature and to turn against that and fall into whatever is currently fashionable or fabulous or self-important is destructive. So, there it is.

CAMILLE ROSE GARCIA (The Real Minx): Growing up with bands like The Clash and Dead Kennedys I realized it was possible to make great music that was entertaining and also have social criticism. All punk rock really started out that way. It came out of an anger and frustration with the current situation. That was my ethos. That's what I wanted to do.

C. J. RAMONE (Ramones): The Clash and Dead Kennedys were both overtly political. Both were at the top of the pyramid of influential political bands. I'm more about people. I try to reach out to people in common terms. I don't really dive much into the overtly political thing. I always see a common thread, the thing that makes everybody kind of the same. That's what I try to get across in my music.

STEVEN BLUSH (author of *American Hardcore: A Tribal History*): Part of my hardcore trip was that I was disappointed with The Clash by the time they were doing *Combat Rock* (1982). I always felt that The Clash was my band! And then they became more rock and became everybody else's band! So, there's that

CHAPTER 1

elitist thing that comes with subculture where you dismiss things because they're popular. But you look back on The Clash and everything they were saying in their songs was spot on. Everything they said about race and politics; it was the musical education side of them. I know reggae music because of The Clash.

I was in England soon after "White Man in Hammersmith Palais" (1977) came out and they're singing about this guy "Ken Boothe for UK pop reggae" and I learned about the history of Brixton ska. I realized half of the songs on *London Calling* were covers. "Wrong 'Em Boyo" is a 1962 ska song. "Police on My Back" (*Sandinista*) was that band called The Equals, which was two white guys and two black guys. Eddy Grant from "Electric Avenue" was the singer. The Clash were doing musicology, politics, gender equality, racial integration. The hardcore bands were influenced by that aesthetic. It was so powerful.

DO THEY KNOW IT'S CHRISTMAS?

A type of political journalism resides within rock 'n' roll and this combination of pop and politics inspired singers like Bob Geldof and Midge Ure to be directly involved in both DIY activism and, at the other end of the spectrum, establishment politics. The Boomtown Rats singer is famous for his compassionate fundraising for the 1984 "Band Aid" charity group and their sympathetic song "Do They Know It's Christmas?" and the 1985 Live Aid Concerts, which reportedly raised one hundred million dollars for famine relief in Africa. A 1986 *Spin* magazine story reprinted on the thirtieth anniversary of Live Aid (July 13, 2015) was titled "Live Aid: The Terrible Truth." Summed up, "Live Aid had, through its missteps, exacerbated the already terrible humanitarian crisis" in Ethiopia, where donated food rotted due to shipping difficulties and charity money ended up in the hands of an oppressive political regime. Though filled with positive intentions, Live Aid is perhaps another vivid argument for punk rock–style DIY and self-organized solutions to social-political struggles.

> *Charity, it fills my heart / To help the poor in Africa*
> —"History of the World" by Gang of Four (1982)

There's a video of Bob Geldof on stage with The Boomtown Rats at a 2013 concert on the Isle of Wight. Geldof introduces the song "Somebody's Looking at You," saying, "This song was written in 1979 about the same thing you were reading about in the paper this morning." Geldof is referring to revelations about government spying revealed by WikiLeaks, ex-US soldier Bradley (Chelsea) Manning, and ex-CIA contractor Edward Snowden. "Somebody's Looking at You" includes the lyrics, "There's a spy in the sky / there's a noise on the wire / there's a tap on the line."

The song is from the album *Fine Art of Surfacing*, which also features "I Don't Like Mondays," a song that became a hit for the band, telling the story of a sixteen-year-old girl in San Diego, California, who shot up an elementary school playground in 1979. Brenda Ann Spencer killed three adults and injured eight children and one police officer. She told a reporter that she'd gone on the rampage because "I don't like Mondays. This livens up the day." Geldof and The Boomtown Rats were touring the United States when the shooting happened. Many more mass shootings have followed, as well as punk songs about them. (In 2017 there were about three hundred mass shootings in the United States [Gun Violence Archive]. From January to June 2022, there were already two hundred.) I always get chills listening to the 2000 song "Colorado" by Fifteen about the 1999 mass shooting at Columbine High School.

ROOM FOR JELLO

> *There's always room for Jello.*
>
> —Slogan for Biafra's 1979 campaign for San Francisco mayor (he came in fourth with 3.79 percent of the vote)

"If voting changed anything, they'd make it illegal." The statement is such a cliché because it holds some truth. Remember that the voting age in the United States was lowered from twenty-one to eighteen in 1971 by President Richard Nixon at the height of student protests against the US war in Vietnam. The Twenty-Sixth Amendment to the Constitution was the quickest ratification in US history, taking only about two months. Some members of Congress called for the age lowering explicitly to shift the focus of activist youth away from mass protest to the state-sanctioned "democratic" process.

Peter Garrett, singer with the punkish and highly political Australian band Midnight Oil, was elected as a Labor Party member of the House of Representatives in 2004 and appointed Minister for the Environment in 2007. Midnight Oil's 2022 world tour was in support of their album *Resist*. The 2021 film *Something Better Change* by Scott Crawford documents the journey of Joey "Shithead" Keithley (D.O.A.) being elected in 2018 as a Green Party candidate

CHAPTER 1

to the Burnaby City Council in British Columbia, Canada. And Justin Brannan, guitarist for hardcore punk metal band Indecision, is currently a council member in New York's District 43 since being elected in 2017. In 2018 Texas congressmember Beto O'Rourke, a former punk rock guitarist in the band FOSS, was on the campaign trail to hold his position and win an election against Republican Ted Cruz. On September 13, 2018, O'Rourke appeared on "The Late Show" (US):

Stephen Colbert: "Can politics be like punk rock?"
Beto O'Rourke: "I think so. I think we're proving that right now."

And during a televised debate on September 28, 2018, O'Rourke used lyrics from The Clash to describe political opponent Ted Cruz: "He's working for the clampdown!"

JELLO BIAFRA (Dead Kennedys): I take things issue by issue because I do vote. National Corporate Cartoon Puppet "A" versus Corporate Cartoon Puppet "B." I'd rather vote for something I want and not get it, rather than vote for something I don't want and get it. Thus, my conscience is clear. I never voted for Bill Clinton. I never voted for Obama and I sure as hell wasn't going to vote for Hillary! What Frank Zappa told me, which turned me around about voting at all, was this: *local elections are where it's at*. Hardly anybody votes on them and that's where people locally decide how a lot of that money from federal and state tax dollars and sales tax actually gets spent. A golf course? A football stadium? Or some public housing and better mass transit? That's how these things get decided. Every once in a while, there's a chance that somebody really cool can win locally. I've even voted for Democrats several times for state legislator; Tom Ammiano has been one of the best. He had to retire, but he said he used to go to Dead Kennedys shows at The Mabuhay.

JACK GRISHAM (TSOL): When I ran for governor (2003), I had no delusions that I was going to be successful. There was no way possible. You just take a little look at my background, and you've got a problem: drug use, underage marriages, arrests. Fifteen minutes after talking with someone they can get on the internet and see pictures of me in a dress! Come on, I didn't have a chance! The main reason I ran for governor of California was to bitch about healthcare. We don't take care of our people. I've got a problem with that. So, it was the one thing I told them, "Look I'll do it, but I'm not going to mention anything about my band. I refuse to talk about music. The only thing I want to talk about is healthcare, healthcare, healthcare! That's basically the whole reason I ran for governor."

PUNK VOTER

SCOTT GOODSTEIN (Punk Voter): Fat Mike from NOFX, post-2000 elections, founded Punk Voter. It started as an internet campaign. We quickly built a roster of over two hundred bands and thirty record labels and registered as an official voter education organization and started doing campaign activities. We're a small organization and Fat Wreck people donate their time. We felt there needed to be an organization giving kids more reasons as to why they need to participate in voting. We have a number of people who have talked about the things they're upset about, within the Bush administration. The war was one issue. The economy and jobs. The youth unemployment rate is 12 to 14 percent. People pay more on student loans than ever before. Young people suffer the most in the job market and are the ones going off to the war.

It's not shocking that young people are going to be mobilized and vocal about a number of issues like the environment and personal freedom and liberties, especially in the punk community; everything from the Patriot Act to Guantanamo Bay and Abu Ghraib. People are starting to wonder: *What type of America do we want to live in?* We do need to make sure these constitutional liberties are protected. And choice issues. It's nothing new for a punk band to be playing a benefit for the local Planned Parenthood chapter.

JM: Are there any difficulties appealing to punk people to get involved in politics? Some punk rock resonates with anarchist philosophy and takes an anti-state stance, where voting isn't seen as the most useful strategy for making change.

SCOTT GOODSTEIN: A lot of these folks rebel against their government. To be able to be in a country and have the right to dissent against your government is something that we stand for. The fact that Ashcroft used the Patriot Act against students at Drake University last November (2003) and then put a gag order on the university for being able to talk about it is bullshit! There's a ton of folks who want to be able to speak out and voice their opinions against the government and we feel that's what makes this country.

The punk idea of "We're all a bunch of anarchists" isn't the case. Most of the bands involved with Punk Voter aren't saying, "We love governments." They're saying that things have gotten so bad it's time to organize and make our voices heard. If you feel that your personal liberties and freedoms are under attack, and you're against the war and want to voice concern about the environment and you're not happy about the economy, speak out in any way possible. Voting is one aspect.

We've sold over one hundred thousand *Rock Against Bush* CDs in conjunction with Fat Wreck Chords. Punk kids are a smart bunch, and they'll take information from our website and put it in their own website and distribute in their own fanzines. We're a resource for a lot of kids to disseminate information. There are millions of kids who don't vote. Five hundred and thirty-seven votes was the magic number in Florida. We're telling people that things could have been different if a few more NOFX fans had a little bit more information.

JM: How effective has Punk Voter been? How useful is the internet for organizing?

SCOTT GOODSTEIN: The internet is one tool. We've also placed ads in cultural magazines like *Punk Planet*. We do media events and had a concert tour in seventeen cities in Western states. We partnered with NARAL (ProChoice America) and did a concert and raised 10K the night before the March for Women's Lives, a pro-choice DC march. We've partnered with Food Not Bombs. We handed out 10,000 DVDs of the movie *Uncovered* by Robert Greenwald, about weapons of mass destruction and the US government. Scott Ritter came out on the Rock Against Bush concert tour with us. There's a Punk Voter booth on Warped Tour.

BRAD LOGAN (Leftöver Crack): I choose not to give a fuck about who gets elected as our next president (2016). I fucking don't give a shit. I'm removing myself from this whole fucking mess.

JM: Do you vote?

BRAD LOGAN: I have in the past. Our system is based on checks and balances, so it's got to be Republicans for a while because it was Democrats for a long time. We don't want it to go too far one way or the other—that's not healthy. I'm not going to go into how I feel about any of the candidates—I don't like any of them. It's time to let somebody else take the reins for a while and for us to fucking deal with it. Why is Holland an awesome place to be? They have a twenty-party system. We have to sprinkle some love and tolerance in there, man. People are so hateful. It bums me out, man. That ain't cool.

KLAUS FLOURIDE (Dead Kennedys): Who people vote in, for president, is really important this year (Obama vs. John McCain, 2008). When people say there's no difference between the Democrats and Republicans because they're all funded by the same people, that's basically a privileged white male stance because they're not affected by the Supreme Court as much as minorities, women, and poor people. For no other reason, the appointees to the Supreme Court make it important that people go out and vote for president. I will easily say "Obama." I'm a flag waver for him. He's intelligent and he's a thinking man and if he leads by example, I think it would do a wonder for this country's self-image. And the world's image of us.

RUSS RANKIN (Good Riddance): Americans are taught to read the paper and watch the news to find out about the world, but it's a narrow sliver of the world we're being shown. If people watch it enough, then suddenly an illegal war against a sovereign nation that poses us no threat, that violates international law and the UN, is now "Operation Iraqi Freedom" (2003). And people buy into it. One of the most tragic things facing our country is this lack of a free press.

I've been to Australia, Canada, and the UK during elections and every candidate from every party is on TV and in the paper. It's a democracy. They ask me questions in interviews like, "Why did Bush win?" I say, "Well, over half of the eligible voters in America didn't vote." They say, "Why not?" I say, "Well, we don't have a free press. Most Americans are told there's only two parties they can choose from. Both are becoming so unpalatable that people are just staying home." They say, "Well what about the other parties?" I tell them, "There's other parties in America, but they're blackballed out of the public arena by the corporate-owned media and the Commission on Presidential Debates, which is made up of Republicans and Democrats, so that when David Cobb, the Green Party candidate last time (2004), tried to get into the debate in St. Louis just to watch in the audience, he was arrested outside." And I had to read about that in a foreign newspaper—it wasn't reported here!

It ought to offend and anger any American that is interested in democracy, that this guy that is going to be on the ballot isn't even allowed in the building to watch the two rich guys debate. Let alone that he's not on the debate floor, where he should be. We've got a real problem in this country. The corporate-owned media is a big part of it. We're not being shown an accurate landscape of what's going on. Other countries are doing it as a matter of course. No one shows up for elections anymore except rich people.

JM: Some of the proceeds from Good Riddance albums have gone to Food Not Bombs.

RUSS RANKIN: Food Not Bombs was our second album. I came up with the idea to do this. I talked to the guy at our label and said, "Would it be too much of a pain in the ass for you guys to chop off some of *our end* for each record sold, and send a check twice a year?" They said, "No." In fact they said, "We'll match you on this record." That was really cool.

Food Not Bombs was the first. Since then, every record we've tried to do something along those lines: Homeless Garden Project, Santa Cruz Aids

CHAPTER 1

Project. The record before our latest we donated money to the Cabrillo Music Department and the Western Service Workers.

PUNK ACTIVISM

KEITH MCHENRY (Food Not Bombs cofounder): A lot of bands had liner notes in their albums with stuff about Food Not Bombs. We were in *Profane Existence* a bunch of times. I did a punk tour with bands all over Mexico in 2005 and that started a huge scene in the Food Not Bombs movement down there. I just went to a lot of punk concerts in the Philippines. A lot of Food Not Bombs activists are punk band members. Bad Brains was a Food Not Bombs house band. Avail started Richmond Food Not Bombs. Fugazi was the DC house band along with Bad Brains. They played a concert in Dolores Park (San Francisco) that over twenty thousand people attended, which became called Soupstock. We gave out food in the park. MDC did tons of concerts for us. There was a punk folk album, a compilation of bands from the Bay Area, and another punk LP in New Jersey. Michael Franti had a whole section in the liner notes from one of his albums about Food Not Bombs. Food Not Bombs has had a big connection with punk. It helped us be global. I've met people who tell me they saw a band that told them about Food Not Bombs.

JEFF OTT (Fifteen): I first got involved with Food Not Bombs as a result of squatting with people in Berkeley and Oakland who had started it a year or two before that. I met Keith (McHenry) the first time in San Francisco when that city thought it was okay to arrest people for giving other people food. When I started to go and cook, I was probably eight or nine years into an eleven-year stint of living outside or in taken-over housing and fairly hopelessly drug addicted and my self-esteem completely through the floor. It really happened to be a thing that I needed to have, just to feel that I was doing something in the world and start putting together some self-esteem and eventually getting sober. I was doing a band already at the time and typically whatever bands I've done have addressed subject matter about whatever is going on around me. And that's what was going on around me at that time.

KEITH MCHENRY: I remember meeting you at one of those arrests where we had a day of action, and the police came. Mostly we got arrested every day, but once in a while there'd be a big event in San Francisco and East Bay Food Not Bombs people would come over and be in solidarity with us. That's how we met.

JM: How did the "Food Not Bombs" song by Fifteen come about?

JEFF OTT: Over a short period of time, I started to be significantly healthier; mainly I ceased being malnourished. I always felt I should write songs about whatever it is that makes me uncomfortable [laugh], usually because the topics are too personal or reveal too much. At that time, I was cooking at least five days a week (with Food Not Bombs) and to me it seemed like, "I'm writing this song about this thing that I do." With years of retrospect, what has become incredibly apparent is that whether it's poverty or militarism or every time they try to bring down the level of medical care that Medicaid delivers in each state—all of these things are violence. And ultimately, I want to live in a society where the organizing principle is people's health. That's food and medical care and emotional health. Every movement that I've ever been involved with comes down to that fundamental equation—as a people, do we want to be organized around massive violence or do we want to take care of ourselves and each other?

KEITH MCHENRY: That's definitely the message of Food Not Bombs. It reminds me that in the news this week (2018) the Pentagon doesn't know where twenty-one trillion dollars went![2] Yet, we're struggling for people to live on the streets, like veterans who should've gotten a piece of that pie. But they're stumbling around trying to find a bush to sleep under and having their belongings stolen by the police.

JM: How does it go serving food with Food Not Bombs in Myanmar? Here in California, it's against the law to serve food on the street and sometimes people are arrested! Keith McHenry is a cofounder of FNB and lives here in Santa Cruz.

KYAW THU WIN (Rebel Riot): Yeah, bro. We found this action in Indonesia five years ago when our band was on tour there (2013). We had the idea to also make this project in Myanmar to help homeless and poor kids however we can. We always complain about the system and governments in our music. But complaining is very easy for everyone. Better than complaining is to do something to change things around us. So, we started this (Food Not Bombs) action in Myanmar. I know it's illegal to feed people on the street (in the US). I know Keith McHenry and we're Facebook friends!

JM: Tell me about your work with the Animal People Alliance in Kolkata, India.

BELINDA CARLISLE (The Germs / The Go-Go's): A friend of mine works with an NGO called Her Future Coalition, which works to stop the trafficking of women and girls. He lives in Kolkata, and I live in Bangkok and he came over for a long weekend and said, "I want to do an animal project" (2017). I said, "I want to do this with you." That was three years ago, and the idea was to provide services for street animals. Anybody who has gone to India sees that there is obviously a big problem with street animals.

CHAPTER 1

Also, at the same time, we create employment for women and girls who have survived trafficking as well as the more vulnerable, lower-caste people that don't have a lot of opportunities. The caste system is alive and kicking in India. It's based on the religion of Hinduism. It's misunderstood and abused. We have a center where we've been training women to become para-vets to service animals on the streets of Kolkata. We just got space at a center called Ashari in the middle of Kolkata where we can perform surgeries for animals and neutering and we do education in schools for children to learn how to treat animals.

I've always been an animal activist and involved with PETA. I have great friends from Seattle who formed the first animal hospital in India about twenty years ago. When I visited them twelve years ago, I thought, "This is what I want to do." It was always a dream. It takes up a lot of my time and I love doing it.

LISA FANCHER (Frontier Records): I spend a huge portion of my life helping the West Memphis Three. Three teenagers in West Memphis were unjustly convicted of murdering three eight-year-old boys (1994). If you watch the movie (*Paradise Lost*) you'll see what a joke their trial was. The only criteria for their arrest was they were the weird kids in town who liked heavy metal. They read Stephen King books and wore Metallica shirts. You wouldn't bat an eye if they lived in Los Angeles. But in West Memphis they thought the kids were devil worshippers and they came up with a whole scenario of how they killed the kids in a satanic ritual. This was 1993 and they're still in prison (in 2010). One got the death sentence and two got life without parole. I belong to an organization called the West Memphis Three Support Fund and we go to hearings and visit the guys in prison. There's a benefit this weekend with Eddie Vedder. I've been involved for fourteen years.

It seems grim and depressing (to visit them in jail), but we spend three or four hours and we're laughing and telling jokes and talking about our lives. Of course, it's depressing when we can leave, and they can't. (Damien Echols, one of the West Memphis Three, was released from death row in 2011 and has written three books including *High Magick: A Guide to the Spiritual Practices that Saved My Life on Death Row* [2018].)

JM: I've read that you work in prisons. Tell me more about that.

JACK GRISHAM (TSOL): It's kind of funny because I have a badge. A little pass to get in. They're inviting me in and saying "thank you" for it! [laugh]. A lot of the problem is—and this goes back to spirituality—people inside don't feel like they're connected. They feel alone, like they're drifting. They are not dealing with the victims of the crimes that they've committed. They don't consider the victims to be real people. I understand what that is, to not think about the people I'm harming.

I love the movie *Runaway Train* with Jon Voight and Eric Roberts. There's a great scene, man. It summed up my life for a long time. They've broken out of prison and they're on the train and the older convict says to the younger convict, "What are you gonna do when you get out of here, man?" And Eric Roberts says, "I'll tell you what I'm going to do, man. I'm going to go to Vegas and I'm going to get some ladies. I'm going to gamble." And Jon Voight goes, "Bullshit." He says, "You're going to get a little shit job that a convict can get, maybe scrubbing floors or something. And you're going to get down there scrubbing floors and the boss is going to come in and say *you missed a spot* and you're going to get down there and scrub that little spot and you're going to keep your mouth shut." And Eric Roberts goes, "Fuck you man. I won't do that." Jon Voight says, "That's your *problem*, youngster. If you could do that, then you could rule the world."

And that's always been my problem. I couldn't do it. "You're not going to make me do nothing!" No humility. Just pride. It destroyed me. It's the same thing for a lot of those guys that are sitting in those prisons right now. And I know how hard it is to have someone come in and say you did it wrong. And for me not to say, "Fuck you! I'll show *you* wrong." So, I go in a lot. And basically, just visit. I do a lot of visiting.

JM: Do you go in as an official chaplain or religious person?

JACK GRISHAM: No, not at all. I go in as a fool that should be locked up! [laugh] And they all know it. And the funny thing is, a lot of times I'll walk on the yard and there's guys walking up going, "Jack! Jack!" My name is basically good in any institution in the States. The brother-in-law of a friend was just locked up in Florida and a picture of her and me together was sent to the brother-in-law in prison and somebody there said, "Hey, how do you know Jack?" [laugh] It was one of those things. So, now they want me to visit this prison down in Florida.

2

DO IT YOURSELF
DIY TOGETHER

> *We snuck in the studio with this kid who was the janitor and cut a record. That's how "A Million Miles Away" came about.*
>
> —Peter Case (The Plimsouls / The Nerves)

DO IT YOURSELF

BRAD WARNER (*Hardcore Zen* / Zero Defects): DIY—Do It Yourself. This is the idea that you don't wait for the big cigar-chomping guy at Chrysalis Records to come and give you a contract. You go and find out where the pressing plant is and how much it costs to make a record and you get that money together and you make the record. And then you sell it at gigs and take it to stores yourself. It's having huge repercussions on the music industry because DIY has become a way of life for many musicians, even outside of punk rock. That's an example of taking responsibility for yourself. You don't wait for somebody else to do it.

PETER CASE (The Nerves): Before the punk rock thing hit, the lesson learned by us was that in the face of the music industry, the artist has to move ahead and take the initiative to do it yourself. If you can't join 'em, fuck 'em! We figured out a way to put out our record and do it ourselves, which is your job as an artist and musician. In 1976 we came out with the EP with "Hanging on the Telephone" and "Working Too Hard."

I've done a lot of my best work in my life on my own initiative, in between record labels. The biggest record by The Plimsouls was "A Million Miles Away" and we cut that when we had no record deal. We had a couple of different

CHAPTER 2

Cover of Adbusters *magazine #91 (2010) "I especially liked this 'No Future' meme that seemed to be at the heart of the punk movement," Kalle Lasn,* Adbusters *publisher and co-creator of Occupy Wall Street (2011).*

record deals from that period, but when we did our best song it was when we were rejected. We were out of one deal and on the street hanging out, playing again and rehearsing, writing songs and playing gigs, but nobody would touch us. That's when we came up with what's our most popular song. We recorded that on nothing at a studio and then put it out on Bomp Records and Cooked Tandem, our own label. That's been the story for me over the years. When you don't get the approval of those people, so what? You just go ahead.

"A Million Miles Away"—we cut that and a B side from midnight until dawn, when the studio was empty. We snuck in the studio with this kid who was the janitor and cut a record. That's how "A Million Miles Away" came about. I knew it was a great song. I knew it was a song that a lot of people were going to be into, it was a powerful song live. So, we went down and cut it. But it got to the point where I was tired of sitting around and waiting for ex-members of Blood, Sweat and Tears to sit there and vote whether they wanted to put out my record or not. So, we just put it out ourselves. Back in those days we got on the radio before we had a record deal. We were supported by KROQ down here. It was kind of renegade radio.

"NO FUTURE" MEME

KALLE LASN (*Adbusters* publisher): The punk rock movement was something I wasn't intimately involved in myself. But it was a very powerful attempt. Music has always been one of those cutting edges of new aesthetics. I did very much admire that DIY—do it yourself—aesthetic behind the punk rock movement. I especially liked this "No Future" meme that seemed to be at the heart of the punk movement. They understood that the way the world was going, it didn't have any future. That was many years before it was becoming obvious that we don't have a future unless we get climate change, [and] ecological and other tipping points in order. That humanity actually doesn't have a future! The punk rock movement was the first time that I caught that idea—that *meme*—that in the gut of many young people, there's a feeling that they don't have a future.

EDWARD COLVER (punk photographer): Punk was DIY and against corporations. Punk was knowing that you can *do it yourself*. Why not try it—you might be surprised! I used to say that there's everything from geniuses to drunken morons in the punk scene, which is totally true. There was a whole cross section of people and they all got along well.

PENELOPE SPHEERIS (*The Decline of Western Civilization* / *Suburbia* / *Wayne's World*): When you've been really hurt you either become more caring or you become a criminal. Most punks have chosen to become more caring. They're good people in general. That's why I like 'em.

Kyaw Thu Win, singer and activist, with Rebel Riot and Food Not Bombs, Myanmar.
Photo: Tom Potisit

DO IT TOGETHER

JM: DIY—do it yourself—is very important in punk rock. And you've evolved that into DIT—do it together.

KYAW THU WIN (Rebel Riot): Yeah, bro, DIY is very important in punk rock. But DIY is only just for you. We live in community with a lot of people and need solidarity to do something together for positive change. So, DIT can be a new version of DIY.

RAMSEY KANAAN (AK Press / PM Press / Political Asylum): My political trajectory was very much intertwined with the punk underground. I was interested in the punk ethics and so-called *do it yourself*, which is a horrible misnomer. It's not a bunch of atomized individuals doing it themselves. It should actually be called "do it *together*." It's about the collective.

JM: I think Joe Strummer once said, "DIY not for yourself but for others."

DAVE DICTOR (MDC): Community is a big part. Ian (MacKaye) was such an important part of that do-it-ourself world. We're still involved in that. You're doing it and you're not paying other people to do it. Some bands do a tour where you're playing for five, six, seven dollars and playing lots of little venues where there's a real ability to communicate with people. And it's not like a cattle call where you're on some gigantic tour where there's thousands and thousands of people out there. Even though it's more work, you're doing it for better communication and because you love people and care about the community. I miss Joe Strummer. I never did meet him. I sure listened to his stuff. I saw The Clash back in Austin, Texas, in the late '70s. I was very inspired by The Clash. It's very sad he checked out so early.

HONEST AND REAL

TAIT REED (Junk Sick Dawn / Noise Clinic): Rock 'n' roll and punk rock inspired me and saved me in a lot of ways. It inspired me to play guitar and listen to music. I thrived on music that had the vibe of being honest and real. It wasn't about guitar solos. Punk was about thinking for yourself. That was one of the primary tenets of punk. Whether you wear a suit and your hair is combed or you've got a four-foot-tall liberty-spike Mohawk, you can be just as punk rock either way. It's about being free in your mind, man. It's about being free in your art and living honestly and doing what you think and following through; being a person of action.

CHAPTER 2

GLOBAL PUNK SCENE

GABRIEL KUHN (*Sober for the Revolution: Hardcore Punk, Straight Edge and Radical Politics*): Punk has had a huge impact. There are the common criticisms that punk has been commercialized, that certain punk bands have sold out, and that it's remained only a subculture. There is validity to some of these arguments, but largely punk has spread political messages at concerts, and within the scene, to people who otherwise wouldn't have accessed those messages. Also, the scene itself was based on particular principles—self-management, self-organization, solidarity, do it yourself—that have created a global punk scene that's had a huge impact on people and changed the lives of many. Even beyond that scene you see a punk attitude, especially a do-it-yourself attitude and way of life, from visual arts to other musical genres and fashion. Even among people and groups who have nothing to do with punk, the principle of DIY has become very strong. In one way or another this is connected to what punk has been doing for the past thirty-five years.

ECSTATIC EXPERIENCES

LAURIE ANDERSON ("Oh Superman"): Punk—this way of playing music that didn't have to stay in formulas—was really important to a lot of very wildly different kinds of people. On the surface we were wildly different people, but I don't think that really there was such a huge difference. They were coming from the same part of the city (New York) and often that music was played in the same clubs at that point, and we really had a lot in common.

Punk rock had a lot to do with Steve Reich, Phill Niblock, and Phil Glass. It had a similar kind of timeframe that was, at the bottom, very meditative. The feedback that was in punk rock and in Lou's (Reed) music and other parts of the rock and experimental world—it came from the same place. It was just trying to find a different timeframe for music and one that would take you really far away. It wasn't so far from the '60s where people had very ecstatic experiences with drugs and music and experimenting with all sorts of things. And then that evaporated from the world in many ways.

JAKE BLOUNT (*The New Faith*): Punk inspired me. I have a very similar relationship to both punk rock and jazz, which is that I listened to almost none of it in its purest form, but it is at the root of so many of the things that I love, and so many of the musicians that I love. I grew up listening to new wave stuff. My mom put on the B-52s on every road trip, and I saw them in concert. That's kind of what

I was going for with the guitar on "Didn't It Rain." So, it's funny that you said that! When I recorded that I was like, "What about Ricky Wilson meets blues meets spaceship?" That was the idea! I'm glad it worked out.

If you play old time and String Band music—banjo and fiddle—you quickly learn that maybe 85 percent of the people between the ages of twenty and fifty also play, or played, punk rock! It's so much overlap it's almost freaky! The punk rock ideology resonates with me. A lot of the sounds that are derived from it resonate with me. Sometimes when I listen to punk, the rushing of the beat isn't always something I can physically get my body into. And that's always been a barrier for me. But I always think of punks as being the good crowd, everywhere I go, and the people who are going to get what I'm doing. Even though it sounds different. I consider punk a very, very, very strong indirect influence on what I'm doing, rather than a direct one. And it speaks to the overall impact of the genre that it bleeds through that much, even though I don't listen to it on its own.

WILLIAM GIBSON (*Neuromancer*): I date from a previous subcultural generation. I actually bought the first Velvet Underground album the week it came out! That was 1967 and it was very important to me. Almost no one I ever met for another decade had ever *heard* that record or heard *of* it. The Velvets were not a big deal for very many people, but by the mid '70s, when I was starting to come up with some sort of strategy to make my living writing, I was looking through my whole life experience for anything that might fit with science fiction and create something new. One of the things that occurred to me was: *What if there was a kind of science fiction that felt very much like The Velvet Underground?* That struck me. The two poles being so far apart, I thought it had some potential. I was already heading in that direction when 1977 came around and the whole punk thing exploded. That was something I enjoyed watching very much, but I was actually a little too old to really be a part of it. I went to concerts. In one season I saw Elvis Costello, Patti Smith, The Clash, and Pere Ubu in the course of two months. That was a very good season.

BREAKING THE RULES

GREG LISHER (Camper Van Beethoven / Monks of Doom): I'm a '70's child so I was submerged in the hard rock thing; Aerosmith, Pink Floyd, Led Zeppelin. I knew there were other types of music, but I had blinders on; it was unfortunate. I started hearing new music and that's what turned me. My cousin lived in LA, and she was managing this punk rock band The Gears and they played a show

CHAPTER 2

in Palo Alto. My grandmother lived in Mountain View and the band needed a place to stay. Because my cousin was family, my grandmother said, "Of course." My cousin got me into the show. The Gears were opening for Young Marble Giants. I didn't know either band. It was so different; it was like I opened some door into another dimension. The stage looked different, the band looked different, the audience and vibe were different. I was mesmerized. I thought, "This is really refreshing."

I had this epiphany and denounced everything I'd been listening to. I sold all my rock records, and I started fresh with new music. Over the next few years, I saw lots of bands like The Cramps, Gang of Four, Buzzcocks. I don't think of those bands as punk rock. I think of them as new music. I've been to a lot of punk rock shows and Camper opened up for Dead Kennedys. The punk bands were entertaining and when punk started, the aesthetic was very positive. People were making music and breaking the rules. Breaking the rules in art has always been really important. There were people who had been considered by mainstream society as not being able to make art and they were making art. And doing it their own way. They were original.

EVERYONE HAS A VOICE

STEVEN LEE BEEBER (*The Heebie-Jeebies at CBGB's: A Secret History of Jewish Punk*): In some ways Hilly (Krystal) is the father of DIY, do it yourself, the rallying cry of punk. He insisted whoever was there at CBGB's do it themselves, play their *own* music. Performers were glad to do so. But up until that point there'd been almost nowhere in New York to play original music. It was usually cover bands, bar bands. There were a few places like The Dom, but it collapsed pretty quickly. That was really wonderful about Hilly. He said even if you don't like the music itself, they should be heard. He really didn't like a lot of the bands like Television and the Ramones, at the beginning at least. But he wanted to give them the opportunity to express themselves. It comes from the Lefty tradition that is democratic. Everyone has a voice. Hilly deserves a lot of credit for that.

PUNK AND REGGAE

RED SAUNDERS (Rock Against Racism): We wanted to break down the fear and punk wanted to do the same. Punk was challenging music and gender stereotypes. Punk was using the great working class, taking the piss. Punk was

DIY—do it yourself—and the reggae movement, and what we call the sound system movement here, was very much DIY. When I went to see the first Black reggae musicians to ask them if they'd join the campaign, we were going to sound systems where Black musicians, Black DJs, toasters, and mixers were literally making speakers out of cupboards and furniture, making it themselves. They'd have these huge speakers where the bass would literally hit your stomach. That was a roots thing, like punk was. It was an extraordinary moment in cultural history when punk and reggae came together. And we came together as a political movement at the same time, to encourage, propagate, and push even more militant anti-racism. We wanted to bring together the cultures and ideas and challenge the conservative, white supremacy at the heart of British society.

SEIZING THE MEANS OF PRODUCTION

STEVEN LEE BEEBER (*The Heebie-Jeebies at CBGB's*): The mainstream doesn't make a lot of room for revolutionary ideas, but the DIY movement does. And now there's technology to create a label out of your computer in your house and put out records. In that sense, seizing the means of production is really available to lots of people now. There's so much music out there now, and a diversity of sounds. The only downside is that I can't keep track of everything. There's lots of great music, but back in the '60s there were only a few bands to follow: Beatles or Stones was your major choice and then there were ten or twenty other bands. Now there are hundreds and hundreds of bands and it's more democratic and more available. Punk was the instigating force behind that whole DIY movement. In certain ways I think punk was revolutionary and still is. The people who were protesting in Seattle at the G8 gathering and the WTO and World Bank, those folks by and large are probably listening to punk and hip-hop.

LISA FANCHER (Frontier Records): I take bands in the studio with the goal of them making the record that *they* want to make. Not the record I wanted them to make. If I didn't like their songs, I wouldn't sign them and I wouldn't back them with my money. But I always wanted them to have control over, not only the sound, but the packaging, too. Obviously, there's some things I couldn't do for them; I'm not Sony. But I can give them creative control. I always promised that, and they always wound up with that at the end of the day. I think those records stand up because they just went into the studio and were ferocious and made the record in three days. That's true of most of those records. And they came out the way they wanted it to. Should all bands have the money they need to put out records?

CHAPTER 2

There's very few bands I know that are together enough to do anything on a consistent basis. The Ian MacKayes of the world are pretty rare.

JM: You did the first Flyboys recording at Shelter Studios in the Valley (Los Angeles). Johnette Napolitano (Concrete Blonde) was working there, answering the phone.

LISA FANCHER: We were sneaking in there in the middle of the night. I did pay them something, but let's just say it was for a whole lot less hours! We probably recorded ten times more than anybody thought we did. It seemed so *guerrilla* at the time. I felt like I had to be in the studio; I wasn't sure if people would just play poker or if they'd really record! As it turns out everybody had a good work ethic.

The Circle Jerks' first record was recorded by them, and I just bought the master tapes off of them. I have no anecdotes about that. The Adolescents were from Orange County, and I made them record it up here (Los Angeles) because I got a really good deal on a studio. I shoved all of them into the most disgusting motel. I didn't check it out first, but I realized it was basically a good place to get stabbed. We made that record in three days. It was grueling, but I think everyone had a good time. The guy who produced the record was perplexed. His name was Thom Wilson and was a nice guy, but he had only worked with super normal '70s bands. He said, "They don't really play that well," and I was like, "I know! That's the whole point." He thought he was doing a Loggins record or something. Thom Wilson went on way later to produce The Offspring.

For The Adolescents record we paid $500 a day and that was the whole day for three entire days, morning 'til night. I guess I paid Thom separately. In those days, everything was infinitely cheaper: record jackets and vinyl LPs. Petroleum is so expensive now; records are way over a dollar. I know the kids love vinyl, but they're a total loss of money. I don't make anything off of a vinyl LP. But those darn kids want them, so I've got to keep pressing them.

Now all I've been doing is reissuing punk compilations. It's so hard to sell records now. I'm talking downloads, too. It's hard to make a noise because there's such a huge glut of product. I don't know how *any* label can make a name for themselves today. I would hate to be in that game now because it's hard to get a guarantee and hard to go on tour. It's all become very insular. I guess you have to have a Facebook page. I don't know how you break a new band, but I'm glad that I'm not trying.

JM: What do you do now? (2010)

LISA FANCHER: I used to have five employees and an office in New York, but those days are long gone. Things started collapsing in the '90s. It's run out of my house now. I did the TSOL and the China White record simultaneously. I was there for both, and it was just exhausting. Thom Wilson produced those; I practically wanted to strangle him by the time it was done! We spent three days on TSOL and maybe two on China White. They were nice guys, polite, and didn't wreck anything. Their record was very heavy metal compared to the demos I had heard, that Chaz Ramirez had made. (A thirtieth anniversary concert for Frontier Records was held on November 14, 2010, at The Echoplex in Echo Park including performances by Middle Class, Adolescents, Flyboys, Rick Agnew, and The Three O'Clock.)

PUT OUT OUR OWN MUSIC!

JELLO BIAFRA (Dead Kennedys): When I was finally able to move out to San Francisco and jump in, in early 1978, a dark cloud had descended on the underground scene. Up *until* then many of the punk bands, especially in the northeast of England, were starting to get signed to major label deals. They were still being seen as the only game in town. One of the best things I think punk gave to the world was the revival of the independent music label. And of course, do-it-yourself independent media and zines. That all traces back to punk. Around late winter/early spring of 1978, it was obvious that a decision had been made by major labels not to sign any more punk rock bands. Only one certifiable punk band was signed by a major label after that—The Dickies. And one of them, it was rumored, had an uncle who worked at A&M Records. No other really legitimate, in-your-face, underground band was signed again until many years later with Hüsker Dü. By then, they probably would not have described themselves as a punk band.

Many high-quality bands were bullied by major labels saying, "If you put out an independent DIY record then we'll never sign you." And for the most part the reaction was, "Well, you probably won't anyway. Why would we want to work for you? We'll put out our music ourselves!" Slowly but surely independent labels like SST started to rise. And even these wannabe major labels like Enigma were chewing into major label profits enough that they had to look back around and see if there was anything there they could do something with.

With Hüsker Dü it didn't work out that well. But with Sonic Youth there was something. Then of course came the Nirvana explosion and suddenly all these dumbbell fat-jacketed executives said, "Oh my god! There's this whole new generation of people and they really aren't interested in what Bob Seger is doing now? What the fuck do we do?" And so now came the dragnet, where all kinds of grunge and even some punk bands were signed up with the majors and thrown like mud against the wall to see if anything would stick. And some of it did. Then of course it happened again a few years later with Green Day.

KERRI O'KANE (*The Gits* film): The Gits had a do-it-yourself ethic. Doug Pray and his film *Hype* captured that a lot. There was a certain attitude. The Gits weren't seeking fame or fortune and constantly turned down opportunities because they felt that they wanted to play music and be self-standing without the big record labels. And do it themselves. They did play with Nirvana. They were trying to steer away from the popularized music, and they wanted to make their own kind of music without the big corporate machine. They had a phenomenal success. At that time, a lot of bands made it big. The Gits sort of stayed away from that to achieve the successes within themselves. They had plenty of opportunities to sell to the corporate conglomerate. Although I'm not a musician, the DIY punk ethic applies to filmmaking. If you have a vision you have to go for it and not be stifled by the powers that be.

JONATHAN RICHMAN (Jonathan Richman and the Modern Lovers): Whenever young groups ask me, "We're going into the studio, what should we do?" I always say the same thing: "Sing and play what you feel. And don't sing and play what you don't feel." They say, "That's it?" I say, "That's it."

CHRIS FREEMAN (Pansy Division): That's the way Pansy Division has operated all of our existence; we get to do exactly what we want, when we want, and say what we want. To have that kind of a career in music at all is insane! When I think about all of the hurdles we've basically jumped right over it's unreal!

MIKE NESS (Social Distortion): To me punk was all about being an individual. That meant doing what you wanted to do even though your best friend thinks it's lame! [laugh] It is respecting each other's individuality. Another one that comes to mind is evolution. I thought of punk as the beginning *of something*. We have to evolve. The thing that fans have appreciated most about Social Distortion is that we were never afraid to evolve and become more of what we were and expound on it and take it to different levels.

USE YOUR LIMITATIONS

MARK HOSLER (Negativland): Punk was an ethic and an aesthetic where you didn't have to be a professional or an expert to create. You could do it yourself and even use your limitations to your advantage. If I only have a four-track recorder, what can I record on four tracks? If I can only play two notes on a saxophone, what can I make out of those two notes? If I can play one chord on a guitar, what can I do with that? It was a very exciting time for exploring and creating music.

A VEHICLE TO SOMEWHERE

GARY NUMAN (Tubeway Army): I developed Tubeway Army as a punk band. Not because I was passionate about the music, and not because I thought punk rock had something long lasting or meaningful to offer. It was because I saw punk as an opportunity. Punk rock created a re-evaluation of what music was about, what it was there for. Why it was not to be taken so seriously and so earnestly. It was just: go out and say what the fuck you want, and do what you want, and just rip the shit up while you can! That's what music should be about! Lots of young people getting out and just being mental and having some fun with it. I loved that side of it. But that's never gonna last. That's going to be a moment in time.

And in that moment, it was as if a whole load of doors suddenly appeared on a wall that had been firmly in your way before. There was no way through that wall—apart from major record company there, massive independent there, who were very arrogant, selective, and very difficult to get into. All of a sudden that wall had a dozen doors in it—big ones—and you opened that door and behind it was half a dozen little punk labels. Suddenly there was lots of opportunity. Not to go a long way, but to get your foot on the ladder. Whereas before you couldn't even see the ladder. That's why punk for me became a vehicle to somewhere. I knew I didn't want to do that long term. But it was a doorway to somewhere. I just didn't know where somewhere was going to be.

GLENN GREGORY (Heaven 17 / Musical Vomit): We didn't want to be punks because punk to us felt a little bit old fashioned. It was like rock and roll, again. It was Teddy Boy and aggressive. But it was new, and it certainly allowed people like us (Heaven 17) and Cabaret Voltaire and Vice Versa, who then became ABC, to suddenly think, "We can get on Top of the Pops. We can get a record deal." I'm forever thankful to punk for that, definitely.

JARBOE (Swans / Neurosis): There's a trajectory of your ears opening, and that process happened for me initially when I started discovering music coming out of England like Soft Machine. Your ears start to expand and what you describe as music expands. The real opener would have to be the experimental noise sound collage art movement around the same time I first heard Swans. Groups like SPK and Nurse with Wound. In college I studied John Cage and twentieth-century classical music that's deliberately atonal. These things can help jar your preconceived notions about what is musical and what is not musical. Punk would have to be one of the elements that has you start questioning what is musical and what is not musical. If you have your ears open, then you start to rethink: What is sound? What is musical? Then your whole universe expands, and the vocabulary opens and there are no rules.

PUNK MAGAZINE—DIY

MARY HARRON (*I Shot Andy Warhol* / *American Psycho* director): Punk was revolutionary as far as it possibly could be. It was music and culture; it wasn't going to change the political structure of society. It could only change the way people felt. But it gave a role model that was really an interesting one. That's what really knocked me out when I first met Legs McNeil and John Holmstrom, who started *Punk Magazine*. I had just left college and all my friends were getting jobs. I had written for the college paper. That was so much fun when we ran our own magazine! "But now it's the real world. It's really hard and you can't do what you want." Then I met these guys, and they were starting a magazine on nothing. It was so inspiring! You could just *do it yourself*. That was the biggest thing. I think about that part of punk all the time when I'm trying to give myself a pep talk about keeping going when faced with obstructions and difficulties. *You can do it yourself.* You can just write something or shoot a film yourself with very little money if all else fails. That independence and self-reliance and not being dictated to culturally—having your own voice—was very important to punk and is important for me. It totally stayed with me. I think it stayed with many people.
JM: The DIY ethic has rippled out.
MARY HARRON: Around the world! That's what is so funny. There are people in Thailand naming their kids Sid Vicious. It's extraordinary.
JM: By the way, I came across a video of a Balinese gamelan cover version of the Gang of Four song "Not Great Men."
MARY HARRON: That's great. I'll have to tell them. That's marvelous!
SARA MARCUS (*Girls to the Front: The True Story of the Riot Grrrl Revolution* / Boys of Now): Riot grrrl was my way into the entire DIY ethos of: publish your own writing, write your own songs, start your own band. Don't worry if you're not super polished at the beginning. The point is that you do something and give shape and form to your ideas. The aesthetics of punk and the DIY ethos and the rituals—the activities of going to shows or record stores, making zines—these are extremely powerful tools for young activists to embrace, feminists and

otherwise. Riot grrrl was the avenue for me to become introduced to these and get involved.

LET'S HAVE A CONCERT!

MATT HERN (*Everywhere All the Time: A New Deschooling Reader*): The thing that impressed me were the DIY aspects of punk rock. I wasn't a musician, but you didn't need a whole lot of stuff to have a show. There were people who were lousy musicians. They were good kids with lots of energy and punk rock attitude and they realized you *can* hold a concert in your living room! And people did. Constantly. It was this DIY aspect that impressed me: "Let's have a concert. We don't have any money? Who cares! Let's do it somewhere cheap. Let's do it in a park. We don't need a mic even." That was the part I took away from punk—there was a certain kind of fearlessness and wrecklessness. A certain urgency and confidence. That's hopefully some stuff I've clung to as I've hit middle age. Hopefully the fearlessness and urgency has stayed with me.

> *Punk rock? I think it was the do-it-yourself movement and the independence, the politics and the activism. Aesthetically the music spoke to me more than even what I was doing sometimes.*
>
> —Amy Ray (*Indigo Girls*)

JM: I remember noticing you wearing a Hüsker Dü T-shirt on the album sleeve of *Nomads, Indians, Saints*.
AMY RAY (Indigo Girls): Yeah, the giveaway! In the late '70s I was in high school and listening to Lynyrd Skynyrd. Right when I started college, I discovered Patti Smith and The Clash, The Replacements, and Hüsker Dü. It was stuff that was considered "alternative" on college radio. Then I went back and listened to what was punk over the years and discovered the DC scene and Fugazi and the riot grrrl scene in the Northwest.

In Atlanta we had a weird punk scene. It's never been documented, which is odd to me. Atlanta had Drivin' N' Cryin' and The Night Porters and Follow for Now. We all hung out together. Emily (Saliers) and I were playing our acoustic music, but we were playing in alternative clubs because the folk scene was a little too narrow for us at the time. It has since expanded quite a bit. At the time it was homophobic. It didn't feel free and as political as we wanted it to be. It was less strident, less about the Utah Phillips of the world and more about apolitical pop-folk. We started playing alternative clubs.

Punk rock? I think it was the do-it-yourself movement and the independence, the politics and activism. Aesthetically the music spoke to me more than even what *I* was doing sometimes. I felt like I was in this space of singer-songwriter because I hadn't been experienced or educated. Our high school was so limited with what we were exposed to. It was a very Southern suburban experience. I know a lot about Southern rock, The Allman Brothers. It's very important to me. But the punk stuff was more of a philosophy and not even so much what you were playing, but how you approached what you do. It was very important to me. I just started discovering one band after another and started a label and that was it.

JM: Your DIY record label—Daemon—produces punk bands and your solo projects have been influenced by punk.

AMY RAY: Yeah, and they're influenced by rock, too. Punk is such a fragile word because what is punk? It is an approach. A lot of the people I play with are from the punk scene and really paid their dues there. It's very influenced by those people.

NORMAN NAWROCKI (Rhythm Activism): The whole DIY ethos inspired me. When we first started recording albums here in Montreal as Rhythm Activism, they were cassettes, and it was completely DIY. That's the way you did it; the method and motives behind producing it were as important as the content of the music. I thank punk rock for that, for giving me the inspiration and showing me the way. Since then, every time I hear great punk rock music a part of me is, "Yes!" I love it.

CLEM BURKE (Blondie): The whole punk rock attitude is based in do it yourself and don't let other people tell you what to do, what kind of music to make or what kind of clothes to wear. But it's not necessary to be right in your face all the time. Culturally, what happened in New York City had more of an impact on pop culture than the bands that came out of the UK in the mid-70s. The intellectualism and vision of New York City won over a lot of people.

FOOD NOT BOMBS

> *We figured that young people are not going to want the revolution if it doesn't have our own music, with our own lyrics that are anti-capitalist.*
>
> —Keith McHenry (Food Not Bombs)

KEITH McHENRY (Food Not Bombs cofounder): When Food Not Bombs started, punk rock was mostly in Europe. We were going to our friends saying, "We need to have punk bands because we need to have our own DIY idea." That's when DIY became a term—it was in '78 or '79. With all our political organizing we said, "We need music." Rock music was the protest music for the '60s, but we needed to do our own thing and keep it away from corporate control because that's part of the main message we want to get across. We figured that young people are not going to want the revolution if it doesn't have our own music, with our own lyrics that are anti-capitalist.

Food Not Bombs fit into this entire new vision that also had art, food, music, and culture. Anarchism was the basic principle. Our idea was that Food Not Bombs would be part of this larger DIY trip that would ultimately support each other. We were against war and capitalism. In those days no one knew about the war in El Salvador, and we were trying to get people to know, "We're killing all these people in El Salvador. Let's protest that." At the same time, I like to remind people that we were already working to stop climate change. We all knew this was going to be a disaster. There was already a movement advocating solar power and trying to debunk the myth that climate change would never happen. All these things are interconnected. I never played music myself, but I did a lot of posters and it turned out that was hugely influential.

3

WE ARE ALL PUSSY RIOT
PUNK ON THE FRONT LINES, RUSSIA TO MYANMAR, CHINA TO MEXICO

When the Soweto Uprising arrived in '76, so did the raw energy of punk.

—*Punk in Africa* documentary, 2012 (directed by Keith Jones and Deon Maas)

It wasn't punk rock that brought down the Berlin wall, but it did have a significant role to play in shaking up the Eastern European communist system.

—Mark Reeder (Die Unbekannten)

They can arrest you and put you to prison. They can send their ultra-patriot activists and beat you. They can take all your money. They have mechanisms. But we have honesty and ourselves. That's why I believe they cannot stop us.

—Maria "Masha" Alyokhina (Pussy Riot)

Punk ideas can help to change society. Punk is freedom.

—Kyaw Thu Win (Rebel Riot)

If punk rock has been a revolutionary force, then we might expect to hear this music manifest in places where revolutions have been ignited to resist authoritarian governments. Indeed, distinct social-political movements and communities have been inspired by punk around the globe. From South Africa to Moscow, from Israel and Iran to anti-WTO protests in Seattle, from Serbians on the receiving end of US bombs to the military junta of Myanmar (Burma) to the fall of the Berlin Wall. In all these cases, punk rock was there.

PUNK PRAYERS

JM: Tell me about performing "Punk Prayer" at the Cathedral in Moscow. (February 21, 2012)

MARIA "MASHA" ALYOKHINA (Pussy Riot): It was very simple. It was just before elections when Putin decided to be president for the third term and Patriarch Kirill, the main guy in the Russian Orthodox Church, used the whole church and the main cathedral as a political stage for Putin. This was very wrong. He said things like, "All Christians should vote for Putin." Also, he owns a huge tobacco business and this particular cathedral he used for political parties. It's not actually a church in the classical meaning. It's a complex of different things and they don't pay taxes for things such as political parties. We made a song about that and performed it for forty seconds, just the first chorus and first verse and that's it.

Pussy Riot (Rio Theatre, Santa Cruz, California; March 11, 2017). Photo: John Malkin

We made several songs before that and I think they started to somehow not like us after the Red Square performance where we sang, "Putin pissed himself." Actually, I believe that in any country, it doesn't matter—Russia or not Russia—it's totally wrong to use a church as a political platform for any president and it's stupid to put people in prison for criticizing this way of using the church. Anyway, I should say thank you to all these guys because it was a totally unique experience that I never had before. Somehow, I think I became stronger than I was before, so I should say thank you to them for doing that!

JM: After the 2012 "Punk Prayer" performance by Pussy Riot three of you were sent to prison. Since you've been out, you've visited prisons in Europe and the US. What did you learn?

MASHA ALYOKHINA (Pussy Riot): Firstly, prison exists in your head. For me it's the most dangerous prison. The one built by the government—it's just a useless, at one point, and terrible, at second point, concept. The *concept of punishment* is a very stupid one. If some person is isolated from their family, it is already punishment. More punishment is sadism. Especially because of the Soviet Union past, we have in Russia a very bad relationship of prisoners and administration because the whole system communicates with prisoners not like they're a person but as a detail of the mechanism, where you should just work. Prisoners are working for twelve or fourteen hours, and they pay them about four or five dollars per month, which is fucking slavery. The conditions are terrible. People are living one hundred in one room, and they have a shower once a week. And this is not really a shower. This is a collective going to barnyard.

This is an extreme condition of those who have power and those who have none. I think the border of this communication is not a prison wall. Prison is just a mirror of how government communicates with society. With this prison I want to fight! Yes, we visited prisons in the United States. We visited Rikers Island (New York City Prison) twice and we've been in a detention center.

It's not a secret that the American system has the same problems as Russia with corruption and relationships with prisoners. We've tried to understand why this is not changing and the answer is very cynical: this topic is not interesting for politicians because they will not have popularity if they're raising this topic. This is totally wrong because people are not prisoners forever. All of these people will go out and their future is in the hands of these politicians and a percentage of their next crimes is also in their hands, so it should be a reason for changing.

CHAPTER 3

REVOLUTION 2017

JM: Is there some chance you'll be arrested for performing this new piece? ("Revolution") Is there some risk that the Russian government will stop the show?

MASHA ALYOKHINA (Pussy Riot): Of course. This is like big percent of this kind of result. It's almost three years since we were released (from prison) and we made a lot of things these three years. For example, in 2015 we made a small auction for political prisoners. It was not a big event, but in the underground oppositional gallery of our friend. He owned this gallery for ten years and it was a historical place for all of us. After our auction they broke the rental contract with him. This is just one of the many examples of how they're acting. They can arrest you and put you to prison. They can send their ultrapatriot activists and beat you. They can take all your money. They have mechanisms. But we have honesty and ourselves. That's why I believe they cannot stop us. But preparation is a very important step.

JM: It seems that the new US president (Trump) has inspired a lot of people to be active now (2017). Sasha (Alexander) Cheparukhin (Pussy Riot producer) said he used to believe America was a model democracy and that Russia was authoritarian. Don't you think both governments seek a similar control?

MASHA ALYOKHINA (Pussy Riot): The main idea of the United States is freedom. My feeling is that the United States is a country of refugees. It was started from refugees. And now to provide the idea of stopping refugees from coming here is schizophrenia. It is really strange. I think at some point this Trump symptom can be somehow useful for the United States because people like him usually appear when people are forgetting what they have. To remind yourself of what you have, you have to kind of fight for these things. And he can be a very good reason to remember what you have. Otherwise, you're in trouble.

Yesterday we just landed to Seattle, and I went to a café near the hotel and I see a paper box with caricatures of Trump. You buy a postcard and write what you don't like about Trump's policy and send it to him! In Russia it's not possible to have these boxes in the café, even in Moscow. I'm always comparing, and I always see the optimistic side. Maybe it's because I'm from Russia. Because if you don't have optimism and sense of humor in Russia then you would have just one choice. [Masha mimics putting a gun to her head, laughing.] And I don't want it.

MASHA ALYOKHINA: The topic of what we are saying in "Revolution," in "Riot School," is about living without borders. It's about uniting and understanding that there's no reason to be separate now. It's time to be together. From one point it's a very simple thing, but this simple thing was somehow forgotten and that was probably the reason why Trump happened and why Brexit happened, because a lot of people thought these rights—democracy and freedom—will exist for forever. It's about 52 percent of people who voted in the United States. Half of the society just stayed at home. Wow! You can look to Russia as an example of what happens if you stay at home and do not fight.

JM: How did this new Pussy Riot performance piece "Revolution" (2017) come to be?

ALEXANDER "SASHA" CHEPARUKHIN (Pussy Riot producer): This idea came to me one year ago. It was already a time when Pussy Riot, especially the most known Pussy Riot girls—Maria Ayokhina and Nadya Tolokonnikova—explored the whole world through meetings and speaking engagements and then created an organization called Zona Prava and a media project called Media Zona, which became one of the most powerful human rights media in Russia. So, they have done a lot after their release from prison.

They wanted to find a new artistic way to deliver their message to people. Nadya started to do these video clips, mostly in America. Masha (Maria Alyokhina) didn't know what is her optimal way to express herself and I found that in all situations when Masha was reading publicly her written texts, it was very, very convincing.

Right after their release from prison we were together at a literature festival in Norway. The Norwegian organizers asked Masha to do some prepared speech and they surrounded this speech with some short documentaries, light effects, and slides; it was quite simple. There was a fifteen-minute rehearsal, that's it. And it was very strong. I liked it very much. Since this moment I thought that it would be good to come back to this form when Masha writes something interesting. And all of a sudden, she asked me to read two books she wrote! They're very different. One is the full story of her personal experience in Pussy Riot. It starts from the action in Red Square and then goes to the action in the Jesus Christ the Savior Cathedral and escaping from police. Then their arrest, jail and investigation process, and court: the trial. Then she writes about the penal colony. It sounds like it's kind of memoir genre, but it's not. It is more like a very strong manifesto, and it looks like real literature. I was really impressed because it was real literature! All of a sudden, I realized that Masha is a perfect writer.

I spent one year trying to convince her to do a play out of this book, and she is very responsible person so she wanted to be sure that it would be a very decent work and that she could deliver her message properly. But what helped me to convince her was her experience with the Belarus Free Theatre, which

CHAPTER 3

is based in London and Minsk, Belarus. They invited Masha to play herself in a piece called "Burning Doors." She also invented her part by herself by just sharing her experience with the audience. She toured with them a lot in the UK, Italy, and Australia and she became much more confident and professional as an actress on stage.

I told Masha, "Listen, now it's ready. You're an actress and a writer. Let's put it together." Finally, she agreed in December after we completed the last American tour. That tour was meetings with audiences of students in universities showing a film about Pussy Riot called *Act & Punishment*. We decided it was time to do something else.

Actually, her book became in high demand and now we have several contracts for US publication (*How to Start a Revolution*) and for UK publication and French edition. A lot of known literature authorities say that this is an incredible book. So, I was right when I found that the book was incredible! Then we abbreviated this book to a much shorter version. We edited it with Masha in a small countryside home near Moscow. Kiryl Kanstantsinau from Belarus, her main partner in "Burning Doors," also helped to make the text shorter and the piece about one hour long.

Then we invited one of my favorite theater directors to participate: Yury Muravitsky. He was unfortunately denied a visa for the United States, so he cannot collaborate. Maybe he will come later. We also invited two best friends of Masha: the band called Asian Women on the Telephone and Taisia Krugovykh, who made the best documentaries about Pussy Riot. These guys were a very essential part of Pussy Riot from the beginning, from the early years of Pussy Riot in 2011. So, it was a kind of, let's say, reunion. Kiryl was a new member, but during his experience with Masha in the Belarus Free Theatre he started to feel Masha very well on stage, so it was a very right choice.

Masha has chosen these three people, her partners on stage, and I have chosen the director. So, we put it together and started rehearsals and then we realized that this is what we've really wanted to do all of these years. Now three months of rehearsals are over. We did part of the rehearsals in Moscow and part in Montenegro because we have the Russian European Art Center there, which is quite active, and they invited us to spend time in Montenegro. Soon they are landing in Seattle. Now we start the first-ever foreign tour of "Revolution." We start in Seattle and go to San Francisco, Santa Cruz, Los Angeles, Austin, Albuquerque, and New York.

JM: Were you at the "Punk Prayer" and Red Square performances?

ALEXANDER "SASHA" CHEPARUKHIN (Pussy Riot producer): No, I have seen this on the internet. I didn't know the girls at this time. How I was involved to this is a separate story. I really was impressed by their action in Red Square (January 20, 2012). I think it was a perfect artistic and political protest action.

Whatever they deserved according to Russian law was maximum five years of public service work, like cleaning the streets or cleaning the church. But instead, they got two years in prison. I was shocked! Since I was the producer and director of big Russian festivals, and I knew a lot of rock stars and managers, I started to involve these big stars to support Pussy Riot.

I involved a lot of celebrities to the campaign for support of Pussy Riot. First was Peter Gabriel, who is my friend. He wrote a personal letter to the girls and made a video statement. He was the most active in the initial phase of the Pussy Riot arrests. My biggest unexpected achievement was involving Paul McCartney to this campaign because I didn't know Paul McCartney so well. But he reacted in half an hour after I sent a letter to him through his press secretary. I realized that it's my unique opportunity to get all of these statements and bring these to court regardless of whether it works or not. Even if it didn't work in terms of convincing the powers to be more soft, it helped a lot for Nadya, Masha, and Katya to feel themselves not lonely.

Then I met the girls because I visited two of them in prison: Masha and Nadya. Katya was already released by parole. I visited them quite often and I brought document of human rights observer; one good thing in Russian legislation is that a human rights activist can visit prisoners as a lawyer. That's how I first met Masha in prison. I visited her several times and celebrated her birthday with some other friends in prison and then I visited Nadya.

Since I played this very active role in getting together the Western artistic community to support Pussy Riot, and I visited them in prison many times, we became friends. After they were released from prison, we started to do some things together and travel together. I organized several trips to visit European prisons and it was very interesting experience especially in countries like Norway, which is far ahead of the whole world in their prison system and especially their concept of why they need prisons. It's a very surprising and human approach. Then we started to do some creative work and together with Masha now, "Revolution." We also call this piece "Riot School." Maybe it's the most creative and interesting thing we've managed to do together.

ALEXANDER "SASHA" CHEPARUKHIN (Pussy Riot producer): It is kind of a mistake to think that Pussy Riot is a punk rock band. They were always a big collective of fifteen or twenty people and really a contemporary art collective. Punk rock was just one of the forms of their protest. But it was one of the most visible and loud forms. When they have done these punk balaclava actions and videos, this was the most shocking and most known to the most people. The three girls were arrested and sent to prison for their punk rock action called "Punk Prayer" in the Cathedral. (February 21, 2012)

They were inspired by punk rock and of course they liked the spirit of punk rock. It was just a temporary form of their self-expression, the form of punk rock protest. They did another punk rock action at the Sochi Olympic Games (February 2014) after Nadya and Masha had been released from prison. By then they decided to find some other aesthetic and musical forms to express themselves. But definitely they still keep this punk spirit.

They met a lot of punk musicians. I introduced them to another famous friend of mine, Patti Smith. I toured Patti Smith several times with different lineups in Russia. I think Patti Smith is a big inspiration for Pussy Riot and definitely Patti Smith could be called the grandmother of American punk music. Patti Smith also sent them a letter and supported them in her concerts.

Also, Johnny Rotten—John Lydon of Sex Pistols and later Public Image Limited—I know him very well. They have done several actions to support Pussy Riot. Right now, punk still remains as a part of the mood and aesthetics of Pussy Riot. Maria Alyokhina, or Masha, she called the "Revolution" play her punk manifesto. She says if you can change something you definitely need to act and fight. She thinks this is a kind of punk spirit.

A POWERFUL MOVEMENT

Serbian band Bjesove was born out of the trauma of war as Yugoslavia was broken apart from 1991 to 2001. Earlier, punk-infused political art had manifested in another region of Yugoslavia, Slovenia, as Neue Slowenische Kunst (NSK), which included the band and art collective Laibach. The 1996 documentary film *Prerokbe Ognja* (*Predictions of Fire*) shows NSK members establishing self-created government consulates and issuing their own passports. Their 2017 mind-bending film *Liberation Day* chronicles Laibach becoming "the first rock group ever to perform in the fortress state of North Korea."

> *Armed only with a stack of old punk records and a dream of freedom, one defiant Belgrade radio station waged a ten-year war against Slobodan Milošević's dictatorship—and won.*
>
> —Matthew Collin, *Guerrilla Radio: Rock 'N' Roll Radio and Serbia's Underground Resistance*

GORAN "MAX" MARIĆ (Bjesove): Punk was a powerful movement in the Balkans. It was an inspiration for many creative artists—musicians, painters, poets, film directors. Young people from former Yugoslavia were bored and angry with the old, conservative, and rigid system of government imposed by the Communist Party. It was a system without any relation to reality. Punk hit in the bull's eye with daring, persistence, and great creativity. The system was exposed for the first time since WWII. We were amazed by some fantastic bands from the US like Hüsker Dü, Swans, Dead Kennedys, Pixies, Ramones, New York Dolls, Iggy Pop, Velvet Underground, RATM, Nirvana, and great bands from the UK like Joy Division and The Clash.

Our view on violence was like this: it is complete madness. We have to look deep inside and find some basic human qualities to appeal to people to stand up for the end of destruction. We knew that music was the most powerful instrument to do that, to grasp knowledge about ourselves, and the world around us. It was a painful experience but also very rewarding. We purified ourselves and we became one of the most important voices of our generation, in the early and mid-90s.

PUNK IN THE MIDDLE EAST

MARJANE SATRAPI (*Persepolis*): When the punk movement started in the mid-70s in the UK the whole thing was during mass unemployment. All the young people of the working class saw no future. The punk slogan was *No Future*. In 1975 I was five years old and the economic situation in Iran was great. So, it was a *Yes Future*. For me it was a post-punk thing that happened almost everywhere because the punk movement was really short.

One year after the revolution in Iran (1978–1979) the war started. We were in economic growth and thought the future belonged to us and suddenly it became no future, too. The country got completely closed. There wasn't a real punk movement. There were a couple of punk bands in Iran. One was half-Iranian, half-German. We were more like having a big bracelet with needles (spikes) and writing "punk" on our T-shirt and jean jackets. Having holes in our pants. But we were too young to understand what it was; we were twelve or thirteen.

Punk really became important to me was when I went to Austria because I ended up in this high school that was very bourgeois. There was one single punk in my whole school, and he was the only one who wanted to be my best friend. In Iran we knew that something was happening, and it gave us some hope. Incredibly enough, this No Future movement helped us know there was something going on. But it was more about fashion than a true thing that touched us. In Austria it was different because they were people who could live outside of the system a bit more. And those were the people I hung out with.

MARJANE SATRAPI: Listening to music is normal for everyone. In Iran it suddenly became forbidden. Everyone wants to listen to music that is forbidden! You find yourself in this situation of risking going to jail just because you listen to music. The music was an opening to the other world. Punk music was a part of the larger rock music, and it was about the sound of anger. We could feel this anger in ourselves. For us, it was a way of surviving and not being told how to become. We were supposed to be extremely religious by brainwashing. We rejected all of that and most of that came through Western rock music. It was an inspiration that meant freedom.

When it was forbidden to have a badge, then we'd have fifty badges! When it was forbidden to have a leather jacket, we'd wear those and feel like we're cool and tough. Then we would write things on the back of our jacket. It was really a way to say we're free. Every human being in this world is made for freedom. The human being is not made to be locked. No matter what you do, at one point, with a little bit of brain and energy you can get out. They can lock you physically, but they cannot lock your brain. They could not close our ears; we could always listen to the music. Incredibly enough, I met a guy from Kansas City, and he said he wasn't allowed to listen to rock music either because of religious reasons. His parents said that rock music was Satan. When people are close-minded in America or Iran, it gives the same results.

> *There's no punk rock in Argentina. There's no punk rock in Afghanistan, Russia, Czechoslovakia, Iran, Nebraska. If you don't keep your eyes open it won't be here either.*
>
> —Jello Biafra opening "Bleed for Me" by Dead Kennedys in the concert film *Urgh! A Music War* (1981)

Michael Muhammad Knight is the American author of *The Taqwacores*, a 2002 fictional story about young Muslim punk rock bands in New York. The novel inspired the formation of a real-life Muslim punk scene including the band The Kominas in 2005 in Worcester, Massachusetts. The band continues to perform and record today with album titles like *Wild Nights in Guantanamo Bay* (2008) and *The Systems Are Down* (2019). Knight's novel was adapted into a well-crafted 2010 feature-length film by Eyad Zahra, *The Taqwacores*. Amazingly, in 2007

Michael Muhammad Knight and a group of radical Muslim punk bands inspired by his story toured the United States and Pakistan, a journey captured in the 2009 documentary *Taqwacore: The Birth of Punk Islam* by director Omar Majeed.

JM: I'm curious how revolutionary punk rock has been on the front lines, confronting totalitarian political regimes. The Taqwacore tour went to Islamabad, Pakistan. Has punk been a revolutionary force in places like Pakistan or Beijing or San Francisco or anywhere?

MICHAEL MUHAMMAD KNIGHT (author of *The Taqwacores*): No. [long pause] Certainly not in Pakistan. Punk rock in Pakistan is luxury. like Western consumer goods. Punk rock in Pakistan is an imposition of attitudes, norms, and values from somewhere else; it's colonialism. You can't be punk rock in Pakistan without being rich. That's the irony of it! Whatever punk was supposed to be here (US) if you're punk rock in Pakistan, you're the rich kids! If you charge 75 cents for your show, most people aren't going to be able to pay that. Who is going to have these guitars and training? Who has a MacBook at home to download songs and have this particular kind of cultural literacy and history of Western rebellious subculture? It's the kids who went to private schools in London. It's the rich kids. There is no revolution happening there.

JM: I just saw Jello Biafra and Guantanamo School of Medicine two weeks ago in San Jose, California (July 23, 2016). Jello and the band were scheduled to play in Israel in 2011 and Useless ID was going to open the show. Biafra decided not to play Israel but toured Israel and the occupied Palestinian territories by himself, posting writings and videos about the trip.

ISHAY BERGER (Useless ID): Any American spending a week here for whatever reason, they're going to romanticize stuff for the sake of making good writing. He didn't say anything that was really surprising. He made his old arguments. His writing was quite lengthy, and I didn't manage to read it all; in the same way I cannot listen to a whole Jello Biafra spoken word album. I can listen to a whole Dead Kennedys album easy!

I'm going to be honest about it because what do I care? We were in touch with Jello. I didn't receive his email, but I did hear about it. When people from production of that show told Jello, "You're going to get a lot of backlash and a lot of emails and threats. And the threats are going to be real. They're going to be like, 'Hey, you're going to play Israel? Then you're not going to play *our* festival in Czech Republic.' Or, 'This promoter in Austria is not down with you anymore.'" Those are the kinds of threats you get when you play Israel and you're Jello Biafra. That was what they told Jello and his reply was, "I'm

CHAPTER 3

going to come to Israel. I like pissing people off. If *I* decide to come play Israel, then I'm going to come play Israel." Production was like, "Okay. I guess it's a bottom-line kind of thing. He'll come at any cost. Okay, cool." We didn't mind if he got to play a show in Tel Aviv or not. Those bands are touring everywhere and if I don't see them in Israel, I'll see them elsewhere.

I think the amount of emails and threats he did eventually get was too overwhelming. If not for him, because he eventually did come, but for at least one band member. Someone there was, "I don't feel like going to Israel anymore when we get way more emails and threats than people actually standing in line for the show." It makes sense to me; it's almost like the show is already ruined. There is so much BDS (Boycott Divestment Sanctions) activity against it.

"State is Burning" by Israeli punk band Useless ID (2016). Contributed: Fat Wreck Chords

We eventually did play the show even though Jello and his band didn't come. Useless ID and an opening band played for free, and Jello came at the end of the show. I didn't want to be unfriendly, but he was like, "What's the plan? What are we going to do?" I said, "I'm going home." I really didn't feel like walking around Tel Aviv after midnight and everyone was talking about whether they're mad about him coming (to Israel) or happy for him coming.

Some people were saying, "Yeah! BDS works! BDS won." And a lot of other people were down, because they canceled. There was this whole conversation and at the time I didn't feel like talking with Jello about it. I would love to hang out with Jello, but in those circumstances I felt, "Aahhh! I'm going home. See you next time." Everybody placed bets on whether they're going to come or not. I like Dead Kennedys, but I don't know about the other band so much.

After they canceled, he wrote a really, really long blog about this whole thing and people asked me, "How did you feel about it?" And I said, "I'm sick of this thing!" Nobody contacted them. *They* contacted Israel. You want the local guy to book your show? The local guy books your show. You want this and that? This and that happens. And then you cancel? Then there's articles and backlash in the press and "Oh my God!" It's like another publicized thing this group is going about. After that The Adicts came to Israel and played. Nobody threatened The Adicts so much. But they had too many stage divers.

REBEL RIOT

Between 2015 and 2017 there were multiple news stories and photo essays about the punk scene in Myanmar (Burma) in a variety of media including *Aljazeera*, the *Washington Post*, *Huffington Post*, the *Daily Beast*, and ABC News. The band Rebel Riot is led by singer Kyaw Thu Win, and they're involved with radical direct-action projects like Books Not Bombs and Food Not Bombs and they often play concerts for human rights. *My Buddha Is Punk* is a 2015 documentary on Kyaw and his band by director Andreas Hartmann.

JM: Is it dangerous to be a punk and play punk rock in Myanmar?
KYAW THU WIN (Rebel Riot): The last ten years were dangerous. But now it's not dangerous anymore." (2018) I think punk ideas can help to change society. Punk is freedom. A lot of people in society are losing their own freedom by money, fame, authorities, etc. . . . Punk music, fanzines, and actions have created freedom in the world and in Myanmar.

CHAPTER 3

WUHAN PUNK

WU WEI (SMZB): Wuhan was one of the first two cities in China where punk bands were born, the other being Beijing. Punk is not for the masses. Most people like pop music and don't like rock music. The kind of person I want to be is quiet, kind-hearted, honest, and brave. This is my idea of punk. Everyone may have a different understanding or interpretation of punk. It does not matter. SMZB began in late 1996. SMZB is the abbreviation of the band's earliest Chinese name, Pinyin Sheng Ming Zhi Bing. The Chinese meaning of the name is "Bread of Life" or "Biscuit of Life." In 2002, the Chinese name was no longer used, only the four-letter acronym was retained. This logo is an attitude towards the government.

JM: What does "naked punk" mean to you?

WU WEI: That's the title of a song; I like it very much. It means very poor: no house, no car, no money; like a naked person.

JM: I read that your last album cover couldn't be printed in China because it had a picture of a fallen statue of Mao.

WU WEI: Yes, there is no factory in mainland China that dares or is willing to print the album cover (*Once Upon a Time in The East*, released August 17, 2020). Finally, I asked a friend in Taiwan to print it and then send it to the mainland. The police closed my friend's record store who was selling the album. No one is allowed to sell this album. His record store has been open for fifteen years. At first, his online store was closed. After that, all the records that went to his home were confiscated. It has happened, if a band is not too famous and influential, that the police have terminated their shows and tours.

JM: Here in the US police violence is a big problem. Is it the same in China?

WU WEI: In China, the violence of the government is worse, and yet no one thinks it's a problem, like it's normal. It's part of our lives, and no one can change it. Over a decade ago my cell phone, email was monitored so they could stop me from contacting other people to go to street protests. They were able to monitor everyone if they wanted to. I don't know why they do this; maybe they're afraid? Just three days ago my friend (now owner of Wuhan Prison Bar) was called into the police station for three hours to be questioned about me and the band and who was helping to sell the band's new album.

EAST BERLIN PUNK
CLANDESTINE CONCERTS BEHIND THE BERLIN WALL

Rock-and-roll music remained the music of hope in desperation. No one was able to shut it down. The more the authorities tried to suppress the sound of the electric guitar, the louder it got. It took exactly fifteen years before the Berlin Wall fell in 1989. . . . For all of those difficult years, rock and roll had been our inspiration, our stubborn friend, and our most faithful ally."

—Rocking Toward a Free World: When the Stratocaster Beat the Kalashnikov by András Simonyi

East German society was based around total control and they considered punk a threat.

—Mark Reeder (Die Unbekannten)

Punk in Western Europe was a pop culture phenomenon with a political background. While on the other hand, Punk in the GDR was a political phenomenon with a pop culture background.

—"Examination of a Circumstance" by Michael Boehlke at toomuchfuture.de (SUBstitut)

Going over the border was always quite scary at the best of times. You never knew what might happen. . . . I told Die

CHAPTER 4

Toten Hosen that East Berlin was the hardest club to get into, so they had to be on their best behavior and look very normal. No jokes and definitely no punk wear or punk haircuts.

—Mark Reeder (Die Unbekannten)

It's spring 1987. After hitchhiking across snowy Europe, I've arrived in the walled city of West Berlin, a front line in the so-called Cold War. I'm at a punk rock club called SO36 in Kreuzberg, a lively district brimming with Turkish grocery stores, tea shops, and aromatic kebab stands. SO36 is a narrow, hallway-shaped venue packed with spiky Mohawks and leather jackets studded with pins and band patches. I didn't know it then, but if I'd shown up a few years earlier I may have run into David Bowie or Iggy Pop.

I ended up living in the white city of lights for the better part of a year and earned some Deutsche Marks hand delivering a thin newspaper filled with ads and coupons. I explored the city while stuffing mailboxes and ringing doorbells, all the while listening to music on my Sony Walkman cassette player, including John Lydon singing, "Now I gotta reason to be waiting—the Berlin Wall!"

One warm summer afternoon—June 6, 1987—I sat on the windowsill of our flat looking out over the city listening to David Bowie and his band play a free concert right next to the Berlin Wall at the Reichstag. The Eurythmics played the following day and on the third day of the Concert for Berlin we joined sixty thousand people to see Genesis. Later we heard that an East German crowd had gathered on their side of the Berlin Wall and had been pushed around by police for trying to listen to the music wafting over the wall, across borders. For three days East Berlin authorities tried to cut off access to the Concert for Berlin, keeping East Berlin residents a quarter of a mile from the wall. Hundreds of East Berlin youth clashed with police, and some were beaten with heavy police batons for trying to hear a few songs. Some reportedly chanted, "The wall must fall," while being carted away. Peter Schwenkow produced the concerts and later said he aimed at least a quarter of the concert speakers toward East Berlin.

The June '87 Concert for Berlin is now viewed as one in a series of political and social events that contributed to the fall of the Berlin Wall, two and a half years later, on November 9, 1989.[1] "It would be a wild exaggeration to suggest that David Bowie brought down the Berlin Wall, but 29 years ago this week, on June 7th, 1987, his concert in West Berlin did play a role in the monumental event two years later."[2]

EAST BERLIN PUNK

Long before the Concert for Berlin, radical folk and rock musicians risked arrest or worse by resisting the authoritarian regime of the DDR (Deutsche Demokratische Republik) with help from churches who embraced the counterculture as a freedom movement. Churches became sanctuaries for clandestine gatherings, political libraries, and punk rock concerts. Pankow, Planlos, Namenlos, Feeling B, Die Firma, and Schleim Keim were East German punk/new wave bands that criticized the authoritarian government during the period before the Berlin Wall was torn down. A July 20, 2011, Reuters report noted, "After a time, East Germany's protestant church provided rooms where punks could meet and play music, feeling it was its duty to shelter youths discriminated against."[3]

East German activists smuggled cassette tapes across the border to West Berlin's Radio 100 where these resistance recordings were broadcast on a monthly program called "Radio Glasnost." Punctuated by punk music, the show informed the German Democratic Republic (GDR)/East Germany's burgeoning resistance movement about upcoming demonstrations and meetings.[4]

One East German Stasi (secret police) officer, Jürgen Breski, told the BBC that he had monitored and infiltrated the East Berlin punk scene. "In 1961, Communist East Germany built a wall across Berlin, and tried to seal itself off from the West. But new research shows how concrete, barbwire and a huge effort by the Stasi failed to silence the seductive beat of rock and roll and punk."[5]

Michael Boehlke, singer for East Berlin punk band Planlos (Aimless), produced an exhibit and film in 2006 about the East German punk scene titled *OstPunk!—Too Much Future*.

> *Wherever you go / your ID card will be checked / and you say a wrong tone / What happens then, you already know it.*
>
> —"Everywhere" by Planlos

> *About 250 punks were forced to sign documents identifying themselves as potential criminal elements. They were warned to stay away from other punks and warned about consequences if they didn't. Most chose to ignore these warnings.*
>
> —East German policy toward punks in the '70s and '80s as explained by Tim Mohr (*Burning Down the Haus: Punk Rock, Revolution and the Fall of the Berlin Wall*, 36) (2018)

CHAPTER 4

Something has to happen / Who wants to stand around passively? / Were you really born / to be subordinate to it all?

—"Überall wohin's dich führt" ("Wherever You Go") by Planlos (1983)

We are the children of the machine republic.

—"Maschinenrepublik" by Die Firma (1988)

The problem in the DDR wasn't No Future, the rallying cry of British punk. As Planlos guitarist Kobs liked to say, the problem in East Germany was Too Much Future.

—Tim Mohr (*Burning Down the Haus*, 40)

In 1979 a young East German named Micha Horschig made a prediction: the fall of his country's socialist government, the German Democratic Republic (GDR), would take 10 years. On Nov. 9, 1989, the Berlin wall fell.

—Andrew Flanagan, "Punks Up Against the Wall: A New History of Punk in East Germany Shows How the Scene Wasn't a Posture, but a Movement towards Liberation," NPR, September 29, 2018

Mark Reeder grew up in Britain during the first wave of the punk revolution and cofounded new wave / punk band The Frantic Elevators with Neil Moss and Mick Hucknall (Simply Red). In 1978 Reeder went to West Berlin to buy records and he's lived there ever since. Reeder was the Berlin representative for Joy Division and Manchester record label Factory Records and in 1981 he formed the darksynth band Die Unbekannten (The Unknown). Reeder cofounded a number of record labels and continues to be a producer, DJ, composer, and filmmaker.

In his 2015 film, *B Movie: Lust and Sound in West Berlin 1979–1989*, Reeder says of Berlin's punk venue SO36, "I went out regularly to places like SO36, which was one of the most popular clubs, deep in the heart of Kreuzberg. . . . Some of the wildest bands performed in SO36." While the Berlin Wall eventually crumbled in 1989, the punk venue SO36 is still standing.

CONSIDERED PUNK A THREAT

MARK REEDER (The Frantic Elevators / Die Unbekannten / *B Movie: Lust and Sound in West Berlin 1979–1989*): Let's get one fact straight: it wasn't punk rock that brought down the Berlin Wall, but it did have a significant role to play in shaking up the Eastern European communist system. As well as the radio shows on West Berlin radio, a lot of young people listened clandestinely to John Peel's BFBS (British Forces Broadcasting Service) radio shows or the one he also had on the BBC World Service. And these shows had an impact. They fueled a desire and a dream to go to the West and buy the music that John played on his radio programs. It was music they wanted to have, not the dreary music that the state dictated they hear. There was a huge desire to listen to this new music, especially in the early '80s.

As punk in Germany evolved with their own version with German lyrics—Neue Deutsche Welle—this desire grew. Unfortunately, in the GDR punk was thwarted by the communist government simply because they didn't like it, didn't understand it, and didn't know how to control it. East German society was based around total control, and they considered punk a threat. Just like most things they didn't understand. In a way, they should have embraced punk and all its ideals, as it had a socialist working-class image and background.

MARK REEDER: The GDR authorities believed it was a form of music that had been born from the failings of the capitalist society, a collapse which had produced mass unemployment, which, in the so-called workers and farmers state, they officially didn't have. In the GDR there was no such thing as unemployment. To the East Germans, punk officially didn't exist. They obviously felt they couldn't embrace punk, as it would've meant that they'd have had to admit the GDR had unemployment, too. Punk started the ball rolling in the East, but it was more the desire to experience a techno dance party that had more of an impact. That too was a kind of vaguely extended version of the punk ethos, as the same rules applied. Techno was revolutionary, too.

DIE MAUER MUSS WEG!—THE WALL MUST GO!

MARK REEDER: I didn't go to the Bowie Reichstag concert in West Berlin (June 1987) as I didn't want to see him looking like a bank manager and jade my image of Bowie as Ziggy. But I did go over to East Berlin to see the Bruce Springsteen concert (July 19, 1988). I'm a Bowie fan and definitely *not* a Springsteen fan, but I thought it would be an interesting experience to go over to East Berlin and

CHAPTER 4

see this open-air concert by a Western musician. Somehow, I managed to get some tickets for it. I went over with my writer friend Dave Rimmer and a Swedish filmmaker friend, Fredrik Lange. We dressed in sharp 1940s suits, complete with collar and tie, baggy pants, and shiny shoes, and without question we looked totally out of place in the sea of thousands of long-haired, Wrangler denim–clad rockers. People stared at us in disbelief, as if we were from another planet. We tried to get a glimpse of the stage, so we crawled up an embankment to get a better look. Suddenly, a Stasi guy appeared and ushered us away. For a brief moment we thought we saw Bruce.

Bowie's Reichstag concert became much more significant because it was the first time that East Berlin fans who had gone near the wall to hear music drifting over were confronted with harsh brutality from the authorities. Normally no East Berliner without a special permit would dare to go anywhere near the restricted zone near the wall. But this was an opportunity to hear Bowie live! So, they decided that in numbers they were probably safe and dared to chance it. They converged near the wall only to be met by the dreaded Volkspolizei wielding batons. The crowd shouted their displeasure, and it was the first recorded incident of East Berliners chanting, "Die Mauer muss weg!" ("The wall must go!").

SECRET PUNK ROCK CHURCH IN EAST BERLIN WITH DEAD TROUSERS

> *If they can't come over to the West to see the bands they like, then I'll take the bands over to them.*
>
> —Mark Reeder (Die Unbekannten)

MARK REEDER: During one of my many visits over the Wall into East Berlin, I struck up a conversation about music with a drunken hippie in a bar. After a few comparisons about our ways of life, he eventually confided in me that he had a Fender electric guitar. In the West, having an electric guitar was no big deal, but in the communist East it was a real rarity.

I asked him if he played in a band and he told me, "No." He was only allowed to play in a church, as he had no permit. I was curious. What did he mean, "Play in a church?" He explained how hard it was to even obtain a guitar, let alone the difficulties performing. He told me about a young priest that put on a so-called Blues Mass in his church, something I imagined was vaguely similar to a Black spiritual church, where they have rock music, prayers, and singing.

I instantly thought maybe it would be possible to perform at such a Blues Mass with my own band Die Unbekannten (The Unknown) like I'd done the previous year at an illegal, secret gig in Czechoslovakia. The first illegal one there, ever, by a new wave band from the West. But as my band was more a synth band with drum machines, it wasn't easy finding such equipment in East Berlin. If getting a guitar was hard, getting a drum machine and synth was virtually impossible! When I asked about borrowing a cassette player, none of my East Berlin friends were prepared to let me use one. These expensive machines were like rare holy relics to Eastie kids. They would religiously record Western radio programs with them, and they didn't want to risk their machine being confiscated. I decided it would probably be easier to do a gig with a more conventional rock line up instead. So, I asked the Hosen (Die Toten Hosen).

It was basically a case of: *If they can't come over to the West to see the bands they like, then I'll take the bands over to them.* A few weeks later, I went with my friends to see the priest and explained to him that I wanted to bring a band over from West Germany to play a gig at his Blues Mass. He looked at me and softly said, "This is not 'a gig.' It's a church service . . . with prayers." We all immediately agreed to cooperate. I think we would probably have said yes to *anything* he suggested. It was obvious he was eager to help.

MARK REEDER: Although religion in East Germany existed, the Christian Church was merely tolerated and existed in passive opposition to the totalitarian state. It wasn't banned like in Romania or Albania where the only religion was communism. But due to its size and influence, the Communist Party was afraid to stamp it out entirely, instead choosing to permit most of its activities while maintaining close surveillance. Consequently, the Church provided one of the few spaces for open political discussion. While becoming a member afforded a degree of protection, doing so was seen as explicitly anti-state and would cause difficulties at work or in education. Therefore, if an East German citizen joined the Church, they were blatantly entering into a silent protest against the regime. So, the Church was infiltrated and constantly monitored by the Stasi (East German secret police) for potential undesirables.

As the Church had a certain amount of freedom within the confines of its own walls, they used this loophole to hold such events as a Blues Mass, where budding singer-songwriters could perform cover versions of their favorite folk tunes. It was all quite safe and therefore tolerated by the authorities. Only this time, our version of a Blues Mass wasn't going to be a conventional blues concert singing bland Cat Stevens covers, but a highly forbidden punk concert!

I was the live sound engineer at that time for what was a relatively new punk band from Duesseldorf called Die Toten Hosen (The Dead Trousers).

CHAPTER 4

I managed to convince the band and my Eastie friends to do this gig in the East. Inadvertently, I had already prepared the ground months beforehand by recording all my Toten Hosen records onto a cassette and smuggling it over the border for my friends. I knew my Eastie friends loved them, so it didn't take too much persuading to get them to help me arrange this gig.

I first explained that what we were about to undertake was quite reckless and that if we got caught, I would just be sent back to West Berlin and never allowed to enter the GDR ever again. But they would be in very serious trouble and would be seen as enemies of the state. My friends were all very excited at the prospect of doing this highly secret gig. I think it gave them the spirit of adventure. The feeling of doing something so dangerous and illegal against their regime just fueled their enthusiasm. They could finally feel that sense of excitement like I always had when I went over into the East. It had a bit of James Bond about it, too.

MARK REEDER: Together with my Eastie punk friends, I set about arranging for the Hosen to play this very clandestine gig in the Erlöserkirche (Church of Our Saviour) in the Rummelsburg suburb of East Berlin (March 1983). It would be a real religious service, complete with prayers. Initially, I still thought my band might be able to perform too, but organizing it was already becoming too stressy and in the end I decided against it.

We decided to use one of the East German punk bands from my friend's circle as a cover; they were called Planlos and they officially applied to perform at the church because you couldn't just turn up and start playing. It still had to be official, even within the confines of the church. The Stasi would therefore be aware, and it could potentially backfire, but we thought they probably wouldn't be paying too close attention and we needed a cover. So, we were able to piggyback on their gig without arousing too much suspicion. Naturally, as it was a very top-secret gig, the Hosen couldn't take their own instruments over the border. We had to use borrowed Eastie electric instruments, which were almost nonexistent there. In communist East Germany you couldn't just walk into a music store and buy an electric guitar and amp, bass, and drums and start a band. Such instruments were not on general sale.

MARK REEDER: Before you could get anywhere near an electric guitar in the communist bloc you had to pass an aptitude test to obtain the permit to allow you to own an instrument. Then pass another test to see if you were musically proficient and if your lyrics were suitable and only then could you apply for a permit to play it in public, which involved another test before a committee of brown-suited, sour-faced, elderly men. A bit like a Stalinist version of "The Voice" or "American Idol." It definitely wasn't easy, but my Eastie friends managed to arrange some guitars, a small shabby set of drums, one amp, and a broken microphone from members of unofficial punk bands Planlos and Feeling B, who later became part of Rammstein.

GOING OVER THE BORDER

MARK REEDER: With my own band partner Alistair (Gray), we successfully managed to bring all members of the Hosen over the border into East Berlin, traveling in small groups of three to avoid detection. I went last just to make sure everyone got over. I told the Hosen that East Berlin was the hardest club to get in to, so they had to be on their best behavior and look very normal, or conservative. No jokes and definitely no punk wear or punk haircuts were allowed.

Going over the border was always quite scary at the best of times. You never knew what might happen. You were going into a country that could arrest you for any kind of misdemeanor or charge you with spying for simply taking a photo of the wrong building. The border crossing at Friedrichstraße Station

Die Toten Hosen play second clandestine concert in East Berlin (1988). Photo: Holm Friedrich

CHAPTER 4

was a bright, neon-lit, no-shit kind of place and you certainly couldn't crack a friendly joke with the border guards, as they all seemed totally immune to humor.

We split the band up and staggered their entrance, simply to avoid being in a big group. I told the band members not to acknowledge each other on the border either, as this also might arouse suspicion. We would all meet up nonchalantly on the other side and then go and meet some Eastie kids who had kindly invited us to their home for snacks.

That afternoon, we all sat around this little East Berlin apartment drinking ersatzkaffee and eating homemade cheesecake while watching a prerecorded TV program on West German TV about two bands. One, an established progressive rock band called BAP from Cologne, and the other, a newcomer punk band called Die Toten Hosen from Duesseldorf! It was priceless to observe the faces of these delighted Eastie kids, as they watched the Hosen performing on TV, then they'd look over and see the band members were actually sitting there in their apartment!

MARK REEDER: We arrived at Rummelsburg S-Bahn Station a while later and some of the Hosen went off with Planlos to collect the equipment. Once everyone was assembled at the church community hall, we took what we believed to be the only photographic document of the day. We had previously decided that there would be no photos, just in case. Little did we know the unofficial Stasi informers within our little circle of Eastie friends had other plans.

That evening, the Hosen performed their exclusive secret gig to about thirty hand-picked and trusted Eastie friends, all packed into the small community hall next to the church. The atmosphere was electric. Would the Volkspolizei come storming in and arrest us all? This wasn't your conventional punk rock show. We couldn't promote it—there were no flyers, no posters, no ticket sales, there was no light show, there wasn't even a stage or a proper PA. After a few songs the microphone ceased working and Campino, the Toten Hosen singer, ended up just shouting out the words instead. It was so exciting. All the instruments went into one amp. It was a massive dirge, but it wasn't the sound that was important. It was the fact the Hosen were actually doing it.

All day the atmosphere had been very tense, which was enhanced by the cold, crisp spring weather. But once the Hosen started playing, we realized, "Fuck! We had actually managed to pull it off!" The band played for an hour and with each passing minute we expected the cops to come. Everyone was elated. But no one could anticipate what the repercussions of this gig would bring.

It was an emotional experience and such a momentous coup for us all. We had beaten the grim Stalinist system of the German Democratic Republic! We had brought a bit of Westlicher Freiheitsgefuehl to the East, and we had done something completely illegal. For the Hosen it was just another gig, this time for their fellow deprived German punk fans in the East. We all thought this kind of thing probably happens all the time. Then we discovered it was the first time that a band from the West had ever performed illegally in East Berlin! It wasn't just any band; it was a punk band! (March 1983)

MARK REEDER: The news traveled fast around the German Democratic Republic of this magnanimous event. The fact we'd used the church as a kind of refuge inspired many other struggling punk bands in the GDR to also use the church as practice rooms or for gigs. It became a symbol of resistance.

The Toten Hosen gig helped galvanize the fledgling East German punk scene with the Church. While brave and principled, the Church movement wasn't seen as cool. Although Blues Masses had existed since the '70s, most punks shunned the Church. Only after our gig did the punks realize the potential, and increasingly began to investigate the Church and quickly came to understand that it could provide both a venue and a degree of protection at a time when punk persecution from the Stasi was increasing. The priests were happy, too, that young people were coming back into the Church.

Of course, it was a potentially dangerous and volatile situation for the Church too. Although the priests absolutely loathed the music, they were incredibly supportive. They understood about freedom and wanted to show that the Church was about doing something good, and they were happy to have young people there. As you can imagine, I was a bit apprehensive about going over into East Berlin after this gig; would the Stasi arrest me? Strangely, *nothing* happened. So, I carried on smuggling cassettes and bringing celebrities over to meet my Eastie friends. Little did I know I was being monitored by the Stasi all the time. They had considered me as a highly subversive element, with an agenda to corrupt the youth of East Germany. They decided to watch me and find out what this agenda was, and where I was heading.

THE SECOND TOP-SECRET GIG

MARK REEDER: In 1988 my dissident friends, members of the Church, my pal Trevor Wilson, and I decided we would repeat Die Toten Hosen in East Berlin, this time in the grounds of the Hoffnungskirche (The Church of Hope) in Berlin's Pankow district (aka Volvograd) of East Berlin. This second secret Toten Hosen gig was disguised this time as a benefit concert for "starving Romanian orphans." Again, we invited only thirty selected friends to this "top-secret" gig.

CHAPTER 4

But when we arrived at the church hundreds of people had turned up including uniformed Volkspolizei and informers of the Stasi!

It was a freezing cold Saturday morning in the church yard. Instead of borrowing instruments this time, the Hosen were able to play on their own. I had meanwhile befriended an American soldier who had a car. As a member of the Allied Forces, he didn't get controlled at the border, so this opened up a whole new way of smuggling stuff into East Berlin. Car cassette radios, cassettes, records, foodstuffs, and also the guitars and bass and a VHS camera to film this gig.

The Hosen were supported by Die Vision, a popular East German indie group whose album *Torture* I would end up producing in East Berlin during the last months of 1989, as their country fell apart. In reality, as before with Planlos, we needed Die Vision to be the front for the gig. However, this particular second secret gig with Die Vision was in fact not as secret as we had hoped. The East German Volkspolizei hung about outside while Die Vision heated up the assembled audience and the Stasi took steps to stop the Toten Hosen from playing.

Moments before the Hosen were to perform it was announced by the priest that "Unfortunately, due to the ice age that had enveloped the Republic," the Hosen were sadly unable to play. A disappointed groan was followed by the usual yielding resignation to the powers of the spoilsport communist state as some of the punky people spilled out onto the streets outside, angry at the denial by their state of an afternoon of music and fun.

We desperately tried our best to resolve the situation, a situation that looked increasingly hopeless. Then we hit upon an idea. We thought the Stasi probably didn't know what the Hosen actually looked like, so we suggested to the priest that they should pretend to be simply another band from Dresden. As he meekly announced to the disgruntled audience that another band from Dresden would perform, I ran about urging the kids (with a wink) to return because "another band from Dresden were going to play instead. And you *definitely* want to *stay* for that." Some just blankly stared incredulously at me and walked off, while others heard the pfennig drop and gleefully hurried back. The Hosen gig went ahead, and they played for about three-quarters of an hour, until our deception was eventually discovered, and the show was stopped.

MARK REEDER: After the gig we took Die Vision, Die Hosen, and a huge group of East German punks downtown for a slap-up meal in the Haus Budapest, a lavish and by East German standards very expensive Hungarian restaurant on the Karl-Marx Allee. To ensure we got a table, I and one of my US Forces friends, dressed in his full Class B dress uniform, had gone into the restaurant a week before and ordered a table for twenty people. Going by the look on his face, the waiter just couldn't believe it. He groveled about in true subservient style and was probably already mentally spending his Western cash tip on frozen peas and coffee in the Intershop as we left the premises.

It was dusk as we approached the red, green, and bright white lights of the Haus Budapest, which cascaded onto the footpath outside. Asking everyone to quietly remain outside for a moment, I walked in first with my soldier friend, the waiter instantly recognized us and beaming, nodded his approval of his eagerly awaited American guests. Then in we all traipsed, a biscuitized, boozed, and bleary-eyed band of punky brothers, some still drinking bottled beer and shouting loudly. Indeed, for nearly all of these Eastie kids, this was the first time they had ever set foot—or even been allowed—into this high-class restaurant. The waiter's face sank. He stared at me with gamma ray eyes. "What the hell is this? And where are the soldiers?"

We were over twenty people, mostly scruffy-looking punks. They all sat about a bit too leisurely, smoking and drinking and feeling what it's like to be decadent. We ordered practically everything on the menu. Paying with the secretly smuggled-in East German cash, which was a long way from being spent up.

MARK REEDER: As midnight approached, we hurriedly left the restaurant for a mad dash back to the border. Our American soldier friend broke as many traffic rules as possible, such as driving the wrong way down a one-way street or skipping the red traffic lights. He wasn't bothered about the police, as only the Soviet military police could stop him.

Once at the Friedrichstrasse station (Palace of Tears) border crossing from East into West Berlin, I met up again with the band. Campino (Die Toten Hosen) was stopped by the first guard and asked to remove his woolly hat. He readily complied, and as he did so, he revealed a head of bright red hair sticking up all over. Startled at this impressive sight, the guard exclaimed dryly, "Which idiot let you in?" To which Campino sharply replied "One of *your* idiots!" Without further ado, he was immediately hauled off to have his personals taken down and have the guard with the brown nose come along with his funnel and rubber gloves.

Die Toten Hosen concert in the Erlöserkirche in Rummelsburg was the very first punk concert to be held in a church in East Germany. I wasn't fully aware at the time of the significance or the impact our little secret gig would have. I certainly had no idea that no one had ever dared to do such a thing before. The audacity of such a show of anti-state fueled the punks throughout the GDR. And everywhere in the Republic, the churches became places to play. The priests

"Remember the 1987 neo-Nazi attack on the punk concert at Zion Church" (former East Berlin) October 2017 concert series. Poster contributed by Horst Edler and produced by Wenke Rottstock

were delighted; it didn't matter that they didn't like the music, they were happy that young people were coming to church again, "And who knows, maybe it will have an effect on some of them?" So, they supported the punks and let them use the halls, even as practice rooms.

STATE-OWNED RECORD LABEL

MARK REEDER (Die Unbekannten): I named my record label MFS after the Ministerium für Staatssicherheit (Stasi—state police). I changed the meaning to Masterminded for Success. After my experience recording and producing the last album of the GDR—for East German indie band Die Vision—I managed to talk the former state-owned record label AMIGA into making a techno label. I obviously didn't tell them I was going to call it MFS. I only ever used the full name in their presence, as I had an inclination they would be horrified. And when they saw the first MFS poster, let's say I had a lot of explaining to do.

JM: How dangerous was it to be a punk in the DDR? (East Germany in 1970s and 1980s)

MITA SCHAMAL (Namenlos): It was extremely dangerous. You couldn't walk one hundred meters without being mobbed by your "own" people. "You should be gassed," "You belong in the concentration camp," and the like. We were constantly harassed. For example, even very small bar owners played tough by asking to see our ID cards before letting us buy a box of matches. But the most annoying were the *Abschnittsbevollmächtigten* (almighty section agents) or other cop types who regularly took us to check our personal details, which ultimately resulted in eternal physical and psychological violence. There was, so to speak, no public space in which we were not harassed. You didn't get into a disco. We were scum.

JM: How did your band Namenlos begin?

MITA SCHAMAL (Namenlos): We wanted to make music and one thing led to another. We were just honest and when there were opportunities to play in the churches, we did it. When we were facing jail time, we didn't say, "No, we don't dare." It's like if you're pregnant with a man you love, you don't just have an abortion because you fear you could die during the child's birth. At least not at that age. I remember that an adult woman had warned me; she was already in jail and knew that it was no piece of cake. I briefly took to contemplation, returned to myself and knew exactly, "I have to perform. If *you* don't tell the truth and say what's going on, then we'll do it, you cowards." Maybe it's like the kids going out on the streets now (2019) because they're damn right.

CHAPTER 4

JM: What role did Ostpunks play in the fall of the Berlin Wall and changing the system in the DDR?

MITA SCHAMAL (Namenlos): You can put on this jacket, and it certainly looks very cool but what do we already know about the larger international contexts? I think if this system had wanted to (East Germany in the 1980s) and got the order from its authorities (Soviet Union), all the dissidents and punks would've been placed in labor camps or shot in the stadium. So many things play an overriding role here. Russia, America, maybe West Germany? The worldwide political situation played a role, which is constantly reorienting itself.

KID CONGO POWERS (The Gun Club / The Cramps / Nick Cave & The Bad Seeds / Pink Monkey Birds): I knew Mark Reeder. I never saw any concerts, but I was aware from my West Berlin friends that there was a scene in East Berlin. I knew they would give people in the East cassettes from the West; there was a lot of cassette trading going on. People knew about The Gun Club and The Cramps even though there were no sales of official records, because there were a lot of tapes in circulation. It was an underground operation. I always thought that was really incredible. I encountered that also because I played a bit with the Berlin group Die Haut, who were part of The Bad Seeds family of people, and we went to Ukraine, and it was a very much the same. They knew Die Haut and Lydia Lunch and Kid Congo. They knew all of this through trading cassettes that were terrible, tenth-generation copies of music, but the music, nonetheless. When we went to Ukraine, we met many kids who were well aware of Western underground music.

I went to a dinner party with Mick Harvey, and he asked me if I wanted to fill in on the tour with Nick Cave and The Bad Seeds. They were doing a tour and Barry Adamson was leaving the band. Mick was going to move to bass, and they needed a second guitar player. I said, "Of course, yes," and I went to Berlin to start rehearsing for the tour. One of my first duties was to film the scene in *Wings of Desire* with Nick Cave and The Bad Seeds.

Coming to Berlin was really opening and amazing. I realized, "This is why they're here!" I could unbutton my shirt, talk louder, and just be myself again and not think about the music industry. I didn't even know what anyone was saying, I don't speak German! I fell in love with the vibrancy and creativity of the scene and the freedom of it. Because we did the film right away, I thought, "This is a place where film, dance, performance, visual art, and all kinds of music all meet up and it all can be collaborative." It's all one thing and all encased in West Berlin, surrounded by the East. It was immediately attractive to me, and I thought, "I'm moving here."

I moved there on May Day, and they're very well known for their May Day rockets and demonstrations. In Kreuzberg there were cars overturned and tanks going down the street and the Aldi Market was burning down and there were drummers in front of it drumming until it was flatly done. I just thought, "This place is amazing." I loved it.

Being in *Wings of Desire* was an incredible experience and I got to meet Wim Wenders. It really captures the feeling of Berlin. Even the beginning of the film where they're flying in; I remember flying into West Berlin and looking down at all of those blocks of buildings and seeing the Alex tower in Alexanderplatz. I'm very proud to have been involved with that film. I knew it was going to be special. Henri Alekan was the cinematographer from Cocteau films and Wim Wenders really made a big announcement, "You're being filmed by a legend, and you are going to look amazing." He wasn't wrong and he was so generous saying, "You are being filmed by one of the greatest cinematographers ever." I thought it was really sweet of him, and everyone applauded. We were all very grateful and the results speak for themselves.

Berlin brought incredible freedom, but also incredible isolation. It was two things. Luckily, I had a ready-made creative community to go into, for better or worse. There were extreme hedonistic values going on. There's a darkness to Berlin as well; I'm well aware of the history of Germany. And you can see war there. West Berlin was half bombed out and half completely modernly rebuilt. If you'd go over to East Berlin you'd say, "Oh, this is where the old buildings are. This looks like other parts of Germany." That divide was very distinct. I just followed my lead in Berlin and of course, got in trouble. That's what I do. Or did. But that's a much bigger issue that I was dealing with at the time. I was set adrift into a culture I had no idea about. I had to make my way into that, and many encounters ensued.

5

MUSIC IS THAT POWERFUL TOOL
BLACKFIRE NAVAJO PUNKS

Politics is inseparable from life. If you have government or other interests that are trying to oppress you as a person or as a nation, as was our case, then there has to be some way of, I don't want to say lashing out, but voicing and expressing yourself. For us music became that powerful tool that people would listen to.

—Clayson Benally (Blackfire / Sihasin)

You can't listen to punk and be a passive person. It just doesn't work that way! Music that inspires change is the very nature of punk rock.

—Jeneda Benally (Blackfire / Sihasin)

A guitar won't stop a bulldozer. If it could, I would use it to smash the state to pieces. But the guitar—metaphorically and literally—can be used as an instrument to educate, inspire, and inform people.

—Klee Benally (Blackfire)

On October 1, 1996, MTV News announced that Joey Ramone would be playing at the Rock the Reservation (Hodiits'a') concert on October 19 at the Navajo Reservation in Tuba City, Arizona: "Ramone will front a new band, The Resistance. He's also expected to guest on a song or two with the punk-ska

CHAPTER 5

band The Independents, who are also performing along with Navajo rockers Blackfire."[1]

A flyer distributed at the drug/alcohol-free concert read,

> A Message from Joey Ramone: Young kids of today, they feel like they've been given a raw deal. Inheriting a nation that's been destroyed. Greed, politics, government, environment, racism. What are they doing about getting over these hurdles? The hurdles known as LIFE. Killing themselves with hard drugs and alcohol. Bailing out instead of getting fired up about the situation and doing something positive about it. Standing idle, they feel a lack of worth and importance. Observing this makes me want to try and help. They need to be inspired.

Navajo punk band Blackfire was started in 1989 by three siblings from the Benally family: Klee (guitar/vocals), Jeneda (bass/vocals), and Clayson (drums/vocals). Their mother, Berta, is a folk singer, and she organized the Hoodíítsa' (Rock the Reservation) concert with Joey Ramone. Blackfire's first EP was produced by C. J. Ramone and the last recording ever made by Joey Ramone appears on the Blackfire songs "What Do You See" and "Lying to Myself" from their 2001 album *One Nation Under*. In the recording from the 1996 Rock the Reservation concert, Joey Ramone introduces one of the Ramones' most popular tunes: "This goes out to all the fucking politicians out there. It's called 'Beat on the Fucking Brat!'" (Author's note: Thanks to Berta Benally for the Joey Ramone flyer text.)

Blackfire's 2005 double album, *Silence Is a Weapon*, features one CD of hard-edged punk rock and a second with their father, Jones Benally, singing traditional Diné (Navajo) music. Often their songs combine both elements. Their mother, Berta, helped produce the band and after years of harassment from the FBI, due to the revolutionary nature of their music, Jeneda and Clayson started another music project in 2012 called Sihasin, which means "hope" in the Diné language. Klee continues to be a media activist and his solo punk albums include *Appropriation* (2021), which he describes as "performance art intervention against cultural genocide."

STANDING UP AGAINST RELOCATION

JM: I've viewed Blackfire as being one of those bands on the front lines of the punk revolution. The 2011 film *Punk in Africa* highlights bands like Suck, Wild Youth, and multiracial National Wake that opposed apartheid in South Africa. *OstPunk!—Too Much Future* (2006) documents the political punk scene in East Germany. *My Buddha Is Punk* highlights the punk movement amid the military junta government of Myanmar (Burma). There seems to be many punk bands on the front lines of revolutionary moments worldwide.

CLAYSON BENALLY (Blackfire / Sihasin): We are from Big Mountain—Black Mesa (Arizona, US)—and we use our music as a voice and mechanism to talk about issues. I never considered myself an activist. We just found our voice through our instruments and started songwriting about what was happening. One of our first songs was called "Resist" about standing up against relocation that was happening to our people.

We were youth then and played our first concerts in 1989, going into our communities where most of our youth were dealing with everything from drug addiction to suicide. We came into the schools and there was that recognition, "Here are some peers that are playing music. Maybe you can reach through to our youth." We started using our music as a form of education. The ability to communicate our message through music enabled us to travel throughout the world and eventually go to places like Sub-Saharan Africa in Mali with the Tamasheq and be on the front lines and see that revolution.

Politics is inseparable from life. If you have government or other interests that are trying to oppress you as a person or as a nation, as was our case, then there has to be some way of, I don't want to say lashing out, but voicing and expressing yourself. For us music became that powerful tool that people would listen to. Because our grandmothers back on the reservation had tired voices. They were going to the UN, and they were speaking, and it was hard to hear them cry and share their stories. Not many people were listening.

JM: Blackfire has combined Diné (Navajo) singing with high-energy punk rock. Tell me about combining these realms.

CLAYSON BENALLY: For us to fully talk about our process and how Blackfire and Sihasin developed we have to talk about the land—Big Mountain, Black Mesa (Arizona). Those are our roots and foundation. Being traditional people, living off the land and being self-sustaining as Diné. We call ourselves Diné which means *the people*. Of course, Navajo was the given name. Being an Indigenous person, there's a lot of parallels between punk rock and being a Native person, being Indigenous. Both have been considered outcasts at one point or another. Being Native wasn't cool. There's a lot of racism and hardships that our people have endured and one of the greatest tragedies in American history is the region of Big Mountain. This is a land with about fourteen thousand displaced people that were forcibly relocated and removed from their homeland. That's right where we're from and our families were all impacted.

JENEDA BENALLY (Blackfire / Sihasin): When we were growing up on the reservation back home, we had a very traditional lifestyle where we would chop wood and work by the light of the day, by the sun. That dictated your day. Having to haul water was such an important lesson because every drop of water meant something; you didn't ever waste water. We had a lot of sheep, livestock, and horses in our family's area. In the early '80s the federal government—the BIA (Bureau of Indian Affairs)—was forcing our people into relocating.

CLAYSON BENALLY: Congress enacted the Relocation Act in 1974 and started forced relocation. Basically, they had discovered one of the largest deposits of coal and there was a very lengthy land dispute. Essentially Blackfire was born from the Peabody Coal Mine that exists here. The BIA stands for the Bureau of Indian Affairs, but in modern terms in the Gulf War they created a similar type of situation also called the BIA—the Bureau of *Iraqi* Affairs. The original BIA was set up by the Department of War to access resources and land, viewing the people as resources as well. There's a lot of historical trauma.

When the BIA created this land dispute, they pitted two tribes against each other: Navajo and Hopi. Two nations that needed each other, that survived for millennia living side by side. When the United States federal government intervened, they spent millions of dollars on PR trying to promote a war that wasn't there. And they utilized that to divide and redistrict the land.

They separated the land; this is Hopi and this is Navajo. And anybody on the wrong side of the fence would be removed. We never relocated. We were part of that resistance. Our grandmothers and elders would go to Washington, DC, to try and prevent relocation from happening. But at the time our people were looked at as wards of the United States government. We had no voice. We weren't allowed to vote as Native Americans in the state of Arizona until the '60s. Even though it was our Navajo language—*Diné*—that was used as the code for Americans during World War II.

Our law was natural law. That is parallel to ideals of anarchism or punk rock—natural law and living off the land. To see that lifestyle being taken away and to have the United States government and mining companies take over, that's really where that fuel and anger started to inspire us to pick up instruments and play music at a young age. We felt the need the communicate the idea that, "Hey, this is not right."

JENEDA BENALLY: What we couldn't understand was: How could this still be happening in modern history? People read about the Indian wars in history books and think, "That's a sad history. But I'm in no way, as a contemporary citizen, contributing to the annihilation and genocide of Indigenous peoples." When this is still happening today and there are still people who are resisting this violence.

CLAYSON BENALLY: Historically we did have a warrior society and when the enemy was approaching you would smother the fire and send up a smoke signal. That would be a warning that the enemy was approaching. In our culture the word for this is *koʼłízhįį*, or Black Fire. "Relocation is genocide" is what our elders would say. Because the moment you sever yourself from your birthplace, land, and the culture, that is when you disappear and cease to exist.

JM: I want to ask you about the violence that began to permeate the punk rock scene. Some paths of punk embraced that, and mainstream media portrayed punk as violent and then kids who came to punk through the mainstream emulated that. I did an interview recently with Belinda Carlisle, singer for The Go-Go's, who was also the first drummer for The Germs in Los Angeles. During the interview she said, "I'm looking at my body now and see the scar from my Germs burn." Darby Crash held a lit cigarette to people in The Germs circle. In the punk scene there have been people like Darby and Iggy Pop who hurt themselves. I'm guessing that's something you wouldn't want to incorporate into your music. What do you think about singers harming themselves on stage?

CLAYSON BENALLY: As an Indigenous person coming from a history of colonization and five hundred years of violence against our people, I do not see the need to harm myself. It was actually the complete opposite response where we were trying to uplift and bring our youth out of that self-harm, out of the dark paths of vicious cycles of violence, where you have some of the worst of it from that oppression. It's first taught to us by colonizers and then it becomes a learned behavior. It was this vicious cycle that we would see happening in our own families: our uncles and relatives using violence against our own people. We are fortunate to have a strong cultural foundation and our traditional songs and healing ceremonies that helped us become a strength and a pillar. We started putting our traditional songs into our music to try to empower and uplift people so they wouldn't feel that hatred toward themselves.

WE'RE ALL HUMAN

JENEDA BENALLY: For me, punk rock is a response to the oppression, injustice, and inequality that we face constantly. Punk rock is organic, it's raw, it's emotion. I felt like the music was about taking an active role to make change. You can't listen to punk and be a passive person. It just doesn't work that way! Music that inspires change is the very nature of punk rock. We were at the protests with our grandmothers, having to be the voices for them because their voices were so soft. Punk music was very much a response to that oppression, injustice, and

CHAPTER 5

One Nation Under *by Diné (Navajo) punk band Blackfire (2001)*. Contributed: Berta Benally / Tacoho Productions / Tacoho Records

inequality. It was really difficult to be a youth at that time. For me, that creative musical outlet was really important, and we used punk music as a way to get the information out to people. "If people only knew about the injustices, about the genocide that our people are still facing in modern days, then they would want to do *something*." Because we're all human.

As Blackfire we utilized every song to address a different issue that we saw happening: Indigenous rights, protecting sacred places, youth suicide. Our traditional songs and staying up all night singing at ceremonies with our father translated so easily into punk rock because it was the same thing. It was about healing, truth, and telling a story. It was very easy for us to move from traditional singing into punk rock.

UPSIDE-DOWN FLAG

CLAYSON BENALLY: Our culture is in peril. We used to get so much flack for burning the flag and putting flags upside down. We were banned from certain areas.

JENEDA BENALLY: We were banned from towns for hanging the flag upside down. We kept telling people, "An upside-down flag is a sign of distress!"

CLAYSON BENALLY: We even had the FBI threaten to pull the plug before we even started playing at our show in Washington, DC, on the mall at the American Indian Smithsonian Institute. They told us we couldn't hang a Leonard Peltier banner. We could not put up a banner that they did not agree with. We could hold it, but we could not tie it or fix it to any part of the area on the mall in Washington, DC.

JM: What did you do?

JENEDA BENALLY: We held the banner. And we sang a song. It gave us a platform to talk about the fact that we were being oppressed at that concert!

CLAYSON BENALLY: Howard Bass, the director of the museum at that time, came to us and said, "This has never happened that the FBI has approached us and told us that a band cannot play until a banner is removed, 'Or they won't play at all.'" We said, "What if we carry it or hold it? We are not physical property of the United States government." You'd think that in Washington, DC, on the mall you would have freedom of speech. But they said, "No. It's actually a zone where free speech doesn't apply!"

JENEDA BENALLY: But it gave us a platform to talk more in depth about Leonard Peltier, an American Indian Movement political prisoner. When we were Blackfire, for quite some time we were followed around by the FBI. All over the world. And it became really intense where my phone was tapped, and we were getting constant calls from the FBI.

CLAYSON BENALLY: We ended up playing world stages. We went to Prague for the WTO (World Trade Organization) meetings and protests. We were invited as an NGO to the United Nations at their draft Declaration of Indigenous People's Rights. We were out there; we were playing in prison yards in military complexes where Leonard Peltier was being held prisoner and working closely with the young Black Panther movement. We were connecting with different groups and uniting them and that became quite a threat.

You hear about COINTELPRO or different events that have transpired throughout history where people were threatened. But to have the FBI question and threaten you and actually *want* you to play certain locations or concerts so they can try and draw out members of communities they were looking for. It's all part of that story and how music and punk rock became a threat. It impacted our family and the disbandment eventually of our group. COINTEL is alive and well.

JENEDA BENALLY: We were being hassled for a long time, being interrogated by the FBI. When you use music for a greater voice sometimes it scares people when that voice gets heard.

CHAPTER 5

CLAYSON BENALLY: That's when you know you're being effective, when you have the FBI calling you up!

RAMONESHEADS

JENEDA BENALLY: The first time I heard punk music it wasn't even about hearing the music. It was more about the feeling of punk! It was this explosive sound that felt honest to me. There were no decorations. There was nothing pretty about it. It's just real. I can't remember what the first Ramones song was that we heard, but we loved it. The funny thing about the Ramones: we saw Johnny, Joey, Tommy, C. J., and Marky Ramone and we thought, "Wow! That's a big family! And they're all brothers—how *awesome* is that!"

CLAYSON BENALLY: We're a band of siblings (Blackfire) and we thought, "We're a family band and they're a family band, too! Sure beats the hell out of being compared to The Partridge Family!"

JENEDA BENALLY: Later on, we realized our mistake! The Ramones were *not* brothers! I met the Ramones after I had just gotten my first car and went to go hear them play down in Phoenix. I ran into an old friend of mine, and we decided, "There's Deadheads and all of these funny groups of people who follow different musical acts." We decided to become *Ramones*heads. We decided we were going to find their next concert and looked on the back of a T-shirt and saw that it was Austin, Texas. So, my friend and I just drove to Austin. I'd written a note to the Ramones brothers because I was really excited about meeting another family band that was punk rock. I wrote the note and gave it to C. J. Ramone. I put our hotel phone number on there and C. J. called me and the first thing he says is, "I'm so sorry to tell you but we are not a family band." [laugh] I was shattered! I was like, "Great, we're going back to The Partridge Family." Not that there's anything wrong with them.

FAMILY BAND

C. J. RAMONE (Ramones): I was touring with the Ramones, and we'd finished a show and we jumped in the van and Jeneda (Benally) passed a postcard through the back window with a picture of her family, and it said, "Hey, we're a family band, too. We'd love to meet you!" So, I started talking to Jeneda, Clayson, and Klee. We had a little giggle when I explained to Jeneda that we're not brothers. It actually comes from when the band was first getting together, and Dee Dee took the name Dee Dee Ramone because Paul McCartney used to check into hotels under the name Paul Ramone so he wouldn't be recognized. Dee Dee thought the Ramones were going to be as big as The Beatles.

I eventually met Berta (Benally) and we really got close. I was amazed at how cool their lifestyle was and what solid people they were. They met Joey (Ramone) and they got to be really close with Joey, too. They were going to go into the studio to make their first album with Joey and I don't remember exactly what happened—if Joey had gone away or got ill—but he couldn't do the record and they already had the studio time booked. And they asked me, "Would you be willing to do it with us?" I said, "Absolutely. I would love to." It was my first time doing anything like that, recording and producing a record. We had such good energy together.

We got together a couple of days before and tweaked all the songs and added little parts and got into the studio and we just let it rip. We were all inexperienced to a degree, but the energy was just so good. I got Jeneda to sing a little bit and Jones (Benally) came in and sang and the final result was pretty cool. It's a little heavy on the bass and kind of what we were going for. I've been friends with them so long that they're my family.

JM: It's powerful to hear Blackfire combining traditional *Diné* (Navajo) chanting with high-energy rock 'n' roll.

C. J. RAMONE: In the beginning I don't know if they had actually considered that. I just thought it had to be, "This is where you guys are from. We've got to make sure you get your dad on there." It might have been Klee who actually brought it up first, but I loved the idea and thought it was great. They had another friend of theirs come in—Robert Tree Cody—and he played flute on a track. They did a great job on the record. They were very young, but they knew what they wanted and had a definite message. I was honored to do it with them.

CLAYSON BENALLY: I always thought the Ramones were completely nonpolitical. You listen to the music: "Beat on the brat / Beat on the brat / Beat on the brat with a baseball bat / Oh yeah!" There were a couple of songs that resonated with us as Blackfire. We only rarely did covers, but every once in a while we'd do "Lobotomy." I remember talking with Joey (Ramone) about it, and I said, "We need a song for the kids to get mindless to—'Lobotomy!'" That was kind of my joke to him, but he didn't think it was funny. He said, "That's a very serious song. That's a political song to me," because Joey was institutionalized. His mom put him through hell—a lot of medication and shock treatment.

He said, "This song is for the voiceless. People who are put into mental institutions have no voice. They're stripped of their identity." That was a changing point for me. I was going to go back and relisten to these songs and try to hear

CHAPTER 5

what the true message and meaning was within those songs. It was pure energy: "One-two-three-four."

Later that was the formula that C. J. (Ramone) brought to our group. When we went to cut our first EP in 1994 it was a five-song disc and C. J. sat down with us and said, "Okay, you have to have a sound." Before that we had different styles, and it was more eclectic. He said, "These are the songs that sound most like you and don't sound like anyone else. Focus on these and think about a formula. For the Ramones, our formula has always been songs that are two and a half minutes, three minutes, tops. Think about it like energy. Give it everything you've got—like 110 percent—and just when the song reaches its highest point, end it there and go into the next song." That was the formula that C. J. brought to us.

C. J. RAMONE: Joey (Ramone) was actually institutionalized at one point. Yeah, it's really not a humorous topic by any stretch of the imagination. But that's who the Ramones stood up for, who they were championing. What Joey was saying in "Lobotomy"—it's pretty straight and to the point. But that was part of the genius of the Ramones: taking such a serious subject and expressing it through their very twisted sense of humor and you get something that is not overtly political, but at its roots it completely is. The Ramones were *socially* political, without a doubt. The Ramones were the voice of the weirdos and the outcasts. They were speaking for everyone on the outside. Just look where some of their catchphrases came from—the movie *Freaks* (directed by Tod Browning, 1932).

If you're talking about politics as in *the political system*: not very. The only song by the Ramones that was really about the political system was "Bonzo Goes to Bitburg." It's one of my favorite songs—it's a great song. But Johnny was very much a Reagan Republican whereas Dee Dee, Joey, and Tommy were much more Left. Joey in particular came from a very liberal family. But Johnny was the boss and because everyone's political opinions were so distant from each other, we just didn't do anything political. "Bonzo Goes to Bitburg" was such a great song that Johnny said, "I like it." That's why on the record the song is called "My Brain Is Hanging Upside Down." He didn't want it advertised as an anti-Reagan song. That's the only song about the political system they had—everything else was social politics. It was about you, me, and us and who fits in with us. And all the weird things that go on. [laugh]

CLAYSON BENALLY: I have a funny story. We spent a lot of time with Joey Ramone. He became our mentor—Uncle Joey. He helped us along on our path in so many different ways, being in the studio constantly. C. J. Ramone also has been there for us. They became part of our family. I remember talking to Joey (Ramone) specifically about the idea of punk rock being dangerous. We were sitting in the studio in Manhattan recording our album *One Nation Under*, and we're at Shelter Island Studio—they're doing some mixing in the backroom and I'm sitting there watching this history of punk rock with Joey Ramone. He's going scene by scene and talking about all the different eras and what happened, what occurred from his perspective, and the moment the Sex Pistols come on the screen Joey Ramone says, "Those fucking assholes! We pissed in their beer!" He was talking about the feud they had and said, "Those guys were fake. They were contrived."

CLAYSON BENALLY: The one thing Joey Ramone said that I really took to heart was, "Punk rock was on a natural path." You look at the history of rock 'n' roll with the energy and the waves that were occurring with music, it was a revolution, and it had a natural course and direction. Punk was the next stage of awakening for music. He was talking about how the Sex Pistols, in his view, undermined that energy because they capitalized off of the fear, and it being dangerous, so much so that radio stations began banning and preventing punk rock from being played on MTV. It became a hidden taboo, a subculture. I think it eventually got there, but it had been popularized to the point where the message, the meaning, and the politics were stripped out of it. You can also see that in hip-hop or other genres where the music and the message start off revolutionary, as a powerful tool to connect youth and bring people together to think and talk and find solutions through music.

SACRED PLACE OF RESPECT

JENEDA BENALLY: When we played as Blackfire, at a lot of punk shows we were always really watchful about what was going on in the pit. If we ever saw violence, we would stop. If we ever saw sexual harassment, we would stop. We made it very clear as a band that anybody who was in that pit, in the audience, that this was a sacred place of respect.

CLAYSON BENALLY: One of my favorite shows would be the Ramones shows. Everybody would be singing along, enjoying arm in arm, singing at the top of their lungs. There was love! It was the coolest thing. But other punk shows you'd go to and the energy would be so down it was like war. You were struggling to just keep your head above the crowd, from hitting the ground. For us, we were very conscious of that energy and how we wanted to use it. We saw it as a powerful tool to uplift. Anger is an emotion—it's a secondary emotion—but we wanted to use that inspiration and emotion to motivate people to do positive change.

CHAPTER 5

COVID-19 AND FOOD APARTHEID

KLEE BENALLY (Blackfire): It's a big challenge right now (March 2020). The Navajo Nation is being ravaged by COVID-19. We have 597 confirmed cases with over seventeen deaths. This is less than a month since the beginning of March, and the cases spiked in our communities. We live in what's called a food desert or a food apartheid. It's the size of West Virginia, with a population roughly of 200,000 people, and we only have about sixteen grocery stores, including small grocers. We're already facing scarcity issues due to panic buying and hoarding. We have a handful of government-run hospitals and some private ones, and they've provided substandard healthcare for years. They're now overwhelmed to capacity. This area now has four times the national average per capita of COVID-19 cases.

KLEE BENALLY: There's a range of analyses you can have of this virus. You can go all the way back to the first biological warfare used against Indigenous people as an act of genocide through the use of smallpox blankets. By some estimates there may have been as many as twenty million Indigenous people that died in the years following the first wave of the European invasion, due to diseases brought by colonizers. That was an estimated 95 percent of our population.

Looking at present-day reality, especially on the Navajo Nation, we have more than two thousand abandoned uranium mines. Back in the 1930s and '40s when uranium was first being mined, our people were not given protective equipment in these mines and today none of those mines have been cleaned up. The impacts of uranium mines in our communities is a grave injustice. We have an extremely disproportionate high rate of cancers in our community. We face a legacy of environmental racism that is directly tied to resource colonialism and has systematically compromised our people's immune systems. This colonial violence, and violence against the earth, has made our people more susceptible to viruses like COVID-19.

MEANINGFUL ACTS OF SOLIDARITY

KLEE BENALLY: The people who are panicking right now, for the most part, are people who aren't as connected to mother earth. This comes from teachings from my father, who is a *hatáli* medicine practitioner. He's saying that the people who are close to earth have an understanding and when this kind of disaster strikes, we are prepared because we listen and work with the land and are not dependent on outside forces. Those who have been removed from that connection have problems. This is the time to remind ourselves to choose ways of life that ensure we can move forward in a healthy and harmonious way with all of creation.

KLEE BENALLY: As an artist, there's no dichotomy between art and life with our traditional teachings as Diné people. There's no separation; our life is creation. So, our creative expression comes in many different ways. What I look at is: What are the issues facing our communities and what strategies can be most effective? Is it going to be through song? Is it going to be through prayer or action? Or can it be all of them?

I never separate and compartmentalize prayer. That's something I always carry with me because that's how I was taught. Every action is a prayer, because that's how I understand my existence. From when I wake up to even understanding how I relate to food. This comes from my father and elders who have educated and imparted me with this. And I do see a need for direct action in our communities. Unmediated action and not waiting around for politicians or other authorities.

A GUITAR CANNOT STOP A BULLDOZER

KLEE BENALLY: I recorded an acoustic album through support from Patreon called *The Unsustainable Sessions* (2019). In weird ways, it's prophetic of these times because every piece on that album is imagining the apocalypse. But also looking at: What is the human response to despair? How can we build and maintain harmony? I helped to found the Táala Hooghan Infoshop, a radical direct-action resource center here in Kinlani, near Flagstaff, Arizona. We started that in 2007 and have always had an orientation of mutual aid and support focused on environmental and social issues primarily through outreach to unsheltered communities and advocating that they're treated justly. Music is sometimes a component of that, but I've put that on hold to move forward with what's effective.

As I mentioned before, a guitar is not going to stop a bulldozer. A guitar might be able to rally people together, and inform and educate people, but right now I think the critical need for intervention is present, especially in this dire situation of food scarcity, with so many in our communities being vulnerable in this COVID-19 crisis. It demands more of us. As long as I'm healthy and able to do this work, I'll be out there. The moment I'm not able or not healthy, maybe I'll start making more music.

Practically, a guitar won't stop a bulldozer. If it could, I would use it to smash the state to pieces. But I think we would argue that the state and structural systems are probably stronger than a piece of beautiful maple wood. The guitar—metaphorically and literally—can be used as an instrument to reach out to educate, inspire, and inform people. Songwriting on that level can serve to mobilize people. But that's limited. When it comes down to direct intervention, I'd rather not be on a stage singing about an injustice when I see it happening in front of me. I'll jump off the stage and address the injustice directly.

JM: Since the pandemic began and life has been turned upside down, many of us are wondering how this could be an opportunity to let go of capitalism and create new systems based on cooperation and caring.

KLEE BENALLY: I don't think it's a question; it's more or less an observation of the failures of capitalism and colonialism. Indigenous people have been saying forever that there are consequences for a way of life that's based on violence against the earth and against all the beings. If we look at the situation before this crisis, the greatest humanitarian threat facing the world at that point was global warming. Indigenous perspectives say that global warming is a consequence of a war against mother earth. We should be making capitalism irrelevant through establishing mutual aid networks and cooperatives so we can restore a more sustainable and natural way of living. This is in line with our natural law as Indigenous people. This is an observation made by the anarchist author Kropotkin, who wrote the book *Mutual Aid: A Factor in Evolution*. Something our elders have been saying and our prophecies have been teaching us is that we have to make a choice to live in a way that is healthy and in harmony with all of creation. I highly recommend that people focus where they're at and build mutual aid groups. This system has failed us for a long time. So, it's up to us to ensure that we take care of each other. We can't rely on these governments. This is an opportunity for all of us to mobilize and dig in deep and ensure that capitalism and this system that failed us a long time ago can't recuperate from this virus.

KLEE BENALLY: If folks are just sitting there, planning what they're going to do after this virus passes and learning some hobby and focusing on some weird personal project and waiting for the crisis to blow over, then that's part of the failure. Then we're not learning the lesson that mother earth is teaching us right now: that we are out of balance.

KLEE BENALLY: This work would be terrifyingly boring without a good soundtrack! [laugh] So keep that in mind. Music can be a catharsis. Music can be that cheerleader that moves us forward. Sometimes music is just as good as coffee.

MUSIC IS THAT POWERFUL TOOL

We all know it's the rich against the poor / class, race, gender, and mother earth just a resource / globalization is colonization and colonization is always war / we know this nightmare because it repeats until something breaks.

—"An Act of Liberation" from *Appropriation* by Klee Benally (2021)

6

TIJUANA NO!
LATIN PUNK ROCK FROM PERU TO MEXICO TO EAST LA

Standing on the border, I got nowhere to go / I'm here in LA I got no place to stay / A man came up to me and he asked my name / couldn't speak his language, they took me away!

—"El-lay" by Los Illegals (1983)

Ceci Bastida grew up in Mexico "in the shadow of the US border wall" and joined the punk band Tijuana No! as a singer/keyboardist when she was fifteen years old. She moved to Los Angeles in 1996 where she continued her own music and activism and recently narrated the podcast series "Punk in Translation" (2022). In eight episodes Bastida explores the Latino/a roots of punk rock and highlights musicians and bands like The Plugz, Los Lobos, The Brat, Los Crudos, and Alice Bag of The Bags, Kid Congo Powers of The Cramps, Willie Herrón of Los Illegals, Victoria Ruiz of Downtown Boys, and Bobby Balderrama of Question Mark and the Mysterians. Bastida points out that one of the first punk rock bands was from Peru; in 1966 Los Seicos released the song "Demolicion," a recording that resurfaced around 2010. Vocalist Erwin Flores growls and the music is raw.

> In 1971, a group made of sons of Mexican migrant workers was the first act to be described as "punk rock" in a magazine. That's right. Latin artists have been instrumental to the creation of punk music, even before it was called "punk." ("Punk in Translation" podcast with Ceci Bastida, episode 1, 2022, referring to a *Creem Magazine* article by Dave Marsh describing Question Mark and the Mysterians as "punk," perhaps the first use of the word to describe a music style.)

CHAPTER 6

MILITARIZED BORDER

Times have changed, no one knows where to go anymore.

—"Conscience Call" by Tijuana No! (1994)

JM: You said you grew up in the shadow of the Mexico-US border wall, and you chose punk rock as a way to criticize anti-immigration politics, the drug war, and gun violence. Tell me about growing up in Mexico near the United States.
CECI BASTIDA (Tijuana No!): There is definitely something that makes people that live next to the border different from people who live in the rest of Mexico. If you live a normal life anywhere in Mexico, you do regular things. But in Tijuana, you would see the border constantly. Growing up near the border marks you in some way. It's really visible every single day. As you're driving through one of the main roads that goes from where I grew up near the beach, to the downtown area, you're basically driving next to the border wall.

Over the years, we noticed as the border wall became more militarized. When I was growing up it was a flimsy chain-link fence. It didn't really do much, but it was there. It became more militarized especially with Bill Clinton's Operation Gatekeeper. It basically forced immigrants to go to areas that are way more dangerous, like the desert. That automatically made it really difficult for people to cross. And for the people that did cross, a lot of them ended up dying. So, the border is something that is in you, because you can't look away.

So, if you're interested or curious, you want to know why there is this fence and why people want to cross the border, and why people want to go to the US? You start realizing that we live in a country—Mexico—that has a wealth gap that's very big. The population that's wealthy is small in comparison with the amount of poverty that exists in the country. So, you understand why people need to leave. It's just something that I couldn't *not* think about. That's what made me want to keep talking about it throughout the years.

JM: Why did you choose punk rock as a way to voice your ideas and concerns?
CECI BASTIDA: I noticed in punk I would hear political conversations happen more than in pop music. I listened to a lot of new wave and all kinds of different music, not just punk music. But I did notice that some music seemed to be more direct in talking about these issues, in the most powerful way. My contribution to my band Tijuana No! wasn't necessarily punk music. I wanted something more melodic. But some bandmembers were really into Black Flag and Dead Kennedys. So, we ended up compromising a lot. I learned a lot from listening to some of that music. I learned from some of the band members who are much

older than I was at the time. And they were very much involved in socio-political issues.

ZAPATISTA REVOLUTION

CECI BASTIDA: When I was playing with my band Tijuana No! back in the early '90s, there was this movement to support a community that was called Ejército Zapatista de Liberación Nacional (EZLN). In English they were called the Zapatista Liberation Army, down in the south of Mexico. A lot of bands were very inspired by them and started playing and being super active. Sometimes it goes in waves; there are moments where people are really passionate, and then it dies down. And then something else happens that makes people really want to fight for something. In Mexico now there is the feminist movement because there's so many women killed every day—at least ten women are killed in Mexico daily. I see some artists talking about these things now, when maybe five years ago it wasn't the case.

JM: The Zapatista movement is powerful. I was part of a group of journalists and international observers who joined the Zapatista caravan to Mexico City in 2001. We thought revolutionary changes would be made to democratize Mexico and ripple out to other places.

CECI BASTIDA: It didn't happen like I thought it would, either. I thought there was definitely this huge change coming. And it didn't. I like that people don't give up. The movement is still doing their thing, but somehow, it's not as popular as it was. Yeah, I thought Mexico was going to be in a very different place. And when I look at it right now—I'm not going to say we're dealing with the same problems—but we're definitely dealing with a lot of cartel problems, extreme poverty, and crazy corruption. This new president (Obrador) sells himself as some sort of liberal Leftist and there's nothing Leftist about him. The opposite I would say—he's Trump-like, in my eyes. 1994 is when the Zapatista movement came to light, and we're now in 2022. A lot of things are still the same.

PUNK BEGAN IN PERU WITH LOS SEICOS

JM: You point out that white European culture tends to view things from its own point of view and say, "We invented everything! Including punk rock!" A lot of punk developed in New York and London, but you point to Latin roots of punk, including the cha-cha-cha rhythm that was used for a punk favorite,

CHAPTER 6

"Louie, Louie." And "Demolición" by Los Seicos was recorded in 1966 and the raw energy and distorted, angry vocals do sound like punk to come.

CECI BASTIDA: Los Seicos were talking about issues of immigration, racism, and things that we still hear bands talking about. Even though Los Seicos recorded "Demolición" in 1966 it doesn't sound old. It sounds contemporary. It's just super raw. They recorded that when popular music was a lot of covers, especially in Latin America, of American rock and roll. Los Seicos were creating this music that must have sounded crazy to a lot of people at the time. It's powerful and it definitely makes you feel what they're feeling.

Narrating the podcast, I was just constantly surprised. I was learning so much. We didn't have social media back then, so people were a little less connected. Now you hear music from anywhere and it doesn't have to be a big band. Back then the music I heard was music that was on the radio like The Clash or all these bands signed to big labels.

I was surprised to learn of this connection between the Ramones and this Mexican guy—Arturo Vega—who left Mexico because the radical social movement was being attacked. He left Mexico and came to New York and all of a sudden he became one of the buddies of the Ramones. He was super creative and designed the Ramones's logo, partly basing it on the Mexican flag. It's interesting to understand that a lot of the music in the US has had influences from Latin America for a very long time. It's good for people to know that punk is not something that was necessarily created here (US). Punk is definitely a mix of things. And that's the way the world is; we're more connected than we'd like to think sometimes.

JM: Tell me about some of the early Chicano/a punk bands in Los Angeles that influenced you like The Plugz, The Brat, Los Illegals, and The Bags.

CECI BASTIDA: At the time I was playing in my band, even though LA is so close to Tijuana, we didn't really play with a lot of these guys. A lot of them were older than I was. So, we didn't really cross paths. I knew Alice Bag. We've shared the stage on different occasions. It was nice to talk to her in the podcast about her identity and things that weren't necessarily evident because she changed her name; she's Alice Bag and not Alicia Armendariz. So, there was no way of necessarily knowing if she was Latina or not. And this was done for the freedom of it. I appreciated the freedom of not being boxed into something like, "You're Chicana punk." She wanted to create music the same as The Plugz, without people having to question her identity.

The Brat are a story that I've heard a million times. The fact that she's the woman; let's make her prettier and make her sound nicer. (Teresa Covarrubias) But at the same time exploit the image of Chicano, which was just so sad because people tend to associate Latinos or Chicanos with a certain aesthetic. I liked that she doesn't fit into that. It shows that not everybody's the same, which is what happens when you're here in this country. People just assume that we all have the same aesthetic and believe in the same things. Hearing these stories makes you realize everybody talks about their identity, and why they want to create music, in their own way.

Los Illegals, for example, rejected the Aztec aesthetic of these murals that you see everywhere, that I don't connect with. They wanted something different, and they were so into art, what they created was so different and fresh at the time. The most interesting thing is seeing this rainbow of different ways of being Latino or Latina, or Latinx, in the US.

PUNK ACROSS BORDERS

JM: Speaking of the wall and border between the US and Mexico, I'm reminded of Mark Reeder. He snuck West German punk bands into East Berlin in the '80s to do clandestine concerts that were revolutionary and illegal. I often think that if punk has been a revolutionary force, it would show up in places that are authoritarian as a fight for freedom and creativity. And it has, in places like East Berlin and Tijuana. Sometimes living inside of an intense political pressure cooker creates revolutionary responses, including with music.

CECI BASTIDA: I think it does create community, and people do connect with it. And they find that it's a safe space for them to be vocal about the things that are not right in their eyes. When you were talking about borders, I was thinking about the Basque country between Spain and France. We worked with a lot of Basque musicians in the past with Tijuana No! and they wrote music against the government of Spain. They were forced to be part of a country that they don't have a lot of connection with. Language wise, it's completely different. They were doing their own fight and a lot of bands were fighting against mandatory military service. They didn't want to go and if you didn't, you'd go to jail. A lot of people ended up going to jail, and they were fighting against it. They were performing shows in front of government buildings, rejecting this mandate that they needed to be in the military at a certain age. So, you see it all the time.

JM: Tell me about your music and activism now.

CECI BASTIDA: I stopped playing with Tijuana No! in the mid '90s. They're all still good friends of mine. But musically, I wanted to do something different. I'm still making music and I have a few albums out. I'm working on my latest one as we speak, which will hopefully release in the fall (2022). I also became a

CHAPTER 6

child advocate for immigrant children in the US with this organization called the Young Center for Immigrant Children's Rights. They connect me to a young girl or boy. During the pandemic, you have to do it through Zoom. But ideally, I'd be with them once a week, drawing and telling them if their case is moving forward or not. I give them information and make sure their needs are met. Ideally, I would go with them to court. I've been doing that since 2019.

That work has been really important to me because sometimes a lot of our socio-political issues seem so gigantic that it's overwhelming, and people end up not doing anything. It can seem like the problem is too big. And then I realized that you can make change even when it seems small. If I'm talking to a girl for a year, every week, I know there's an impact and I'm helping one person. It seems very small, but I think in the end it's very satisfying. I feel like I'm actually doing something.

There were so many other people that felt the same way I did, that it gives you power; it makes you feel more empowered to keep fighting. When you're doing it alone, it just feels lonely. When you have a community that supports you and you're all focused on a certain goal, you feel supported. We've seen it in the Arab Spring. There is power in numbers. The more people are connected

Ceci Bastida, singer/keyboardist, with '90s Mexican punk band Tijuana No!.
Contributed: Fresh Produce Media

and really vocal about what they're opposing, we can create change. And I think music is a big part of it.

JM: You mentioned that you have an album that is going to come out in the fall (2022). Do you have a name for the album? What kind of music is it?

CECI BASTIDA: The music is hard to describe. It's very rhythmic and melodic with a lot of electronic elements. I originally wanted to write an album that's mainly inspired by displacement, immigration, and migration. Most of the songs talk about displacement from the point of view of characters and stories I created. The working title is *Everything Will Be Taken Away*, which is based on an exhibit that I saw by an artist called Adrian Piper.

JM: A punk band from Orange County, The Vandals. performed for US troops in Iraq. Henry Rollins also performed for US troops. In the case of The Vandals, some of their fans protested after they heard the band had performed for troops. There's actually videos of The Vandals on the back of this flatbed truck in Iraq singing the theme song from Team America, which is "America! Fuck Yeah!" a sardonic black humor song that criticizes US militarism. Henry Rollins told me that the soldiers don't want to be there, so he's offering them a little relief by entertaining or hanging out with them. He said that his anger isn't directed toward the soldiers who were sent there. It's with the people who create these wars.

Similarly, in a different way, in 2008 at the US Guantanamo prison, guards there played music extremely loud to augment torture, including music by Rage Against the Machine. Tom Morello was angry about this and tried to stop them from playing his music to torture people. Sometimes a revolutionary force can end up being used in a funky way. What do you think about punk rock people entertaining US troops?

CECI BASTIDA: I don't like it. I would understand this idea that the soldiers don't want to be there if it was back when there was a draft. But a lot of people want to join the military, and they know exactly what the military does. They're probably aware that there's wars all over the world, and there are US bases all over the world. We're not talking about the '60s. We can talk about the Iraq war that started thirty years ago. I wouldn't perform for troops. In the end, you're supporting the government and something you claim to oppose. Even if it's about the soldiers, I still wouldn't do it. Also, we've known through the years how many abuses soldiers do around the world. This is not a new story. There's murder, killing of civilians, rape. I would stay away from it. It's something I would not do. I agree with Tom Morello; if somebody were using my music to torture people, I would be upset and try to stop it.

CHAPTER 6

1968—MEXICO CITY MASSACRE

JM: There's a popular notion that punk rock was a deliberate cutting off from the hippie '60s movement. But lots of punk musicians drew on the revolutionary elements of the '60s. 1968 saw huge political movements worldwide as well as authoritarian responses like the terrible massacre in Mexico City. What do you think about the qualities of communalism and creating a new culture that were brewing in the '60s that are present in punk rock?

CECI BASTIDA: The messaging is similar. I was going to mention the 1968 student killings in Mexico City. A lot of artists were imprisoned, and a lot of art came out of it and many musicians started singing about it. It goes in waves. During 1968, there's definitely movements, artists, and movies, and then it dies down. And then something else happened. It was in the early '70s when this Mexican guy created the logo for the Ramones: Arturo Vega. He left Mexico during another confrontation with government. The music of the hippie movement was different. But I think the message of punk is similar by rejecting war, rejecting authoritarian governments, and rejecting policing. I think it's part of the same thing, in a weird way.

JM: Would you say something about The Clash? Mick Jones once said, "We're a news band." *Sandinista* is very specific. They're talking about Victor Jara in the Santiago Stadium, Castro in Cuba, the US versus Russia battle, which unfortunately we're still in. They sang about resisting military service, the Sandinista Revolution, and damage done by the CIA and US imperialism.

CECI BASTIDA: The Clash are one of my biggest influences because musically, they didn't sound the same all the time. They did different kinds of music. I like that. Their songs also have a structure that is not that different from a pop song, perhaps, in terms that you can sing to it. It's melodic and rhythmic. But the lyrics are smart, and they talk about, like you said, specific things. It makes you appreciate the fact that there's a band that is looking to Latin America and talking about issues that a lot of people don't talk about.

People will criticize war, but The Clash were very specific in one of the things that infuriates me with the US. It's this lack of knowledge about the presence of the US in Latin America and what it's created throughout the years, especially in the '70s, by supporting dictators that hurt their own countries. They killed and disappeared thousands of people and made it so that the poverty was even worse. Violence everywhere. If you're living in a place like that, of course you're going to want to leave. They come to the US and people are like, "Why are they coming here? It's not our fault your countries are shit." Well, it kind of is, in a lot of these cases. It really is. I'm not saying that the governments in Latin America are not to blame, but there's an influence from the US that was very present in the '70s and it's going to have consequences.

It makes me mad when people think Mexicans want to come here to get a big house or they want to take your job. That's not why people leave their homes. People generally don't want to leave; people want to stay in their homes. They leave because they're desperate. Because there's no way of providing a better life for themselves or their families. It's not an easy decision. It's a very difficult life they choose to embark on. I find that really maddening. We are all connected, and the actions of the US have affected the world for so many years. And there is a lack of responsibility from a lot of people here that's just mind blowing.

CECI BASTIDA: My biggest issue is that sometimes I do not have enough faith in human beings in power. So, there's always going to have to be somebody leading. And corruption always seems to enter when there's a leader. Anarchism—I haven't really thought about it in my life as something that I aspired to. I'm not saying I'm anti-anarchism, but I have never said out loud, "Oh. Yes, anarchism." That being said, I do appreciate the idea of there not having to be a government. Not having police would be an ideal situation. I'm just not sure what that would actually look like.

JM: John Lydon sang about anarchy and recently supported MAGA! He told me he never really embraced anarchism.

CECI BASTIDA: I was very disappointed and saddened to see what's happened with Johnny Rotten. At the same time, I know the Sex Pistols started out as sort of a boyband. Somebody put them together and created them. But even that, it just seems like an extreme. I've seen photos of him with a MAGA hat. It's baffling. He lives here in the US, in Venice Beach or somewhere. I don't know what to think about that.

JM: I talked to him about it. Lydon embraced this notion that was pretty widespread about that president guy, "He's not a politician. He's an outsider. He's going to shake things up." Lydon also said, "Sometimes you need to build walls between people."

CECI BASTIDA: Oh, God! It's stupid. To me, there's nothing you can say to me that would make me understand why you support Trump. He is the example of everything that's wrong in this world. If you're supporting Trump, you're supporting anti-immigration, anti-LGBTQ. I can't justify it. It's really a bummer Johnny Rotten became this weird person.

I think about somebody like Morrissey, who started off in The Smiths. They were singing against the queen and the government. They were anti-so-many-things, and then all of a sudden, he's anti-migrant! He supports this idea that England should look a certain way and that migrants are changing that. It's

CHAPTER 6

similar to what's happening in the US now with the Great Replacement theory; this idea that immigrants are going to change what the US is or should be. It's basically this fear of the US not being white dominated anymore. So, it's upsetting to see some artists that started off connecting with people all of a sudden go the complete opposite direction. It's crazy.

PANSY DIVISION
OUT OF THE CLOSET, INTO THE SLAMPIT

In those early Pansy Division songs, even though a lot of them are riotously funny, there is a lot of anger in them. I felt that was an important way to deal with the reality of the situation but do it in a way that feels like I'm doing something that's positive and makes me happy.

—Jon Ginoli (Pansy Division)

Television, Blondie, Patti Smith—none of those people sounded like each other. And they sounded very different than anything else that was happening. I thought, "That is the spirit of punk rock!"

—Chris Freeman (Pansy Division)

They hate me but I resist / Still their hard looks persist / Violence is a glance away / If the average men get their way.

—"Average Men" by Pansy Division featuring Jello Biafra from the album *That's So Gay* (2009)

Jon Ginoli entered the punk milieu by booking shows in Illinois with some early punk and post-punk bands like Jonathan Richman & The Modern Lovers, The Replacements, The Feelies, The Minutemen, and Guadalcanal Diary. Ginoli went on to form the first out gay pop punk rock band, Pansy Division. Chris Freeman joined Pansy Division in 1991, and the band has produced twelve studio and live albums, most recently *Quite Contrary* (2016). ACT UP (Aids Coalition to Unleash Power) was founded in NYC in 1987 to address the AIDS crisis.

VERBAL BOMB THROWERS

JON GINOLI (Pansy Division): ACT UP got a lot of very bad press because they were too radical for a lot of people back then. But I noticed from having been involved with it that ACT UP was creating space for people. Here were people at the margins who were verbal bomb throwers, people who were very loud, angry, and demanding. And for good reason: they were trying to save people's lives because it was the AIDS crisis. When people are pushing at the edge, pushing the envelope, as they push forward and expand the boundaries of what is possible, all these other people are able to fill in behind them. Let's say you've got a bunch of radical activists chanting in the streets with bullhorns. Because they're able to push the envelope, you've got people who work in public health or in government who want to do things but aren't really allowed to because it seems too radical. Then suddenly someone else seems *more* radical and the center moves. I see the way ACT UP was doing that in '89 through '91 when I was involved.

I saw Pansy Division as a way that I could do something that was in a field that I wanted to do, which is music. And create that same effect where people just thought we were outrageous in the subject matter that we were singing about. Especially when we first began, we were singing about sex so much because it was the time of the right wing. People like Jesse Helms and Pat Robertson were just pounding on gay issues. I thought, "I am not going to be cowed by these people." That was the debate back then: Should we be assimilationists as gay people and try to placate the mainstream? Or are we more liberationists? Do we try pushing for what we want as hard as we can? I can see both ways of doing it. I thought with Pansy Division we were out there pushing the envelope in a way that had political meaning but wasn't as overtly political as something like ACT UP.

CHUCK WILD (Missing Persons): I'm openly gay; I came out in 1976. I joined ACT UP LA. We'd go with cans of red spray paint in front of city hall and lay down in the outline drawing of a body. Ronald Reagan never mentioned the word AIDS. Now it's called HIV. There was little movement by the government to let people know it was a sexually transmitted disease. I had over fifty-five friends die. There was this zeitgeist of anger. We were feeling that we had to do something and make a difference. There was also a feeling of helplessness, especially when you're in your twenties or thirties and everybody you know dies. It's not only tragic, it shakes the foundations of who you are. There was a real feeling that society could be changed, which was some hangover from the '70s. I'm glad I had an outlet for all that energy. It was quite an interesting time. I still live in Hollywood, but I've never experienced anything since then like that window from 1979 to 1986. It was an experience.

PENELOPE HOUSTON (The Avengers): The scene in San Francisco was really diverse with a lot of different kinds of music and people in it. There were a lot of women in bands. You had bands that were artsy and bands that were noisy. The Mutants, Flipper, Crime, The Dils, The Avengers, The Nuns. A lot of bands had gay people in them like The Offs. There were some political bands. It was really a broad palette. Everybody knew everybody else. When we traveled to LA, we would stay at friends' houses like The Screamers, X, and The Dils. When bands came up here, they stayed at our house. It was this really tight community of musicians and people that were into punk. You could meet a lot of people and go places without having any money or transportation or a place to stay. You would find all that when you got there. You would get fed and taken care of.

KID CONGO POWERS (The Cramps / Nick Cave & The Bad Seeds): Punk was about freedom. I was a teenager coming out of the glam rock scene. David Bowie had liberated all of us! He'd given us hope and an example to identify with. Whether he was really bisexual or not, if he was really an alien or not, it didn't matter. These things fed into a teenager's fantasy. I was completely into that rock and roll fantasy and glam rock gave me a green light to be a gay, flamboyant young creature.

So, when punk rock came around it was quite liberating. I was able to dress up and prance around and be obnoxious but free, at least within that world. That didn't make me free in the rest of my life or at home with my parents. But when punk rock came, it was the very logical extension as I was getting a little bit older and wanting to take matters into my own hands about my own identity. Punk rock was perfect because so many people I met were queer people, of all genders. There were already trans people in punk rock then. So, it was a great gathering spot. I would go between Los Angeles, San Francisco, and New York and meet my tribe. It was a meeting of the tribe, and there was a definite openness with people about freedom of sexual expression.

I go back to the earliest days of pre-punk of the Ramones and Patti Smith in 1975. That was the real meeting of the misfits, because that was hippies, punks, and weirdos. Like people in a crowd scene from *MAD Magazine*! People with

CHAPTER 7

their tongues hanging out and someone hammering a nail into it. Other people with their eyeballs popping out! That's what I thought when I first went to Ramones and Patti Smith concerts; the audience looked like it was just madness. That was punk rock.

The lifelong Holy Grail of music for me is about finding my tribe and people who identify with you and the music that you make. I loved bands that created new communications, like The Cramps, Nick Cave, The Gun Club, Devo, or the B-52s. People who created a whole world and language for people to learn and pass on. I loved the high concept of bands and I always thought punk rock had that, even though at first its credo was *live fast, die young, and leave a beautiful corpse*. It was about creating a world for people to escape to, to live in and to communicate with each other. That's what I chose to go for.

CHRIS FREEMAN (Pansy Division): The thing I also loved about punk rock when it started was that it was hilarious! Devo, The Dickies, the Ramones were hilarious. Put on "Orgasm Addict" by The Buzzcocks and you're going to smile. "Teenage Kicks" by The Undertones; all these songs just put a big smile on your face. Musically, we wanted to capture that original spirit of fun that was in punk rock.

At the same time, we were doing double duty because right when we started, we were coming out of the '80s, which was really a drag for the gay community. AIDS had basically desiccated our community. I've had dozens of friends die. I've had five boyfriends die. At that time there was so much dour art about HIV. It was all so heavy. We didn't want to reflect that heaviness. We wanted to bring some lightness and say, "Look guys, just put on a condom and enjoy yourselves! Who knows how long any of us have got? Let's try and be happy and embody the word gay: be happy." A lot of us were told growing up that if you're gay then you're going to have a horrible life. "You're going to hell." Whatever excuses they told you to keep you from being gay, those things you internalize, and a lot of gay people end up being depressed. We thought, "We've got to fight that with humor!"

STAN LEE (The Dickies): Something makes us laugh, we write it down and make a song out of it. I've always been against that heavy thing, all those bands in England: "No future! Parents suck! Hittin' the dole and it's all fucked." We never played it that way. We were more like, "Where's the water slide? Where's Bob's Big Boy? Who's got a swimming pool?"

TAKE A STAND

> *Pansy Division happened at the moment when the word* queer *was suddenly on everyone's tongues. It reclaimed an epithet and brandished it as a weapon.... When I came to San Francisco in '89, the word* homocore *was being spread; by '91, it had evolved into* queercore, *with which PD was tagged ... and we don't use it to describe our band anymore. It presents a misleading image of raw noise with gay lyrics that doesn't take into account the pop qualities of our sound.*
>
> —Jon Ginoli[1]

JM: You wrote that when you first heard "Anarchy in the UK" it took a bit for that to grow on you, but it did. You said it was "angry but really fun and funny at the same time. It articulated an anger I felt but couldn't really spell out." Similarly, you've said the music that tended to be played at gay bars was connected with gay culture and there wasn't necessarily a lot of openness in the gay community for heavy rock and roll, especially punk rock.

JON GINOLI (Pansy Division): The band I was in prior to Pansy Division made three albums in the '80s—The Outnumbered. That was when I lived in Illinois. It was the Reagan era, and I was writing songs about the state of mind from that period, which was political in some sense, sometimes overt and other times not. I listen back to those songs and remember playing those songs and expressing anger in the way I did, in a serious way, not using humor as a weapon. It got to the point that my own songs would depress me. I thought, "I want to be honest, but I don't really think it's good for my state of mind to be going out there and re-depressing myself by singing these songs." I think they're successful as songs, as art. But I didn't like the effect they had on me. So that group broke up. I moved to California and four years later started Pansy Division.

When I started playing music again, I decided that I wanted my music to have substance, but at the same time I wanted it to be joyful. When I was starting Pansy Division I thought, "I want to channel this energy, which has a lot of negative aspects I want to talk about, but instead of playing defense I wanted to play offense. I wanted to go out and be bold and take a stand and be pro-something rather than anti-something." In those early Pansy Division songs, even though a lot of them are riotously funny, there is a lot of anger in them. Sometimes people have noticed that. Other times people don't really get that. I felt like that was an

CHAPTER 7

important way to deal with the reality of the situation but do it in a way that feels like I'm doing something that's positive and makes me happy.

CHRIS FREEMAN (Pansy Division): If you're going to try and sell any kind of a message to anybody it's better to do it, as Jon (Ginoli) puts it, "political with a small p." Our politics are from our stance, not from our lyrics. In his mind, if The Clash sang about a specific event, it dated their music immediately. And we didn't want to have our music be dated. We kept it so the politics are internalized. If we slipped in a little line about using condoms in a song like "Bunnies"—"Put on the condoms"—we felt like we were injecting our politics in there by throwing in lyrics that illustrate what we were talking about rather than say, "Everyone needs to use condoms."

Nobody wants to be preached at, especially if we can tell stories that make people laugh. Basically, once you laugh, you're disarmed. That's something we noticed all along, on the Green Day tour as well (1994). We came in contact with thousands and thousands of opposition teenagers that were completely opposed to what we were saying! But, by the end of the show a good majority of those people were finally laughing and getting the joke of it. They'd come up later and say, "I didn't like you at first and then you made me laugh and then I got it!" That's the secret for us. To keep the humor involved like, "A spoon full of sugar helps the medicine go down." The politics are there, but they're more personal politics. And how we conduct ourselves. It's not preaching. It's just sharing our experiences, or other people's experiences, that we've extracted and turned into songs. We've always wanted to maintain that level of humor.

JON GINOLI: If the straight edge thing had been around when I was in high school, I probably would've embraced it. But I got out of high school a couple of years before Minor Threat were around. My parents drank. They were social drinkers and had a lot of parties. My parents are pretty fun, actually. But I knew people who drank and did drugs and seemed pathetic to me. I remember thinking, "These people are drinking so they can do things and the next day say, "Oh, I didn't know what I was doing!" They can pretend they forgot what they'd done. I didn't want to live like that. I was idealistic. It seems patently obvious that people are using these substances to do certain things. I drink now, but I didn't start drinking until I was almost forty. I said, "I had these ideas about drinking that were valid at a certain point and now I don't really agree with that anymore." But that was my thinking at the time.

JON GINOLI: I've never been much of a fan of hardcore punk. As punk became more hardcore oriented it's been driven into directions that I don't find appealing. My version of punk rock is to harken back to the early period of punk. I like punk that's a combination of the '60s pop ideal, British invasion music like The

Jon Ginoli and Chris Freeman, Pansy Division concert in Santa Cruz, California (Sept. 16, 2009). Composite Photo: Matt Fitt

Byrds mixed with the punk sound of the '70s. As far as punk goes, there are a lot of pissing matches going on. "Are they punk enough?" I don't really care! [laugh] We're coming from a place; people will either get it or not. If you ask me if I'm in a punk band, "Yeah!" But we're other things, too.

AT LEAST I'M NOT CHRISTIAN

It's a warm evening—September 16, 2009—and Pansy Division is playing at the Blue Lagoon in Santa Cruz, California, with The Avengers. A sticker on Chris Freeman's bass reads, "At Least I'm Not Christian." During Pansy Division's set Chris rips up a Bible on stage, launching pages into the audience. The Avengers open the show with a lot of energy, and I'm standing right up in front. When Avengers guitarist Greg Ingraham holds his guitar out to us, I reach over and bang on the strings.

CHAPTER 7

The documentary film by Chris Freeman *Pansy Division: Life in a Gay Punk Rock Band* (2008) begins with a quote from George Bernard Shaw: "The secret to success is to offend the greatest number of people." This reminds me of the photo of a young Elvis Costello from the June 8, 2009, "Culture" section of *Newsweek* magazine with the quote, "My ultimate vocation in life is to be an irritant." In the spring of 1994 Pansy Division toured the US with Green Day (*Dookie*), and it was during this cross-country tour that Green Day's popularity exploded, and larger concert venues had to be arranged to accommodate the surge in fans. Concert promoters actually tried to remove Pansy Division from the bill twice and Green Day demanded they remain included. Pansy Division songs during that tour included "Fem in a Black Leather Jacket," "The Cocksucker Club," and "Fuck Buddy."

CHRIS FREEMAN (Pansy Division): We call Green Day the gift that keeps on giving! Just the fact that fifteen years later we're still talking about it! It was a pivotal moment for a lot of people, especially them because they were making a big statement by putting us up front and center at the biggest moment of their existence. It was incredible. What a whirlwind and what a learning experience for us, too! I got to see firsthand what happens to a band that goes from nothing to selling fourteen million albums in one year. It was a good look for myself because I'd wanted to be a career musician when I was in my twenties. I gave it up when I turned twenty-eight because I figured when you're starting a band it usually takes three years before the band gets anywhere. And I knew there was this unspoken rule in the music business that you're not going to get signed if you're over thirty. I thought, "I'm already going to be too old, so I might as well give it up and cut the career aspect out and just do music for the fun of it." So, here comes Pansy Division after I'm thirty-one.

I was thirty-three when we were touring with Green Day and Jon (Ginoli) had turned thirty-five at the end of the tour (1994). So, there we were in our mid-thirties having this tour that would've been better in our twenties because I could've gotten what I wanted earlier. But watching them go through all the things they went through with their bad management at the beginning and everyone who was their friend started to turn on them and either called them "sellouts" or leached on them for money. They didn't know which way to turn, and they pulled the walls up immediately, as soon as that tour was over. I got to see how this whole machine can ruin people if they're not prepared.

I don't think I would've been prepared at that age. I would've been less prepared than they (Green Day) were. But they were really insulated, inside themselves. The three of them, you can't separate. A lot was riding on them, and they were turning into huge stars. Every month we'd say, "Oh my god! Look how big these guys are getting." Every month we'd get the new set of magazines or playlists and it was like, "You guys are taking off! Right under our feet!" We had to move shows from smaller places to bigger places. They'd say, "We're going to have to play a bigger place," and we were like, "Okay!" It was quite a learning experience.

JM: There can be this idea that if you get good at playing your instruments and become popular like Green Day, then you've sold out or you're not punk anymore.

CHRIS FREEMAN (Pansy Division): Punk rock happened when I was sixteen. I got to look at all these different bands. I was a big Iggy fan to start with. I think he's the godfather of punk, and Velvet Underground before. The Ramones and those bands out of New York were happening when I was in my mid-teens. They were all on major labels and they all wanted to be huge stars. You can read any Ramones biography, and they'll all tell you, "We wanted to be as big as Bay City Rollers." It's this underdog mentality, but it's ill conceived. They all wanted to do something different than the status quo. They wanted to separate themselves from everybody else and sound like nobody else.

The Ramones sounded like nobody else. If you listen to any of the other bands in that circle—Television, Blondie, Patti Smith—none of those people sounded like each other. And they sounded very different than anything else that was happening. I thought, "That is the spirit of punk rock!" It's to say, "Screw the labels, screw what everybody else is doing, we're not going to try and sound like Pink Floyd. We're not going to try to sound like any of these other classic rock bands that we're tired of. They've gotten to be so overblown with their musicianship." I really love prog rock. I love all that stuff, but there is a time and a place for it, and you've got numerous bands trying to copy that sound. That's ridiculous! There only needs to be one Pink Floyd! There only needs to be one Yes.

I think the same is true with the Ramones. Why do we need another Ramones? Try and sound different somehow: unique. Punk rock over the years has been modified so that now, you have to sound as much like certain other bands as possible so that you can be aligned with this punk sound. That has nothing to do with what punk originally stood for! There was no punk sound. There was a punk idea of trying *not* to sound like everybody else, trying to be different than what the mainstream was offering. And to bring back some energy. All those guys were just bringing back the '60s garage sound of The Seeds or The Sonics. They said, "That stuff didn't get all that popular and we loved it. So, let's do that!"

CHAPTER 7

When we started as Pansy Division we said, "Yeah, we've got some ties to the Ramones." But when we started, the Ramones hadn't yet gotten their due. Punk rock hadn't broke like it did a year or two later with Nirvana and then two years after that with Green Day. We were going back and saying, "We love The Buzzcocks, and it didn't really get its due. Let's use that as our format and try and sound like ourselves." I think we achieved that.

JON GINOLI: The thing about punk rock that was the most appealing initially was that it was simple enough so that people who weren't trained musicians could do it. Almost anyone could do it! You have to start somewhere, and you'll end up somewhere else hopefully. But none of the first punk rock bands had punk rock to listen to! It was something they created based on other influences. They weren't influenced by punk; they invented it. Part of the problem is that people who are just influenced by punk, that takes away the vast number of sources that actually fed punk in the first place. But if you're starting out and forming a band it's easy to make that early punk rock sound.

DISCO VERSUS PUNK

JM: You write in *Deflowered*, "Disco celebrated pleasure and materialism and punk was suspicious of it."

JON GINOLI: Really, we're kind of lightweight as a punk band. But if you listen to a lot of the '77-era punk rock it does sound kind of lightweight now in light of what's happened in the last thirty years since the first punk sound. It's the initial punk sound that I tend to like the best. Listen to the first Ramones album and compare it to any new punk band today. The Ramones seem kind of tame, but it was so startling back then!

JM: When you came out you realized that the music in gay clubs was not very interesting. You were counterculture (punk) within a counterculture (gay).

JON GINOLI: The thing I wrote about disco versus punk was that the '70s, as the stereotype goes, are remembered as being a time of indulgence, a time of pleasure. I was in high school at that time, and I rebelled against that. Punk rock was one way I was able to express that rebellion. But let's not be too pure about punk. I know a lot of punk rock fanatics and they have huge record collections that cost thousands of dollars. I'm not saying that's bad. I'm saying let's be honest about where punk does fit into a system of commodities. That's the way American life is: you buy things. Some people have tried to minimize that or undercut that because they see the contradictions. But even though it tries to be alternative, punk is still part of the same culture. You can't just separate yourself that easily. I related to punk because it asked questions about how to approach capitalism and materialism. The fact that it's full of contradictions doesn't make it any less valid.

JM: One of your early loves in the punk realm was Patti Smith. You write that "she's the only rock star I tried to look and dress like."

JON GINOLI: Yeah! I was as skinny as she was when I was in high school. In 1975 and '76 there were not a lot of people walking around with white button-down shirts in school in Peoria, Illinois.

CHRIS FREEMAN (Pansy Division): I was a fan of KISS back in '75. They were sort of an underdog, and in fact they were called "punk" because of the leather and makeup. I didn't really understand it, but I knew I loved it. And all of a sudden, they went disco, and they had little kids in their audience, and I thought, "Now you're selling out. You don't sound like KISS anymore. Now you sound like bubblegum, and you have this disco song." I lost track of a lot of those bands in about '79. And I was very happy to go deeper into punk and post-punk music. I don't think today's version of punk aligns with what punk started out with at all. It's free to change. That's the way Pansy Division has operated all of our existence; we get to do exactly what we want, when we want, and say what we want. To have that kind of a career in music at all is insane! When I think about all the hurdles we've jumped right over it's unreal!

JELLO IS GOING TO LOVE THIS!

JON GINOLI (Pansy Division): Alternative Tentacles, despite being around for thirty years, is a pretty small label. They put out our records, but they don't really spend a lot of money or time promoting things. They do have somebody who does press work and mailings, but they're not out there trying to twist people's arms to hear the music. They're just putting it out and it either finds an audience or it doesn't. That suits us fine. We always had a great deal of respect for Dead Kennedys and Jello (Biafra), though they don't get along well with each other anymore. Jello was always a fan of ours from the beginning. I wanted to have our records on a label that really believes in our band. And the fact that they were local in the Bay Area was helpful, too. It seemed like a good fit. It's been a good experience.

Jello being on our record is partly because we were doing this song in the studio, and we had already finished singing it. It was a song where I sang the lead vocals and I said out loud, "Wow, Jello is going to love this!" Because I know his taste to some degree. I knew he was going to love the song "Average

CHAPTER 7

Men" (2009). Chris said, "Why don't we get him to sing on it?" We gave him a copy of the song and asked him if he'd be willing to do a duet. I'd sing part of it, and he'd sing part of it. He came to the studio, and it turned out great. I'm thrilled that he's on our record and that it sounds so great. Watching him do his stuff in the studio was pretty amazing. He's a legend. I'm really glad that the contribution he made fits really well with what we're doing.

JELLO BIAFRA (Dead Kennedys): It means far more to me than someone asking me for an autograph, let alone a selfie, if they come and say, "Your music really means a lot to me and here is something I did that I want you to listen to, or read, or watch." Even, "I practice law at a public interest firm now." Or, "I changed my major in college from business to something else and I'm a lot happier now." Or, "What you've done has influenced how I teach high school history." The whole planting seeds and spreading positive seeds; you never know where the payback is going to come from.

POLICE RIOT

JM: You write about going to an ACT UP demonstration in San Francisco on October 4, 1989, and experiencing a police riot. You saw someone clubbed and then they had a newspaper stand kicked onto them by a police officer.[2] Later you spoke to the SF Police Commission about the incident and found it totally ineffective. Activists and people in the punk rock realm have often become radicalized after directly experiencing police abuse. Say a little more about how that affected your path.

JON GINOLI (Pansy Division): During the ACT UP days there was always the threat of getting arrested and there were a few times when I was prepared to get arrested. I actually never did get arrested, unlike a lot of other people who were involved with ACT UP. So, maybe I would have a more radical viewpoint if that had happened to me. But it happened to a lot of people I knew. One of the big problems in this country right now is, how do you hold police accountable? That's something I think the gay community isn't so worried about anymore, now that cops aren't raiding gay bars like they did twenty-five years ago. But whenever there's a big demonstration, they've got more surveillance tools than ever! It's something that concerns me, that's on my mind. But I'm not sure that it had a direct influence on what I'm doing now.

PANSY DIVISION

John Wayne wore an army uniform / Didn't like us punks and fags that didn't conform.

—"John Wayne Was a Nazi" by MDC (1982)

JM: I'm not certain, but I think maybe you're gay and I wonder how that's been in the punk community?

DAVE DICTOR (MDC): It's one of those things where I've been very ambiguous. I've never truly been gay. I've never really had a male partner. I've worn women's clothes. I lived in an apartment with three gay men and one gay woman, and people would ask me if I was gay and I'd say, "Of course I am!" I'm even listed in the homosexual Who's Who as being gay! It's online, but it's one of those things that is so not important for me to clear up. Someone recently told me, "Dave, you're my hero. I realized I was gay when I was twelve." This person was seventeen. I said, "Okay." I feel gay, but I have this thing where I kind of enjoy the smell of women, and there's all these other levels like maybe there are parts of me . . . a woman trapped in a man's body. I relate to the female dress code and parts of the sexuality.

I left it ambiguous because so many people in the music scene would say, "That guy's a fag!" I would say, "Yes, and I'm the biggest fag you know! I probably scare you and I'm glad, because you should be scared! For a forty-year-old man to have so much fear, you hold on to that fear! I'm not going to take it away from you by making you feel less afraid! I've reached a certain popularity in punk rock, and it's disturbed you!" This is true even of some bigger bands who know who I am and have talked disparagingly about me, or gay people in general. So, "Yes. I'm Black. I'm gay. I'm Asian." You can hold onto that fear.

DAVE DICTOR: My brother was online, and he Googled my name and it said, "One of the famous gay people." He asked, "Dave, are you gay? Have you been hiding something from me?" I told him just what I'm telling you. This is how I've gone about my life, and I haven't cleared it up. What does it all mean? I don't know. I've chosen to let it be ambiguous. There's a famous, definitive book on hardcore, and it basically calls me the gay Che Guevara of the punk rock scene. The guy sent me a copy of the book, and I said, "That's very flattering!" [laugh] "To be the gay Che Guevara of the punk rock scene! Gosh! Thank you!" Let him take away from it what he wants.

JM: It sounds like you're not comfortable being labeled. We're complex human beings that have a lot of different qualities simultaneously.

DAVE DICTOR: That's very true. Who knows, I might be everything! I'm omni- and multidimensional, and if we have to go for a label to define ourselves, which

CHAPTER 7

people seem to love to do, then people can just hold that label. I just thought, "Screw everybody! The people who don't get it don't need to know any better." I don't want to make straight people feel better thinking I'm straight. And I don't feel so straight. There is a sexual outlaw in me, though it's not quite clear as a gay man. I'm a multidimensional person that's got many different facets.

JM: There's a song you have, "America's So Straight." On the one hand it's talking about sexuality, but you probably had a broader intention.

DAVE DICTOR (MDC): The song actually goes, "Rebel, rebel on the street, makeup on my face, stockings on my feet, all the American people ask me why I'm not a typical American guy, why is America so straight, and me so bent?" It alludes to this Lou Reed drag thing and people wanting to put a label on me. There was a disc jockey from Toronto who has a gay radio show, and he plays that song once a month and is very happy that I wrote it because definitely gay punks are a minority in the whole scene. Especially out gay people. Very small minority. Punk, for all its rebellion, can be very sexually conservative. Or just as conservative as many parts of the classic rock world. "Enjoy yourself. It's later than you think while you're still in the pink." There are people getting hurt all across the world fighting for rights. Can you imagine living in some of those Eastern European places and going on a gay march where you're totally bashed by these right-wing and skinhead elements? It's an intense world out there.

WAKE PEOPLE UP

D. H. PELIGRO (Dead Kennedys): A lot of people have been inspired by our views and those of The Clash and Crass and some other bands that are outright more political. People confronted their fears and went, "Wow, this is opening up a whole new horizon." Yes, it is a learning tool. It is a kind of weapon. Yes, it was meant to wake people up to what is going on, as opposed to a bunch of silly love songs. I was hoping to influence some people, but it's kind of a worldwide thing where a lot of people found that starting-off point and carried it further. They got involved with protests. People in Berkeley were standing up for gay rights and human rights. Even all the way trickling down to getting out and voting Obama into office. I think it's had quite a rippling effect across the globe. Politics in punk started off with the MC5 doing political stuff.

JELLO BIAFRA (Dead Kennedys): Even though early grunge seemed to be a deliberate reaction against how political and cookie-cutter hardcore had become, many of the grunge pioneers of Seattle came out of hardcore bands. In the long run a lot of those bands did turn out to be very socially conscious. The only time I got to see Nirvana was when they played a great big gig at a horseracing track with Helmet and Poisoned Idea in Portland. It was designed to be a rally against an anti-gay amendment that was on the state ballot that fall. Coming out in support of gay or LGBTQ rights at that point was a little shocking to some people. That a rock band—especially like Nirvana—would do that. But they did. And then when the abortion doctor was gunned down by a probable future Trump supporter in Pensacola, Florida, who showed up down there to play a combination concert and rally for choice? To let people down there know they weren't alone and shouldn't be afraid? It was Pearl Jam and L7.

JESUS WAS GAY

NORMAN NAWROCKI (Rhythm Activism): One of our last albums, *Jesus Was Gay*, was put out by Propagandhi and the G7 Welcoming Committee record label. That album was so controversial! We were on tour in the United States, and we asked for extra copies of the album to be mailed to us, to sell on the road. But we'd never get them. They'd be put in the mail and the box would arrive at our tour destination and we'd open it, but there were no *Jesus Was Gay* CDs. Inside it were Christian fundamentalist pamphlets telling us that Jesus was going to save us! Somebody at the post office had sabotaged the shipments! This happened to us constantly on the road, and we ran out of albums to sell. It's one of those Canadian-American-cross-border-Christian-fundamentalist-rock-and-roll stories.

JM: I didn't know that the post office provided that service.

NORMAN NAWROCKI: The disciples of Jesus obviously do! We have a photo of Jesus on the cover smiling. The title song, "Jesus Was Gay," went, "Jesus was gay and moved to Alberta (Alberta is one of those super redneck provinces, like Alabama, in the US), opened up a bar for all his friends, bought a pickup, and got a tattoo saying, 'love your brother, amen.'" The story is about a gay man who opens up a bar in a small town. The bar gets attacked. He reopens and gets attacked again, spray painted and windows smashed. He continues to reopen, and they physically attack him. He physically fights back, and then they all become friends and they realize he's okay. That song came out in '97.

DAVE WAKELING (The English Beat): There was a certain fearlessness to punk. To be in some of them punk groups you had to be willing to face enormous ridicule. Now everybody says, "They must have been so cool with their spiky hair and chains and pins in their face." But half the time they were running around town with skinheads and Hells Angels trying to rip the chains out their ears! You had

CHAPTER 7

to be kind of fearless. "Hello! I'm six foot three with orange hair, a pin through my nose and I'm gay! Run!" [laugh] There was a degree of fearlessness. The people weren't doing it to be rich and famous. They were doing it try to find out who they were.

8

POSITIVE FORCE
MARK ANDERSEN AND FUGAZI IN WASHINGTON, DC

The politics of punk are deeper than political parties. The politics of punk are a deep critique of modern corporate society, consumerism, and conformity. The punk music I was listening to was opening my eyes to a broader universe of possibilities and giving me a sense of my own power. There were things wrong in the world and I needed to take a stand and speak out.

—Mark Andersen (Positive Force DC cofounder)

Karl Marx said the revolution has to begin in the ruthless criticism of everything existing. Mikhail Bakunin said the destructive urge is also the creative urge. There you have the philosophy of punk.

—Mark Andersen in *Positive Force: More Than a Witness: 30 Years of Punk Politics in Action*
(2011, Robin Bell, director)

Mark Andersen cofounded Positive Force DC in 1985 and organized concerts, protests, and political events with Washington, DC activists and punk bands Minor Threat, Bad Brains, Fugazi, Anti-Flag, and others. He helped establish direct action groups, a communal house that hosted meetings for activists, anarchists, riot grrrls, and others and participated in punk percussion protests against South African apartheid and US militarism that caught the attention of then US President Bush. Political posters from Positive

Force also caught the attention of the FBI. In 2004 he helped establish the We Are Family Senior Outreach Network, which he continues codirecting today. Initial funding of $15,000 for We Are Family was donated by punk band Good Charlotte to collaborate with St. Aloysius Catholic Church. Andersen is author of a number of books, including *Dance of Days: Two Decades of Punk in the Nation's Capital* (2001) and *All the Power: Revolution Without Illusion* (2004). Andersen is featured in half a dozen films covering the Washington, DC punk scene including *Positive Force: More Than a Witness: 30 Years of Punk Politics in Action*.

US POLICY IN CENTRAL AMERICA

MARK ANDERSEN (Positive Force DC cofounder): Punk as a music or a social/cultural movement predates Ronald Reagan in the US or Margaret Thatcher in the UK. Having said that, when Reagan came in, there was a counter-revolution happening. There was a backlash that was gaining ascendancy. There were a zillion issues to be struggling around. The issue that I grabbed ahold of was US policy in Central America. There's a long history of US involvement in Central America, much of it very sad and unsavory. Even Carter was not perfect in that region. When Reagan came in it was a full-on confrontation with the Soviet Union, the Castro regime in Cuba, and stopping the tide of communism. Reagan was fighting the Sandinista regime that had overthrown our dictator Somoza and the rebels fighting against US-backed military regimes in El Salvador, Honduras, and Guatemala.

Reagan was a powerful symbol of pretty much everything that punks opposed, especially when you paired him with some of his fellow travelers like Jerry Falwell of the Moral Majority. It radicalized young people who were coming to an awareness of a concrete political situation; it made you want to do something. As dramatic as this current moment is in 2022—and it's pretty dramatic—that was a very dramatic moment as well. It was a turning point whose reverberations are still with us today. It was only logical that folks began to sing songs opposing not only Ronald Reagan, but also specific policies. Although the great Dead Kennedys song "Bleed for Me" is the quintessential attack–Ronald Reagan song, it was originally written during the Carter administration. Just as "California Über Alles" was attacking Jerry Brown and not Ronald Reagan. So, there's some problematic politics involved.

> *In the name of world profits / America pumps up our secret police.... When cowboy Ronnie comes to town / Forks out his tongue at human rights.*
>
> —"Bleed for Me" by Dead Kennedys (1982)

ROCK AGAINST RACISM

MARK ANDERSEN: There was this movement called Rock Against Racism (RAR) in the UK that was extraordinarily powerful. It was a big inspiration for me from afar. I first heard about it through the Tom Robinson Band record *Power in the Darkness* (1978). It had information about RAR. Robinson played at a 1978 RAR concert in London with Aswad, X-Ray Spex, and The Clash. He also famously sang "Glad to Be Gay."

It's fair to say that the template for what Positive Force would be was essentially stolen from that original RAR movement. I was not the only one who noticed RAR and thought it was a great idea. There were efforts here in the United States to create Rock Against Racism and a couple concerts happened in DC with Bad Brains, an all–African American punk band who grew up in southeast DC or just across the border in Prince George's County (Maryland). In 1979 and '80 Bad Brains took young teenage punk bands to play at one of the troubled low-income housing complexes there, Valley Green. Ian MacKaye remembers those concerts fondly as an actual Rock Against Racism event because it was causing folks to step across the racial boundaries here in Washington, DC. All of those kids, including Ian, would never have been at Valley Green if it weren't for those concerts. And Valley Green is just as much part of DC as the Lincoln Memorial.

However, the organizers of Rock Against Racism here in the United States tended to be the leftovers of the Yippie movement—Youth International Party—the politicized hippies whose major cause seemed to be legalization of marijuana, or just consuming marijuana, and wanting to do that more freely. That might be a valid cause to support. I'm one of these straight edge guys, so I don't do drugs at all. But I also don't want people going to jail for doing drugs, unless they're harming someone else. But Rock Against Racism was kind of tainted here because it was tied into drug legalization. With the exception of these shows I just described in DC, RAR didn't seem to have the relevance or impact it had in the UK.

That began to shift a little bit when it became Rock Against Reagan in '82 or '83. Rock Against Reagan was also tied in with the Yippies, but it seemed

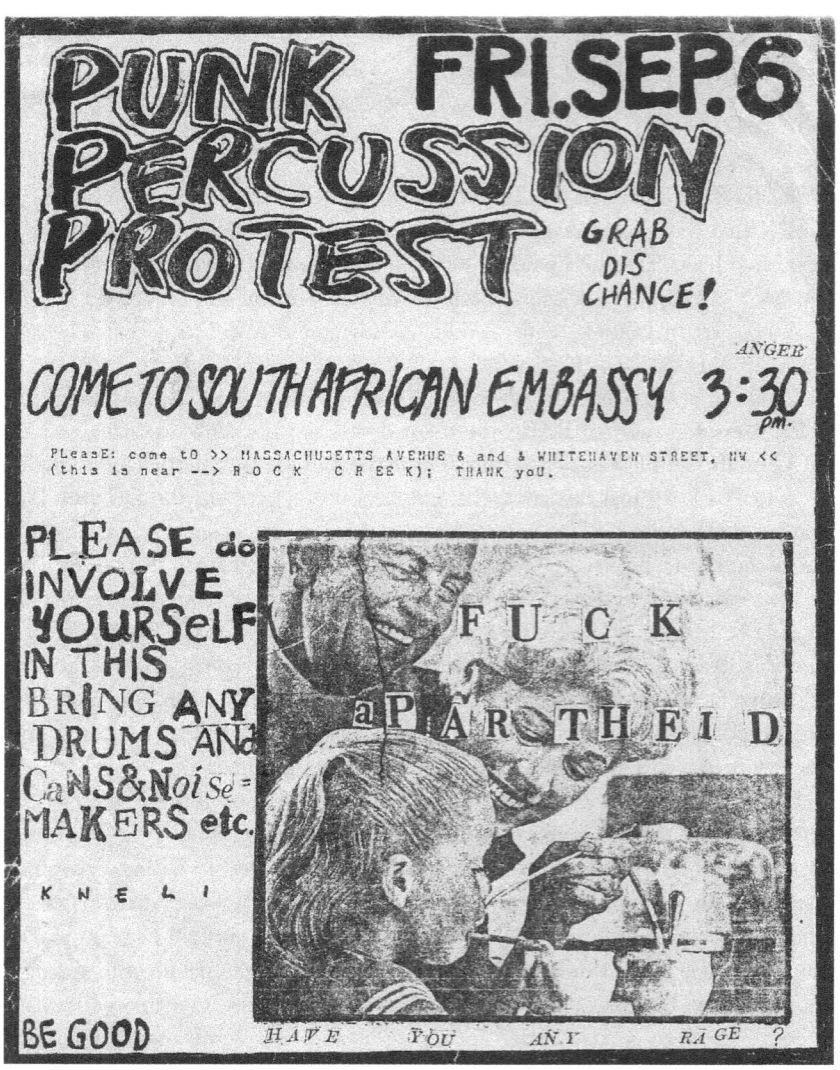

Punk Percussion Protest "Fuck Apartheid" flyer (1991). Contributed: Mark Andersen

to be more of a logical connection. MDC was a headliner for the original Rock Against Reagan and then in '83 Dead Kennedys were the headliner. It was the first DC punk show Dave Grohl went to and he was just blown away by what he experienced on The Mall on that day in '83 with Dead Kennedys. It certainly impacted his trajectory playing with Scream, Nirvana, and Foo Fighters.

DAMN DRUMS ARE KEEPING ME UP ALL NIGHT

JM: Tell me about the punk percussion protests you helped to organize that kept US president George H. W. Bush awake. He was quoted, "Those damn drums are keeping me up all night." That must have been thrilling to hear that he was disturbed by the protests.

MARK ANDERSEN: It was, in a certain juvenile way. We were scrambling around in our subterranean world and didn't feel like we were particularly significant players politically. We were trying to do our part. But, when somebody on that level takes notice of what you're doing it means something. The same thing happened when we made the "Meese Is a Pig" posters. In a weird way, all the attention from the police—or in my case the FBI—was some of the biggest compliments they could've given us! Who's going to pay attention to a bunch of ragtag punk rockers? It meant everything to us. (Edwin Meese III was US Attorney General under Reagan.) With the punk percussion protests, punks wanted to speak and act. But they wanted to do it in a way where they weren't just tag-alongs to the real activists; you wanted to approach it in a way that felt in keeping with your general ethic. There's a number of other ways it played out as well with this whole other phenomenon of the Warzone Tours and No Business as Usual, these roving, spontaneous disruptive marches.

> *The mysterious posters appeared overnight last week, pasted on walls and utility boxes all over Washington, and many people found them objectionable: They said, "Meese is a Pig."*
>
> *The posters contained a commentary in smaller type on the bottom, which upbraided Meese's personal ethics and approach to law enforcement, noted his relationships to people connected to the Wedtech scandal, and called him a "weasel."*
>
> —"Anti-Meese Poster's Source Is a Mystery" by John Mintz, *Washington Post*, December 25, 1987

CHAPTER 8

MARK ANDERSEN: It's weird to think back that apartheid was not that big of an issue in the minds of most people in the early 1980s. Randall Robinson at TransAfrica helped make it an issue by doing daily or weekly demonstrations at the South African Embassy. The punk percussion protests came about because of this work by Robinson and TransAfrica. They realized there was a DC representative of the apartheid racist regime that was torturing and murdering so many people there, including people the same age that we were. You can critique the way TransAfrica approached it because it was definitely a Capitol Hill, news media thing. They wanted to bring big name people down there and have them be arrested in symbolic ways to draw attention to the horrors in South Africa. They did a good job of that.

My friend Amy Pickering worked at Dischord Records and later was in a really important band, Fire Party. She saw the news reports with South African teenagers, our own age, putting everything on the line and being imprisoned, brutalized, murdered. It really shook her up. There was a lull at that moment in the DC punk scene and it seemed like the punk scene was kind of eating itself or falling apart. And then you see your peers in this other place, putting everything on the line, and you feel, "I'm not much of a rebel. I'm not risking very much. What am I doing?" That's the spark that ultimately becomes Revolution Summer and leads to the punk percussion protests. The idea was, "We've got to turn our rhetoric into action!"

One of the obvious ways was to go to the South African Embassy. But we didn't want to just go down there with Congress people and religious leaders and stand in the street to get arrested in this kind of show-arrest thing. We wanted to go and be punk rockers! And what are punk rockers good at? Making noise and making a disturbance! We brought noisemakers, drums, paint cans, plastic tubs—whatever you could bring to make noise. We set up three blocks away because at that time in Washington, DC, the regulations said you had to be two hundred yards or something from the South African Embassy. So, you could make this unholy racket, and it's going to be heard at that embassy. It felt like a creative way for us to participate in this larger action.

Without TransAfrica the whole thing wouldn't have been happening, but we wanted to operate in a way that was in line with who we were. Also, the idea for noise protests wasn't created by us. It existed before at least in Argentina, with the Mothers of the Disappeared. And it wasn't only us who did it after that. I led the last of the percussion protests at the South African Embassy in January of '90. Mandela was freed and South African apartheid began to crumble shortly thereafter. We thought, "This form of protest worked in this context. So, let's do it over here, too."

POSITIVE FORCE

FUGAZI SHOW WAS A PROTEST

MARK ANDERSEN: In late 1990 I had been chatting with Ian MacKaye and he wanted to do a show with Fugazi. It's now the Bush administration because Reagan has finished out his two terms, and then his vice president was elected. Overall, it was a continuation and was viewed as such. Ian's idea was that we have so much money in this country and yet here in Washington, DC, you can't hardly walk around without seeing all these homeless folks living and dying in the shadow of these beautiful monuments to our country's idealism. Ian's idea was to go to a place that's going to be hard to ignore—right in front of the White House. "Let's do a free concert in the middle of winter and dramatize the reality. People will find it uncomfortable to be out there for a couple of hours." Well, how do you think it is for the people who have to live there all the time, who are suffering this dysfunctional and inadequate shelter system?

That was the original idea and we were working way in advance to get a permit because Fugazi was about to go off on a long tour of Europe. We got the permit in August 1990, and around then Saddam Hussein invaded Kuwait and this horrid series of events played out which led to the invasion of Iraq by US-led forces. We were extremely concerned about the Kuwaiti and Iraqi people who would die as a result. So, the event was shifted from focusing specifically on

Ian MacKaye and Mark Andersen commune before Fugazi concert at Lorton Youth Correctional Facility in Virginia (Dec. 26, 1990). Photo: Jim Saah

CHAPTER 8

homelessness to a larger focus against the war and against the way that expenditures for war making take away resources that could feed, clothe, and house poor people. So, we ended up playing in front of the White House two or three days before the bombs started to fall. It was not just a concert; it was a protest (January 12, 1991).

The Fugazi show itself was a protest. It wasn't an entertainment event. Before the concert there was this enormous punk percussion protest in front of the White House. The day was powerful enough that some of the demonstrators, who essentially lived in Lafayette Park, picked up that drumming and continued it. And it was that continuation of the Fugazi show that leads to the famous statement by President George Herbert Walker Bush, "Those damn drums are keeping me up all night," which was reported by *USA Today*. Of course, we felt validated by that. It was important for us that these big entities were taking notice, just as with the "Meese Is a Pig" posters. It suggested to us that a small number of creative, committed, and persistent people can have an impact.

MARK ANDERSEN: What did we end up with? We didn't stop the war. Many people died and that war sets the stage for the disastrous, illegal invasion of Iraq by George Herbert Walker Bush's son, George W. Bush, in 2003. Part of the reality of activism is that just because you take a stand and speak out, it doesn't mean you win in the short term. Or the long term. What it does mean is that you have done something. That is critically important, because you never know how history is going to go. Do I know what's going to happen here with the insanity that on the one hand Trump unleashed on America? And the other hand, the insanity that was there already that Trump simply exploited? I don't know. I have no idea how it's ultimately going to turn out. But I know I've put my heart on the line and my back into the struggle so that it turns the corner towards greater democracy, freedom, and justice for all.

We fought the Civil War, the bloodiest war in terms of the loss of American lives. And you would have thought in 1865—after the shock of the assassination of Lincoln, but the rise of Reconstruction—that we're actually making a huge step forward in realizing the promises about human equality and justice. But then we had another century of a quasi-form of slavery and oppression with Jim Crow and segregation. I don't know what's going to happen. But I'm going to try to do what's right, no matter what the cost and no matter what other people think.

ANTI-FLAG—THE FIGHT OF OUR LIVES

MARK ANDERSEN: The band Anti-Flag are like family to me. They're very skilled musicians. They're very good-hearted people and they're very serious about their activism. Moments before I got on this interview, I saw their new video for the song called "The Fight of Our Lives" that's just come out (August 10, 2022).

On one hand, it's truly inspiring. The song is great and the video is very powerful. However, one of the things that disturbed me watching the video was that there was so much focus on confrontations in the street, fighting with the police, trying to break police lines, and fucking shit up. I know the band to be thoughtful folks so this is not really a critique of them. It's more of a critique of what we look for in protest or activism. There are things that are really glamorous and catchy for the media, these violent, showy confrontations in the street.

That's why the Black Bloc—somewhat related to Antifa, although quite distinct—has gotten so much attention. It's why the big story from the Seattle protests in 1999 focused on trashing Starbucks or Nike. This stuff plays really well in the media and it was easy for the protesters to be portrayed as vandals, as people just fucking shit up, as opposed to people who actually are trying to fix shit up—that means all the patient organizing that led to the ability of that movement to stop this major international meeting of the World Trade Organization. It was an astonishing accomplishment! And it had absolutely 0.0000001 percent relation to the Black Bloc trashing Nike Town or Starbucks. And yet, how much coverage did that get?

My one fear with the Anti-Flag video is that it gives people an unrealistic, skewed vision of what activism is. It's not only, or even mostly, fighting the pigs, quote/unquote, in the streets. It's about talking to people and building neighborhood organizations. It's about connecting different communities to change minds and change social structures. It's not something that you'll see on the evening news much. Yet, it is this method that shut down the World Trade Organization and shut down the bus system in Montgomery until segregation was done. We believe we're part of an expansion of democracy and respect for life in general. I do believe that is the right approach and that the overall trajectory of American history is towards that greater freedom. It's about the earth and everything that lives in it, not just humans.

CHAPTER 8

WTO ANARCHIST RIOT

JELLO BIAFRA (Dead Kennedys): In my "What Would Jello Do?" (video blog) about Antifa I say that nonviolence is the better way to go long term. Even in pure tactical terms, the minute anybody from the anti-fascist, anti-corporate side says anything *remotely* violent, that's *all* the corporate media tells everybody else in the country. At the Seattle demonstrations (1999) I was at, there were fifty thousand strong with everybody from the pilots union to the Teamsters, everybody swarming peacefully to put a stop to the WTO. Even trapping President Clinton in his limousine so he couldn't get to the hotel for hours! Then somebody throws a newspaper vending machine through a Starbucks window. We're all, "Woo-hoo! That's hilarious! I love the sound of breaking glass." We also realized, "Oh, shit. That's *all* CNN is going to talk about now." Sure enough, from that point onward, corporate media's rewriting history, spinning the thing as "anarchist riot." The pilots union were not rioting anarchists. The nurse's union are not rioting anarchists. The unions got written out of the story. Which makes it all the more reason never to give anybody with a mouthpiece the size of Trump any ammunition to say, "Well, both sides were at fault in Charlottesville because both sides were violent" (2017).

PANDEMIC ISOLATION

MARK ANDERSEN: There's also extraordinary suffering going on from the pandemic itself, but there's the additional isolation that itself poisons us. I work with low-income seniors in inner-city DC and these folks are extraordinarily isolated to begin with. When the pandemic hit, it was even worse and I was working with probably the single most high-risk population: mostly nonwhite, very low income in the inner city, with many preexisting conditions. It was extraordinarily intense.

I've spent over thirty years of my life working with very mundane stuff that is meaningful. I helped found a group called We Are Family Senior Outreach Network (2004). I work with low-income seniors, most of them African American and Latino. Many are immigrants, people who are not considered to be significant in the overall scheme of things in our society. Most of what I do is not flashy, making sure people have food, that they're getting to the doctor and don't feel like no one cares. It's about drawing people from different communities together so we recognize each other as human beings, as sisters and brothers in one family. This is not glamorous work. And it is not there in the Anti-Flag video. Although I will say in defense of Anti-Flag: they came and played at one of our volunteer events. In the film that Anti-Flag put out about the band there's a brief portion of me speaking at that event (*Beyond Barricades: The Story of Anti-Flag*, Jon Nix, director, 2020). I just think they're more sophisticated, politically, than that video would suggest. They're correct that we are in the fight of our lives! It's just that the fight won't necessarily look like what's in that video. That is, if we want to win it.

MARK ANDERSEN: Marching in the streets is extremely important. I'm a big fan of flesh-and-blood activism, no offense to cyberactivism. It's all important. But I do think there's a special power that people have when we're together in the flesh. I'm so glad that the pandemic is mostly behind us because it was so hard on human beings to be kept apart like that (August 2022).

However, marching in the streets can only go so far. If I have a critique of marching in the streets, it's not that by confronting the state we're going to get killed. The fact is that there are structures that operate that you have to acknowledge and engage with. Even if you don't ultimately accept them as the best way, or the right way, they exist and they must be dealt with. I think the right wing has done a great job on this. They have run candidates in local and state elections and have gained control of the levers of power in many places.

Even when I disagree with people, I'm reluctant to call anyone my enemy. Although maybe that's the reality we're coming to; maybe there's going to be another civil war in this country. Sometimes it feels like there might be. But more fundamentally, I want to see you as my brother or sister. I want to see creation in general as part of our family including the animals, plants, and all of life.

PEACE AND LOVE: THEY'LL SHOOT YOU!

RAY MANZAREK (The Doors): I saw punk as an outgrowth of the hippie thing. Now, there's two ways of looking at hippies. You can look at hippies like The Doors, who were really *not* hippies but were existentialists. Or you can look at hippies as those going to San Francisco to wear flowers in their hair. Punks were definitely not of the peace and love generation. The punks realized that peace and love will get you nowhere. They'll shoot you! If you're a hippie and you go up against the establishment, the military will kill you. I think everyone realized this after Kent State (May 4, 1970). Certainly, the punks did. They'll kill you! Your fathers will send the military out and they will shoot you dead. You've just killed students at a college. The military has come out and fired upon the word.

CHAPTER 8

Is this America or some Latin American banana republic? Or Romania? If you keep it up, they'll bring in the tanks. Everyone realized, "Holy shit!"

So, everyone realized *hippie* isn't going to get you anywhere. The punks thought, "Holy fuck!" The punks didn't have any power yet and they looked around and saw that peace and love would get you nowhere and that money was the only way to go, and they had no way of getting money. Punks said, "Let's just play our music. Let's attack our music with all the fury we can possibly muster." What the punks were doing was an attempt to get beyond that whole hippie thing. I don't think they really knew what they were doing. But they felt it coming.

CAPITALISM AND DEMOCRACY?

MARK ANDERSEN: I don't know about what Ray Manzarek had to say. I was not under any illusions about what could be done to protesters. But it didn't stop me from protesting. We're relatively protected here in the US compared to other places, Kent State and Jackson State notwithstanding. It's not like South Africa, Myanmar, or Russia.

One of the fundamental challenges we'll have to face if we're trying to more fully realize democracy here is these archaic structures that enable minority rule. We have to look deep at the way our society is structured. I'm glad for the rise of politicians like Bernie Sanders, Elizabeth Warren, and AOC who raise questions about the nature of capitalism and, "How compatible is capitalism with democracy?"

To have political democracy you need something closer to *economic* democracy. Look back at '67 when Martin Luther King Jr. started the Poor People's Campaign, shifting the focus of his activism away from racial justice to also encompass anti-militarism and economic justice, highlighting the huge gap between the rich and the poor in this country. And look at us now; it's over fifty years later and economic equality is off-the-charts worse than it was back then!

Occupy Wall Street did a great job of reframing things and getting a focus on this economic inequality. It did *not* do a great job of suggesting how we might actually build a movement that could realize advancements on that front. Democracy and economic equality are not reflected in how our government and society operates. It's maybe a feature of the system rather than a bug; the US wasn't set up to lift up the poor and have them run things. An elite was created to run things.

MARK ANDERSEN: If punk builds a wall between us and other people, then it's part of the problem. There's the line in "Smells Like Teen Spirit"—"Our little group has always been, and always will be, until the end." Cobain would sing it as, "Our little *tribe* has always been, and always will be, 'til the end." If it's all about making us feel better than other people, then it's not revolutionary. It's not even progressive. It's just another way for some people to feel good about themselves by putting down other people.

That deeper reflection has led me not away from revolutionary politics, but to a deeper understanding of what they require of me. For anyone who is inspired by punk and is still trying to have an impact on the righteous path, just keep asking questions, keep taking your stance, and keep rolling, reflecting, and learning. The real sellout is when we are complacent. That's the end of the revolution. If punk can be redefined away from just loud, angry music or extreme hairstyles, piercings, and tattoos, to understanding that it's a spirit that challenges us individually as much as it challenges the world, then it can help us accomplish these great things for humanity, the earth, and all of creation.

We might discover that punk rock as a spirit didn't arrive in 1975 with Patti Smith and later with Sex Pistols, The Clash, Fugazi, Minor Threat, Bad Brains, Bikini Kill, or Anti-Flag. It was there all along. It was the creative, compassionate spirit that pushed human beings to do just a little bit better. It is the fuel for the revolution. It's not easy. But it's worth it.

CHRISTIAN REVOLUTION

MARK ANDERSEN: I visited Emma Goldman's grave. I would not consider myself an anarchist, although I'm inspired by anarchist ideas just like I'm inspired by Christian, Marxist, Socialist, Islamic, and secular ideas. But the quote on her tombstone is profound: "Liberty will not descend to a people, a people must raise themselves to liberty."

The revolutionary tradition in this country says there is something of extraordinary value in the Christian revolutionary tradition because Jesus Christ was hung on a cross. Everybody knows that, but do people understand what that means? It was the most torturous, brutal, publicly humiliating death that the Roman Empire could devise. He suffered that death like thousands of others. For what? For sedition, for being a rebel against the empire. You can understand why Jesus was viewed that way when you read about his life and what he said. He presented a fundamental challenge to structures and the powers that be. Have people taken those revolutionary ideas and turned them into

CHAPTER 8

ways to oppress rather than liberate? Yes, they're doing it right now. But those ideas have power and we must not surrender that power. We should do our best to take at least the next tiny step towards realizing those ideals.

There is an almost inevitably slow trajectory of progress towards justice. This is what's implicit in that famous quote from Martin Luther King Jr.: "The arc of the universe is a long one, but it bends towards justice." There's also a Jewish proverb, "It is not up to you to finish the task. But neither can you forsake the work." I'm paraphrasing. But the idea is that activism is not blinded by illusion. We know we're not going to make as much difference as we'd like. But it is essential that we do it anyway. And we never know exactly how much difference it might make.

JM: You're reminding me that even though we like results and ending points, the revolution is a process. The revolution is a dynamic, alive thing.

MARK ANDERSEN: It is, absolutely. It's a living thing, a process. Paulo Freire inspired me and said that being Christian is a process of becoming. You're never done being Christian, you're never done as a revolutionary. You keep living, growing, questioning, and learning. Punk is also a living thing. It's not over until your life is over. And then it continues on in someone else's life who you may have touched. That is both sobering and liberating. And empowering because we know we make a difference and our life has meaning.

MARK ANDERSEN: What an extraordinary cosmic accident that I turned up here in DC when I did. It's meant everything to me. The DC scene probably was the most influential cutting-edge punk scene of the '80s to the mid '90s. Musically and pushing boundaries politically. And then the mechanics of doing it yourself and Dischord Records and so many other record labels. And then of course the example of bands like Fugazi. It's not surprising that not long before Joe Strummer died, he was asked by *Spin* magazine who he felt epitomized the spirit of punk as he knew it. He didn't hesitate a second and said, "Fugazi." And there is no Fugazi without that larger DC scene. I'm blessed to be part of it.

9

"FIGHT WAR NOT WARS"
PUNK ROCK, MILITARISM, AND WAR

I had to regain my self-respect / So I got into camouflage / The girls, they love to see you shoot.

—"I Love a Man in a Uniform" by Gang of Four (1982)

Fight war / Not wars.

—Crass (1978)

When World War II ended in 1945 it was hailed as the end of mass modern warfare. In 1947 the United States changed the name of the Department of War, established in 1789, to the Department of Defense. Despite the pacifist-marketing facelift, the United States continued to expand weapons production and warfare. The Central Intelligence Agency (CIA) was also established in 1947, beginning decades of devastating worldwide economic violence, weapons sales, "low-intensity" warfare, political surveillance, covert assassinations, coups d'état, and secret torture prisons that continue today. The period following World War II was euphemistically referred to as the Cold War, even as US control and influence spread to include more than 750 military bases in eighty countries.

Punk rock exploded from the frustration and anxiety of living in a time of corrupt politics, a lack of social services, rabid anti-communism, and a culture of war. In 1971 former US military analyst Daniel Ellsberg became a whistleblower by releasing the "Pentagon Papers," exposing the failure and devastation of the US war on Vietnam. Also in 1971, Quaker activists broke into the FBI

CHAPTER 9

office in Media, Pennsylvania, and "liberated" documents that revealed a secret program of the FBI based on counterintelligence and counterinsurgency. Called COINTELPRO it was designed to disrupt domestic Black, Chicano, and Left political organizations. President Nixon resigned in 1973 after it was discovered he'd helped consolidate COINTELPRO and the CIA's Operation Chaos to illegally spy on and sabotage political activists in the United States. Nixon also secretly bombed Laos and Cambodia and employed mafia-style thugs to break into the National Democratic Party headquarters at the Watergate Hotel in Washington, DC in 1972.

During a televised speech in 1984 US President Reagan thought he was "off the air" when the former actor was captured joking about nuclear war. The recording was used by John Lydon and Afrika Bambaataa on their 1984 punk/hip-hop fusion hit "World Destruction."

> *My fellow Americans, I am pleased to tell you today that I've signed legislation that will outlaw Russia forever. We begin bombing in five minutes.*
>
> —US President Ronald Reagan (August 11, 1984)

> *Yes, the world is headed for destruction / Is it a nuclear war? / What are you asking for?*
>
> —"World Destruction" by Time Zone (John Lydon, Afrika Bambaataa, and Bill Laswell, December 1984)

Since the end of "the war to end all wars" the most esteemed US scientists and political leaders have supported a safety policy regarding nuclear war based on world destruction appropriately called mutually assured destruction (MAD). The intensity and absurdity of life under imminent annihilation inspired many punk rockers to scream into microphones, strum guitars, and slam out rhythms on drum kits.

NUCLEAR HOLOCAUST

JM: When I graduated from high school (1981) I took a poster from a classroom wall that illustrated what to do to survive a nuclear attack. I think we were the second generation that rehearsed for nuclear war, so we grew up thinking about the devastating possibilities. Many people are overwhelmed and don't think there's much of a future on the planet for humans.

DICK LUCAS (Subhumans): Well, there isn't if we all sit back and accept how it's going—from bad to worse.

EDWARD COLVER (punk photographer): I grew up thinking we might be annihilated the next day. Like hitting a light switch: flick and we're gone. That's inspired a lot of the ridiculous greed. People are out for themselves; there's no tomorrow. It's the nihilism stuff that inspired the punk scene in a lot of ways. I have an old *LA Times* photo and downtown is in the foreground and you can see the nuclear blast from Nevada in the background. The glow at night.

JON KING (Gang of Four): Our song "In the Ditch" is about the absurdity of living in Leeds (England) in the 1970s, as we were all living under the expectation that there would be a nuclear strike between the Soviet Union and NATO forces. Being in Britain, we were about a twenty-minute flight time from East Germany. So, there wasn't much time between launch and landing.

Every household in Britain was sent a pamphlet, "You and the Bomb." There were localized versions of it so in Leeds we all got, "Leeds and the Bomb." The key advice of these really helpful pieces of literature, which I found really funny in a black, absurd way, was, "Whitewash the insides of the windows and fill up large plastic bin liners with clothes and put them on top of a table, because it will absorb radiation. And get under the table." It's quite a lot to do in twenty minutes! I've tried to put shelves up, and it's taken me more than twenty minutes to find the screwdriver!

The book showed the different blast areas and the big joke in Leeds was, "If a nuclear bomb went off, how could anyone tell the difference before and after?" So, you hoped to get to the blast area where everyone is vaporized. We all expected to be vaporized. Or we all *hoped* to be vaporized and not to survive. Because the only people who were going to survive were billionaires down in their bunkers. So that triggered the writing of "In the Ditch." It became a comical song.

JM: The first song Bl'ast recorded was "Holocaust."

CLIFFORD DINSMORE (Bl'ast): That was when we were still called M.A.D. (Mutually Assured Destruction) before Bl'ast. We were really young and that was the first song we wrote together. Then M.A.D. evolved into Bl'ast when Mike Niter joined the band. When Bl'ast started we were growing up in the '80s, which was the Reagan era. It was like nuclear holocaust hanging over your head at any second in time. There was a lot of anger towards that insanity of war.

CHAPTER 9

Democrats are out of power / Across that great wide ocean / Reagan's president elect / Fascist god in motion.

—"(We Don't Need This) Fascist Groove Thang"
by Heaven 17 (banned by the BBC in 1981)

GLENN GREGORY (Heaven 17 / Musical Vomit): "Fascist Groove Thang" and "Let's All Make a Bomb"—we wrote those songs because we were genuinely scared. We were very worried about nuclear attack and we thought Ronald Reagan was going to lead us down a path to destruction. We wanted to shake people and say, "This is really happening. This is more than a possibility." That's why we were specific about lyrics and naming politicians and past warmongers. "Fascist Groove Thang" also happened because fascism at the time in England was really on the rise. People were getting beaten up by racist skinheads.

It's heartbreaking to think that these songs—"Fascist Groove Thang" and "Let's All Make a Bomb"—could have been written last week and are as relevant as they were forty years ago. How can we still be there? It seems impossible. You keep getting false horizons where you think things are going to get better, but then we're pushed back down and it's all happening again. I was listening to a newscast this morning (August 2022) and someone actually used "mutually assured destruction." And I thought, "Wow, I haven't heard that for a long time." It's always been there. But now they're bringing it back up as, "This is a thing. We should do this. If we haven't got nuclear bombs, they'll get us." No! How can that be?

ANTONINO D'AMBROSIO (*Let Fury Have the Hour*): The Clash had a giant moment when *London Calling* was the biggest record in the world. It was a critical sensation and continues to speak to today's concerns; the title song is about war and the threat of nuclear catastrophe.

In 1978 British anarcho-punk band Crass released the song "They've Got a Bomb" on the album *The Feeding of the 5000*. The middle of the song has a purposefully awkward fifteen seconds of silence and during live performances the lights were turned out and film was projected of an atomic bomb exploding. The band's 1980 song "Nagasaki Nightmare" came with album art that included images of nuclear war victims in Nagasaki. Crass were supporters of the Campaign for Nuclear Disarmament (CND), described in a secret July 1984 CIA report as "by far the most influential peace group in the United Kingdom."[1]

PENNY RIMBAUD (Crass): I've lived my life coming out of another pandemic, which was the horror of the Second World War. The war itself was no more horrific than any other war, bar the Nazi camps and Hiroshima and Nagasaki. Those were total statements of a new age.

HIDE FUJIWARA (Ultra Bidé): Japan got the atomic bomb not only two times. Three times. Hiroshima first, Nagasaki second, and the third was Fukushima (2011). All three times were by America. The Fukushima nuclear plant was made by General Electric and they're an old part of the nuclear war system. Of course, it didn't survive. They didn't build a wall or design the building to survive an earthquake. And the Tokyo Energy Company are cheap motherfuckers.

During World War II America and England fought the Germans, Italy, and Japan. Why must the US finish the Japanese war first? Germany was much stronger. America and England wanted to use Japan for testing. Japan made a stupid mistake after the First World War: they joined Mussolini and Hitler and became fascist. Nice idea. It was a mistake and we had to pay for that.

RAMSEY KANAAN (Political Asylum / AK Press): A lot of bands sang about the threat of nuclear war because in the '80s that was the zeitgeist of the time. The bomb could be dropped at any moment. You'd get a four-minute warning and then you'd duck and cover.

C. J. RAMONE (Ramones): The whole threat of nuclear war, after Ronald Reagan, disappeared for a good long time. There really wasn't much trouble in the nuclear sense from the end of the Reagan era through the Bushes, Bill Clinton, and President Obama. We had a good little stretch because the USSR came apart. That introduced new problems with possible nuclear weapons getting sold to bad actors. But in those years, I could actually feel how much it made a difference to me, to not be worrying about that.

OH, SAY CAN YOU HEAR? VIETNAM

When Jimi Hendrix played "The Star-Spangled Banner," the national anthem of the United States, at Woodstock on August 18, 1969, it was an intense audio collage dripping with meaning and fervent noncollaboration with the powers that were. Perhaps the last time an instrumental song had such an impact was in 1958 when "Rumble" by Link Wray—a half-Shawnee Native American musician—was banned from US radio airplay. Wray's guitar playing inspired Iggy Pop, Pete Townsend of The Who, and the MC5's Wayne Kramer.[2]

CHAPTER 9

JON KING (Gang of Four): When Hendrix played that song, it's very interesting that although all he was doing was playing the American national anthem on an electric guitar, everyone knew it was about Vietnam. Reactionaries wanted to take away his passport and revoke his American citizenship. They knew it had a certain content beyond what it was on the surface.

I wouldn't put myself up with Jimi, but that's kind of where you want your music to be, where everyone knows what it's about. Andy (Gill) and I wrote "I Love a Man in a Uniform" as a pop song. It was in the charts and it was banned in the UK because it came to be understood to be about the (1982 UK) invasion of the Falkland Islands. The song had to be banned; it was dangerous. Obviously, we didn't make any money out of these things. It was quite pleasing to have been banned twice in the UK and have records thrown off the air. ("At Home He's a Tourist" was banned by the BBC in 1979.)

> *I'm American. So, I played it. . . . They made me sing it in school. It was a flashback.*
>
> —Jimi Hendrix on US TV with Dick Cavett (September 9, 1969) on playing the US national anthem at Woodstock Festival (August 1969)

Jimi Hendrix enlisted in the US Army on May 31, 1961, after being stuck with this choice: join the military for three years or go to prison for two. This was after being arrested for stealing cars. Hendrix was assigned to the 101st Airborne Division at Fort Campbell, Kentucky, but the guitarist was (surprise!) not a good fit for the army and apparently often missed midnight bed checks and kept other soldiers awake with his guitar playing. Hendrix was honorably discharged after one year due to an apparent ankle injury sustained during a parachute jump.

EDWARD COLVER (punk photographer): I avoided the Vietnam War draft because I was underweight. I was up in 1968: eighteen, six foot, and 138 pounds. They called me in and I was scared to death, man. My father had been wounded in the Battle of the Bulge and that was a war worth fighting. But every war since then, what's been accomplished? Nothing!

"FIGHT WAR NOT WARS"

NUMBER THREE AT THE CIA: MILES COPELAND JR. AND THE OVERTHROW OF GOVERNMENTS

> *I suppose you know who Miles Copeland Junior was? Number three at the CIA for several US presidents. How do you think The Police got to play in places like Egypt and Chile who had brutal, fascist totalitarian regimes?*
>
> —Jello Biafra (Dead Kennedys)

Miles Copeland III was born in 1944 and he and brothers Stewart and Ian grew up in Syria, Lebanon, and Egypt, where the family had a chauffeur, two nannies, five gardeners, a chief cook, assistant cook, and several maids. The Copeland family often picnicked at the pyramids in Egypt where Miles carved his name. It wasn't until their father, Miles Copeland Jr., wrote the first of four books in 1969—*The Game of Nations: The Amorality of Power Politics*—that his children discovered he'd been secretly organizing assassinations and political coups for the CIA, including the 1949 overthrow of the Syrian government. Miles Jr. helped build the Mukhabarat, the Egyptian version of the CIA, and installed US-friendly dictators like Saddam Hussein.

Miles Copeland III later carved his name in the music business by starting I.R.S. Records in Los Angeles in 1979 and released albums by punk and new wave bands like The Go-Go's, The Bangles, The Buzzcocks, Squeeze, Wall of Voodoo, The Cramps, and Timbuk 3. His brother Stewart became a drummer and formed the band The Police and Ian founded the Frontier Booking Agency (FBI). Miles's exciting 1981 concert film *Urgh! A Music War* has footage of energized bands like Gang of Four, X, Oingo Boingo, Pere Ubu, Devo, and Dead Kennedys.

JM: When you were a kid, your dad helped to found the Central Intelligence Agency and participated in assassinations and overthrowing governments. He helped to install Saddam Hussein and said, "He's a bad guy, but he is *our* bad guy," which became one of the mottos of the CIA. In a 1986 *Rolling Stone* interview he said, "My complaint has been that the CIA isn't overthrowing enough anti-American governments or assassinating enough anti-American leaders." Tell me about your dad.

MILES COPELAND (I.R.S. Records, former manager of The Police and Sting): You have to take things in context. During World War II my father was OSS (Officer of Strategic Services), counterintelligence against the Germans. At the end

CHAPTER 9

of the war, he was brought in with Kermit Roosevelt and Roger Roosevelt and they helped build the CIA. But pretty quickly, by 1948, just a few years after the war was over, the world pretty much divided into two between the Soviet Union and China on one side and the democracies on the other. So, the dynamic of America was, "It's us or them. The world is binary."

So, a lot of the decision making in the CIA was based on that very real issue between, "Do we let the guy go over and help the Russians or Chinese? Or do we have him on our side, even if we don't particularly like him?" Like Saddam Hussein, as my father said, "He's a bad guy, but he's *our* bad guy." He was on our side. He was not on Russia's side. Up until the fall of the Berlin Wall, the world was basically divided into two and we wanted to make sure that our side was going to be on the winning side.

Was Saddam Hussein a killer? Absolutely. But he was nowhere in the league of Hitler or Stalin or any of those people who really did kill millions of people. Or the Khmer Rouge, who killed two million people. Saddam was very careful who he killed. He killed the people that would cause some trouble. Putin is doing it now. He picks people causing trouble and makes sure he fixes them. He either assassinates them, or whatever. Anytime somebody stuck his head up and said, "I'm going to be a problem," even if he was a relative, Saddam would cut his head off.

MILES COPELAND: When my father was saying, "We should have overthrown more governments," it was because he really hated the idea of a war. Like Vietnam: what a waste of time that was! His view would be, "If we had just assassinated one or two people here and there, we would have never needed to fight a war." He was looking at it from a numbers standpoint. His view was that there's no point hating a dictator, they're gonna do what they do. The point is, let's get a guy that's least bad.

DIABOLICAL CIA PLOT

PAT MACDONALD (Timbuk 3): There was a time when I thought Miles (Copeland) was the devil. I thought he was sent by his dad to corrupt the music industry. And defang it politically, so to speak, through offering rewards, monetary and otherwise. I never really completely trusted that he wasn't some kind of operative in some big CIA scheme. But I can laugh at that too, because that's doubtful in retrospect. But at the time that was a little conspiracy theory in me that was very much alive for a while. I actually met his infamous dad one day when I was at Miles's house. Maybe it was a diabolical CIA plot that we were entangled in.

I have no idea. If anything, it might have been a casual flirtation with the devil, rather than a deal with the devil.

KID CONGO POWERS (The Gun Club / Nick Cave & The Bad Seeds): I made records with The Cramps and we went to play in London. The Cramps were on I.R.S. Records at the time, which was Miles Copeland's label. Miles was out of town and offered us to stay at his house, to save on hotel fees. So, we stayed at Miles's beautiful house and the first night we were there I noticed all these artifacts. I said, "These look like museum pieces, these replications are really good." And Lux said, "His father was in the CIA. These are probably things they just picked up overseas."

The weird thing is that I woke up in the middle of the night and I really felt like I was on acid. The room was tipping to the side and I was trying to walk down a hallway that went on forever. It was so strange! The next morning we're at breakfast in the kitchen and I said to Lux, Ivy, and Nick, "I got up to go to the bathroom and this weird thing happened." I described the hallway and this hall-of-mirrors-type thing and Lux said, "The same thing happened to me, exactly like you're describing." So, we thought, "This place is haunted!" I asked Lux, "How does Miles live in this house with this?" Lux was like, "Oh, Miles has no conscience. This wouldn't affect him at all!" So, we had some strange, ancient intervention going on and we're convinced it happened because two people experienced it, not just one. It's a strange story. You know, you meet some strange people. I hope those pieces found their way back to their rightful homes.

ROCK AGAINST REAGAN

STEVEN BLUSH (author of *American Hardcore*): When I wrote the book and the film the subtext was "radicalism in the Reagan era." These were radical misfit kids who came of age in this conformist late '70s/early '80s monolithic world and were raging against it. That's where I was coming from. There was always a political component to all of this. "If you're looking for radicalism in the '80s you have to look at hardcore" is the opening line of the film *American Hardcore* from Vic Bondi (Articles of Faith). Look at Dead Kennedys and MDC and what they were saying.

The 1984 Rock Against Reagan Tour had Dead Kennedys and Millions of Dead Cops touring the country. Come on! It was on. I remember seeing that show played in front of the Washington Monument and we felt we had a revolution going. In 1984 Walter Mondale got his ass kicked and it was after that election when punk pretty much flames out. I can't even express the disappointment

CHAPTER 9

after that; I was done with thinking that this revolution was going to change the world. Flash forward to today (2020) and many of the ethics certainly start with hardcore. Almost all of it. Antifa—I remember those guys from the Dead Kennedys-Oakland-crusty-punk-radicals.

DAVE DICTOR (Millions of Dead Cops): We played Rock Against Reagan and we were in front of up to five thousand people with Dead Kennedys at the Lincoln Memorial playing with six, eight, ten bands and there'd be thousands of people. We played celebrations of the Tompkins Square riots about seventeen years ago in New York City. We played shows with Leftöver Crack and some of the NYC bands and there were three thousand kids there and three or four hundred cops in the background, all literally gripping their nightsticks. You can see there's a deep tension in the air and you just don't know where it's going to end up sometimes.

"5.45"

A June 2014 essay published in the *United States Naval Institute News* was titled "A Brief History of Punk Rock in the Cold War." The author writes that Talking Heads "channeled the mystique of the loner guerrilla in the big city in their hit, 'Life During Wartime,' and offers details about punk bands like National Wake that supported direct action in 1978 in South Africa to bring down the apartheid system."

> Punk rock is no stranger violent politics. [*sic*] From decrying statist militarism to embracing revolutionary upheaval to reveling in the nihilistic specter of nuclear war, the genre has a lot to say about conflict.
>
> Name any war, police action, popular unrest, and there's a good chance somebody sang, shouted, screamed or spat about it to a crowd.
>
> The scale of irregular violence surrounding the better known clashes between Cold War superpowers is staggering. U.K. post-punk band Gang of Four memorialized the omnipresence of irregular conflicts in the 1979 song *5.45*, emphatically declaring: "guerrilla war struggle is a new entertainment." Many of their contemporaries seemed to agree.

DAVE ALLEN (Gang of Four): When we wrote "5.45" originally there was a sense that you could bring these subjects to the fore and people would be upset and that some shift would happen by presenting the idea that guerrilla warfare is on the news as a form of entertainment. "Guerrilla war struggle is the new entertainment." Whereas now, it doesn't even get ten seconds! The news in America is amazing: "And now here's some news from Iraq," and then straight to, "Today, the Mariners won their baseball game." It's not *even* entertainment any longer.

ANDY GILL (Gang of Four): "5.45" is quite cool and in many ways feels to me like it was written about now (2005). When you think about it, when that song was written (1979) the Soviet Union was apparently doing well and was very powerful. Now it very much *is* about guerrilla war struggle, with covert operations rather than superpowers standing off against each other. One of the other things about that song is that it is a bit odd musically.

PEACE IS NOT PROFITABLE; WAR IS BIG BUSINESS

Long before punk rock emerged in New York and London, US president Dwight D. Eisenhower famously warned against the dangers of the "military industrial complex." He coined the term in his leaving-office speech on January 17, 1961, and pointed out that "three and a half million men and women are directly engaged in the defense establishment. We annually spend on military security more than the net income of all United States corporations. This conjunction of an immense military establishment and a large arms industry is new in the American experience." Unfortunately, Eisenhower came to this critical perspective only after commanding US troops during World War II and overseeing the fusing of militarism and capitalism, including the proliferation of US nuclear weapons.

Now, even Eisenhower would be shocked at how the business of war has grown. In 2020 weapons sales by the world's one hundred largest arms companies totaled $531 billion, according to a report by the Stockholm International Peace Research Institute (SIPRI), which also pointed out, "Arms sales increased even as the global economy contracted by 3.1 per cent during the first year of the pandemic." US arms manufacturers rank highest with a total $285 billion in sales.[3] For many corporations that profit from war, weapons are only part of their conglomeration. For example, although General Electric has been a top producer of war planes and nuclear weapons components, most Americans know them for their lightbulbs. Similarly, from 1979 to 1997 the British EMI Record Label was merged with Thorn, one of the United Kingdom's largest "defense" corporations. During that period EMI Thorn released albums by hundreds of bands.

LYDIA LUNCH (Teenage Jesus & The Jerks): Violence—that especially men are allowed to create in this abomination of a killing field that stretches everywhere, the war being a virus that just travels around the world—is mainly exported from America at this point. There is no end to it because peace is not profitable, but war is big business. Bottom fucking line. It's just fascinating to me because it's a subject that always obsesses me as someone who has a natural tendency—as my hormones are insane, as if I had a dead male twin who I consumed—feeling both male and female, it's just a subject that I'm forever exploring. War is big business. The American way of life is the American way of death. I'm tired of talking about it, although I won't stop talking about it. We go on. Or as Samuel Beckett said, "I can't go on, I'll go on." We have to.

JM: A two-word phrase has always stuck with me since I read Beckett's *Worstword Ho* when I was a teenager: "Fail better."

LYDIA LUNCH: Well I've succeeded in everything I've tried to do. I'm the most successful person I know and that does not reflect in my bank account however. But that's not the point of my existence; it never was. I've done everything I've wanted with everyone I've wanted to do it with. And I'm not stopping. So, period. Or dot dot dot.

JM: It seems there's plenty of money and resources for the US to continue multiple wars . . .

JOHN LYDON (Sex Pistols / PiL): Oh, yeah. Because they benefit the powers that be, the corporations making the arms. There's a lot of money to be made by the sale of guns. I'm quite surprised, considering the number of guns that are in America, that there's so many of us still alive! There has to be something genuinely decent in the American psyche because there should be a lot more funerals.

PETER CASE (The Nerves): It's so natural for Americans to support war. It's like a solution to everything. I guess it's been sold to everybody. Even Obama has to either give lip service to that or he buys it. War is our main export product. It's appalling. We need to be a leader in peace. America has exported so much war that it could be part of the price that's going to be exacted now. This country could be paying for it all the way if we don't watch it. The war thing is super evil. The thing that's so appalling is there's never been any mass appraisal of the effects of war and what it really means. For example, we're still feeling the result of the Vietnam War and Vietnam is still feeling it. It affected generations of people. It affected children who were born at that time, who are grown up now. Their families have been destroyed.

This new war (Iraq 2003) is going to be paid for when these guys come home and they're crippled and we've kept them alive. In Vietnam fifty thousand men were killed and how many people were wounded? How many people were traumatized? It's a huge impact on society. We're so bought into it. It's like what Dwight Eisenhower said about the military industrial complex.

DICK LUCAS (Subhumans): Jesus, we're in the twenty-first century! Why are there any wars whatsoever? It's not that we haven't learned. It's just that the *leaders use war as an opportunity to gain resources and profits in order to keep power structures in place.* They think in terms of possession and personal gain. They are beyond my fucking comprehension. They can have anything they want, they can all retire now on a life of luxury, golfing forever, wherever they like. They can build all the space modules they want. Fly off to the moon from a desert in Nevada. They can do all of this stuff without going to war at all. But their head's been filled by tradition and the past, politically, in terms of power structures, and they think they're at the top of the power. They think they're doing people good. The illusion is complete. Once they've got control over the media and the way that people receive their ideas, then a lot of people *also* believe that this truth is the only truth there is. That's what's called the status quo and that's what a vast majority of people are actually fighting against, one way or another. To most of us it becomes common sense and it's just obvious.

JON KING (Gang of Four): The state has always monopolized violence and it does very well and they allow us to participate in it. It is quite an ugly part of our collective world. If you were in space you'd say, "These people living in these rich countries outsource their violence somewhere else." We live in the most amazing luxury and comfort now, in these amazingly safe environments, actually because of this outsourcing movement. In the punk rock time, there was a sense that the violence was a lot closer to home. Not quite so now. I use this business term *outsourcing*, but the word outsourcing hadn't been invented. All of these sort of brilliantly Orwellian words about moving something that should be somewhere, to somewhere else.

OBEY TO HOPE TO DRONE

In the 2010 documentary by artist Banksy *Exit Through the Gift Shop* illustrator Shepard Fairey is seen wearing a Sex Pistols T-shirt as he talks about his early days plastering the sides of buildings with the OBEY posters he crafted, a design that spread to urban settings worldwide.

Fairey later designed a poster to support presidential candidate Barack Obama in 2008 that once again included a single word: "HOPE." For many, the excitement and hope generated by the election of America's first African American president shifted to despair upon realizing that Obama was continuing America's violent legacy by participating in mass warrantless surveillance

CHAPTER 9

and daily reviews of an extralegal kill list for US drones, a program that included murdering Americans abroad without trial.

Perhaps Jello Biafra and the Guantanamo School of Medicine hit the irony on the head when they parodied the title of Barack Obama's 2006 autobiography by changing the word "Hope" to "Hype" and titled their 2009 debut album *The Audacity of Hype*.

In 2013 Fairey told TMZ that the word "HOPE" on his poster should be replaced with "DRONES."[4] And during a 2015 interview with *Esquire* magazine, when asked if Obama had lived up to his HOPE poster, the artist answered, "Not even close . . . drones and domestic spying are the last things I would have thought [he'd support]."[5] In the *Esquire* interview Fairey also mentions the punk inspiration for his own art: "When I was 14 years old, I was into punk rock—The Clash, Dead Kennedys—and skateboarding."

IMPULSE AGAINST VIOLENCE, THE NATURE OF WAR

JM: There is pretty much constant war, with some thirty-five wars since World War II. Some people argue about whether violence is natural or not. Do you have any thoughts about why this planet is in the state it's in?

CHRIS HANNAH (Propagandhi): I have thoughts. They're speculations. There is no hard science that I have consulted. But on this idea, there is a Chris Hedges book called *War Is a Force that Gives Us Meaning*. He cites a study that says there have been twenty-nine years of recorded human history where there's been no war. So, is it natural? Is it the consequence of negative social relationships that evolved early on? I don't know. So many of us have an impulse *against* violence that I think it's just as natural. But violence is naturally the thing that people tend towards when they want to consolidate power and wealth.

JM: It seems to take a lot of effort to educate people to be violent. If it were natural to us, people wouldn't have to go to military training to be taught to view others as nonhuman and be able to act violently towards them.

CHRIS HANNAH: Yeah. We were actually having a huge talk about this last night with friends in San Francisco that went into the wee hours of the morning. It was about ideas on violence and related things, like responses to third-party violence. For example, the death of a US soldier in Iraq. You might hear somebody say, "Yeah, I cheer every time I hear that." I think, "You cheer when you hear that someone has been killed? Are you talking tactically or do you enjoy that a human has died?" So, a discussion evolved from that.

DAVE WAKELING (The English Beat): "If Killing Worked, It Would've Worked by Now." That's a new song we've been playing. We were practicing it at the sound check: "Turn on the TV, see what they've done, they made our culture look like a setting sun, but we're better than that because we know how, if killing worked it would've worked by now." How many piles do you have to pile up before you realize that it doesn't work? I couldn't imagine human beings doing anything else for ten thousand years that always has the opposite effect of what you fancy.

C. J. RAMONE (Ramones): I was in the Marine Corps and I hate war. I hate killing. I hate violence probably more than anything else on the planet. I despise it. We throw away the most beautiful part of our youth and throw them into a meat grinder. It's horrible and I guarantee you that any learned military person will always tell you, "We don't want to go to war. That's not what we're here for. But in the way our world operates, it's a necessary thing." We're just caught up in this thing that's been part of human nature since the beginning. All these guys you see going into the military overseas, it's just part of who we are. Now you have women in combat roles, flying jet fighters and helicopters.

This is how it will be until we find something to replace or redirect that warrior spirit into something more creative. To me, being a warrior is not going out and killing people. Being a warrior is defending your people and your land. But it's also helping those who can't help themselves. If you're a warrior in your community and there's an older person that lives on your block that struggles with something, you go over and help them out. When there's natural disasters overseas and they send our military over to help them out, that's part of being a warrior, too. It's taking care of people who can't take of themselves, and defending them.

DICK LUCAS (Subhumans): The idea of not harming others is the foundation of most religion. That's the really ironic thing! Most religion is founded on being nice to other people. If you take the worship of God out of it, the rest of it is based on being nice to people and *don't fuck each other over*. Yet religion is used as an excuse to create an enemy: my God versus your God. George Bush's final excuse for going to Iraq was *God told me to do it*. Whoa! We are dealing with a fundamentalist lunatic! Fundamentalists are partially running the government in America. It's very dangerous.

CHUCK D (Public Enemy): You can't think of violent means because you got the powers that be and the attitude at hand is in charge. Their game is violence and they will take it all the way. They will destroy the planet if they have to. So, there has to be a better way. My thing is that *the human family is the most important thing*. The beautiful thing about culture is that it brings human beings together for our similarities and knocks aside the differences. That's a beautiful thing about music and culture. Being able to enjoy the human family together and go

CHAPTER 9

forward in a proactive type of way. That's very important. What it boils down to, thinking that you can have a violent advantage is far fetched. That's just a belief in death without any movement.

JM: A main point in your book *Population Wars* (2015) is that war is inevitable. I sense that you hope war can be decreased and less destructive. Yet I'd like to see a world that doesn't have war. What can you say about the inevitability of war?

GREG GRAFFIN (Bad Religion): The current explanation of biologists is that war is inevitable. That's based on a Malthusian construct, where Malthus came up with the idea of struggle for existence; if you explain life in any way, you have to see it as the inevitability of war and warfare. However, my book ends with a chapter called "Evolution Management" and the whole point is that the war metaphor does not apply. Therefore, when you say, "Yeah, there's war everywhere in the world," you have to ask yourself, "Is this a product of mankind? Or is this a product of evolution?"

I would say that most examples are products of mankind. Mankind is not managing our environment, and if we don't manage our environment then the Malthusian war narrative has to take over. But if we're managing our environment, not only can we decide which species live and which die, we can also eradicate warfare as we know it. That's one of the most pressing objectives of this book: *How can we ever end war if we don't understand the narrative?* I show that the war narrative is basically a biological construct and it goes back to Darwin's reading of Malthus and Darwin's incorporation into the explanations of most phenomena of life today.

There is a war on everything. "The war on *blank*" is one of the most common things you'll see in newspapers. Why do we have so much war? It's mostly because that's a narrative we can all understand. We're told that from childhood. What I'm trying to show in *Population Wars* is that this story is worthy of being questioned very severely.

JM: I think the philosophies of Darwin that were misunderstood to emphasize competition, coercion, and control have been utilized by the war makers.

GREG GRAFFIN: Not only the war makers, but also the profiteers, the markets. Everything is explained under competition. That's why chapter 6 talks about it in a historical perspective and says, "Look, it's time to put this in its proper place; competition belongs on the playing field. It doesn't belong as a narrative for why we exist and for everything we depend on."

JM: It sounds like nonviolence is something that resonates with you?

JACK GRISHAM (TSOL): Yes and no. Sometimes I'm a fan of violence. Sometimes I think it's necessary. I'm still working on it. But sometimes I do think it's necessary. If we can completely separate ourselves into the spiritual, then violence is *never* necessary. Being destroyed by someone else will not harm me. But the trouble is I'm a human being and I just don't float like that. I don't have enough faith in the spirit to believe in that. I just don't.

JM: Some people have recognized that the greatest violence to transform is inside of themselves. And that we all need to find our own answer.

JACK GRISHAM: That was a very disturbing day for me when I realized that *they* didn't have my answer. That no one had my answer. It set me up for a lot of study to find out where my answer was going to come from. They all had little pieces of my answer, but not a whole. The thing I've found is that I'm my own tool. We didn't need another Gandhi tool, another Martin Luther King tool; we needed a Jack tool. It was important to find my answer, which was a little bit of a letdown. I wanted it to be easy. I wanted to come up to somebody and say, "Hey, tell me what the deal is. Thank you." And it just didn't happen.

PRESTON JONES (co-author with Greg Graffin of *Is Belief in God Good, Bad or Irrelevant?*): It was the late '80s and I was on this huge aircraft carrier with five thousand men and no women. We were doing circles out in the Indian Ocean for forty-five days and then they'd set us loose in some port. There were fourteen and fifteen-year-old girls in brothels not only being prostitutes, but doing all sorts of shows that were absolutely degrading. You'd hear normal, middle-class American guys who were in no way sinister talk about what they'd done with a thirteen-year-old girl they'd rented for a week. In the Philippines and Thailand there were fourteen-year-old girls and they didn't have a choice. Some are basically prisoners. It really depressed me.

What blew my mind after I got out of the Navy was seeing that no one was writing about it. I wrote articles for national magazines, but they were politically conservative and wouldn't print anything denigrating to the military. I just got shut down one place after another. Eventually *Christianity Today* opened up its pages to this topic. It's hard to hear the US promoting democracy in Iraq and meanwhile see these guys spending their money on thirteen-year-olds in Thailand who don't have a choice.

> *Everyone knows it's us niggers get most of the combat missions, while all them rich kids finish college. We get R & R. We party, man. Stoned out of our fucking trees. That Saigon puntang, them bitches are fucking wild.*
>
> —"FMUSA" by Gang of Four

CHAPTER 9

AGAINST ALL WARS?

RAY CAPPO (Shelter): It might be the collective karma of our country to be at war. That doesn't mean we can't do more protests. But if I'm yelling at you to change and I am myself completely contaminated, what good is that? The spiritual solution is looking at yourself. I truly believe you can change the world by changing yourself first. That might sound like a cop out, but if you set a good example, people follow.

RAMSEY KANAAN (AK Press & PM Press): When I was fifteen, I really thought everyone dressing in black and singing along to "Fight War Not Wars" (Crass) was really going to change the world. It wasn't the fault of singing along, but as I got older and my politics developed, I started to see the limitations of those politics. They actually didn't have a fundamental critique of how society works. They focused on what we'd now call *single issues* which different bands were angry about—the threat of nuclear war, the treatment of animals, and this instinct for freedom. These are all good things, but they're not a coherent, sophisticated political idea, nor a set of practices.

JM: A song on your 2004 album *Duckwork* titled "By What Right, America?" features a young schoolgirl listing countries the US has invaded. It goes on for six minutes.

NORMAN NAWROCKI (Rhythm Activism): That song could've gone on for *thirty* minutes! That song has only a partial list of countries the United States has intervened in militarily over the last hundred years. The idea was that this is material that isn't taught in schools. We're taught to look at the United States as the savior of the world. Rarely are we taught the real role of the US government and military in world history. I've received many letters about that particular song. People are shocked at how far back US military intervention goes. What does it mean? It means that today in 2011 the empire is everywhere! They're now on the verge of attacking Iran. It's frightening and consistent with the history of American policy. You have to ask yourself: What gives the American government the right to do this? We have to occupy the White House. It's obvious. Oh, I shouldn't have said that! I can see the SWAT team descending on my place!

NORMAN NAWROCKI: I believe we can effect radical social change nonviolently if we have the mass. We just have to mobilize the mass. There's more of us than them. We don't need to pick up guns or bombs. We need to pull the plug on the entire military industrial complex and break all those guns. Whether it's with a hammer, chainsaw, or pickaxe, we need to make it physically impossible for them to use those weapons against us. We have to be prepared to fight back—the best way to do that is quite obviously if they have nothing to fight with. People can't keep going to war. We have to stop fighting wars and stop the idea of war itself. This is something that Crass once upon a time sang about.

JM: You're going to tour soon (2007). Will you address things like militarism and wars the US is currently involved in?

ROB FISH (108): We've done that quite often since we started playing again two years ago (2007). With 108 back in the early '90s, most of the scene was anti-war. It never made much sense for 108 to talk about it because we felt, "Everybody here believes the same damn thing, so why would we bother talking about it?" This time around, it seems people don't really care. They don't feel involved in determining what the United States does. Because of that, there are a few songs on the new record that deal with political-oriented topics. That was inspired by the fact that we play shows and talk to these kids and they don't seem to be talking about it. It's strange.

LYDIA LUNCH (Teenage Jesus & The Jerks): I feel like I'm one of the last war whores standing who's still there with a bullhorn and will find within rock songs a rhythm to make a complaint about the never-ending war. I just had an installation/exhibition in New York in June (2015) and part of that was called "The War Is Never Over." I had to find a photographic way to talk about that which has forever obsessed me: man's homicidal tendency. I don't even know why. Well, I do know why. It's because I have homicidal rage as well! But American men especially—men who believe in God or war or greed—they have a homicidal rage to dominate or destroy.

JIM LINDBERG (Pennywise): When people from all walks of life, from all faiths, start to let in a little more tolerance for other ways of interpreting the universe and letting people experience their spirituality the way they want to, *then* we'll be able to consider the end of wars. And start creating a bill of rights for humanity that says *war is illegal*. Until you have this cultural change in our collective way of thinking on this planet we're condemned to keep making the same mistakes.

GREG GRAFFIN (Bad Religion): I'm a pacifist when it comes to war. Any reading of history shows that wars were not responsible for the changes that came after them. The changes were already in motion. I look at war as a kind of an *unfolding of previous events*. I hesitate to say "inevitable," but there's certainly a spontaneous unfolding of events. I don't know if war can be stopped. Western civilization is a history of wars. I think it's a little bit naïve to think we can stop them. But we can change the rules involved in war and I don't think it has to involve so much violence. In other words, we can accept that cultures take over other cultures.

CHAPTER 9

If we accept what the scientists tell us, that there are only thirty years of oil left, then we have to start recognizing that our way of life is going to be different in the very near future. Maybe the wars of the future will be scientific wars. Again, we might not be able to get rid of war in terms of the sweep of human progress, but we certainly can come up with new methods that would be far more invigorating than the ones we've practiced for thousands of years.

GLENN BRANCA (Theoretical Girls): Things are changing, but very slowly. They're going to continue to change very slowly. I wish I could live for another thousand years and I might see a real world that makes sense instead of this horrifying sickening, disease-ridden shit house that we live in. Which is what it is. I don't know how anyone could disagree with that. My point of view is: you have to live your life. You have to do the best you can to enjoy yourself while you're here. And you may have a chance to make what little change you personally might be able to make. But I think to sacrifice yourself to change—I shouldn't say it's a waste of time—but we're living in the Middle Ages! This is a nightmare! We still have war? What morons!

We allow completely self-absorbed, sickeningly egotistical assholes to dominate our world. Nothing really has changed. We don't have kings anymore? Big fucking deal! We still have rulers. We're still serfs. As John Lennon said, "You're all fucking peasants as far as I can see." And he said that in a song! That wasn't in an interview. If there was anyone who knew what he was talking about it was certainly John Lennon.

PENNY RIMBAUD (Crass): It's not much of a future, is it? I haven't been able to avoid my own childhood, which was knowledge of the Nazi camps and Hiroshima. If that was what life was, then no thanks. It's a bit of a *"no thanks"* moment now, isn't it? (COVID-19 pandemic). And a tease as well, because everything is so much more beautiful: the air is better, it's more silent. Colors are radiant because the light is better. I'm looking out the window, and it's just profoundly beautiful at the moment. I can see distances that would normally have a slight haze. We're twenty-five miles from central London and we can see from here as the pollution intensifies above the city. To be able to see the Eden that we live in for once in our life, that's something. To be able to look at the sky and not see airplanes and at night to see constellations. It's staggering.

PENNY RIMBAUD: We are all in this together. That's one of the unique things about this particular pandemic: we are all in this together. There isn't hardly anywhere in the world it hasn't reached. That has a great beauty to it. Why shouldn't we

"Fight War Not Wars," Crass (1978). Contributed: Penny Rimbaud, Gee Vaucher, Steve Ignorant.

all be in it together? We can live so comfortably when people are blasted off the earth in Iraq or wherever. We can be very comfortable with that. But now we're engaged and we need to be engaged. And that's the lesson to be learned through what's happening at the moment.

10

JUST ANOTHER GULF WAR
PUNK, US WARS IN IRAQ AND AFGHANISTAN, AND 9/11

The best way to avoid warfare is if no one shows up.

—Justin Sane (Anti-Flag)

In 1991 US President George Bush began bombing Iraq in what he called the Gulf War. A decade later, in 2003, his son George W. Bush was president and he attacked Iraq again, declaring a military strategy of "shock and awe." One war flowed into the next and included economic sanctions that devastated millions.

The longest war in US history began after the September 11, 2001, "terrorist" attacks that targeted the Pentagon, the White House, and the World Trade Center in New York City. The 9/11 attacks were carried out by nineteen al Qaida militants who brutally hijacked four US commercial airplanes and crashed them kamikaze style, killing almost three thousand people. Fifteen of the hijackers were from Saudi Arabia and the others were from the United Arab Emirates, Lebanon, and Egypt. US President George W. Bush said he would enact retribution for 9/11 by bombing the countries of the hijackers, but instead of bombing Saudi Arabia, a close ally of the United States, Iraq was targeted again with Afghanistan. Some who later criticized the US military response were imprisoned and tortured (Bradley/Chelsea Manning) or went into hiding to avoid the same fate (Julian Assange and Edward Snowden).

The legacy of US wars in Iraq and Afghanistan included "extraordinary rendition" (kidnapping) and "enhanced interrogation" (torture) at US prisons like Abu Ghraib (Iraq) and Guantanamo Bay (Cuba), tactics that flowed back

CHAPTER 10

to the United States, along with military gear, to become further integrated into US police departments.

Some punk rock musicians protested loudly against these and other wars and have sung and screamed out against colonialism and militarism worldwide. Ian MacKaye and Fugazi headlined a concert in front of the White House in January 1991 called the Punk Percussion Protest. Originally organized by the Washington, DC, punk/activist collective Positive Force to bring attention to homelessness, the focus shifted to stopping the imminent US war on Iraq.

Tom Morello from Rage Against the Machine countered President George W. Bush's 2002 declaration that Iraq, Iran, and North Korea were an "Axis of Evil" by organizing a music/education nonprofit organization and concert tour called "Axis of Justice" (2003). Billy Bragg joined the Axis of Justice tour and released his own song about the war, "The Price of Oil." Bad Religion teamed up with political philosopher Noam Chomsky to produce a 2001 seven-inch record called *New World Order: War #1*. Anti-Flag supported legislation to stop military recruiters from having access to students' personal information. Fat Mike and his band NOFX spearheaded a Rock Against Bush tour and compilation album in 2004 to stop the re-election of President Bush. And Black Flag singer Henry Rollins lampooned President Bush by naming his 2003 spoken word tour "Shock and Awe My Ass." Ironically, Rollins also performed for US troops in Egypt, Qatar, Japan, South Korea, Iraq, and Afghanistan. The 2011 Gang of Four song "Do As I Say" is about torture at the US prison in Cuba: "You say you're innocent, so you must be guilty. . . . They dress in dayglo robes in Guantanamo."

FIRST GULF WAR

JUSTIN SANE (Anti-Flag): I wrote the song "Die for the Government" in 1992. It was about the original Gulf War (1991) and soldiers coming back with Gulf War Syndrome, which was due to exposure to depleted uranium. It's incredible to sing that song now and look at those lyrics and realize we're doing it all over again and making all the same mistakes! (2003, second Gulf War) War is very profitable for many people who are in power. There are so many examples of the United States supplying weapons to both sides of a conflict—like the Iran/Iraq war. Somebody was making a lot of profits off of that.
JM: Tell me about collaborating with the punk band Bad Religion.
NOAM CHOMSKY (author of *Manufacturing Consent: The Political Economy of the Mass Media*): At the time of the first Gulf War, in 1991, somebody from the

Photo and text from the 1992 book Just Another War. *Photo by Kenneth Jarecke, text by Exene Cervenka.*

CHAPTER 10

group Bad Religion got in touch with me and asked if I would record eight minutes of just talk on the Gulf War. I'd never heard of the band, but I liked the name. I said, "Fine." They sent me a tape and I sat in front of a tape recorder and talked for eight minutes on the Gulf War. I mailed it back to them. Next thing I knew, it came back on a 45 RPM disc. One side was punk rock music, which they told me was an anti-war song. I couldn't make head or tail of it. On the other side was my eight minutes.

Actually, I sent the disc to a friend who had a fourteen-year-old daughter and asked if he would ask her to explain to me what the song was about. She wrote me a very interesting and thoughtful letter explaining what the song was. It's just not a part of my culture. I'm kind of an old-fashioned conservative. But I have to say that record—around the world, not just here—after talks and at meetings, people come up and ask me to sign things. I doubt if I sign anything as often as I've signed the cover of that disc, or whatever that's called!

Although Exene Cervenka has described her politics as *personal*, she's been engaged in sharing information that is clearly political. In 1992 she put together a book with journalist/photographer Kenneth Jarecke called *Just Another War*.
JM: What was your interest in punk rock and how has that affected your attitude toward photojournalism?
KENNETH JARECKE (photographer *Just Another War*): The proper attitude toward photojournalism is the punk rock attitude. There's no difference between the two. It's pretty unlikely you're going to get paid anywhere's near what you're worth to do this job. At least when you're starting out, you're going to have to figure out a way to finance it. You're going to do it on your own without any support from magazines. Just like punk rockers didn't have support from record labels. You're going to go out and do it because nobody's going to pay you to do it. Punk rock came out of the '70s bland radio scene. Nobody would play punk on the radio and nobody would record it. So, they made the music for themselves. That's the proper way to make pictures as a photojournalist.
JM: How did you hook up with Exene from X to make the book?
KENNETH JARECKE: A couple months after the war I had these pictures. The black-and-white medium-format pictures that make up the book, I did on the sly. The book has fifty-four images. I did those because in the (US military) pool system you were required to shoot *color* negative film. Color negative film isn't archival and limits your palette as a photographer. I decided to shoot square format, medium format black and white that is archival to beat that system. And not let anybody know I was doing it. I offered that work to the magazine that I was

under contract to: *Time* magazine. They passed on it. I had the box of prints and thought, "What am I going to do with this?" I was listening to X at the time. I was looking through the liner notes and I was thinking about George Bush Senior and he was talking about this philosophy of "Just War" and I thought, this is *just another war* for us. That's how that came about.

If you pick up any X album you can see what Exene does with the liner notes. Literally the whole vision for the book came together one night. The title and everything popped fully formed into my head. I called up some agent, and I was going to LA the following week. I set up a meeting and walked into an office with a box of prints. We were in the hallway. I saw Exene and John Doe was with her and we sat down and looked at the prints. We didn't even get into the conference room where we were going to meet and she said, "Well, what do you want me to do?" I said, "Just by looking at the photographs I want you to write whatever comes to your mind. We'll do this book: your text will be on one side and the photograph will be on the other side."

The working philosophy was, *how do you communicate something like war to someone who has never been in a war?* It's like how do you communicate something like giving birth to someone that has never gone through that process? How can a man understand what a mother goes through? It's one of those things you can't describe. In a way, there's no real way to do that in photos, words, or music.

JM: You contributed poems to *Just Another War*.

EXENE CERVENKA (X): Right, the *first* Gulf War. In the Gulf War in the early '90s they had press pools and everybody would go out with a military guard and be taken to a safe place and shown something. All of the pictures in the book are in black and white. Kenneth actually got a second-place Pulitzer Prize for one of the photos. The reason he contacted me to do a book with him is because his photos were censored—they weren't shown in the United States, but they were published widely across Europe. He came back and was quite angry that no one had seen his war footage. Since I hadn't covered the war, I was just not sure of what my role would be. But I figured it out. I wrote captions for the photos that referred to World War I, World War II, Vietnam, and the current Iraq crisis that we were in and how we got there. The photos in the book are very stark and interesting because they show the military kind of sitting around a lot, looking out into the desert, not really having much to do. The fourth largest army in the world, which was then Iraq, wasn't very formidable. It was an easier war than the one we're in now.

CHAPTER 10

9/11

> *I remember the day that the planes crashed. I thought, "Wow, this is really kind of the end of the world." If people are outraged by the loss of three thousand lives, wouldn't they be even more upset about the death of one hundred thousand? I should think so. Except if it's Iraqi lives.*
>
> —Ian MacKaye (Fugazi / Minor Threat)

IAN MACKAYE: If you think about the experience of having planes crash into buildings, it's an absolutely horrific thing to contemplate. They are such brutal acts. Human beings have been brutal, I guess, since the beginning of time. Those planes crashed into buildings, things were blown up, and all of these people disappeared from the earth. At the time, I was living about three-quarters of a mile from the Pentagon, so it was raining down essentially on my neck of the woods. I had friends saying, "What are you going to do? Are you going to get out of here?" I realized all I could think about was that I have no control over any of this. I never had any control. It's sort of like the weather.

One thing I did decide was that I was *not* going to watch television. I knew that all the television could do was repeat the images over and over. And in that repetition, by watching it enough, people thought that maybe they could get some meaning. They hoped that they could comprehend what had occurred. My belief is that this sort of brutality is incomprehensible. All that you can really do is become numb and then accepting of it. If you watch it that many times, you are never going to understand it. You are just going to stop feeling it. And in that numbness comes disconnection.

I thought that it was a time of serious grieving and some introspection. It was like, "Well, what just happened here?" I was not surprised, but once again appalled, by the reaction, which was just bizarre. Almost like national religion taking over. I remember reading about Congress going on the steps of the Capitol and singing "My Country 'Tis of Thee" or the national anthem. It just reinforces that as a holy song! It's so twisted. And flags everywhere. There was a disconnection and they jumped in and gave people something to hang onto. This disconnection is very serious. The idea that we don't want to feel is a central part of why things are going to be so painful. When we wake up, we are in a world of hurt.

IAN MACKAYE: I'll tell you what I did that day: I answered the mail. I had a lot of letters. People had been writing. I actually predated my letters; I dated them all the *tenth* of September. I did it as sort of a *vote for the future*. I didn't want people to think that I was insane, writing letters all day on the eleventh. But I did want to write because I believed that they would arrive on the twelfth or the thirteenth. That was a vote for the future.

I was looking out of *this* window and it was a beautiful day and I have this pond of fish in my backyard and I thought, "They don't give a fuck." I was looking at the trees and I thought, "They don't care." It didn't matter to the birds. They are just going about their business. I don't know if humans are really any different than any of those other things. It's our decision to get emotionally involved. Emotionally, things have been switched off. It's not a human condition. It's a nationalist conditioning.

I remember thinking, "The world will be okay." If the world can survive something like World War I, where the loss of life in that conflagration was absolutely insane; we're talking about two-week battles where 200,000 or 300,000 people lost their lives. And somehow the world continued to rotate. I felt that was the case with this situation as well. But I was very concerned about the repercussions.

I was involved with anti-war marches a couple of weeks later, trying to voice that we were opposed to the idea of invading Afghanistan. Iraq was just coming down the pipe. But right off the bat saying, "Let's not spin it again. Let's try to stop this madness." But with big and kind of clumsy entities like nations, especially one of this size, it was almost inevitable that something like this was going to occur. It's a shame. I don't know what to do about all of that. Well, I do know what to do: I live my life in a manner that is opposed to war.

CHRIS HANNAH (Propagandhi): When the towers went down, I watched it. We were in the States at the time and my first response was almost some sort of excitement. I knew it was happening and I knew the scale of the horror. I was brought up to confuse vengeance for justice. Through every movie that I ever saw—whether it was an underdog who punches out the bully, like *Rocky*, or all of this shit—it was a part of my upbringing. I was taught that violence is conflict resolution and when someone rises up and strikes a blow against the bully, we should cheer. As radicals or dissidents, there are very few opportunities to cheer. It's a Pavlovian response. It is learned. And it's something I have grappled with because I grew up in a military family.

JM: It's interesting to notice we're taught that justice comes by causing pain to others. The whole police and prison system is based on the idea that if you make people suffer . . .

CHRIS HANNAH: . . . then that's justice.

JM: Supposedly, making others go through suffering improves their behavior.

CHAPTER 10

CHRIS HANNAH: Clearly it is too one-dimensional. It's too narrow of a way to define justice. I think that it has done some damage to all of us.

JM: There are ongoing debates about how television violence or other imagery affects people. There's an idea that television images helped to end the US war in Vietnam, but I'm now hearing that that wasn't necessarily so.[1] I've grown up in a time when I was told that if people had information, they would take action to stop atrocities and war. It doesn't seem to have happened.

CHRIS HANNAH: Clearly there has to be a new way of looking at this. There is a lot of information out there. Everywhere we go in North America, so many people have information. They know that things are wrong and they know *why* they are wrong. Sometimes they know details that are incredibly archaic. But the next step, which we haven't moved towards, is taking that information and actually doing something with it. So many people, and I would count myself among them, are people that have information and should feel haunted by how little they actually do to connect with others and take chances and do things to concretely affect radical change around them.

C. J. RAMONE (Ramones): I did work at Ground Zero after 9/11. When the towers went down, in the buildings directly surrounding the site, most of the guys running the buildings just ran out and they didn't shut down the air intakes of the buildings. I'm not saying there is anything wrong with that—I'm sure most people would've done the same thing. But what happened was, before the power was severed, those buildings were taking in all of the toxic dust that was coming up. Our job was to climb through the duct work and we dragged Hypervacs behind us and vacuumed out all of the dust. We were exposed to some high levels of some nasty stuff and I ended up with some long-term issues because of it.

My dad actually worked down in the pit immediately after and he ended up with Asbestosis. Over time he's gotten better. He moved up to Maine from New York and he's been able to recover. His health improved and he'll be seventy-seven this weekend (February 2018). All the years I had spent hanging out and having fun in the city and partying and having a good time, I felt like I had to do something to pay back. That was the best way I figured I could do it.

DICK LUCAS (Subhumans): Since 9/11, the freedoms being curtailed are enormous. The freedom of speech, movement, protest—if we lose the freedom to protest against things, then where are you going to go from there? If you can't protest then you can't do anything about it. England is getting like that and I imagine America is as well. There's the Patriotic Act in America and a whole bunch of words put together with the word "act" at the end of it in England.

Brian Haw has been protesting outside Parliament for so long they actually put a subclause into the anti-terrorism act to ban people from protesting within a mile of the Houses of Parliament. It was supposed to include Brian, but because he'd been protesting since before the law was invented, he was the one person exempt from the law! So, he just carried on. It's a superb example of one person sticking up for what they believe in and then going through a loophole that the government created for him by mistake! (Brian Haw died in June 2011.)

JAY BENTLEY (Bad Religion): The attack on the World Trade Center of September 11 was only different from the Oklahoma City bombings in that it wasn't an American driving a Ryder truck. Let's be realistic—it wasn't like a new phenomenon. America was just living in a bubble of, "We've never been attacked other than Pearl Harbor." The war in Afghanistan was a continuation of the 1991 war in Iraq. They just sent over 320,000 troops and did nothing. Snipered some shit and blew up some caves and then promptly marched the troops straight into Iraq. That was so predictable. Now they're saying, "The US is eyeing Syria. Let's march the guys over to Syria." It's almost predictable, this entire thing. It's about control of the Middle East. That's been an agenda since Reagan. Wolfowitz, Rumsfeld—it's the same people that were involved from '85 onward.

Americans act surprised that there are so many angry people in a certain region of the world. How about a twelve-year-old embargo that's killed 300,000 (Iraqi) kids because they can't get medicine? "Saddam keeps the medicine." Well, why was he in power? We gave him all of his money and weapons to fight Iran. That's the way it's always been: "Who's fighting the Soviets now? Let's give them weapons." Osama Bin Laden was the same. We gave him weapons because he was the leader of the rebellion against the Soviets. "We don't like the Ayatollah Khomeini, so let's give all this money to this Saddam guy! He seems okay!" [laugh] Twelve years later: "Give us our ball back. We don't want you playing with it anymore." The concept outside of the United States was that America is a bully. Now, it's just a fact. Now we are the fucking assholes that everyone thought we were.

THE WAR ON TERROR—LET'S KEEP EVERYONE AFRAID

JAY BENTLEY (Bad Religion): Fifty-one percent of the people still think Saddam Hussein was the guy flying the plane into the World Trade Center! Fifty-one percent! No! Ignorance is bliss. And we're proving that every day. Once again, it's all about the War on Terror. Let's keep everyone afraid and not have everybody questioning us because we really can't defend ourselves. We don't have

CHAPTER 10

any answers. If anybody came out and said, "Where are the weapons of mass destruction?"—"We're finding them."—"Really? Where are they?"—"Well, we found a trailer."—"What was in it?"—"We don't know; some powder."

All biological and chemical weapons have a shelf life of about six to thirteen months. After that they turn to harmless jelly or powder 'cause they're living. They don't live very long. They're not like Twinkies! For twelve years of embargoes these guys (Iraqis) have had nothing. There are no weapons of mass destruction. Saddam Hussein is crazy and doesn't deserve to be running the place, but at the same time the principles that we used to justify the invasion were incorrect. They're lies.

JM: The US government fabricated that stuff and even said there were nuclear weapons components that had been sold to Iraq from an African country.

JAY BENTLEY: All the UN inspectors in '91 said, "We found some laboratories but just blew them up. There's no way they could rebuild them 'cause they have no money and no resources and we were watching all the people who could've sold them anything and they never did." It's not like pirating a CD. There's not a lot of downloading plutonium-grade nuclear weapons. All it takes is a person of authority to have five minutes of airtime on national television to tell people that's what's happening and people say, "Okay. I don't want Saddam to have that." Well, that's why he *doesn't*. We took care of that a long time ago, twelve years ago to be exact. It's frightening that people don't know all of this about the Middle East. They think it's some sandy place where people are angry. [pause] Okay, that sounds kind of like Vegas!

JM: Do you have any hope for change? This time (2003) there were protests against a US war *before* it started.

JAY BENTLEY: As we get older, the hope is that the people start to have more influence on politics and that politicians are more like us. Right? When you look at people running things now, you can say they are naïve about the world. They believe this crap because they're from a different timeframe and mentality. All it takes is a couple of guys coming out of California that know who Black Flag is and that changes a lot—"We can't keep doing that anymore, it's not okay."

All I can do as a person who would like to see more tolerance and humanity from my government is wait for these people to die and be replaced by younger, more worldly men or women who actually understand what it must be like to live in Afghanistan or Iraq as a mother of three kids whose husband and father is dead, who can't get medicine or food because there's an embargo.

When they showed (Iraqis) cheering in Baghdad, I saw a hundred people waving American flags and cheering. I can gather a hundred people in Santa Cruz (California) right here to get Iraqi flags and run around and cheer! Where are the crying women and children huddling in the corner because they're scared shitless? They don't show them because that's not what they want to broadcast to us. When will everyone—media, politicians, artists—become more honest and finally accept reality? I'm not talking about being Sean Penn going to Iraq. That's okay, but that's kind of a publicity run anyway. There's got to be more to it than you flying over there and leaving. There has to be a collection of individuals who people take as seriously as George W. Bush. That's what is so insane about it: people are far more willing to believe George W. Bush than Noam Chomsky!

Here's a guy coming in with zero history of foreign policy basically putting us on the brink of World War III, but that's who people choose to believe. Anyone who you put in there is going to be believed by the people. It doesn't matter if it's Bill Clinton, George W., or Reagan. As long as the guy is talking, most people are believing. Our hope is that whoever it is that gets in there, he's at least educated in the ways of the world and not just, "Hey, we're America. We live in a bubble and we don't care." That's what this government has been doing since the beginning.

THE IRAQ WAR: "HOW MANY IRAQIS PER GALLON?"

All the young people down the ages / They gladly marched off to die.

—"The Call Up" by The Clash

IAN MACKAYE (Fugazi): I remember the day leading up to the invasion of Iraq (2003). I had been involved with anti-war protests and other things. I was contacted by a school in New Jersey to speak about the anti-war movement. Suddenly this ultimatum came down and they (the US government) said, "If you don't do this, we're going to start bombing you tomorrow." I talked to this fellow that had invited me to the gathering and he said, "I don't know if there is any point in having this gathering now because tomorrow there's going to be a war. We failed to stop them." I said, "I don't think it's actually going to happen." And he said, "Are you crazy? It's obviously going to happen." I said, "No, I just feel that up until the moment that the first bomb drops, I don't believe they're going to do it." I'm just going to continue with the idea that they can be stopped. If you don't operate with that idea, then you're doing their work for them ultimately.

CHAPTER 10

JM: In *Sit Down and Shut Up* you write, "The war in Iraq is an ultimate expression of anger." Tell me more about that and if you have any further thoughts about the current US wars in Iraq and Afghanistan.
BRAD WARNER (*Hardcore Zen* / Zero Defects): I probably shouldn't go there. My opinions about that are probably a little different from what people expect. I wasn't trying to say that the war in Iraq is especially, in and of itself, a big expression of anger. War is an expression of anger. But by the same token, I think that wars happen because they need to happen. It is a very sad thing and we should do our best to avoid getting to that point, but sometimes things get to a state where the only thing that is going to happen is war. It is not a good thing, but it happens. So, I don't have any great desire to go out and protest the war. It's just something that may be a sign of improvement in a certain way. But I am not a very political person.
JM: I'm guessing you would rather that people aren't starving and being bombed.
BRAD WARNER: Oh, yes.
JM: Certain conditions lead to extreme violence. Yet the conditions for war don't come from nowhere. I think that compassion and direct action can transform conditions in incremental ways before there are wars.
BRAD WARNER: But if you want to go that route, you're talking about a really fundamental change among people. That would be difficult. And it takes a long time. It won't happen overnight. Sometimes the worst thing that you can do is say, "Let's all be peaceful." Because there's somebody who is going to knock you on the head and grab your wallet as soon as you do that.
JM: In Julian Temple's documentary about Joe Strummer, he's really upset that the US military were dropping bombs on Iraq that had "Rock the Casbah" written on them.
MILES COPELAND (I.R.S. Records): Yeah, well c'est la vie. Whether you're right wing or left wing, you would think that dropping a bomb that's going to kill villagers is not a good idea. But the reality is, the invasion of Iraq was stupid in the first place. We should have never done it and it caused a lot of problems. George Bush has a lot to face from the fact that he decided that we're going to war. They basically lied to get us into the Iraq War. Whereas my father (Miles Copeland Jr.) would have said, "Just assassinate a few people. That's all you need to do." [laugh] So, who was right? Do we go into Iraq and kill hundreds of thousands of people? Or do we just allow a few to be killed and then we keep a lid on the place? I think it could be argued either way.

INVITED TO THE PENTAGON

MILES COPELAND (I.R.S. Records): The Pentagon approached the Recording Institute of America and said, "Are there any Americans that know anything about Arabic music and entertainment? We need some help to win hearts and minds in the Middle East." They were told, "There's only one American who knows anything about it. That's this Miles Copeland guy." So, that gets to the Donald Rumsfeld office, who calls up and says, "We hear you're the guy. Would you come and tell us what to do?" [laugh] I have to admit I was thinking, "My God, what a great chapter of the book that will be! Getting invited to the Pentagon to advise them how to win hearts and minds!" Here I am, just some little rock and roll manager. Of course, I went to the Pentagon and I did exactly that. I listened to all the programs they had in mind, which were all pretty much nuts. And I told them what they should do. And they didn't do anything.

But a couple of years later Tori Clark, the Deputy Secretary of Defense, calls me up and says, "You pitched something at the Pentagon that I really thought was a good idea. And PBS is now doing a series of films and they might go for that idea. Would you mind if I pitched it to them?" I said, "Be my guest." The next thing I know PBS calls me, "We love your idea. We're gonna film it." So, I did this project called "Arab Music Goes West." I went to the Middle East on PBS's dime and filmed Arabic acts and said, "Would you come to America and play with American acts? Let's see these two cultures working together and find common ground." We created this documentary which Al Jazeera bought and aired all over the Middle East. PBS didn't play it very much.

The April 11, 2005, issue of *Newsweek* magazine featured an article about resistance against US militarism by Anti-Flag:

> Military recruiters are already scrambling to enlist enough soldiers to meet wartime demands. Now they're facing a new obstacle: punk rockers. With militaryfreezone.org, an anti-war band from Pittsburgh, Anti-Flag, has started a campaign against an obscure provision of the No Child Left Behind Act dictating that public-school districts supply high school students' names, phone numbers and addresses to military recruiters. . . . Justin Sane, Anti-Flag's spokesman, lead guitarist and lead vocalist, tells Newsweek, 'Schools should not be turned into military-recruitment centers.'

Justin Sane grew up in Glenshaw, Pennsylvania, where he and Pat Thetic were the only punk rockers in town. They formed Anti-Flag in 1988 and the band has been part of the Free Mumia Abu Jamal movement, and historian

CHAPTER 10

Howard Zinn wrote liner notes for their 1999 album *A New Kind of Army*. In 2003 they formed the not-for-profit organization Underground Action Alliance and teamed up in the recording studio with Rage Against the Machine / Audioslave guitarist Tom Morello to produce the *Terror State* album. They helped register hundreds of thousands of new voters during the 2004 Vans Warped Tour and other events. They also contributed music to the *Rock Against Bush* CD/DVD.

JUSTIN SANE (Anti-Flag): My dad is from Ireland. He was involved in activism trying to kick the British out of Northern Ireland. Both of my parents were. My dad tells me that my mom was the first person he ever knew who opposed the Vietnam War. It was very early on. My parents have always been very progressive. I can remember as a kid my dad telling me *never* to join anyone's military. I'll never forget that! From a very young age, trying to solve the world's problems by using militarism is something that has always resonated with me as being a bad idea.

We were 100 percent opposed to the invasion of Iraq and Afghanistan. Now they're trying to target kids in high school at such an early, impressionable age to join the military. They're going into schools with propaganda that's ridiculous, driving tanks onto campuses. There's a provision buried in the No Child Left Behind Act (2001) that says if you attend a public high school your school system is required to turn over your private information to the US military unless you opt out. "Opt out" means that you need to turn in a form signed by a guardian or a parent stating that you do not want the military to have access to your private information.

It's basically the exact opposite of the age-old school permission slip where if you wanted to go on a school field trip or you wanted the school to give out your private information, you had to turn in a form signed by your parents saying that it was okay. Instead, the school is going to give away your private information to the military, specifically for recruitment targeting, unless you hand in a form telling them *not* to do so. Of course, 99 percent of the population knows nothing about this provision in the No Child Left Behind Act and most public schools haven't bothered to tell their students and they're simply giving students' information out. Anti-Flag felt that we needed to make kids aware of this.

> *Anti-Flag. . . . Don't let their stage name fool you, these kids care about their country. Yeah, they have mohawks and rings, but in the '60s we were considered radical because of the long hair and beads. And we changed this country. And these kids*

will, too. They're straight edge punk. Just kids from Pittsburgh with colored hairdos and a great message for young people: register and vote or be told to go and fight by an administration that will not talk straight to the American people. . . . Voting is going to be the in thing in 2004.

—Rep. Jim McDermott (US House of Representatives speech, October 3, 2004)

JUSTIN SANE (Anti-Flag): We don't want more kids going off to fight and kill in Iraq. This is a war based in imperialism. It's a war based on lies. We don't believe that militarism is the way to solve the world's problems. We think the best way to avoid warfare is if no one shows up. That's why we're pushing so hard to let young people know what the military is really about.

There are ways to serve your community, help people, and help your country. More important than helping your country is simply helping people in general. We talk to so many soldiers. Before, when soldiers would come out to see Anti-Flag, they usually came to kick our asses! [laugh] They didn't like us turning the American flag upside down and they didn't like us criticizing the government. But now they're coming out to thank us! I have talked to literally hundreds of soldiers saying, "Thank you guys for speaking out because I joined the military because I thought it would be a way for me to earn some college money. Now I just got back from a tour in Iraq and it's basically destroyed my life."

We have a really close friend who, right before 9/11, was feeling down and didn't feel like his life was going anywhere and he wasn't sure what he was going to do with his life. He came very close to joining the military. We talked him out of it! [laugh] We had some late-night discussion about it and luckily, we did talk him out of it and now he's so thankful. He's not somebody who is old enough to remember any kind of major warfare that the United States has been in. I think that's one of the reasons that a lot of people joined up to be weekend warriors.

JELLO BIAFRA (Dead Kennedys): Military recruiters are very aggressive and skilled liars. The more a person is living in poverty and doesn't see a lot of options, they will fall for it when the recruiter promises job training and, "We'll get you into a good college." They don't realize that it's really, "We're bringing you in here to send you to Afghanistan or Iraq. You didn't bank on that when you joined the National Guard, did you?" I'm surprised, and crossing my fingers, that we haven't had more mass shootings in this country by people who are trained to do that.

CHAPTER 10

JON KING (Gang of Four): Of course, the victims of all of these things always are lower-income young men and women (in the military). You're trying to write lyrics about that where you're not being negative about the decisions of these young men and women, but it's about this whole framework which got them screwed.

JM: On March 19, 2003, the US government began bombing Iraq in another full-out war on that country, in retribution for the attacks of September 11, 2001. That evening I saw you perform in San Francisco with Audioslave. There was a sign on stage that read, "How many Iraqis per gallon?" There was a large anti-war movement worldwide and it seemed that the bombing might be stopped.

TOM MORELLO (Rage Against the Machine / Prophets of Rage): The anti-war protestors predicted that an invasion of Iraq would lead to *more* terrorism around the globe. That's happened. We predicted that there were no weapons of mass destruction, that it was a deceit on the part of the Bush administration, and that has proved to be true. There were no tethers between Al Qaida and Saddam Hussein's regime. All of the justifications for going to war were proved to be deceitful. The question then is: If the Bush administration was lying about these things and if all of the justifications were false, what were the real reasons? All you have to do is look at the price of oil and the contracts that have been given out after that.

I've just come off of the Tell Us the Truth Tour where myself and Billy Bragg, Steve Earle, Lester Chamber, and Boots Riley from The Coup, as well as Mike Mills from REM and Jill Sobule, have been touring the country and talking about two issues: media consolidation and corporate globalization. Both of those issues are very much tied into the Iraq campaign. Media consolidation being one of the reasons why the very complicated issues that everybody needed to process in the wake of 9/11 were simplified in this deceitful, patriotic fog to get this administration's geopolitical agenda across. That managed to jam their agenda down our throats.

Corporate globalization is really at the heart of the matter. Working families here and throughout Latin America and now in Iraq are suffering very much from the multinationals' grip. What they didn't count on, however, was the fact that this corporate globalization has brought into effect the movement that will be its undoing. From the WTO riots in Seattle (1999) to the enormous protests that we just participated in against the FTAA (Free Trade Area of the Americas) in Miami (2003) to protests around the globe. The issue of corporate globalization as a tentacle of capitalism has an unintended consequence of uniting people across the globe against the injustices they are perpetrating.

I think it's wrong to look at the United States government as separate from the corporate entities that bolster it. Transnational organizations like the IMF (International Monetary Fund), WTO, and the World Bank very much control what our air, water, politics, and working conditions will be like. And we do not vote for them and don't have anything to do with the decisions that they make which effect many people's lives.

ISIS AND THE WAR IN SYRIA

EAST BAY RAY (Dead Kennedys): One of the causes of ISIS and the war in Syria is they've had a drought for five years. This is climate warming. All the people moved from the countryside into the cities and the government there—the dictator Assad—did not take care of them. There was the start of ISIS. Where there's climate change and overpopulation it's getting harder to be nice to people. When there's more and more people and less resources it's harder to be generous. The example of Buckminster Fuller is the problem of the commons: you have a meadow that can support ten sheep and ten sheepherder families and everything is fine. But as soon as you have the *eleventh* family with an eleventh sheep in a commons that only supports ten, you have war. A problem going forward is that people thought the green revolution was going to solve our problems. But the big war is probably going to be over water. People fight over resources. That's survival and human nature. The human tendency is *me first and other people second*. That's the way people are hardwired.
JM: You think people are born with that?
EAST BAY RAY: Yes, absolutely. Or we wouldn't be here now! What's the saying? *The nice die young*. The tough ones last longer. Genetics. It's not the only reason; I haven't studied it much, but one of the reasons that people cooperate or are nice to each other is because they see there's an advantage to it. Right?

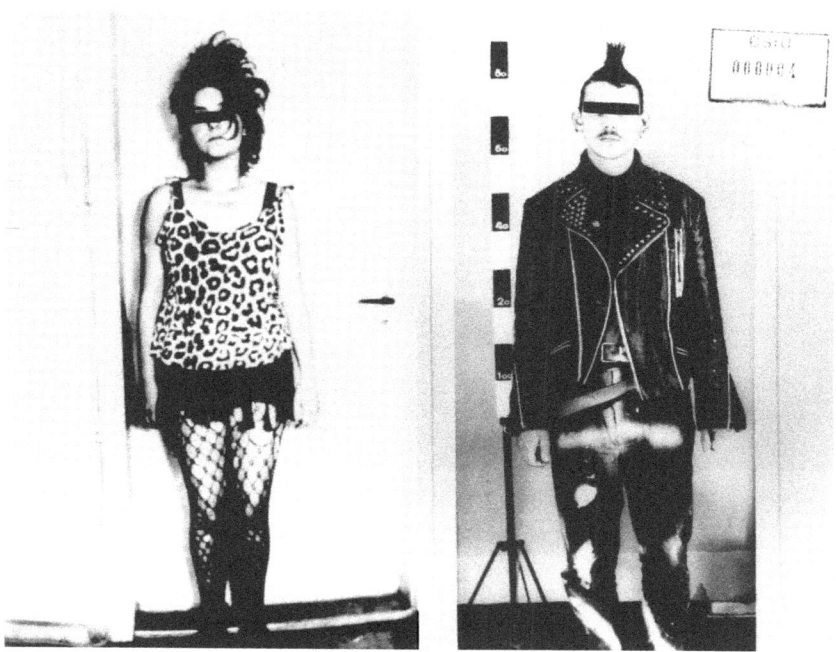

East Berlin Secret Police booking photos of two punks in about 1985. Contributed: Bundesarchiv Stasi-Unterlagen-Archiv, Berlin, Germany

"Punk Is Not Ded" from Persepolis *by Marjane Satrapi.* Contributed: StudioCanal

Subhumans performing in Santa Cruz, California (2008). Photo: Matt Fitt

John Malkin interviews Stan Lee of The Dickies in 2008: "'No future?' We never played it that way. We were more like 'Where's the water slide? Where's Bob's Big Boy? Who's got a swimming pool?'" Photo: Matt Fitt

James Williamson plays guitar with Iggy & The Stooges in San Jose, California, at C2SV (Creative Convergence Silicon Valley) Technology Conference and Music Festival (Sept. 28, 2013). Photo: John Malkin

Andy Gill of Gang of Four creating rhythmic feedback. (Santa Cruz, California; Oct. 18, 2015). Photo: John Malkin

Fugazi concert in front of the White House (Jan. 12, 1991) to bring attention to economic disparity and preemptively protest the US war on Iraq, which began four days later. Photo: Unknown

Lenny Kaye with Patti Smith during performance of "Horses" for the album's forty-year anniversary (Santa Cruz, California; Jan. 2, 2016). Photo: John Malkin

Cowboys and Indians: cover of Entertainment! *by Gang of Four (1979).* Contributed: Jon King

Feel like things are bad now? Remember Ronnie? T-shirt from JFA (Jodie Foster's Army). Contributed: Brian Brannon / JFA

Rock Against Bush Volume 2 *(2004)*. Contributed: Fat Wreck Chords

The Day My Kid Went Punk *ABC Afterschool Special (1987)*. Contributed: Fern Field, director

Punk for Ukraine Volume 2 *benefits Doctors Without Borders (2022).* Contributed: Dave Dictor / Grimace Records

Klee Benally (Blackfire) delivers supplies at Big Mountain, Arizona, when the COVID-19 pandemic hit Native Americans hardest (2020). Contributed: Klee Benally

11

"AMERICA! FUCK YEAH!"
PUNKS PERFORM FOR US SOLDIERS

Many of them have even said, "I loved Dead Kennedys in high school," and I thought, "Holy shit! They enlisted anyway? Where did I fail?"

—Jello Biafra (Dead Kennedys)

I remember one time we were on tour and we stopped in Virginia right near a Marine Corps base. It was packed full of Marines and they were drunk and listening to Offspring. [laugh] I thought, "Wow, this is weird." It's like if Jimi Hendrix could see his music in a soda commercial today.[1] And it makes sense that we weren't going to be immune to this stuff.

—John Stockberger (Sense Field)

THE VANDALS

In 2004 The Vandals performed for US troops at forward bases in Iraq, using a flatbed truck as their stage. Their setlist included a rousing version of "America Fuck Yeah" from the over-the-top political satire film *Team America: World Police* (2004), which depicts the United States as a destructive force under the guise of fighting for freedom and democracy. This juxtaposition has something in common with Slovenian band Laibach performing their anti-authoritarian brand of avant-rock to audiences in North Korea in 2015. Laibach delivered

CHAPTER 11

a critique of controlled society to people living within one, all orchestrated through lyrically amended cover versions from *The Sound of Music*.

In one video titled "The Vandals at PB Volunteer Baghdad, Iraq 2004," singer Joe Escalante is heard introducing a cover version of the theme song from *Team America: World Police* saying, "We worked on this song on the way here. We're probably going to fuck it up." To which guitarist Warren Fitzgerald adds: "If you can sing 'Fuck yeah' you can sing along."[2]

Another video, "The Vandals Play for U.S. Troops in Iraq (Sadr City)— Nice Army Moshpit," shows The Vandals performing at Patrol Base Volunteer in Baghdad, Iraq. One of the comments posted about the video on YouTube is by a soldier named Matt Fisk, who was at The Vandals's show:

> I was in audience for this one, thrashing about in the pit. The amusing thing about reading some of the comments regarding the Vandals' punk credentials is that the people making those statements don't have the nut to step foot in the arena that the Vandals played that day. While Toby Keith and a host of others regularly played Camp Victory, only two groups had the courage to come out to our small, wild-west base: the Vandals and Henry Rollings. [sic] Our base had such a reputation for being in the shit that other soldiers would request to convoy there as they were guaranteed to get a combat patch on the way.[3]

US soldiers stage diving during a concert by The Vandals in eastern Baghdad during the band's tour of Iraq and Kuwait (Dec. 28, 2004). Photo: Specialist Jan Critchfield

ISHAY BERGER (Useless ID): I learned something when The Vandals played shows for American soldiers in Iraq. It was such a big punk rock backlash. I realized you cannot fuck with the punk police.

JM: The Vandals played for US troops? And punk rock people were saying that was not a punk thing to do?

ISHAY BERGER: No, even worse. Not just punk people, these were promoters. The Vandals had a blog at the time where they would write about their experiences in Iraq, meeting the soldiers and touring the army. Then they had big protests outside their shows when they went to Greece later. They had promoters canceling shows saying, "We don't want to work with The Vandals anymore after they supported Bush and went to Iraq." I think it damaged them, having protests outside their shows. That sucks. Having a riot—that's cool. Having a protest—that's shit.

JM: Henry Rollins has told stories about going to Iraq and entertaining US troops. I was surprised he would do that. On one level that does appear to be collaborating with a government that's causing a lot of suffering. Later I saw his photo essay book *Occupants* (2011) where Rollins has traveled a lot by himself with a camera to places of suffering and war, and he's been interested in how to change things. I was confused why he would go to Iraq as it seems like supporting US militarism.

ISHAY BERGER: It's not very politically correct? They may have done that, but The Vandals are an incredibly fun live band! When a band does something like that, obviously it's political. But I see it as a nonpolitical thing. They just have fun shows in a shit situation. I don't want to defend them or go against them. They're playing for nineteen-year-olds, for people who are practically kids. I see that all the time where I live (Israel) because kids of eighteen already have a rifle and want to shoot terrorists. I'm not for or against the soldiers. I'm against giving an eighteen-year-old kid a rifle.

I don't think it's horrible what The Vandals did. The Vandals make good songs and shows. When you think about bands being politically correct or not, if you get behind the scenes the whole point is to enjoy the music. This is something I do. If a band is wrong politically but really great musically, then I listen to them. And there are plenty of politically minded bands that are not very good. I sometimes like to hear a band that is not too serious or politically correct. I love The Vandals so much that whatever they're doing I think, "Yeah!" Joe (Escalante) is a bullfighter and people ask him, "How can you bullfight?" When I see the bullfighter and the horns in the stomach on TV I think, "You had it coming. You're stupid!" But somehow when Joe does it, I think it's cool!

CHAPTER 11

JM: I don't like the idea of people entertaining troops who are squashing people in the Middle East. Henry Rollins also entertained the troops.

JELLO BIAFRA (Dead Kennedys / Guantanamo School of Medicine): Henry's always kind of had that code and the disciplinary side of it has served him very well. But to go back to The Vandals, there's a difference between performing for the troops and taking away, for an hour or so, all of the hell that they're going through as well as the hell that they may be inflicting on others. And for some troops, that's tearing them up inside because it wasn't what they expected when military recruiters lied to them in order to get them to join.

But another thing that came down hard on The Vandals is that their leader (Joe Escalante) is very outspokenly right wing. He provoked a huge backlash in Germany when he came out on stage and gave his honest opinion of George W. Bush, whom he whole-heartedly supported. The audience was furious! A music-booking agent claimed to me that Joey wound up going to an American Embassy hoping they'd protect him from the people who were so angry at him![4]

Another really scary one would be Godsmack because they're overtly pro-military and pro-war: "We want to inspire people to join the army!"—"Well in that case, why don't you join yourself, motherfucker?" You're no better a chickenhawk than Dick Cheney or Donald Trump when you tell everybody else to go join. I don't know what would happen if I was asked to do anything for the troops. I would be totally shocked I was asked in the first place.

JELLO BIAFRA: It's one thing to perform at a café right outside the grounds of the military base that's being run by Iraq Veterans Against the War or another group doing active counter-recruiting. I've been supportive of Iraq Veterans Against the War. I've often asked, "Why did you join in the first place?" and the attitude every time is, "I don't know." Many of them have even said, "I loved Dead Kennedys in high school," and I thought, "Holy shit! They enlisted anyway? Where did I fail?"

My father, who was drafted and sent to the Korean War against his will, told me, "After a few weeks or months of combat a soldier is useless because they're in such shell shock, combat fatigue, and PTSD." If somebody does come back gravely wounded or maimed, I'm not going to judge. That's part of what being involved with Iraq Veterans Against the War, in a peripheral level, taught me—*regardless* of what you think of war and the military, you don't shit on people by denying them their pension, denying them treatment for PTSD, and letting them wind up on the street as hardcore, long-term homeless people.

JM: There's a video of The Vandals performing in Baghdad in 2004 and they're playing the theme song from *Team America*, a politically astute film with a clear anti-war message. It seems absurd they'd play this song to US troops in Iraq.

JAN CRITCHFIELD (Department of Defense journalist - 112nd Mobile Public Affairs Detachment): I don't recall them playing "America Fuck Yeah," but they definitely played "Oi to the World" and people seemed to enjoy it. *Team America* was definitely a popular movie while I was there. I saw copies of it around, and it was for sale at the post exchange. I'm not sure how many got its message. It's pretty clearly satire. A similar phenomenon is when "Born in the USA" by Bruce Springsteen is played during patriotic events. It's almost like people don't listen to the lyrics.

JM: While you're curious about Henry Rollins' motivation to visit US troops in Iraq, you don't seem to have the same concerns about The Vandals.

JAN CRITCHFIELD: I don't hold The Vandals to the same standard. I think it's because I associate The Vandals with skate punk, and I met a lot of guys who were into that kind of music in the army. The bit about "Rock the Casbah" written on a bomb doesn't surprise me at all, either. Maybe my assessment of The Vandals is wrong. Maybe it's because Black Flag always seemed angrier and more aggressive. Both are definitely counterculture, but I associate BF more closely with the hardcore scene, and so boot parties. And I associate the army with being a haven for white supremacists. The Vandals, on the other hand, I envision chilling on the beach with longboards and a doobie. A demographic also generously represented in the army: the slacker.

The motivation of anyone deciding to support in any way the things we did in Iraq is worthy of at least a little scrutiny. The problem is that the guys they were entertaining, those 1st Cav soldiers, were also doing a lot of shooting and raiding. They were in the thick of Operations Iron Fury one and two. They undoubtedly sent quite a few people to Abu Ghraib and I witnessed some pretty aggressive interrogation techniques on the base. Not at all punk.

JAN CRITCHFIELD: The Vandals—minus their drummer; the dude from Pennywise stepped in—played a good show in one of the most violent parts of the city for the 1st Cavalry Division unit that had taken among the most killed in action, if not the most that year. The soldiers fucking loved it. I loved it, too. Still one of the best concerts I've been to. They brought a lot of energy and seemed to be having fun. I have other shots of soldiers stage diving, moshing, and a few other angles of the band from that performance. Unfortunately, I didn't get to take photos of the band firing machine guns on the range that day. Since it was against the rules and very illegal, I was supposed to keep that part of their visit hush-hush.

> *Punk rock and military discipline—not exactly like shampoo and conditioner. More like fire and ice.*
>
> —Jan Critchfield, *US Department of Defense News*[5]

CHAPTER 11

Henry Rollins signs autographs for US soldiers in Iraq (2004). Photo: Specialist Jan Critchfield (112nd Mobile Public Affairs Detachment)

JAN CRITCHFIELD: I have a few snapshots of Henry Rollins signing autographs for soldiers. Unfortunately, I didn't get the shot of him signing a shotgun shell, but that's what he was doing when I walked in the room. I sometimes wonder whose door that shotgun shell was used to breach during a no-knock home raid. Or maybe it was smuggled back unused? Who knows?

I interviewed him and wrote a crappy story about him being on the USO tour, but the editors went with a different story written by another soldier. I had heard of Rollins prior to meeting him, but I only knew him from the films *Lost Highway* (1997) and *Johnny Mnemonic* (1995). Not his music. I read a little about him and Black Flag before interviewing him, and the thing that kept going through my head was, "Why is this guy here?" It seemed so strange that a guy with an anti-establishment reputation felt the need to honor the boys fighting Bush's vanity war.

By that time in my deployment, I was pretty thoroughly convinced that what we were doing in Iraq was deeply wrong. So, I was a little disheartened to see a guy like Rollins, or what I thought he represented, on a USO tour. That seemed like a square peg/round hole combo.

Years later, maybe 2008, after listening to some of Rollins' spoken word and hearing him brag about wandering around in some Pakistani city by himself despite being warned of danger, I kind of wondered if it was just war tourism. The motivation for touring Iraq he gave during my interview was to support the soldiers whether he agreed with the war or not. Fair enough, I guess. He certainly had fans there that punk music apparently hadn't saved from being duped into army service.

I also recently read an interview in the book *More Fun in the New World* by John Doe where Rollins said national politics was never something he cared to engage with. Local politics were more important. Which might explain why I've never heard him described as anti-war or seen him say word one about ending occupations and state-sponsored murder. In the absence of outspoken opposition, à la Rage Against the Machine for instance, it's hard to know where he stands exactly.

JM: I was surprised to discover Henry Rollins's 2011 book *Occupants*, a sort of photojournalistic book with prose about traveling to war zones and other intense places like Antarctica, Sudan, and Haiti after the earthquake, where he handed out soccer balls and bottles of water to children. He seems to have hoped that bringing stories back to the US about political injustice and environmental degradation might inspire positive change and diminish US militarism. I wish he'd plugged some of that into his lyrics over the years.

JAN CRITCHFIELD: I definitely don't think Rollins is supportive of people like Bush and Reagan. I think he's probably an anti-imperialist. But the optics of being more vocal about wounded soldiers than murdered civilians is strange for a punk icon like him. It's been a curiosity of my experience there, in a packed field of surreal curiosities. There were definitely quite a few centrist Dems and some genuine lefties that I met in the army. Even some anarchists. They probably evolved quite a bit after getting out, like I did.

C. J. RAMONE

JM: How did you go from the US Marine Corps to punk rock?
C. J. RAMONE (Ramones): This is how it went: out of high school I worked in an aircraft factory, Republic Fairchild. It was great-paying job. When I got out of school my dad worked there and he got me right in. But I was only there about a year and a half and the factory closed down. Back when Reagan was president, the aircraft controllers had gone on strike and he gave permission to fire all of them, even though they were all union workers, and rehire new people. So, it

CHAPTER 11

sent a message to corporate America that you could get out from under unions and no one is going to say boo about it.

All of the government contractors on Long Island, the entire economy, was based around aerospace government contracts. We had Grumman, AIL, Republic Fairchild, Raytheon. If it flew or exploded, we made it on Long Island. All of the factories on Long Island closed down all at once and the economy went in the toilet. I was twenty years old and I was cutting people's lawns—there were just no jobs. I woke up one morning and thought, "I'm not going to live and die in my hometown. There's no way that's happening." I was playing in bands, but when all the jobs went away and the economy took a hit, it affected the clubs too.

My dad and his oldest brother were Navy and my uncle Kenny was Army Airborne and served in Korea, so it was an easy choice for me. I wanted to get out and see the world and make some kind of contribution so I went down and enlisted in the Marine Corps.

I was in the Marines when I auditioned for the Ramones. A friend of mine called me at home, "Hey, the Ramones are auditioning bass players." I was like, "I'm in the Marine Corps." [laugh] But I thought about it and said, "You know what, I'll go down and meet the band." So, I went down for the open audition. I was the first one there. Being a Marine, I got there fifteen minutes ahead of time so I was the first one to go in and audition. I went in and introduced myself, "Hey Johnny, great to meet 'cha." Joey wasn't there yet and we played through a song and Johnny asked me how many shows I'd seen—that's how he gauged how big a fan you are. And we talked a little bit and then we played the song again, and while we played it the second time Joey walked in. My buddy who told me about the audition played drums with Joey's brother, so I said, "Hey, I'm Mickey's drummer's friend." We played and I went home and I called up everybody I knew and said, "I jammed with the Ramones!"

The next day my mom said, "Monte Melnick called." He was the Ramones' tour manager their whole career. "He wants you to call him back." I immediately thought, "Did I leave something at the studio?" [laugh] I had no expectation to get the gig! They said, "Okay, learn a couple of songs and come back." And I did. It went like that for weeks and I went back and forth.

When I realized I might get the gig I called back to base and they sent a police car right over to my house and they picked me up and put me in jail. I spent one night in the local jailhouse and then a bounty hunter picked me up in the morning, took me over to Fort Hamilton over in the Bronx. Two Marines picked me up from there and took me to the Philadelphia Naval brig where I spent the night. Then I got picked up in the morning by two Marines who took me down to Quantico, Virginia. So, it was three days after I got arrested that I got to Quantico.

We went in and they gave us uniforms and they took us to the barber, and we're sitting in the common area where the TV was and the corporal on duty came out and said, "Hey, Ward. You got a phone call." I thought, "Oh, it's my mom and she's going to be crying." And I picked up the phone: "Chris?"—"Yeah."—"It's Johnny Ramone." I said, "Oh, man. I'm really sorry. I should've told you what was happening, but I didn't expect it to get as far as it did and when it did, I wasn't sure what to do." He said, "Well, what did they say?" I said, "I'll be here two weeks to a month and then they're going to discharge me." Johnny said, "Alright, do your time and don't get in trouble. When you get out, you got a job." I was like, "What?"

I got out about two and a half weeks later and took the Greyhound bus home, called up Monte, and told him I was home and he said, "Alright, take the weekend off and we start rehearsing on Monday." Five weeks later—September 30, 1989—I played my first show with the Ramones in Leicester, England. I had five weeks to learn forty songs!

C. J. RAMONE (Ramones): It was a strange transition. But had I not been in the Marine Corps I never would've made it in the Ramones! By the time I got there Johnny, who was the leader of the band, was pretty much tired of babysitting people. Dee Dee had just left the band, who was a drug addict and out of control. Marky had been kicked out of the band once for being an alcoholic and Joey had just recently stopped drinking because he was in bad shape from alcohol, too. Johnny did not want to deal with anything, especially from a new guy. So, when he started giving me the speech I said, "Hey, I can follow any rules you got. I just don't want to get in trouble for things I don't know about."

The discipline I got in the Marine Corps—the focus and understanding of being part of something that's bigger than myself—it all really paid off. I got into the band and got locked in and helped them through seven years of their career. The years that I was in the Ramones were their most successful years. They never played more shows or made more money than the years I was in the band. And they had fifteen years before I was there! I'm not trying to say that was all because of me, but I definitely helped them get through. Both Joey and Johnny said in interviews that when I got in the band, and the energy I had on stage, they suddenly realized that they needed to start moving again, you know? [laugh] They weren't going to be able to just stand there anymore.

JM: I wonder what you think about how the US military has sometimes co-opted punk rock? A couple of disturbing examples—they've blared loud music at prisoners at Guantanamo as a form of torture, including music by Rage Against

CHAPTER 11

the Machine. Tom Morello protested this. And the US military played "Rock the Casbah" by The Clash to gear up troops during the Gulf War. Fans of The Vandals protested after the band performed for US soldiers in Iraq and Henry Rollins has gone to entertain the troops. I feel uncomfortable with punk rock people entertaining US troops. Others say, "The music provides some relief for soldiers who don't want to be there anyway; they can dance for a little while."

C. J. RAMONE (Ramones): Having been a Marine, I will always be a Marine. The Marines will always be my brotherhood. It's not a brotherhood of political opinions. I was in with guys who were conscientious objectors, guys who did not agree with a lot of what the US does around the world. But you have to understand that it's a warrior brotherhood. It has nothing to do with politics. It has nothing to do with hating the people that you're fighting against. There's a part of this culture that boys grow up in that makes them into warriors. It's not something that is taught consciously and some of it is almost genetic. Men and boys are programmed to be fighters and warriors. I'm not saying all. But there's a very large segment of men in our culture who have a need to be part of a warrior brotherhood.

C. J. RAMONE: When you ask, "How do you feel about punk bands going over there (Iraq/Afghanistan) to play for the military?" They're not going over there to play for the military! They're going there to play for guys and gals that are far away from home and going through a whole lot of misery and suffering. That's who they go to play for. I'm sure you've heard a million cases of guys who served in every war who come home and say, "What we're doing there is wrong. I don't agree with what's going on there."

In my experience most of the guys and gals I served with were good people who were not in there to kill. And I was in the Marine Corps; that's what we're known for! But most of the guys and gals I knew weren't hoping for war. They were in there because they didn't have a lot of options. Those are the people I don't mind going to play for. But the bands that are going there aren't saying, "We support the war!" You don't have to support the war, but we should be supporting our troops.

JM: Have you played for US troops?

C. J. RAMONE: No. I left music for a while when I started a family, just after the Ramones retired, and by then my oldest was diagnosed with autism. I put music down for a while and focused on my family. I was in the Marine Corps and the only way I would've seen Havana, Cuba, or Moscow in 1987 would've been with fixed bayonets. However, fast forward twenty-five years and I played in Moscow and St. Petersburg. I was the first US punk rock artist invited by the Communist Party to go play in Cuba. I'm going back this November (2018). If changes like that can happen in my lifetime, I have plenty of hope.

"NAZI TRUMPS FUCK OFF!"
PUNK IN THE TRUMP ERA

It's July 23, 2016, and I'm standing directly in front of the stage at the Ritz Club in San Jose, California. The last time I'd seen Jello Biafra perform was *thirty-two* years earlier at a 1983 Dead Kennedys concert in San Diego. Biafra now has a super-sized discography that includes spoken word albums, collaborations with numerous bands, dozens of albums distributed by his Alternative Tentacles record label, a series of info videos called "What Would Jello Do?"

Jello Biafra with Dead Kennedys (1981). Photo: Edward Colver

CHAPTER 12

and a new band formed in 2008 called (no pressure coming up with the *second*-best punk band name) Jello Biafra and the Guantanamo School of Medicine.

For tonight's show Biafra and guitarist Ralph Spight and the band have updated the DK's song "Nazi Punks Fuck Off" to "Nazi *Trumps* Fuck Off" and the merch table offers T-shirts emblazoned with the slogan. After the 2016 US presidential "election" Chris Shearer at Alternative Tentacles told me they could barely keep up with orders for the "Nazi Trumps" T-shirt. On a similar note, Ronald Reagan's 1980 presidential campaign slogan resurrected by Donald Trump in 2016, "Make America Great Again," was also creatively modified by Prophets of Rage and Jodie Foster's Army to read, "Make America *Rage* Again" and "Make America *Skate* Again!"

During the concert everyone seemed to know the lyrics to "California Über Alles" as Jello held his microphone out into the audience. A slam dance circle swirled most of the night and Biafra was mashed into the crowd after stepping down into the audience. As he performed, Jello revealed deeper layers of costume as he stripped off a black plastic leather East Berlin Stasi-style trench coat and matching black hat adorned with a bright red Christian crucifix. He ended wearing a "Bernie Sanders 2016" T-shirt.

Jello spoke between songs about politics, including the importance of voting, especially when it comes to local city councils and referendums, and the specter of widespread state surveillance. He asked, "Do you think Edward Snowden is cool?" and went on to talk about Chelsea Manning and other pro-democracy whistleblowers. He also suggested that the Black Lives Matter movement would do well to include all people of color and marginalized people. One Guantanamo song was about for-profit private prisons and another—"Three Strikes"—covered the drug war. Another tune spoke of the prevalence of homelessness. Biafra also noted that right-wing politicians were gaining power not only in the United States but also across Europe.

JELLO BIAFRA (Dead Kennedys): When my new band came out—Jello Biafra & The Guantanamo School of Medicine—I wanted to play new songs. But I haven't forgotten about the old family recipe. I wrote most of Dead Kennedys' music and lyrics after all. The Melvins talked me into playing Dead Kennedys songs when we played shows together, but we didn't play "Nazi Punks Fuck Off."

Guantanamo School of Medicine were able to get gigs in a lot of countries Dead Kennedys—the real Dead Kennedys—were never able to go to. The old former Soviet Bloc countries, Balkan peninsula countries, South America; places where people had very vivid memories of putting their necks on the line fighting real live fascist regimes. They would ask me, "Where's the song? 'Nazi Punks Fuck Off!' That song was part of our anthem when we were fighting against the fascists. It helped pull us together!" So, it came back.

And then [laugh] worst of all possible worlds—we now have a neo-Nazi, white supremacist, old-school, fascist pig who's stolen the White House and is very heavy handed in trying to bring as many violent bigots out of the closet as possible for his red, white, and blue brown shirts. It was a no-brainer to change it from "Nazi Punks Fuck Off" to "Nazi *Trumps* Fuck Off." Especially because early on after Trump announced his campaign, I did one of my YouTube rants called "What Would Jello Do?" warning people who thought it was kind of hip to say, "This guy is shaking up the establishment." I said, "Wait a minute! This guy is a hardcore fucking racist! He's rich beyond belief and that's the only thing he cares about. You shouldn't fall for this dude." And we got all kinds of angry [laugh], you know, Twitter-sized-attention-span messages saying, "Dude, Trump is punk! What's the matter with Jello? Is he some kind of Muslim now?" Then I did a second one about *that* because I found it so disgusting.

JELLO BIAFRA (Guantanamo School of Medicine): We don't do enough on this side to fight back against soulless media perceptions. Now when people hear the term pro-life, they think of anti-abortion zealots who don't give a damn about life—some of them are pro death penalty! Some are willing to kill abortion doctors and, once the fetus is born, they don't care about it at all. These pro-life people are the same Trump and Paul Ryan types who want to cut all assistance to the underprivileged to zero and let the market run its course. If the market says you starve to death in the richest country in the world, "No problem, the market's doing good!" They're not pro-life, they're anti-life!

Aside from alt-right there is religious liberty, where people claim they want religious freedom and they're really trying to force their own narrow interpretation of one strain of religion down everybody's throat by law, or by violence. They're not interested in religious liberty at all. They want to take everybody else's away and run this country like a Christian supremacist Taliban.

I did a "What Would Jello Do?" recently taking issue with that element within Antifa who consider it jolly good recreational fun to go to demonstrations hoping they can beat the crap out of some neo-Trumpkins, Nazis, or white supremacists. I'm not going to call those people *alt-right*, that's for sure. That was a mainstream media term that was put on from above in order to defang their impact so that less people would feel threatened by them and consider it a little more normal. You know, "Alt-right. Like alt-country! Oh, cool!"

CHAPTER 12

VOTER FRAUD

JELLO BIAFRA: And then we get to voter fraud. There is no bigger or damaging form of voter fraud than monkeying with the results through digital means, first to make George W. Bush president and now to make Trump president. It just astounds me that people like Bernie Sanders and Elizabeth Warren haven't even mentioned that the real voter fraud is the interstate Crosscheck program. Greg Palast is the only one who's gone out of his way to expose this.[1]

Crosscheck is the program initiated by Kris Kobach, Secretary of State of Kansas, the right-wing wunderkind behind the scenes. He got twenty-nine states to dump all their voter databases into one big one controlled by *him*. And cross-check with programs to look for so-called voter fraud by seeing how many names matched in different states. And if you get a match you take everyone with that name off the voter roll. It was designed to take the vote away from people named *Washington* because, according to Palast, 75 percent of people with the last name Washington are African American. Of course, if your name is Jose Martinez, all hundred of you were kicked off the voter rolls of twenty-nine states because obviously you were the same person and committed voter fraud. A lot of people who voted don't even know that their vote didn't count. All this hype about "shockingly low turnout" and how African Americans didn't turn up for Hillary Clinton and all that; I will wonder to my dying day how many of them actually *did* vote but had their votes tossed out in this Crosscheck.

JELLO BIAFRA: It's no surprise to me that Trump is now using another one of his psycho tweets of how Hillary actually got millions of illegal votes. I think a lot of those tweets are put under wraps ahead of time and used when they want to suck the air out of the room. But this whole premise to investigate these stolen votes for Trump—he knows that ain't true. Mike Pence, cochair of the Voter Fraud Commission, knows that's not true because his cochair is Kris Kobach, Mr. Crosscheck himself. The goal of this so-called Voter Fraud Commission is to commit much bigger voter fraud than we've seen even in the 2016 elections. So that by the time 2018 is rolling around, all kinds of other people who are being suspected of being people of color or young people or old people are all kicked off the rolls, and anybody dreaming of taking back the House and Senate from Trump in 2018, they can just dream on. Because Crosscheck will make sure it goes in the other direction again and again and again. This is why even some mainstream media pundits are referring nonchalantly to post-democracy America. This kind of puts punk rock in perspective compared to all the really bad shit going on in the world, doesn't it?

SLAVE TO THE SYSTEM

> *The Dead Kennedys were great! Love 'em.*
>
> —John Lydon (PiL)

John Lydon has often connected his music and lyrics to politics. He told me, "Politics has always been there in my writing. I can't help it. I just feel naturally inclined to help the disenfranchised, and I'll always feel that way myself." Lydon has said he's confronted racist systems like apartheid with songs like "Rise" (1986) where he chants melodically, "I could be black, I could be white." In his second memoir *Anger Is an Energy* (2014), Lydon writes, "'Rise' was looking at the context of South Africa under apartheid. . . . Lines like 'They put a hotwire to my head, because of the things I did and said,' are a reference to the torture techniques that the apartheid government was using out there." In the same autobiography he notes that "hotwire to my head" also referred to his own hairdo at the time. The title of Lydon's first autobiography, *Rotten: No Irish, No Blacks, No Dogs* (1994), recounts signs that the author saw displayed in boardinghouse windows as a child of Irish parents in London.

JOHN LYDON (Sex Pistols / PiL): I'd love to see a more transparent society, but there's a point to transparency that has to stop. What are these new robot things that people are introducing to their house that you talk to and it listens and answers you? Those things also spy on you! So, now people are willingly paying good money to be spied on. So, there's no privacy at all. That really is stage one in slave to the system. And they're selling like hotcakes!

JM: It's a dream come true for the surveillance state.

JOHN LYDON: I think the precursor to that was the really horrible, awful reality TV shows. You've got entire young generations just wanting to be talking about themselves all the time! With cameras on them all the time. No privacy, no nothing. Just fame, for no good reason. Poor old Andy Warhol got it wrong when he said everybody wants fifteen minutes of fame. [laugh] Cut out the fifteen minutes—they just want fame! But fame as in vain, glorious. So silly. So not thought about. So not talked about, so not discussed. So not observed. Where will technology be taking us?

JM: We don't have collective discussions about new technologies and whether or not they're beneficial and if we want them or not.

JOHN LYDON: Yeah. I understood years ago that parents worried about their children and they wanted them to have a phone when they went to school, because

CHAPTER 12

there are crimes in schools. But now look what that's turned into. It's bizarre when a ten-year-old is demanding for their Christmas present the latest Samsung. Everything attached. Wow! They're being robotized. We don't need the robot parts; we've already watched our young giving up their brains willingly, to be suckered into a machine that is supposed to answer all your problems. It's unhealthy. But then again, all the best things are. But this is much more destructive than drugs. Modern technology is a very challenging problem. It makes people incredibly stupid. They don't know how these things are using them, how or why these things are manufactured, and they don't know where their information is going.

There was a TV program when I was very young called "The Prisoner" that starred Patrick McGoohan. It was a terrific program but at the time was viewed as being slightly paranoid about the future. It's here—it's right now. One of the key lines of it is they held him prisoner in this facility, this village, of everybody being nice to each other and, "Why aren't you happy?" He asked the powers that be—whom he wasn't allowed to know—what they wanted and the answer was, "We want information." Lo and behold, that's now our reality. Very clever writing. "The Prisoner." It's very hard to take, I admit. But the idea of it, when I was very young, really impressed me! The idea of people having access to your innermost thoughts is just not right. If that happens then you have no thoughts at all. And you don't need armies any longer, because you're already being controlled. Well, maybe temporarily, the way the Russians are.

> *A population that feels lost and weak and powerless can be led / by any volumatic twat who says things that are never said / Racist, sexist, vacuous bullshit.*
>
> —"Trump Song" by Dick Lucas (Subhumans, November 2016)

NOTHING RHYMES WITH ORANGE

Although Amanda Palmer of The Dresden Dolls optimistically declared, "Donald Trump is going to make punk rock great again," there wasn't exactly a plethora of politically charged punk albums released during his time as commander in chief.[2] The Boston band Hallelujah the Hills even made fun of the notion with an acoustic song, "Punk Rock's Gonna Be Great Now that Trump's in Charge." Singer Ryan Walsh reminded us that political music might come from other directions, "It's not going to be folk music, it's not going to be punk music. This isn't a science. It's not going to happen the same way, and no one knows how it's going to work yet."³

Oakland-based pop punks Build Them to Break did hit the new president with the 2016 song "Nothing Rhymes with Orange." And "Fuck Donald Trump" was released by hip-hop artist YG. Sri Lankan singer and former refugee MIA rapped about boat people escaping US wars of 9/11 retaliation in her 2016 song "Borders"—"Politics / what's up with that? / Police shots / what's up with that?" Grindcore band Brujeria recorded "Viva Presidente Trump!" as another contribution to anti-Trump art.

The slight uptick in politically charged punk has focused on Trump and seems to be partly inspired by widespread condemnation of the one-time reality TV star turned president. Even though all US presidents since World War II have committed war crimes (according to Noam Chomsky's 1990 speech "If the Nuremberg Laws Were Applied"), Trump was so openly racist, classist, and misogynist that he was perhaps an easy target.

In 2018 Gang of Four (with single original member Andy Gill producing) released the EP *Complicit* featuring a photo of President Trump's daughter and advisor Ivanka on the cover, with the word "Complicit" in both English and Russian (замешанными). In her mother Ivana's 2017 memoir Ivanka is quoted, "During my punk phase in the nineties, I was really into Nirvana. My wardrobe consisted of ripped corduroy jeans and flannel shirts. One day after school, I dyed my hair blue. Mom wasn't a fan of this decision."⁴

> *In the morning daddy wants me in his room, it's where we get together / It's not true that daddy calls my name in stormy weather.*
>
> —"Ivanka (Things You Can't Have)"
> by Gang of Four (2018)

JM: On the new EP, you have an image of Ivanka Trump. The word "complicit" is also in Russian, which reminds me of the back cover of an early Gang of Four EP, with a map of the US in Russian. How'd you decide to focus on this US administration?

ANDY GILL (Gang of Four): On previous occasions we've steered clear of being particularly current affairs related or naming particular current political individuals or situations. But we live in particularly interesting times. I think it's

CHAPTER 12

entirely appropriate that Gang of Four in 2018 would give some commentary that is politically charged: amusing backdrops to the life we're living at this point in time. It's easy to lash out at Trump as being a symbol of everything which is retrogressive. That would be easy and that's not what I'm doing on the new record. But what is particularly interesting about Ivanka Trump in this situation is that when *The Donald* was installed in the White House, he then in turn installed Ivanka Trump in her own office in the White House. When he was questioned about that he said, "It's nepotism. And nepotism is great, isn't it?" It's an extraordinary thing for an American president to say, but there you go!

Ivanka was in there and she was wheeled out to do interviews, which obviously were going to attract massive worldwide attention. And she came out with this extraordinary speech and parts of it were this brilliant statement of, "Complicit? I don't know what it means to be complicit." Which, if I'm not wrong, somebody said at the Nuremberg Trials after the Second World War.

This is suddenly a very interesting and novel situation where you have this apparently innocent-looking girl trying to give a sugarcoating to the Trump ideology. And I thought this is something which has to be described. But there was nothing I needed to do, really. Most of the words in that song are the words of Ivanka Trump, not mine. In all honesty, I feel that I should share my royalties with her, as she's one of the main lyricists of the song. Of course, when Ivanka Trump was on the digital cover of the download, it was reported all across America. I woke up one morning and someone said, "You're in the *Washington Post*." I checked out the link and it was like, "British post-punk band quote Ivanka and have her picture on the sleeve." That was reported across America.

JM: In her mom's book Ivanka Trump is quoted saying she went through a punk rock period. What do you think about that?

ANDY GILL: Not that much. Apparently, her favorite band was The Police, which is sort of ironic on a certain level. Good luck to her. I don't care what she did or does. She's not that interesting. But for her one phosphorescent moment in history, she certainly burned brightly. I don't think anybody expected this and nobody expected that he'd (Trump) become that open about what he was doing. The difference between Trump and previous US presidents is that, to a certain extent, he knows that he can be as brazen as he likes and it's not going to affect his project.

JM: Maybe the last time Gang of Four was so specific in your lyrics about political people and events were "FMUSA" and "Money Talks" (1991) with the lyrics, "Curtain tear but Bush don't care / fights on like General Custer. . . . Here's the dope on Noriega's jones / a pineapple on the US payroll."

ANDY GILL: Yes, well remembered. That's a good point.

JM: I know a lot of songwriters believe if they're too specific, it dates a song. But I love "Money Talks." And I love "Fascist Groove Thang" by Heaven 17.

ANDY GILL: I don't know. It's sort of a fine line. I don't want to define exactly and precisely what Gang of Four can and cannot do because it's a movable feast. I don't want to be tying myself down with certain rules. In the past we actually made a song that Jon (King) and I did—a spoken thing—called "Banned Words." We semi-jokingly listed a few things that we thought we'd talked about in songs in the past and wouldn't talk about anymore. I remember money was one of the things on that list. That's what you think at a certain point and six months later of course the rules have changed again. Sometimes you can talk about current political affairs and sometimes you want to write songs that are more generalized.

PAT MACDONALD (Timbuk 3): I don't even want to put his name in a song. I don't want to dirty up my song with his name. The closest I came was writing a song called "A Most Despicable Man." I wrote more songs about Trump in the '80s when I didn't realize I was writing about him, when he was part of the '80s *greed is good* thing. I wrote about that a lot back then. I'm kind of tired of writing about that now.

PENNY RIMBAUD (Crass): There was a terrible time for about eight years where I thought, "I don't want to go to America. It's shit." Then something brought me there again and I was so relieved to find that the people are the same, nothing's changed. The dynamic and directness, all the things I love about America were still there. There just happen to be fools in the White House, as there always are. It doesn't matter what color they are or what background they are. Well, they're always Yale and Harvard.

ANDY GILL (Gang of Four): One big problem with the American constitution is that it was written by a bunch of old, white Englishmen over two hundred years ago. America is so keen to have absolutes carved in stone forever that they've held the constitution up as almost a religious text that must be obeyed at all cost. The problem is that the world changes, history changes. We learn things and move on. We discover that people can't be relied upon to always be anti-fascist. Owning a gun is not always a good thing!

The years 2018 and 2019 saw significant offerings from punk (and other musical genres) addressing war, oppression, racism, police abuse, and economic violence. The video for the 2018 song "This Is America" went "viral," won four Grammy awards, including song of the year, and inspired political analysis from *The Atlantic* and the *New York Times*.[5]

CHAPTER 12

"The Kids Are Alt-Right" by Bad Religion was also released in 2018 with a video featuring an animated Donald Trump chasing a shotgun hanging from a string.[6] Also in 2018, German punk band Abwârts released "Smart Bomb."

February 1, 2019, brought the first new album in twenty years from The Specials and has feminist/humanist songs like "10 Commandments" and "Vote for Me." Anti-Flag released their twelfth studio album, *20/20 Vision*, with an image of Trump on the cover and songs like "Don't Let the Bastards Get You Down" and "Hate Conquers All," which features an audio clip from Trump discussing political protesters: "In the good old days, this doesn't happen because they used to treat them very, very rough. And when they protested once, they would not do it again so easily." The year 2020 saw a new album from The Pretenders, also directed toward the US president, titled *Hate for Sale*.

> *You're all so drunk on money and power, inside your ivory tower / Teaching us not to be smart, making laws that serve to protect you.*
>
> —"Vote for Me" by The Specials (2019)

WORSE BEFORE THEY GET BETTER

In early November 2016 Green Day performed at the MTV Europe Music Awards and updated the lyrics for "American Idiot" from "Subliminal mindfuck America" to "Subliminal mind-*Trump* America." Articles in mainstream media had described the 2016 US presidential campaigns of Hillary Clinton and Donald Trump as *literally* making people sick. Clinton was one of the least popular presidential candidates, while Trump referred to Mexican people as "rapists" and advocated for a larger US military, the building of a wall along the US–Mexico border, increasing the use of torture, and requiring Muslims in the United States to register. He also seemed to feel comfortable talking about the size of his penis as a symbol of strength and that he could grab any woman's "pussy" whether she consented or not and get away without consequences. On January 23, 2016, during a speech in Iowa, he said, "I could stand in the middle of 5th Avenue and shoot somebody and I wouldn't lose any voters! It's like, incredible!"

Twelve days after Trump's surprise "election," Green Day played at the November 20, 2016, American Music Awards. They began their song "Bang Bang" with a rousing chant of "No Trump! No KKK! No fascist USA!" This slogan was heard in marches across the United States following the November 8, 2016, "election," though many probably didn't know the words were modified from the 1988 MDC song by Dave Dictor "Born to Die"—"No war! No KKK! No fascist USA!"

MARK REEDER (The Frantic Elevators / Die Unbekannten): I don't like the idea that President Trump is planning on building a wall. He obviously has learned nothing from history. If the US legalized drugs and invested in Mexico and really helped them to educate their people and build their economy, then they would have no need for a wall. People in Mexico have no hope and no prospects, except for maybe moving to Mexico City or fleeing to a supposed better life in the US. Building a wall is certainly not a long-term solution, even if it's a thick, big wall like in a John Carpenter movie.

The cost and infrastructure to maintain such a huge wall would certainly provide many Americans jobs and cost the taxpayers billions. Maybe this is President Trump's main aim? He could give all his business mates the contracts to build and keep the wall in perfect working condition and upgrade it whenever needed. However, as the USA starts to go into decline, I'm sure many will be lining up, trying to get out, too. I don't like the idea of separation. I'm all for sharing and collaborating. Unity is the only way. That's why I called my album *Mauerstadt*, to bring awareness to the subject of being walled in. I mean not just physically, but mentally too.

JOHN LYDON (Sex Pistols / PiL): I think everybody needs a wall! You have to have a line. "This is my space—do not cross into it!" We do this mentally and we need to do it physically from time to time. There has to be a demarcation line. I think that's just common sense! Do I go as far as what's going on at the moment? (2019) It's insane! Both sides of the argument are totally missing the point. If you can do it electronically, that's fine because the physicality of a brick wall doesn't solve very much. Particularly in mind of all the drug tunneling. (From Mexico to the US.) It's easy to crawl under. Just as easy to go 'round. Economics are part and parcel of all this; if you don't want a huge influx of desperate poor people that can't live in those societies, well then help those societies! Help them! Help them live in their own places. Why not? Charity begins at home and guess what? Everyone wants their own home.

It took me years and years to get my green card, to become an American, and I have a personal resentment that you can kind of waltz in out of the desert and that's it. The Democrat concept that there is no such thing as an illegal alien or illegal immigrant? [laugh] Really? This is a minefield, mate! And what does it have to do with music? It has *everything* to do with music. I'm very sad to see

CHAPTER 12

so few Americans take this on. And the few that do, do it in such a silly way—a Kid Rock way. Play golf with Trump! What? You'd be ashamed to mingle with any powerbrokers on that level! I treat all governments as civil servants and if they're not civil to me, I won't serve! The art of the individual is too much for either Democrat or Republican philosophies, isn't it?

AMERICANS FIRST

JOHN LYDON (Sex Pistols / PiL): It's about time we had a mad man in there to sort out the rest of them (Trump). I think everybody is showing their true colors and it's all really a dull shade of gray. I take it as a momentous moment in history. Our future decides on where we go with this, but we can't be extreme. Since I've become an American (2013) it's vitally important to me that people understand that. I do appreciate the idea of *Americans first* because I'm living in California and I'm surrounded by homeless people. And they're all Americans and nobody is doing nothing to help them. Tent cities are now up and down the coast, all the way to Oregon. They were born and raised here. They come before you can even deal with the concept of illegal aliens. It took me a long time to get my American passport. I don't understand why! I could've just hopped and skipped across the desert! I quite like the desert.

JM: You said that at colleges now, you're being heckled because students have been hearing ideas about you that aren't true.

JOHN LYDON: Modern comedians are finding it very difficult to play universities now because they're instantly booed if they tell a politically incorrect joke. That's *the point*! You should welcome speakers and challenge everything you believe. Those should be the ones you're dying to get a ticket to listen to! Don't heckle—Listen! You might learn something. College campuses are no longer the bastions of free thinkers.

JM: What is something people are hearing that you've said, that you have *not* said?

JOHN LYDON: Just about everything, really. Where do I begin with that one? Bloody hell. I'm not a nasty-minded person. Left-wing students demonstrating now sound bitter, twisted. And at the same time deeply hilarious cartoon characters of what humanity should be. You don't listen and you ain't got nothing to say.

KID CONGO POWERS (The Gun Club / The Cramps / Pink Monkey Birds): The thing with Lydon is you don't know: Is he pulling our leg and being the ultimate sarcastic person? Or is he another libertarian? Is he being contrary, or is he really invested in those people's ideology? If he is supportive of MAGA (Make America Great Again) or the Brexit referendum, then that loses me immediately. I'm from an immigrant family. I'm Mexican American. I was born in America and my parents were born in America, but beyond that we were immigrants. I'm a queer man and all of these shady ideologies are against that. I see racism, homophobia, transphobia. I see just phobia. From history I know where that leads; it can go somewhere really awful, even to genocide.

DON REDONDO (JFA): We now (2017) have another idiot in the White House (Trump) who believes that giving tax breaks to the rich is the way to go! So, we haven't accomplished shit! And this guy is probably more unstable than Ronnie. When I was a kid, my friends had older brothers that were hippies or whatever and they'd say, "Hey man, someday we're going to be in charge." And it's like, "No you're not! The Hitler Youth guys that are class president right now are the guys that are gonna be in charge!" And it's the same with the people in our generation, right? It's nobody like us! It's the jerks and they're all right wing.

BRIAN BRANNON (JFA): I think of things like a pendulum. Obama did a lot of things to change and some of those things were a little too much for some of these people that weren't ready for it. In some ways we're feeling a backlash against that. I think he did a lot of good when he was in office. Now there are some things going on that are pretty far right. They're pushing it so far that the pendulum is going to have to come back. But I don't think these wild swings are where we need to be. We need to find a middle ground. We also need to remember that we're all Americans. It was *us against them* back at the time and there was a lot of them and not that many of us. Theoretically there's more of us, now that you can buy punk at the mall. But we're all people. When you hear this stuff about *libtards* and *wingnuts*—we forget we're all Americans. We're supposed to be the *United* States of America. But now we're so divided we can't even talk politics or anything. We need to get back to where we're all Americans and go from there. And get away from calling each other names and labeling stuff.

JM: So many people are stunned about the new president of the US. Coming from Russia, what are your biggest concerns about this new guy?

SASHA (ALEXANDER) CHEPARUKHIN (Pussy Riot producer): The very fact that Mr. Trump became president of the United States is the result of a weakness of American democratic and liberal forces. We always think that America is so different from Russia, but the last several years we realize that many things are not that different. We were thinking that the American system is so experienced in democracy and could prevent anything that is anti-democratic and anti-freedom. But I found that this distance is not that incredible as we sometimes think, the distance between Russia and America in a political sense.

CHAPTER 12

When young people see Putin on TV every day, he is all the time delivering this message in a direct or indirect way: "Guys, be obedient to power. Power and money mean everything. Everything else is bullshit. You have to follow whatever power tells you and then you can get everything." This is a very cynical thing and I see how it works. A lot of young people started to share this conformist ideology much more than it used to be at the end of the Soviet Union when people were inspired by Gorbachev's changes and the wish to be with the whole world in the democratic way of development. People were much more open and free in whatever they said then than now during Putin's time.

SASHA (ALEXANDER) CHEPARUKHIN: In America all of a sudden it seems the same. Maybe it's my own personal experience, but I know Masha feels something like the same. We actually meet (in the US) many more people now who are more open in their racist statements and much more rude with foreigners. I don't know if it's connected, but based on my personal experience I see that the police in airports who decide whether you are allowed or not allowed to enter the United States, some of them have become much more rude and suspicious. We definitely see much more control in the United States. It happened way before Trump. 9/11 definitely influenced these kinds of decisions of more control and more information about everybody. But America is not the kind of free country as I remember in the '80s when I first visited America during the Gorbachev Perestroika times.

Also, we see separation of American people. We see how people in some universities literally say the same as people in Russia; they feel themselves surrounded by a kind of different nations, by the nations of people who like and elect people like Trump. We see that is not *that* safe and not *that* stable a system despite the fact that America has a long history of democratic development. But it could be reversed, especially in people's minds. It seems like a dangerous trend and we are worrying about this. We don't see America as a perfect example for us anymore. We don't like what happens in Russia, but we don't think America nowadays could be an example that could be the model we should see as our goal. What happened with American democracy that led to people like Trump to get much more power in the States I cannot really analyze because it's a very complex thing, but it's unfortunate.

13

"I AM AN ANARCHIST"
ANTI-AUTHORITARIAN SOUNDTRACK

If we conceive of a world that doesn't have government, what that means is not only experiencing the freedom we want, but also the responsibility that we might be less eager to take on.

—Mark Andersen (Positive Force DC cofounder)

I am an anarchist / Don't know what I want, but I know how to get it.

—"Anarchy in the UK" by Sex Pistols

I tend not to call myself an anarchist anymore. I'm just an angry sixty-one-year-old man.

—Steve Ignorant (Crass / Slice of Life)

Anarchy has played a role in many punk bands and projects but not the majority. For those punks who have experimented with anarchist philosophy and practice, the intentions and results have been diverse and even contradictory. While some bands have attempted to *be* anarchy, others have *described* anarchist philosophy, with some doing both. On the other side, some punk artists use a familiar punk *style* or *sound* associated with anarchy and choose to leave behind the core principles of mutual aid, free association, and self-reliance.

Many punk bands have been self-designed and are based in shared power, freedom in creativity, and challenging structures of authority. Before any script is written—when any and all clothing, haircuts, and sonic experiments are

CHAPTER 13

valid—punk offers a pulsing sense of *anything can happen*. Improvisation and surprise naturally collaborate with planning and structure. Indeed, a healthy balance of structure and freedom is a common way of viewing one of the philosophical progenitors of revolutionary punk: anarchy.

NOAM CHOMSKY AND BAD RELIGION

JM: Your voice is heard on records by punk bands like Bad Religion. For some young people punk rock is an introduction to anarchism. What's your take on punk rock as a manifestation of anarchism?

NOAM CHOMSKY (author of *Manufacturing Consent*): Around the world, after talks and at meetings, people ask me to sign things. I doubt if I sign anything as often as I've signed the cover of that disc (Bad Religion). And does it contribute to anarchism? A lot of young people have told me that's the kind of thing that got them interested in activism and anarchism. I can see from places I've been it really works. It's certainly perfectly reasonable. Like in the 1960s and a long time before that—the '30s and so on—folk music was having that effect. And for others, classical music may have it. Or other art forms. Murals are a case of popular art that often has remarkable aesthetic value and has been amazingly effective in Mexico. A friend in Northern Ireland who does research on this sent me a great book of murals in Northern Ireland. I've seen murals everywhere in the world. So, music, too. If that's what people find stimulating and exciting, it's a wonderful thing.

JM: Do you connect with ideas of nonviolence and anarchy?

GREG GRAFFIN (Bad Religion): I connect with a lot of these ideas. One of the leading advocates of anarchy is Noam Chomsky, who we've collaborated with. I have read a lot of his stuff. But I must say that a lot of times I lose him at the point where he starts to talk about anarchy, because anarchy is not well defined. I am a naturalist. That is my focus. That's my position in life and the social science slant of anarchy is something that does not interest me. I am far more focused on what unites people from different walks of life through our *biological* connections than I am interested in our *social* connections.

JM: On the new album (*Dissent of Man*, 2010), you sing about paradise and a vision of the future. Do you have specific ideas about how a positive, different world would look?

GREG GRAFFIN: I don't know what society will look like in the future, but I know that we have a long way to go in order to educate people. My idea of paradise is simply an enlightened society where you can walk up to someone and ask them what their ideology is and what it means to be that kind of a person and they can actually give you an answer. I think that you would maybe find one out of a hundred people who could answer that question today. If they have an ideology or a coherent theory of what life means. Until MTV and the things that children are watching take that issue seriously, we are going to have an uphill battle.

NIHILISM AND ANARCHIST PHILOSOPHY

JM: Part of punk rock went down the road of nihilism.

GREG GRAFFIN (Bad Religion): In my observations, nihilistic punk did not go very far. It certainly is not the stuff that is most popular today. I think there's an element of nihilism that goes back to the early days and the Sex Pistols with "Anarchy in the UK." But their nihilism was more of a stylistic feature and less of a serious doctrine. It also didn't produce some of the most beloved, long-lived punk bands.

EXENE CERVENKA (X): The beginning of the punk scene was nihilistic and anarchistic because it was about erasing everything that came before and starting over with something new. New ideas, new music, new people, new everything! In that way, punk was extremely revolutionary. I don't know if that's spiritual, but I think it is. That's the roots of punk: nihilism and anarchy that would erase the mistakes of the past and give us a clean slate to come up with something brand new that reflected a different society, a different way of interpreting experience.

KLAUS FLOURIDE (Dead Kennedys): Lots of people confuse nihilism with anarchy. That's what you're taught to do in high school. We were taught that anarchy was something to stay far away from because it meant total loss of civilized behavior. In fact, it's supposed to be just the opposite! Instead of having some outside force telling you what to do and treating you like children, you're supposed to behave like adults because you know damn well what's good and bad. This world has a bit of maturing to do—a couple hundred years' worth—before we can come anywhere near being able to live in real anarchy. It's like a four-way stop. The guy on the right gets to go. It's like stuff we learned in kindergarten about taking turns. Anarchy is simple: take your turn and make sure everybody else gets their turn at life.

My favorite representation of working anarchy came out of Italy, and Rome specifically. When we (Dead Kennedys) first went there, a communist march was going through town and this person in the front row carrying the banner

CHAPTER 13

was wearing a Fiorucci outfit! [laugh] Communism was more of a fashion statement! And the fascists were on the other end.

DAVE WAKELING (The English Beat): I liked the Italian anarchists. They've got the best salads. Nicest trousers and shoes—blimey! I thought they had the best anarchy as well. Their notion of it was that the problems in society were inherent. You didn't need to go railing on about it—it was dead obvious. All you needed to do was keep working its contradictions against itself and it would wind it up so tight that you wouldn't need a real hammer. You could use a toffee hammer: just hit it once on top and it would crack to its foundations and shatter. You didn't need to attack it like it was a truth. Just keep on rubbing its contradictions against itself until it becomes too tight to operate. I thought, "Yeah, that's good."

We tried to do that with the lyrics. We wanted to point things out in a funny way. There's nothing better to take the steam out of something than deride it and be accurate! [laugh] "Margaret Thatcher—what a joke!" Much better than, "Aaaahhh! We're going to fight and set up barricades!" That's just what they want! I'm not going to play into their game. They *like* killing, *that's* the point. You don't want to play that game. They're so scared of life, all they know is how to take it.

JM: Does anarchist philosophy resonate with you?

DAVE WAKELING: Anarchist philosophy was the whole basis of The Beat. But we tried to use it in its purer form: "anarchos"—without rulers. The way we saw it was that the equation of anarchy was *freedom divided by responsibility*. You could have as much freedom as you could be socially responsible. You could do anything you liked as long as you don't hurt nobody with it. It got a lot of bad press by the Russian crowd with the bombs.

I'm afraid that too many people in punk just heard, "ANARCHY! DESTROY!" [Dave sings this out loud in his best Johnny Rotten impersonation, with a bit of a nasal squeak.] It was like, "Yes, but that's only the first chapter, isn't it? You didn't read the rest, did you?" We were very fond of anarchist philosophy. That was quite a lot of the original ethos, in a responsible way. Freedom divided by responsibility, without rulers. We're old enough to look after ourselves now.

DAVE DICTOR (MDC): Anarchist philosophy does resonate for me. What it does within punk rock is the whole idea that a government shouldn't run your life. Anarchy means that we conduct ourselves autonomously. It's a popular notion that we don't need certain things from the federal government, whether it's them collecting your money or putting you in jail because you get caught with some controlled substance. Those things are used as a political tool to control people. People lose their voting rights because they get a felony.

There is an anarchist-individualist streak going through the punk rock community. Now, who is actually practicing anarchy? That's all up for personal interpretation. Who even knows who Bakunin is anymore? Or Emma Goldman for that matter?

DAVID LESTER (Mecca Normal / Horde of Two): One of the many things that are compelling about (Buenaventura) Durruti is that during his fight against fascism during the Spanish Civil War, he put into practice the ideals of anarchism. Things like workers operating their workplaces in a democratic fashion and making sure no citizens would go hungry or without shelter or medical care. We see in the twentieth century incredible examples in Spain of people operating under a system that wasn't based around capitalism. It's ironic during that time, where he was trying to create a freer and more democratic world, that we see the rise of authoritarianism and fascism across Europe. Franco in Spain, Mussolini in Italy, Hitler in Germany. And fascist parties throughout Europe, including Britain with the Union of British Fascists, and in America with the German American Bund, which wanted essentially to see a Third Reich in America. If we fast forward to today, we see once again the rise of authoritarianism and fascism across the world with the US Republican Party fully embracing authoritarianism and a cult leader (Trump).

PENELOPE HOUSTON (The Avengers): When we started, we saw this great openness in culture and we wanted to step into that space. We didn't really think, "We're going to be *this* kind of band or *that* kind of band." We just got together and started writing songs and my attitude toward life was where people should be able to speak out and live their own life and not follow a bunch of set rules. I was nineteen years old. I felt like there was a noise to be made. We didn't have any set beliefs that we were trying to put forward that we had talked about or worked out. The lyrics were pretty much all mine and were an expression of who I am and some righteousness that I felt about the world, and how screwed up stuff was. It wasn't studied in any way. It was a pre-expression.

SOCIAL STRUCTURE AND RESPECT

JM: Does anarchism make sense to you?

JOHN LYDON (Sex Pistols): No. Even the words I used with a sense of humor way back then, because I'm aware that you cannot be an anarchist unless there is a society providing the equipment necessary—the roads, the infrastructure, the rucksacks, the Doctor Marten rebel boots, the airplanes to fly you around to go and demonstrate. All of the accoutrements of society you need in order to

CHAPTER 13

complain—and try to drag it down into what? Rubble? I don't want to live in a world of Mad Max! So, there has to be some kind of sense of social structure and respect for each other, and you don't get that achieved at all by turning your back or arming your enemy. And the enemy is, of course, partially yourself.
JM: What do you mean "the enemy is partially yourself"?

"You cannot be an anarchist unless there is a society providing the equipment necessary." Public Image Limited (left to right): Lu Edmonds, John Lydon, Scott Firth, Bruce Smith. © PiL Official Ltd photo: Tomohiro Noritsune

"I AM AN ANARCHIST"

JOHN LYDON: Your own phobias, prejudices, resentments. Your own sense of pressures, spite, and lack of empathy for others. The songs are filled with this! A daily battle in my own head is to sort out what is right and what is wrong. We all need a certain amount of barrier between us, otherwise we get on each other's nerves. The art of the individual is really as an individual. This is my space and stay out of it! And I'll stay out of yours. And out of that common respect, we have civilization.

JM: Anarchism is often associated with punk. Have you been interested in that realm?

STAN LEE (The Dickies): Fighting establishment? Is that what that means? Hate your parents? Hate the government? It's all nonsense. No! Too negative.

BRAD WARNER (*Hardcore Zen*): If anarchism means *get rid of the government,* then that is no good. We are not ready for that as a species. We have to have social controls and, I hate to say it, people with guns to make sure that people will stay in line. It's just a fact and to ignore that is to live in a fantasy world. If that is what anarchism means, then I'm not interested. But if anarchism means you don't accept authority *because* it is authority, then I can understand that.

You have to be moral to live in a world of anarchy. This is one of the discussions we always got into in the punk days when I was in the band Zero Defects. Everybody was saying, "Anarchy!" and spraying letter As with the circle around them everywhere. We all really hated the police, but you really wouldn't want to live in the year 2004, or the year 1982, without police because the rednecks would get us! I wrote in the book how the police saved our punk asses from a bunch of *Deliverance*-type guys that wanted to kill us. If there is ever to be a world where anarchy actually exists, it would have to be a world where everybody is extremely moral and able to take responsibility for their own actions. Real anarchy has to be intensely moral.

TRUE ANARCHIST?

JELLO BIAFRA (Dead Kennedys): I don't know if I'm a true anarchist or not. I'm not even sure what that's supposed to mean. Anarchy defined by The Exploited is different than anarchy defined by Crass, which in turn is very different from anarchy defined by some academics. Let alone whoever may or may not have thrown the Haymarket bomb.

STEVE IGNORANT (Crass / Slice of Life): Anarchism has been really important. And I have to stress that my idea of anarchism is totally different to everyone else's [laugh] in the world! And it's totally different to Penny Rimbaud's idea of

CHAPTER 13

anarchism. I tend not to call myself an anarchist anymore. I'm just an angry sixty-one-year-old man. My anarchism I got because I was never into politics. I called myself Steve Ignorant because I didn't know anything about politics; I was totally ignorant. My sense of anarchism came from black-and-white movies in the '60s which were mostly about injustice. And books I read about loss of innocence.

I never thought I'd be saying this, but I think the aging process does do something to you. At the age of sixty-one (2019) I'm not going to go on another protest march and get locked up. Christ, have I not done that enough? Can someone take over for me? With Crass, we called ourselves anarchists because at the height of our powers, if I can put it that way, we were being courted by the right wing *and* the left wing. To stop all that, we called ourselves anarchists. We weren't political and our politics was the personal politic. *Think for yourself* and *take responsibility* and *respect*. That was incredibly important because going to a Crass show back in the '80s, you were setting yourself up for a good kicking from the skinheads. We attracted the real misfits, even within the punk rock or anarchist movement. Anarchists in those days were incredibly boring, patronizing, stuck-up wankers. I couldn't stand them! I went to two anarchist meetings and I was so fucking bored. Same with anarchist books as well! Put some pictures in it for Christ's sake!

PENNY RIMBAUD (Crass): We operated as libertarian. Libertarian being a very different word to how it's now measured in America. Anarchism is far too organized for my taste. And it never actually manages because it's so organized that the usual ideological battles occur. Libertarian is quite simply, "Where are you in all of this? So, get on with it." I headed very much towards libertarianism. Or Taoism, in the sense of being in deep resonance with one's own consequences.

D. J. BONEBRAKE (X): I realized from being in the scene that the idea of anarchy wouldn't work because people are destroying toilets at their only music club, The Masque (Los Angeles—1970s to '80s). And someone has to play daddy and it was always Brendan Mullen (Masque owner). He was always going, "They broke the toilets!" So, we were supposed to be this tribe, but no one is in charge. It's like this funny experiment that went wrong! [laugh] You could see the difference between the performers and the people who were just hanging out. The performers wanted to go on stage and be able to have the PA work. Whereas someone else might say, "Hey! Anarchy! Let's unplug the PA!" Or, "Let's jump on the drum set." Of course, The Germs were the exception. They went on stage and said, "Hey, we don't have any guitar strings!" Everything would fall apart.

JOHN DOE (X): It's a rite of passage and it represents a lot of freedom to go to a punk show when you're seventeen. It's anarchy in a classic definition: you take care of yourself, there are fewer rules and not as much security. Usually there's not a lot of violence. If there is, maybe somebody gets a black eye or something like that.

CAMILLE ROSE GARCIA (The Real Minx): When I was younger, anarchy used to resonate with me. But when you see how it ends up in real life, it's not a realistic option. When people think about getting rid of the government there's a blank spot in their minds in terms of what they're going to fill it in with. Anarchy is the absence of any order and it's not real pretty in reality. With all the gloom and doom with the state of the world now, a lot of young people don't have a lot of hope for the future and they fall into a well of despair. That is not a viable option either. I'm gloomy and nihilistic, but ultimately, I'm a positive person. I want to be part of something good. Anarchy sounds really good in songs!

JM: Leo Tolstoy said, "Government is violence." I'm curious if anarchism is important to you? Russia of course is famous for some of its anarchists like Peter Kropotkin.

MARIA "MASHA" ALYOKHINA (Pussy Riot): I believe that community is stronger than any government. What we are doing is building community. I was born in the Soviet Union, so I know a lot of bad sides of communism. But bad sides were actually made by people like Stalin, who changed one modern punishment concept to another one. We can have community without controlling and constraining somebody; that's what we are doing. This performance at Cathedral of Christ the Savior was near the metro station called Kropotkin Square, who's named for Peter Kropotkin. So, we have very interesting topography in Moscow!

In our schools there's a cult of normal, which I hated from the very beginning because I don't think that normal is something we should cultivate. Every person is unique. The protest riot is a way to check because every rule has to have a reason. If you're just writing rules and do not have reasons for them, why should they exist? Punk protest is really about that. It's not a protest for the protest. It's a protest for checking the honesty of the rules. I hate hypocrisy. That's why I really hate official politics. They provide plastic life without any honesty.

The Russian name of our show is "Riot School" (in the US: "Revolution"). My whole life I am learning and now at this current political situation, when conservatives are taking a new role, I think we should do cultural revolution. This protest and women's march, especially in United States this year (January 21, 2017), is an independent strong thing. Like Woodstock, for example. Trump? He is just a much lighter reason.

CHAPTER 13

ANARCHO-PUNK

RAMSEY KAANAN (Political Asylum / AK Press / PM Press): Music can be energizing and inspirational and a comfort. Music is very successful at providing all of these things. It's vital for the human condition. Punk rock as a particular genre of music has done all of the above. There is the more political end of punk rock such as the so-called anarcho-punk scene which I grew up with and was a part of in the UK in the late '70s and '80s.

Firstly, as a musical genre punk rock has more elements within it that are explicitly political. The only real parallel would be the folk music revival in the '60s. But that didn't last in the same way punk has lasted. The anarchist politics of punk is the most explicitly political, though aficionados of blues and jazz might argue with me over that one. Secondly, punk has persevered over the generations as an entryway to politics. Hip-hop folks would also argue that it has political elements, which I'm sure is true. In terms of being a gateway into politics, punk has been that consistently for almost forty years. I find that remarkable and very gratifying.

RAMSEY KANAAN: For me politics and punk were really indistinguishable. The things that attracted me to punk rock were politics and anger. I remember in 1979, when I was thirteen, I bought my first Crass T-shirt. I had heard of Crass, but I hadn't heard their music. I bought the T-shirt because it said "Anarchy, Peace and Freedom." Then I thought it was a bit embarrassing to wear the Crass T-shirt without knowing what they sounded like, so I decided to get a Crass record. I wasn't that impressed by the music, but I liked the ideas.

RAMSEY KANAAN: Anarchism is a particular history, set of ideas, and practices. One of the problems that anarchism has is lack of definition. We need to be able to define what anarchism is and what it isn't. What's the difference between an anarchist and a Marxist? An anarchist is a liberal. Part of what I've been doing as a publisher is draw upon and record those histories, ideas, and practices. I've also been inspired by, and published, all kinds of writings which are not anarchist. As someone who wants to make a better world, I'm going to take whatever set of tools and ideas I can. Personally, I think anarchism is one of the best. Since the age of thirteen I've called myself an anarchist. Most of what was articulated by so-called anarchist punk bands had very little to do with actual anarchism. Of course, the grandfathers and grandmothers, in a few cases, of political punk were of course Crass. Actually, The Poison Girls. But their politics had very little to do with anarchism.

WHAT'S THE SITUATIONIST IDEA?

Life Is Elsewhere.

—Situationist slogan written on Paris walls in 1968

Could I be happy with something else? / I need something to fill my time.

—"What We All Want" by Gang of Four (1981)

MARK ANDERSEN (*Dance of Days: Two Decades of Punk in the Nation's Capital*): What's the situationist idea? That we don't want to be simply caught in routine. Life becomes a living death when you're so structured and caught up in the norms of society. That situationist idea was very liberating. You construct your life—your identity—moment by moment. At the same time, people also need stability, a foundation. Sometimes having structures and conformity can, if you choose wisely, give you the foundation to seek freedom and truth more successfully.

GLENN BRANCA (Theoretical Girls): When people started talking about the French situationists, who were anarchists, relative to the Sex Pistols, the band said they had no idea what the hell that was and that they had nothing to do with the situationists. The situationists and anarchist theory were very interesting to me.

ANDY GILL (Gang of Four): Situationism. I do sometimes think it's easy to rewrite it a little bit in retrospect, looking back. In many ways situationism is a branch of pop art with a bit of meaning tagged on. For example, when we did the artwork for *Entertainment!* a lot of it is just about the context. The pictures on the inside I took from the Belgian TV guide and we wrote something that goes with them. Jon (King) found a picture of the cowboy and Indian from a well-known series by German author Karl May. We didn't get it in Britain, but they used to get it in Europe. It's like the European equivalent of the American one with Tonto and the Lone Ranger. The Gang of Four approach to songwriting and lyrics very much mirrors pop art. It's about putting things into a different context and trying to find irony.

JON KING (Gang of Four): I've been hugely interested in situationism since I was seventeen. I thought the critique was really interesting. It seems even *more* interesting to me now: the idea that you are participating in some way as a passive consumer of a spectacle. The world parades in front of you and you consume

CHAPTER 13

it. It becomes your substitute for life. Something that underpinned my lyric writing was the idea of this spectacle.

(Michel) Foucault was all about the fact that if you don't actually act in your own life, then you're powerless to express yourself. I reached around lyrically in that subject area in a number of different ways. "What We All Want" was one of those songs. The character in that song is unable to find a way in which they can participate in their own life. Until you get to that point of clarity, you're doomed really. The song "Return the Gift" was again in the same domain. It was full of quotes from marketing offers. You apply for a subscription to some book club and you get yours-to-keep-free-in-any-case the complete "History of Art Before the Romans" or something like that. And of course, the moment you keep it you're doomed! So, you have to send the gift back. In the song "Why Theory?" I have: "We've all got opinions, where do they come from?" Well, it comes from where you're born. I also enjoyed doing rhymes with exactly the same word. "At home he feels like a tourist" then rhymes with "At home he feels like a tourist." [big laugh]

Bob Dylan in 1964 sang, "You're only a pawn in their game." That was this idea that you are some passive cannon fodder. A later idea was that you're *not* passive! You're an active collaborator in your own misery. That is quite a conundrum. The point of realization is that if you're a collaborator and you're in misery, what do you do? You have to say, "No." And that is quite hard to do. That filled lots of my thinking time. What's it like if you don't say, "No?" The two dominant sets of ideas for me at the time were situationist critique and feminism. It was an offshoot of the new left to recognize that what you do on a daily level is what makes politics.

UTOPIA

> *I would love to see anarchism work. With a country this size you'd have to have a lot of localized structures, networks. I hope for it. I don't want to live in a police state. To a frightening degree I think we do. Look at us, compared to other first world nations and the proportion of our population in prison. Prisons are one of our main growth industries in economic terms. We went from being a military industrial complex to a penal colony as well. Something has to change.*
>
> —Steven Lee Beeber, *The Heebie-Jeebies at CBGB's*

CLIFFORD DINSMORE (Bl'ast): Early punk did have a utopian sense. I definitely did when I was younger. That was expressed in my lyrics, trying to enlighten people to the fact that they could actually live life the way they wanted. Anytime you rely on a government to govern you—as opposed to governing yourselves—you're in trouble and you'll just be herded around like sheep. I have read anarchist stuff. I'm interested in it to a certain extent, but you have to realize that anarchy on a mass scale is exactly what the word implies: sheer chaos. No stop signs! [laugh] There has to be respect towards others and some element of structure and order to the world. But I think we're better off doing that ourselves, as opposed to having other people do that for us.

JM: Without punishing people.

CLIFFORD DINSMORE: Yes. Totally. People need to be schooled in the fact that if they're going to fuck with people on a certain level, then they should be punched in the face. It's just the natural order of the universe. Some people can see through the bullshit and other people need to be slapped in the face. One of the things with Bl'ast was that we felt we were doing that, musically. There was a complete violence to the music. Playing music was a violent outlet as opposed to real physical violence.

JM: Does anarchist philosophy resonate with you?

RAY CAPPO (Shelter / Youth of Today): Why don't you explain to me anarchist philosophy first, and then I'll tell you my opinion.

JM: My understanding of anarchy is self-managed groups based in cooperation and choice rather than coercion and authority.

RAY CAPPO: I'm not sure if that's the definition of anarchy or not. When you define it like that it sounds like utopia. Anarchy to some people means complete lawlessness. I know a lot of people who would use lawlessness to take advantage and dominate people. The way you said it sounds much nicer than the way I've learned it. I'm also open to saying I have no clue what it is.

JM: A lot of people think anarchism is some utopian impossibility.

DICK LUCAS (Subhumans): They possibly think that way because they imagine anarch*ism* must be like all the other *isms* and there must be a certain structure and form with leaders and a hierarchy who do certain things to make anarchy happen. Am I an anarchist? I'm not sure. I don't like this label because I don't know if I'm good enough to be an anarchist.

    I generally avoid the label "anarchist" and would say it is about thinking for yourself. *And* it's about giving a shit about other people. And having your eyes wide open to what is going on around you and considering it to be actually part of your problem. If you don't like what's going on, don't wait for somebody else to change it. It's up to you.

CHAPTER 13

Within a collective, there's nothing wrong with a little bit of leadership. If people are too scared of being leaders, or opposed to being led, no one is going to be able to suggest anything without being accused of forcing it on other people! If somebody's got a good idea, let them lead the idea and join in with it. If you've got your own idea, expect other people to follow you as well. There's a major difference between oppression and a good idea.

JM: The popular image that's developed of anarchism is leaderless chaos.

DICK LUCAS: Right. That's the version that gets put over in the media. It's all bomb-touting people with hoods on. Every time there is a riot with people in balaclavas chucking stuff, they're labeled anarchists. And they might be. But that's the *only* sort of anarchist you're going to see through the media.

HIDE FUJIWARA (Ultra Bidé): Anarchy started more than two hundred years ago in France. It was against having humans be slave workers. That was especially true in America. At the Chicago Haymarket Square, the guy with the bomb used to be working on making the Brooklyn Bridge. Of course, he's the guy with the bomb! He was a slave! He wants to have freedom. We still need freedom.

CORPORATE PUNK ANARCHISM

ADAM NIGH (Craig's Brother): There's a lot I resonate with in anarchy, but at the same time I've been aware since I was an adolescent that there's a danger. Our culture is just screaming that at kids: *think for yourself, drink Sprite, obey your thirst.* There's a lot of marketed anarchism. Anarchism has sort of become corporate. I teach high school kids. They get the less mature idea of anarchism in their head: "Why do I need to listen to what anybody else says?" But let's not reinvent the wheel every generation. Especially where there has been truth, compassion, beauty, and love. As long as I've been a fan of punk rock, I've always seen an imbalance in that side of it. I remember getting into Pennywise when I was in high school and they had a lot of songs like that. *Unknown Road* was one of my favorite albums and there were a couple of songs about "I will make my own rules." I always thought, "That's great." But I could see a lot of self-destruction coming from that if you're not willing to listen to the wisdom of others.

JM: Punk and anarchy were connected in popular media. Some bands become a parody of punk and have used anarchist symbols as a sort of branding tool.

GABRIEL KUHN (*Sober for the Revolution*): The connection between punk and anarchy has been huge. Although it seems like an overstressed cliché, there is no way to overestimate the connection between punk and contemporary anarchism. I've talked to anarchists from a lot of different countries and a huge amount of younger contemporary anarchists have had a direct connection to the punk scene. Some bands have taken anarchist principles very seriously and tried to relate their music and artistic expression to very concrete political activism. There are other bands who've adopted anarchist symbols and slogans as a part of the *punk identity package*. There are differences in the level of commitment. At the same time, I think it's problematic to create too big of a division between *true* punk anarchists and *poser* punk anarchists. It's difficult to say what level of commitment you need to be an anarchist. To be honest, I don't think there's anything wrong with starting with an identity package. You never know where people will go from there.

KIM FOWLEY (Runaways producer): Anarchy is now just another perfume or T-shirt. You have to define rebellion. Maybe rebellion is going into a vegetarian restaurant and asking for a cheeseburger. Or going on an airplane and saying, "I'd like a vegetarian meal please."—"We don't have it. We demand you eat chicken." You can go either way. Anything extreme I'm not interested in. Unless it's sexual. I'm into sexual extreme and clothes extreme. Everything else, moderation and balance.

"FUCK AUTHORITY"

JM: Pennywise has a song called "Fuck Authority" and in one section of your book you write about going to school with one of your daughters and discovering that her teacher knew your band. You were embarrassed when she said, "Isn't that your song playing on KROQ called 'Fuck Authority'?" You write, "How do you reconcile the fuck authority attitude that punk rock has always championed when you're trying to teach your kids to respect authority, especially your own? How can I go out every night and sing that song at the top of my lungs and the next time I tell my six-year-old to quit goofing around and go to bed not expect her to come over and flip me the bird and tell me where to cram it because I'm the man and I've been repressing six-year-olds like her for centuries!"—I'm curious how you've resolved this issue?

JIM LINDBERG (Pennywise / *Punk Rock Dad: No Rules, Just Real Life*): I haven't! I wonder how we'll *ever* answer that question! That's why it's called, "No rules, just real life." There's a lot of rules people will give you about how to be a parent—"Here's the perfect three-step way to raise the perfect child." You realize soon enough that nothing is that easy and every child is different.

It's up to all of us to present some form of authority to our kids without being overbearing. There are some rules that we have to follow that, one, keep us alive and, two, keep us out of dangerous situations or out of jail. Those are the laws that you should probably pass down to your kids to help them go along in life. If you stand up on the table, you can fall off and hurt yourself. If you run out into traffic, you may get run over by a car. That type of authority has to be respected. Police and teachers need to be respected if you want to get ahead in life. And there are certain figures of authority that *aren't worthy of respect,* especially if they're abusing their privilege. When the government doesn't respect our needs as a society, they shouldn't be respected. They should be disrespected. That's what the song is about.

JM: Jim Lindberg with Pennywise sings the song "Fuck Authority" and when he's at home he wants some authority over his daughters.

KLAUS FLOURIDE (Dead Kennedys): The more you try to lay down authority the more you're going to have a rebellious kid. Especially when the kids come around to the age of my kid, fourteen. Basically, it goes back to tribal stuff. At that age in lots of cultures the kids go out on their own. They may have an extended family, but they're considered grown and it's time to leave the home. And it's easier to leave something that you're really angry with than something you're crazy about.

HARMONY—THE BALANCE OF LIFE

LENNY KAYE (Patti Smith Band): It only works if your anarchism is very well in sync with the rest of your band. You can really go wherever you want, but you have to realize that you are playing with other people. Anarchy for its own sake is chaos. Anarchy in the service of everyone, allowing themselves to be free, and placing itself within *harmony,* that's the end result of a band truly playing together. It's all about us learning to live together as human beings. You don't have to have a specific system with its rigorous rules, but then you also have to realize that there are moral precepts because we live in a communal situation, not just one solo object. That's the balance of life.

JENEDA BENALLY (Blackfire / Sihasin): As a traditional Diné person, I am most guided by our traditional philosophies and our natural law. It's about respecting oneself and the community, the environment—respecting everything and living in harmony. We say, "To be in beauty." When we're talking about beauty, it's not a material beauty, but it's being in harmony and balance. Traditionally we never had any governance; the federal government has been forced upon us. We didn't have a tribal chairman or president. We had our own traditional leadership which often times came back to the women, who were our decision makers, our leaders. And when a woman made the decision to end even a relationship, to have a divorce, it was up to her.

CLAYSON BENALLY (Blackfire / Sihasin): As you move towards the concept of anarchy, it's like having natural law. It's not lawlessness. It's working with your environment and community. That's something we've seen within our generation kind of stamped out. Unfortunately, the word anarchist has a negative connotation now. To call someone a punk back in the '70s and '80s also used to be an insult. It would be like saying, "Fuck you." Or to call someone an Indian at that time. All three of those had the same kind of connotation of an insult.

HUGO BURNHAM (Gang of Four): Nobody really understands what true anarchy is, but anarchy has nothing to do with *destroy!* It's not the 1976 punk rock version, which almost everybody thinks anarchy *is*. People think it means lawlessness. But to be without law does not mean to be without responsibility, care, and consideration. *That* is true anarchy.

RUSS RANKIN (Good Riddance): When I was a lot younger, I was all into anarchy. I've met a lot of people over the years who are peripherally involved in the punk movement who were anarchists. They weren't the kind who said, "I'm going to get drunk and throw a rock at that cop car." They were anarchists who started food co-ops in their hometown.

DAVE ALLEN (Gang of Four): This is where I have a bit of a problem with punk rock and anarchism. "Why are you buying the clothes you wear from the top retailers on Oxford Street in London? Are you thinking about the exploitation of labor in Thailand, India, and China, where everything is made really cheaply?" Most likely the punks weren't thinking that.

JM: You've said Buddha was an anarchist. How important is anarchism to you?

JOE CLEMENTS (Fury 66 / The Deathless): Buddha was definitely against the stream, an anarchist. And in a sense, I am too. I never bought into the American dream. Buddha was an anarchist! He was saying, "You don't need to look outside yourself for freedom." People said, "Yeah, fucking right. You're out of your mind!" And he kept going, inviting women and different nationalities; anybody could be part of the sangha (community) in a time when there was a caste system.

FREEDOM AND RESPONSIBILITY

MARK ANDERSEN (*Dance of Days*): It seems to me that if one is serious about anarchy, it is the highest demand you could make of yourself. The same is true of

CHAPTER 13

Christianity. This is the challenge: if we believe that human beings are able to live without "government"—an externally imposed authority that forces us to do certain things—that means not only experiencing the freedom we want, but also the responsibility that we might be less eager to take on. The only kind of anarchy I would support is one that embraces both freedom and responsibility firmly rooted in compassion.

The danger I've seen with a lot of punk anarchism is that it's so much about *me*: "I live my way and fuck you! I live by my rules." That *is* a place in the journey that has reality, meaning, and truth. But if we get stuck there, we're nowhere closer to being revolutionaries. Parts of the anarchist tradition I find very compelling, like mutual aid. I was in an organization years ago—Positive Force—that was almost destroyed by people who were trying to live out what I would consider to be a situationist approach. I guess it always comes down to, *what is it that we're talking about?* What's behind the label?

AMY RAY (Indigo Girls): Anarchism is a good thing that many people don't understand. I feel that it got bastardized into this thing that means chaos. It's really not about that. It's about self-discipline and being accountable to us and the world in a way that's engaged. It's important to look at anarchy as being responsible and accountable rather than this idea that everything is just crazy and chaotic with people breaking things. That's not what people mean when they talk about anarchy in a serious sense.

NORMAN NAWROCKI (Rhythm Activism): I first encountered anarchy at the high school library. I was this fourteen-year-old kid hungry for a book to read. On the shelves was an anthology called *The Anarchists* by Irving Horowitz. A collection of essays by Emma Goldman, Bakunin, Kropotkin, and Proudhon. The kid takes the book home and starts reading. My mom comes to the door and says, "Time to turn the light out." I turn the flashlight on and read under the covers. Get up and go to school and come home and read again. In three nights, I finished this anthology. I thought, "That's it. I'm an anarchist!" All the ideas resonated: freedom, questioning authority and the system we live in, standing up for people around me, and trying to fight for a better world. Nothing's changed since then; I'm still fighting for a better world. Freedom still is one of the things that motivates me as a writer and person. How do we get it? Where did it go? How do we get it back? Things haven't changed; I'm still an anarchist.

LIVING WITHOUT THE RULES

JM: Some of your songs with TSOL reflect an interest in anarchism: "Property Is Theft," "Abolish the Government." How important has anarchism been to you?

JACK GRISHAM (TSOL): The more I read about it, the more I realized how unattainable of a goal anarchy is. The trouble with anarchism is that it's an amount of responsibility that we're not capable of achieving. A lot of these kids don't understand that. They're ready to throw anarchy on their jacket and they have no idea what they're talking about. It was the same thing with me, with a lot of those songs. I liked the idea of no one having control of me, but I didn't like the idea of having to do the work myself. [laugh] It's like, "Hey, fuck the government," however I'm not willing to pick up a shovel. Now, I consider myself more of a socialist.

JM: Have you identified with anarchist philosophy?

JAMES WILLIAMSON (Iggy & The Stooges): No, not at all. In fact, before I got in the band, they were very, very tight with the MC5, John Sinclair, and The White Panthers. But even then, the band was apolitical. When I was in ninth grade, I marched on Washington, but I didn't have a strong sense of politics. It seemed like the right thing to do. The band, before I was in it in the very beginning, was called The Psychedelic Stooges. They did very bizarre theater. They would play oil drums and vacuum cleaners. Nothing even remotely to do with politics, although if you were alive at that time I don't know if you could separate yourself from political events. If anything, it might have been a predecessor to industrial music in that it had to do with the Detroit automaker environment that we lived in.

JM: Your 1994 *Symphony #8* has a movement called "Spiritual Anarchy." Does anarchist philosophy resonate with you?

GLENN BRANCA (Theoretical Girls): I consider myself an anarchist in the philosophical sense. Not in the bomb-throwing sense of the turn-of-the-century anarchist. I found a great writer named Peter Lamborn Wilson (Hakim Bey). "Spiritual Anarchy" wasn't the name of one of his books, but I got that term from him. In fact, I think I dedicated the piece to him.

EXENE CERVENKA (X): I'm not an anarchist. I'm not a communist. I'm not any of those things. If I believed in any of those things, I couldn't be spiritual. I have to be a completely open-minded free spirit. I don't get caught up in political movements.

14

"TO HELL WITH POVERTY"
CAPITALISM AND CLASS IN PUNK ROCK

It's time to make some money / It's time to get rich quick / It's the wonderful world of capitalism.

—"Demolition" by The Kinks (1973)

I hear this year's Vans Warped Tour is "going green!" / I guess they heard that money grows on trees / Hope they ship all those shitty bands overseas / like they did those factories.

—"Rock for Sustainable Capitalism" by Propagandhi

I'm so tired of hearing you whine / About the revolution / bringing down the rich / When was the last time you dug a ditch, baby!

—"Capitalism" by Oingo Boingo

One day old and I'm living on credit.

—"Capital (It Fails Us Now)" by Gang of Four

You and those gringo bosses / you're always talking profits and losses / Capitalism is cannibalism.

—"Chock Full of Shit" by MDC (1987)

CHAPTER 14

It's a war on the we that wanna stay free / They're looking back to slavery / They want the world down on its knees / Well we been there already and fuck that.

—"Trump Song" (2016) by Dick Lucas (Subhumans)

Economic and political disparity between the haves and have-nots is often hidden from popular analysis, although it's in plain view. Managers/workers, owners/consumers, teachers/students, pop star/audience, masters and slaves. Punk music has toyed with the Robin Hood archetype of stealing from the rich and giving to the poor, often with a dark sense of humor. "Punk in the Supermarket" by Adam and The Ants (1978) features a mellow acoustic guitar and Adam singing in his lilting style, "There's a punk in the supermarket / and she's carrying a waterbasket / and she's putting lots of food in it / and a big box of shreddies / There's a punk in the supermarket / and she's got a little chain through her tit / and she doesn't seem to mind it / and a packet of digestives." Here are additional punk song titles that point to themes of anti-capitalism and class struggle:

> The Dils, "Class War" (1978) and "I Hate the Rich" (1982):
> "They should dig the ditch."
> The Clash, "Lost in the Supermarket" (1979):
> "I can no longer shop happily."
> Dead Kennedys, "Kill the Poor" (1980):
> "Unsightly slums gone up in flashing light."
> The English Beat, "The Limits We Set" (1981):
> "Shoplifting, shoplifting, shoplifting."
> Gang of Four, "Capital (It Fails Us Now)" (1982):
> "They say, 'We're bankrupt.'"
> Crass, "It's the Greatest Working-Class Rip-Off" (1982):
> "They box us up and sit pretty."
> Billy Bragg, "To Have and To Have Not" (1983):
> "There's only a future for the chosen few."
> Gang of Four, "To Hell with Poverty" (1984):
> "Some are insane and they're in charge!"
> The Smiths, "Shoplifters of the World Unite" (1987 single):
> "Unite and take over."
> The Business, "Do a Runner" (1988):
> "'Cause Mr. Bank Manager's a nice ol' man."

The Slits, "Shoplifting" (1977): "Babylonian won't lose much."
Green Day, "Shoplifter" (2004):
"It's not considered stealing / Unless you're getting caught."
The Clash, "Bankrobber" (1980): "Some is rich and some is poor."
The Coup, "I Love Boosters" (2006):
"The stores make money off of very low wages."
Fifteen, "Landlord" (2000):
"Why is it that you own seven homes and I own none?"
TSOL, "Property Is Theft" (1991): "Money runs the world."
Gang of Four, "Cheeseburger" (1981):
"No classes in the U.S.A., improve yourself, the choice is yours."

LAND OF "OPPORTUNITY"

JM: There is the idea in this country that if you work hard enough, you'll have whatever you want. And if you are not successful, you haven't made enough effort.

GREG GRAFFIN (Bad Religion): Right. That's just all part of the poison. We are taught that in the land of opportunity it's somehow your fault if you don't succeed. The truth is that all of the people whom we admire for their success had completely different conditions and sets of events that led to their success. So, if we measure ourselves on those terms, it's really futile. We each have a completely different set of events and experiences leading up to our present moment. This would mean that all the CEOs, celebrities, all the important money managers, and all of the people we think of as the most successful, they would have to admit, freely and openly, that they were *lucky*! That they just happened to have a more favorable set of circumstances than those who were not in their position.

JUSTIN SANE (Anti-Flag): The greatest myth is that capitalism keeps order and everyone who works profits. Then you realize there's all these homeless people. "All those people are lazy or something," according to them.

REVEREND BILLY TALEN (The Church of Stop Shopping): We have a system that controls us on a level that competes with Roman Catholicism in the 1400s. Consumerism is all the more powerful because it pretends that it is freedom. It advertises itself as American democracy.

MARK HOSLER (Negativland): One of the systemic problems in our country is that we've created a political and economic system that rewards you, and you get to the top of the heap, the more you're willing to make choices that are sociopathic, psychopathic, and cruel. You don't succeed if you make choices that are humane, fair, and just—in fact, the choices that Jesus would've made, if you do a careful reading of the New Testament. We've got a system where quite literally the people who are in charge are mentally ill. They're drawn to black-and-white thinking, fundamentalist thinking, and hierarchies.

STEVEN LEE BEEBER (*The Heebie-Jeebies at CBGB's*): I teach a course on making monsters. One of the things I'm going to be talking about is zombies. Zombies are our ultimate monster now and they're speeding up all the time. It used to be that they were slow and they'd get you no matter what because there were so many of them. Now they're turbo charged. I think a lot of that has to do with capitalism. They're literal manifestations of dog-eat-dog and these people who feed on others with a compulsion and are kind of brain dead. There's actually some evidence that the original zombie stories came out of early practices in South Africa with the colonial powers. What we need is a punk revolution at the very least. Probably more! I don't want people going into the streets shooting other people, but some major change.

SYMPTOMS OF WANT

JM: The Good Riddance EP *Phenomenon of Craving* has an image on the cover of a guy who I used to see around Santa Cruz (California). The man later froze to death, sleeping in a park.

RUSS RANKIN (Good Riddance): I got that title out of a book about the disease of alcoholism. It described the medical diagnosis of why somebody who's got drug addiction or alcoholism does what they do. A normal person takes a drink and they're cool with it. An alcoholic takes a drink and they develop the phenomenon of craving where they can't stop. It could also be used to describe the *symptoms of want* for people who are less fortunate in our town, country, or the world. It's a world with so much excess and resources and there is such a massive underclass, especially here in America. To find a guy who is indigent like that puts a face to the whole thing. A lot of people said, "I know that guy. I see him around." He'd crack people up. He walked around the Pacific Garden Mall and yelled at bushes! The fact is that he was a messed-up dude. He'd fallen through the cracks.

We can spend $95 million a week on an illegal war, but we can't afford to make healthcare a right instead of a privilege in this country. That's a shame. And when I see people like that, I'm not a person who can look the other way and ignore it. It hurts my heart to know that we are the richest country in the world and then see people falling between the cracks and dying left and right without much public outrage.

Our bass player Chuck (Platt) was the person who approached him about the picture. Fortunately, Jim was in a lucid moment. They talked about it for a while and we gave him some money and some food. For about a year after that record came out, he'd always go into Streetlight Records where Mario works—who is our T-shirt guy and had been our roadie forever—and Jimmy would ask how many records he'd sold. And if anyone was talking about "his" band. He was pretty stoked on it. It's sad that people still die outside because they have nowhere to sleep and no roof over their head. In a country that's able to spend so much money on other things that maybe aren't quite as important.

CRUSHED BY CAPITALISM: SELLING OUT?

JON LANGFORD (The Mekons): I don't know how successful punk has been as a revolutionary force. It was a moment in time where everything seemed possible and it passed very quickly and we crashed head-on into the mechanics of the music business. I totally believed in the idea that you didn't have to play that well to make music exciting. We were art students, and at the same time there were a lot of heavy metal bands speeding up their music and getting their trousers taken in and playing speeded-up heavy metal. That's punk rock!

The music industry, while at first completely confused by punk, got the lid on again pretty tight, quite quickly. But the thing was moving and evolving. The music industry wanted to identify something and then sell it. Particularly in the provinces of England outside of London, people were making stuff that was not really that commercial: very experimental and very political. It was stuff that was really hard to commodify and make it have a broad appeal.

We were a part of that, but we got sucked up in the major label thing. We thought we could change the beast from the inside. We were quite naïve and optimistic at the same time and we fell afoul of that. Punk rock isn't a postcard of a kid with a Mohican standing in front of Houses of Parliament. It was a moment in time where we said everything must be questioned, anything is possible, and you don't have to follow the rules. You can have a band and it can be people who can't play. You can do whatever you want and it's valid.

JM: How did that experiment go, with getting inside the major record label to make things more egalitarian from the inside?

JON LANGFORD: We were crushed by capitalism. It's as simple as that, really. The band didn't survive the first encounter with the major labels. We didn't

CHAPTER 14

understand what we were doing. We basically said we wanted control. As my friend Kevin (Lycett) says so eloquently in The Mekons documentary, "You gave them absolutely no reason whatsoever to promote or support us in any way" (*Revenge of the Mekons*, 2013). Once the accountants got involved and saw what was going on, it was over. So, we were one album—swoosh—and we were gone. It was devastating for us as people. It was a total failure. It took a while for us to recover, but for some reason we did! What's kept the band going across all the years has been camaraderie and social grouping.

CHUCK D (Public Enemy / Prophets of Rage): There's been a lot of money made off the roads we've paved and I'm at peace with that. Like I said, "I don't count 'em, I just make 'em." I'm not going to fool you and tell you how I'm going to go off on some Kurt Cobain guilt trip either. I make music and I have a whole bunch of people that surround me and they actually make a living doing this. I do think that *making a living* is what this thing could be about. Not *making a killing*, which wipes out the cultural ecosystem of it all. I'm a firm believer that you're not going to stop people who say, "I want to get into the music business because I want to get rich." You're not going to stop that. But we can at least put our own conditions onto it. I'm twenty years in. The temptation's to, what? Be more famous than I've been? I could be more *infamous*. Or somebody wants to make me a star and put me in a bunch of movies? I'm usually hardheaded when it comes down to somebody else giving me an itinerary, so if it hasn't happened yet, it probably won't happen.

JACK GRISHAM (TSOL): The trouble is the minute something gets popular people want to capitalize on it. I don't know what's really going to make people wake up. I'm a big fan of civil disobedience. I just read *The Kingdom of God Is Within You* (Leo Tolstoy, 1894). I love it. It's just great. I think we need a class war in the United States, actually.

RAMSEY KANAAN (Political Asylum / AK Press / PM Press): If The Clash argued that they had to play stadium shows to feed their kids, well, is that selling out to the man? No more than any other job is selling out to the man. We have to put it in that context. We want to encourage people to do what they can using whatever platform they have for positive reasons.

I was recently in Sweden and friends there told me the two main songwriters in ABBA, the two men, are both down to earth and donate loads of money to Sweden's Feminist Party (Feminist Initiative). I think that's fantastic. Neither are revolutionary anarchists, but when high-profile folks do genuinely radical things with what they have it's wonderful.

It's weird that we put certain workers on pedestals and then criticize them for not being perfect. I say "certain" workers because I'm referring to workers involved in cultural production like actors and musicians. For some reason those people are held to an impossibly high standard by everyone else and that includes within the radical underground counterculture spheres where they're put under the microscope for any action or nonaction, so to speak. But let's not forget that under this capitalist system that we work in, they are workers! They may or may not be paid and may or may not be professional.

MARJANE SATRAPI (*Persepolis*): Now a band makes music and it's on YouTube and people "like" it or they don't "like" it. You have to sound good and be very well produced. "Oh, you have more than 200,000 views," and they start giving you money. Everything goes into this economic system very quick before even knowing what you want to say. They become a slave to how much people "like" them. Then how rebellious can you be, really? Who gives a fuck if people like me or not? I don't care personally.

CAMILLE ROSE GARCIA (*Tragic Kingdom* / The Real Minx): The title *Soft Machine* (William Burroughs's 1961 novel) I've always loved because I think that's what the capitalist machine really is! It lulls you to sleep and tucks you into a nice comfy bed and you're sort of being enslaved the whole time, but you don't mind because you're so comfortable. Capitalism in America is like that: as long as everyone is comfortable no one wants to know about the horrible substructure that supports their lifestyle.

The capitalist machine that extracts everything from nature and turns it into a commodity—they'll never be able to extract that thing that is the soul in everything. But they're certainly going to try. So how do you remember that? For me, what I have to do is be in nature. Growing up in LA I was in the city most of the time. I recently moved to the redwood coast in Northern California and I'm looking at a river right now. I might start wearing tie dye! Anything could happen!

CORPORATIONS ARE PEOPLE

EAST BAY RAY (Dead Kennedys): Here in the United States corporations are considered people by the Supreme Court. They're *not* people! They're like a psychopath. And they're giving corporations more and more power. That's what the corporations are designed for: to get more power. Who's going to stop them? The market? Bullshit! People don't understand that to have a free market you need regulations.

Imagine two thousand years ago and you brought in some cotton and were trading it for gold pieces. How did you know it was gold? They used to put the government's stamp on it: "Yes it's gold." Or if you're trading olive oil for stuff, the con guys would have olive oil that's crap and disrupt the market. So, they'd come in, "Okay, these people are good olive oil sellers," and they have to approve you before you could sell oil in our "free market." Otherwise, *free market* would just be a rip off. People would just be stealing from everybody else. The reason it never lasted is because it's unsustainable. If you steal from a farmer off his farm, he's not going to grow food, is he?

We have a market setup where if you steal food from a market, a sheriff comes out and arrests you. Same thing with private property; it's socialized, isn't it? We have a court system, a sheriff, the county clerk, and property boundaries. So, you don't have to hire guards. The sheriff's your guard for your property. Socialism. Socialized private property. Crazy, isn't it?

JM: It's an interesting combination. I think people would probably say that within capitalism some people's property is protected better than other people's property.

EAST BAY RAY: That's true. But the theory behind the court system and property deeds is basically that private property is supported and socialized by taxes. If you took away all of that system, how would you define your property? What right do you have to property—a piece of earth—anyway?

G-7 WELCOMING COMMITTEE RECORDS

> *Conventional wisdom would have one believe that it is insane to resist this, the mightiest of empires ... but what history really shows is that TODAY'S EMPIRE IS TOMORROW'S ASHES, that nothing lasts forever, and that to not resist is to acquiesce in your own oppression. The greatest form of sanity that anyone can exercise is to resist that force that is trying to repress, oppress, and fight down the human spirit.*
>
> —Mumia Abu Jamal's notes for Propagandhi album
> *Today's Empires, Tomorrow's Ashes*

JM: I've read that your record label G-7 Welcoming Committee Records uses a *participatory economics* structure. Tell me how you learned about this structure and how it functions.

CHRIS HANNAH (Propagandhi): There is a collectively organized bookstore and café in Winnipeg that started in 1995 called the Mondragon Café and the people who started the place were very familiar with Robin Hahnel and Michael Albert's writings on Parecon—Participatory Economics. We were interested in a collectively run record label and we saw what the Mondragon was doing. They had a statement of principles and they had a constitution. We thought, "Wow, where is this all coming from? How are they collectively arriving at this?" They said they'd been inspired by the Parecon model and we took a look at it and said, "Yes, this really resonates with us." It's a values-based system rather than a profit-based system. It's not a rulebook. There is not a Parecon book that you get from Michael Albert and you run your business based on it; it's a set of values that resonated with us and makes a lot of sense. He speaks of it in terms of not just businesses, but in terms of how interconnected societies may actually operate. You can check it out at www.parecon.org.

"NOTHING WRONG WITH CAPITALISM"

DANNY ELFMAN (Oingo Boingo): Oingo Boingo started as a ska band and became a pop band. I'll never claim to have any punk cred because I considered that to be a young man's domain. But the attitude was everywhere. Everything I wrote in that era was intended to annoy people. It was meant to be irritating. Even in Paris last week (September 2019) people were asking me about lyrics to Oingo Boingo songs. They asked about "Only a Lad" and was I really right wing? I told them, "Don't you understand? The thing all of these songs have in common is their sole reason for existing: to annoy people." I was out to annoy everybody! What in the world was I trying to say in the song "Little Girls"? I said, "Look at the lyrics. It's about a disgusting, vapid man who wants a girlfriend that doesn't question him. He wants a dumb girlfriend because he's a dumb older guy. It's about that."

"Only a Lad" is about a right-wing attitude towards juvenile delinquents. I wrote it taking the perspective of that character. In "Nothing Wrong with Capitalism" I sing, "Middle-class socialist brat." That was criticizing middle-class socialist brats. But the point is that I *was* a middle-class socialist brat! [laugh] I grew up in a far-left liberal Jewish family. I was out to irritate everybody! And that's exactly what I did.

MILES COPELAND (I.R.S. Records): Sting said to me, "You can't go on TV saying anything nice about capitalism because that will label me as a capitalist and I don't want to have that label. I'm gonna fire you if you do the show." Then it just so happened that the TV presenters came when Sting was staying with me in my house and they presented the reason why they thought I should speak.

CHAPTER 14

And Sting turned around and said, "Well, I don't have to agree with what you say, but I'll fight for your right to say it." And then I did the show. Needless to say, when Sting and I parted ways, he was worth half a billion dollars. So, I don't think one could say that he and any other successful rock star were really all about *not* making any money at all. He gave a lot of money to charity, and he's done charitable things, as do a lot of rock stars and movie stars. But do they live in shit houses? No!

KLAUS FLOURIDE (Dead Kennedys): Things are awful bleak looking for the next hundred years down the road. It's driven by corporate greed. Finally, people are getting slapped in the face with it enough and they're realizing that their best interests aren't being looked after by their great leaders and protectors. They realize they have to do some of their own work on it. The whole work ethic—that you have to work hard to earn something—doesn't seem to creep into their minds that you have to work hard to make the planet not dissolve, also.

Now people are starting to realize that they're going to have to give up some stuff in order to have their children and grandchildren have a decent place to live. Let alone the fact that there's already masses of places on the earth where people are already dying by the millions that would be considered, by any standards in the '40s, a holocaust. It's caused by warlords and people who are not controlled by governments but by greed and/or corporate power and sometimes by fundamentalist religious thinking.

ANTONINO D'AMBROSIO (*Let Fury Have the Hour: Joe Strummer, Punk, and the Movement that Shook the World*): In some ways punk has been very effective. In some ways, it hasn't. There's beautiful moments throughout the history of punk that offer models for us to think about the system differently, and how to change it. The challenge that makes it ineffective sometimes is that we're sitting within capitalism.

JELLO BIAFRA (Dead Kennedys / Guantanamo School of Medicine): I guess I'm closer to being a socialist more than anything else. (Tim) Yohannan of Maximum Rocknroll, in better years when we were very close, did tell me that he was a socialist and not an anarchist because he felt we did need a government entity to transfer the wealth from people who have too much to those that don't have enough. And I agree with that. I'm all for socialized medicine, transportation, and I think a maximum wage is a great idea and everything else goes down for the public good. Originally, I thought—cut it at $100,000. Now I compromised—cut it at one million. What do you need a second million dollars for after you've made your first? You could live off that forever! "Oh, look how much money I made! I win! I've got to win, therefore somebody else has to lose." Instead of having crack addicts we have wealth addicts!

I think even Trump's monster children or the Cheneys could do good if they were put in rehab for their wealth addiction long enough via a maximum wage. What would we get in return? Free education for all, all the way to law or medical school. Free transport, including air travel. Our infrastructure would be in a lot better shape, as would our parks and everything else. Maybe even subsidizing someone who has good ideas for art or invention. People say, "We don't want people to be on welfare. They should get a job." Well, maybe if they're on welfare they'll have the time and where-with-all to create a *bunch* of jobs. We could be losing our next Steve Jobs or our next Kurt Cobain simply because they can't get welfare so they can concentrate on what they really want to do. I say, "Fine! Give welfare to anybody that wants it!"

KLAUS FLOURIDE (Dead Kennedys): It'd be really powerful if everybody, not just stockholders, got to vote for who runs the multinational corporations. And for who is in charge of decisions that Exxon makes, for example. I understand why people are angry at the government and, yes, it is fucked up. But Google and Facebook invade your privacy willy-nilly. They have these monopoly oligarchies. They're filthy rich. It's like the robber baron days of the 1890s. You know Google's slogan? "Don't Be Evil." How *1984* can you get? It's a con job. It isn't going to be government-run fascism. It's going to be corporate-run fascism. Kind of like East Germany, in a way. At this time there is a greed thing. It drives everything. It's all about wanting more and more. The top 2 or 3 percent own most of the wealth of the world.

JON KING (Gang of Four): I'm white bourgeois, so it's quite hard to stop being like that. Not that I honestly want to stop being like that, but it's hard to not automatically think like that. You can find certain ways to liberate yourself from your social class. There is a sort of grimness about some of the things we do when you're just trying to make the best for yourself. In Europe, when the Nazis occupied places like France, Belgium, and Holland, they were all a bunch of collaborators. And yet, you may wonder, what would it have been like if *you* were under some fascist regime which told you what to think and how to behave? What would *you* have been like? Well, the majority of people just try and get by. Actually, we do live in countries like that at the moment—I'm talking about Iraq, where there's this terrible debacle, tremendous shambles, and shocking pointless waste of young men and women's lives, whether they are Americans or Iraqis. It's like a machine that's chewing people up. That has made me think a lot.

CHAPTER 14

Jon King smashes a microwave oven, as usual, while performing "He'd Send in the Army" with Gang of Four (San Francisco, 2021). Photo: John Malkin

PETER CASE (The Nerves): I remember when communism fell in East Berlin, when the wall came down. I was talking to my friend Martin Rowe over in England and I said, "They wiped out communism," and he said, "One down and one to go." *Capitalism*. We took out the one big economic system and we have this other one left. It's just as fucking evil. Capitalism is a complete failure! The whole idea that capitalism works is a joke. There's got to be a third way. That is where some spiritual third way would work. Hopefully the third way isn't world fascism! [laugh] It seems like that's also possible. We're right on a precipice.

I don't know where music fits into all of this except that: people like me that sing, we're down here way underneath the radar singing for these little groups of people. Which is part of trying to maintain an emotional environment on some level of change and hope. And some form of revolution. You're trying to create an atmosphere with music where that kind of change could be thought about, discussed, and activated. Every once in a while, you see the things that we've been working on jump into the mainstream for a second. My friend says, "It's the second bird that gets the worm." It was Nirvana that made it big, not Black Flag or The Nerves.

JUSTIN SANE (Anti-Flag): Anarchism is certainly possible. You see it in all kinds of communities all over the world. In my own state of Pennsylvania, we've got Amish communities where it's really all for one. All reap the rewards of their work, and the community takes care of those who can't take care of themselves. The priorities are much different: people are concerned about taking care of one another. Unfortunately, a lot of society is rooted in this idea of capitalism where you're looking out for number one first and if it produces something good for someone else, well that's nice, but it's not a priority. Anti-Flag is a band that's been singing about questioning your government and not trusting your government.

JON KING (Gang of Four): I was just in Africa and these Masai guys I visited, it was absolutely life-changing for me. To see these people that don't use money, they don't have any property. They live in a place where there's no buildings, signs, communications. There's nothing. It's an area the size of Texas and there's not a single brick building. It is quite interesting. Their life is about acting within their environment. Without a colonialist mentality about it. It was really thrilling to see that as a possibility in this world of us all observing things going by and staring at screens.

DAVE WAKELING (The English Beat): Unfortunately, because punk was built on a slightly unstable foundation—it wasn't a genuinely working-class movement, but a middle-class artistic movement that had spread to the working class—it fairly quickly degenerated. Just like hippies. Hippies started off as spiritual beings and ended up as junkies. The same happened with punks. Three or four years later somebody who might have had an occasional line of speed was now sitting at home fixing heroin and that was that. You could see the difference between the people who moved on and the people who got stuck. Any of those little movements tend to decay and if you hang around a bit too long, then it always ends up the same: people cooking heroin in silver paper boats. They can all end up that way, if it becomes hedonistic.

"WHITE RIOT"
RACE AND ANTI-RACISM IN PUNK

White pride, you're an American /
I'm gonna hide anywhere I can.

—"White Minority" by Black Flag

Black people gotta lot a problems / but they don't mind
throwing a brick / White people go to school /
where they teach you how to be thick.

—"White Riot" by The Clash

Punks and n*ggers are almost the same thing. . . . When I
come to America I'm going straight to the ghetto.

—John Lydon in *Rolling Stone*, October 20, 1977
(quoted by Paul Gilroy in *White Riot:*
Punk Rock and the Politics of Race)

We're white! Strong and Free! / White supremacy!

—"White American Youth" by White American Youth

I'm sorry for something that I didn't do / Lynched somebody
but I don't know who / You blame me for slavery /
A hundred years before I was born.

—"Guilty of Being White" by Minor Threat

CHAPTER 15

Punk is rap for white people.

—Kim Fowley (Runaways producer)

JAMES SPOONER (director of *Afro-Punk*, author of *The High Desert: Black. Punk. Nowhere*): When I first got into punk rock, I was thirteen and living in Southern California, in the desert. I got into it because I was into skateboarding, and they went hand in hand at the time. I lived in Apple Valley, which is near Barstow. It is blatantly racist there in the way that you can't deny when people are yelling "nigger" at you out the car window. The punk scene was not really different. Most of my friends were the few punks of color because most of the white punks had no issue with wearing swastikas. Even if they didn't really believe that stuff, it was just the norm.

That was my introduction to punk, and I definitely had a lot of hatred toward myself because I just wanted to fit in like everybody else. Luckily about a year and a half later, my mom decided it would be much better to live in New York, where I was born. Just to have more variety of people. We moved to New York, and I ended up going to the High School for the Performing Arts. It was easy to find all kinds of people of various backgrounds who were interested in the stuff that I was interested in musically.

But I wasn't feeling the New York scene so much. Forget race; the kind of violence that was going down in New York hardcore at the time was really reminiscent of gang culture. I found myself searching for other things. Eventually I found the DIY, hardcore, straight edge scene in Jersey, Pennsylvania, Boston, and Connecticut. My mom was pretty relaxed with me. Friday after school I'd be out and come home Sunday night, going to these different places.

In that punk scene I found my DIY culture and the politics—all the things that to this day I still believe in. But it was a very white, suburban, privileged set of kids that I was hanging out with. In pretty much every state, that was the norm. You'd go to these shows in rich kids' basements. Again, I started to feel alienated. Not because they were racist, but because they were privileged. I didn't necessarily have that vocabulary then, but they would never come to New York to stay with me. When I was living on my own, my place was too dirty for them. This kind of stuff was really based in their white suburban privilege. I stuck with it for a few years.

When I was twenty or twenty-one, I moved to Seattle. The all-ages scene sucked at the time. I dropped out. Nobody from the hardcore scene knew me there. I was able to reinvent myself. I hung out with a different set and tried to acclimate myself to what I then considered mainstream, which was people who listened to bands who had *barcodes* on their records. Then I moved back to New York. I got into the dirty underground rock and roll scene and was a party promoter. When I was twenty-two, I started questioning what I was doing and who I was hanging out with. I started questioning my identity. I took a step back from myself and realized: though I had friends of color, I didn't really have any Black friends. That was a problem for me.

JAMES SPOONER: After taking a trip to San Lucia (Caribbean) where my family's from, I realized how much I didn't know about myself and where I'd come from. All I knew was the *punk rock* me. I started thinking about punk rock and how it raised me, and how, despite being totally devoted to it, it didn't really take care of me in regard to my racial identity. I wanted to do a critique of it. That's where *Afro-Punk* the movie came in. That started getting me more involved in the scene again. I got to know some of the newer bands and some of the kids who were running things. It took about two years to make the film.

As I started showing the film, I started meeting more and more kids. It became apparent that it would be possible to have a scene something like the Latino hardcore scene. I remember going to a Los Crudos show in Arizona in '94. I was one of five not-Mexican kids there. It blew me away! I thought, "I wonder if this would be possible for Black people?" Not because I wanted to separate people, but because I wanted to feel the things that I knew they were feeling as a community, being together. When I first started putting together shows and inviting Black kids, I realized the reason that there are so few Black

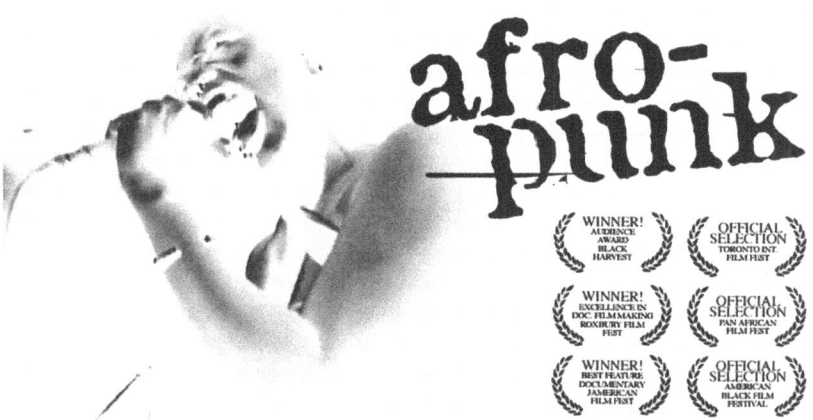

Afro-Punk *movie by James Spooner: "In that punk scene I found my DIY culture and politics—all the things that to this day I still believe in."* Contributed: James Spooner

CHAPTER 15

kids at shows is simply because they're not invited. I started inviting them and all of a sudden, we're having shows and there's three hundred Black kids in the crowd and twenty white kids. That was amazing!

JAMES SPOONER: I pretty much credit every amazing American music movement to Black poverty. You can name any American music, and at its roots are Black people needing to be able to speak to one another in a language that only they understand. The moment that outsiders start to understand it, and other outsiders realize they can make money off of it, then it starts to slip away. It takes a couple decades, but eventually it looks nothing like what it started like. It has no connection to its origins and a new language begins to form. For several years now I've been waiting to see what that new language will be.

I saw this movie made in 1955 called *The Cry of Jazz*. They were talking about how there will be a new sound in jazz. Everybody in the film was saying, "That's crazy! Jazz is amazing. It's the biggest selling thing there is! How could there be a *new* sound? What could come after jazz?" They couldn't *possibly* think there could be anything after jazz. I feel to a large degree that's where we're at now. Hip-hop's got nothing to do with Black people anymore. Black people love it all over the country and all over the world, but it's got nothing to do with that original intent of speaking to one another in a special language.

JM: Your film *Afro-Punk* opens with a dedication: "This film is dedicated to every Black kid who has ever been called a nigger and every white kid who thinks they know what that means." How revolutionary has punk rock been in terms of transcending race and class?

JAMES SPOONER: As far as punk being revolutionary, in certain ways it is. It's influenced me for a lifetime. I still live DIY in as much of life as I can. I'm still vegan. I still care about the same things that I did back in the day. It would be unrealistic and short-sighted to think that the kids who are part of the scene are exempt from the socializing that they came up in. It became very clear to me when I was sixteen that the straight edge kids that I hung out with that came from really rich families were mini versions of their Republican parents. They were more apt to be on one side of a pro-life debate. These kids never had to deal with these issues.

Whereas when politics came up in the hardcore scene in New York City, it was a lot different. Being a kid from Brooklyn, I was always having to fight to even be part of a scene like this, constantly having to be checked by your family on your identity. It's a completely different reality. Just because we listen to the same bands and we want to talk about "You stabbed me in the back" and that kind of junk, that doesn't exempt you from privilege. Punk rock has a lot of privilege. Shit, we're a bunch of kids who can go on tour and not think about bills at home and anything. Just getting to the next gig because we don't have any responsibilities. At sixteen you don't have to get a job to help pay the rent. That's a reality for a lot of people, but not for a lot of people in the punk scene.

WHITE, WHITE, WHITE

> *Since its beginnings, punk musicians have directly confronted ideas of whiteness and have wrestled with America's white supremacist history. And although the punk scene is less white than it has ever been, punk is still considered one of the whitest styles of music.*
>
> —Evan Rapport, *Damaged: Musicality and Race in Early American Punk* (2020)

> *That's right motherfucker /
> we're that spic band /
> You say you call yourself a punk /
> Bullshit! /
> You're just a closet fucking Nazi.*
>
> —"We're that Spic Band" by Los Crudos

CHRIS FRANTZ (Talking Heads / Tom Tom Club): Especially in the hardcore punk scene, but even in our punk scene, there was a good degree of racism. It wasn't necessarily overt. No one was talking about Black music unless it was Jimi Hendrix. Even the punks could admire Jimi Hendrix. But nobody was talking about James Brown, The Temptations, or Aretha Franklin. It was all white, white, white. I remember the first time we invited a reggae band to be our opening band at CBGB and people walked out on the reggae band. They went out on the street and smoked cigarettes. It was not cool. The whole racism thing became more blatant with hardcore punk, with the exception of the Bad Brains. But they were an exception to the rule.

LISA FANCHER (Frontier Records): Except for bands like Pure Hell, punk was a white person's thing. The OC thing was also kid's rebelling against their parents and the wealthiness. Perhaps you didn't get the grunginess of the Hollywood punks. (Orange County is a wealthy, right-wing suburb of Los Angeles.)

KIM FOWLEY (The Runaways producer): Punk is rap for white people. It's rebellious music, the way music used to be. White suburban mobs need to protest against restrictions, censorship, and complacency. White people in America, or people who think white, need some sort of edge to propel them and possibly punk music fits the bill.

LENNY KAYE (Patti Smith Group): With our song "Rock and Roll Nigger" we try to reclaim the word "nigger" as a positive place within society, beyond its racial connotations even. It was the principles of rock that we believed in, which was something really common enough that anybody could play it. You could reach out and touch the instrument, learn those three chords and be there. That sense of immediacy and quick understanding. We wanted to short-circuit certain elements within music that were getting a little too weighty, toppling under their own weight.

JM: There's a Propagandhi song, "Resisting Tyrannical Governments," where you sing about the sense of privilege you have *and* that it doesn't stop you from taking action in the world.

CHRIS HANNAH (Propagandhi): It really shouldn't. You should try to be engaged however you can. And people shouldn't feel guilty about what they were born into. They should leverage what they have and do what they can, instead of pretending they weren't born into privilege, which is very common in the punk scene: people pretending they don't have access to things.

RUSS RANKIN (Good Riddance): I've never believed in having pride for something you had absolutely nothing to do with. There are people who say they're proud to be white when it was just a genetic crapshoot. If someone raised four kids and put themself through college and achieved things that were maybe above their abilities, that is something a person can take pride in. But to happen to be born a certain color or in a certain country and have chest-beating pride about it is really self-serving and narrow.

DAVE DICTOR (Millions of Dead Cops): MDC was in Texas at the time. There were farmworkers being murdered and there were famous pictures of Ku Klux Klan people dressed in Klan outfits sitting in police cars. This was quite difficult. We were angry about that and a lot of songs expressed that.

PETER CASE (The Nerves): We were opposed to the Vietnam War, racism, and any kind of authority that tried to control youth. I was really political.

NOAH LEVINE (*Dharma Punx* / The Deathless): Buddhism and punk are both about the desire for happiness, freedom, and seeing the truth about life. As a kid I saw the truth about life. I was in a lot of pain and there was suffering everywhere: inequality and oppression, war and racism. Capitalist-driven media crap. I just knew that happiness couldn't come from that.

PENELOPE HOUSTON (The Avengers): I wasn't going to stand for any sexism or racism or homophobia in anybody that was around me.

JELLO BIAFRA (Dead Kennedys): I didn't like the racism. I didn't like what Dirk Dirksen (The Mabuhay Club) called the "wolf pack mentality." I wondered, especially at the Fleetwood in LA, where the real thugs looked to be a little bit older, how much of this was the work of undercover cops? And so out came "Nazi Punks Fuck Off." It wasn't directly aimed at neo-Nazis; there were so few of them in the scene and around the country in general, let alone ones who were open about it. But the main focus was, "No! You people are beating the crap out of other people on the dance floor. Stage diving so you can punch somebody in the back of the head and then run away before they can go after you; that's chicken shit jock violence. You're acting like a bunch of fucking Nazis!"

JM: Punk rock has largely been a white movement. Bad Brains stood out as a band of young Black men. What's been your experience being Black in this mostly white rock 'n' roll scene?

H. R. (Bad Brains): What we've learned is that within our hearts and minds everyone has a soul, and in that soul there's what we would call their inner spirit. And there is a heart that beats. We're dealing with the wisdom time now. You've got to remember that when we're talking in wisdom time, it does get a bit idealistic and it's a joy. We're not doing it for the money, but our generosity. Nevertheless, what it brings to us is an upliftment of spirit. One of our influences years ago was the ever-so-popular Mahavishnu, who was a fine guitar player. His new music is a little different than his earlier compositions. His earlier compositions were a great inspiration. Also, Kitaro, Stevie Wonder, and the ever-so-popular Earth, Wind and Fire.

D. H. PELIGRO (Dead Kennedys): DEATH is an all-Black sort of punk band way before The Bad Brains, right around the time of the MC5. But the name DEATH wasn't so kosher back then and they didn't get a whole lot of airplay.

CHICANO PUNK

JM: How important is it that your Chicano/Latino heritage is recognized?

KID CONGO POWERS (The Gun Club / The Cramps / Pink Monkey Birds): Oh, it's incredibly important. This is something I didn't think a lot about in my younger years. But it was always there. Actually, when I say that I didn't think about it, I mean that I didn't use it as a platform in my younger years. Jeffrey Lee Pierce is a Chicano as well, from The Gun Club. We always spoke about this and identified with Mexican American culture. We always spoke about our families and Cholos and Cholas at school and we talked about the music of the lowrider community. That was very influential to us. They loved "the oldies," as we

CHAPTER 15

called them. They were into Jimi Hendrix, Black Sabbath, and Santana, mixing psychedelic music with Latin culture. Jeffrey and I hardly ever talked about it in an interview, but it was definitely important for us.

As an older person, I became aware that a lot of Chicano people were very proud of the fact that I was a Chicano in these bands. I don't take it lightly. I think back to my sisters in the '60s, loving Thee Midniters and being so proud there was this local Chicano band from Whittier that had a hit record. Latin music has always been there and I've been influenced by it all along. I take great pride in that. Chicano culture was very important and I'm still very much in touch with Alice Bag and my Chicano contemporaries, and we let people know that our stories are the stories of weird immigrants and that it can be a beautiful thing. If it doesn't destroy you.

One of the reasons I wrote a book was for younger people to know that there is a Chicano musician out there who went his own way, for better or worse, and ended up for better in the end. That's my story today. A lot of my problems and the things that held me back, my own self-deprecations, came from the fact that I did always feel like a second-class citizen and an outsider. I was Chicano, immigrant family, queer man, weird artist, punk rocker. It was like, how far away can you be from white, mainstream, American Anglo culture? That led to childhood trauma and demons and the only way I could figure how to quell them was to take drugs and numb myself out until that didn't work anymore.

JM: Tell me about leaving heroin behind and finding a new path.

KID CONGO POWERS: If you're lucky, you realize that doesn't work. That's not the answer. I started out with drugs wanting to experience everything, and I ended up experiencing nothing except numbness. I realized, after many years, "Here I am, staring at the abyss." I had lost all passion about music and art. Luckily, I came to a point where I got a glimpse of that, and it scared me. I thought, "I don't even know who I am anymore. I used to be exploring the world and on a search for inspiration, hope and music."

Part of my writing this book was for Chicano culture, queer culture, weirdo culture, and self-starters, untrained musicians, and people with a passion for life. I was writing my truth. I started writing it in 2006 and it now comes out in 2022. It was a bunch of tiny stories that we weaved together. The book is about a fan who bumbled their way into musicianship. Luckily, I had an aptitude and appetite for it. Writing the book also showed me how incredibly single-minded I was from a youngest age about pursuing music. I didn't need to look to another subject; I always knew that music, film, and the arts is where I'm going take it.

H.R. with Bad Brains (Santa Cruz, California; 2010). Photo: Matt Fitt

WHITE SUPREMACIST COUNTRY

> *I am an Islamist, I am the antichrist . . . the Feds had bugged my red toy phone / So I devised a plan for heads to roll.*
>
> —"Sharia Law in the USA" by The Kominas, from 2008 album *Wild Nights in Guantanamo Bay*

MICHAEL MUHAMMAD KNIGHT (*The Taqwacores*): Punk is supposed to be about freedom, but there's people that get very authoritarian about what being free means! There's something very white about that, in the sense of claiming a universality from this very privileged place and imposing that on other people. So, if you say there is a punk position regarding religion, *can punks be religious or not?* That ends up being informed by race as much as it is by religion because certain people are making these pronouncements.

I've done film screenings and book readings, and I've encountered the same dude with a million different faces. This white guy who stands up in the crowd and says, "You can't be punk *and* religious." And he's a white guy who has never dealt with race and has never experienced the intersection of race and religious identity. In other words, he has no idea how being Muslim in a white

CHAPTER 15

supremacist country plays out. You can be Muslim and that's a statement about the government and the media and every aspect of living in this country (US). It's always this white dude saying, "Punk is all about rebelling against religious authority and Islam is all about oppressing people." That's not how it plays in the United States of America. In the US, Islam is more punk than punk. All these white dudes can put long-sleeve shirts on and you don't know what they got on their skin. It's a lot harder being a brown Muslim woman than being a white punk dude in this country. The hijab is more dangerous than those things people put in their ears now that I don't even know what they're called. "Oh, you have a big disc in your ear! You're fine at the airport." Know what I mean?
JM: Have you been contacted or surveilled by the US government because you're Muslim?
MICHAEL MUHAMMAD KNIGHT: I know there's a file on me. I've tried to get it and haven't been successful, in terms of Freedom of Information. I've had problems at the border when I try to re-enter the country. I get detained every time. I'd written a letter to John Walker Lindh in 2003 and in 2009 they're asking me about that at the border during a six-hour hold. They had to actually wake up the local FBI agent because I was trying to cross the border at four in the morning. This guy had to wake up, get dressed, and come over. A lot of it is because I have a publishing record. I've tried to cross the border with the wrong kind of books and that becomes a problem. Your basic pamphlet-type stuff from the mosque, not anything crazy. It's always at the border when it happens, for me.
JM: Taqwacore bands tend to be very political, but I don't hear many other bands singing about Abu Ghraib and US torture, for example. Jello Biafra's current band name refers to this: Guantanamo School of Medicine.
MICHAEL MUHAMMAD KNIGHT: It's something I was really thankful for with the Taqwacore kids. There are blind spots that whiteness and white privilege create. I have my blind spots. I came to Islam through Malcolm X and Public Enemy. But Islam became an internal religious thing for me. Taqwacore, as I envisioned it, was a religious project. It was kids who had no place for themselves at the mosque or they felt alienated from what you'd call "organized religion," but they still clung to it in some way.

I had the experience of being a white convert and I wrote about my emotional disillusionment with religion and then I'm just back to being a white guy. I'm no longer paying a price for being Muslim if I stop wearing the hat. So, my relationship to Islam was different than The Kominas's. Maybe religion wasn't the top priority for them, but they still paid a price for being Muslim in the world, whatever their internal condition.

"WHITE RIOT"

CLAYSON BENALLY (Blackfire): Here in America, there is so much racism. Going to schools, I ended up getting branded in the locker room from racism by people that don't respect Indigenous cultures or viewpoints. They tell you to keep your views and identity on the reservation. That's part of the reason I identified with punk rock. I was a social outcast and misfit, just to have long hair and my cultural identity and have my hair up in the traditional Navajo way with the hair in a bun: *tsiiyéél*. I was different. I needed to find the group that respected and valued me as an individual. Naturally, that's where punk rock came in.

JM: You just said that at school you were branded. You don't mean physically?

CLAYSON BENALLY: I was held down in the locker room and they took a lighter and held it upside down until it was nice and hot and then held it to my stomach and they branded me. I still have the scar. I carry that with me.

FROM "WHITE RIOT" TO "NEVER BEEN IN A RIOT"

> *An' everybody's doing just what they're told to /*
> *An' nobody wants to go to jail!*
>
> —"White Riot" by The Clash

JM: Joe Strummer said about the DIY ethic, "Do it yourself, but not *for* yourself. Do it for others."

DAVE WAKELING (The English Beat): That's nice. He was probably doing that interview in the CBS office in London, I imagine. My feelings about punk are a bit controversial, really. As a working class myself I tended to get a little bit irritated by it. Although punk, in England at least, tried to express itself as some sort of spontaneous uprising of the working-class, of course it wasn't. It was instigated by an artistic Bohemian upper-middle-class that could afford to travel between London and New York. They caught what was going on in New York and brought some elements of that back.

I did have a conversation with Joe Strummer about it. I said, "It's all right to want to have a riot of your own. Because once your street is all burned you can go and live at your dad's house in the country, can't you? But when the streets in Hemsworth burn down, guess what? There's no shops where I live. So, it's not so glorious having a riot of your own, really."

I was a little bit concerned that there was this sort of nomenclature that was pretending to be the driving force behind a working-class revolution. Paul Weller was more of the grit and grist. He actually believed that the working-class

CHAPTER 15

would rise up! [laugh] I was like, "They're in the pub, Paul! They're not rising up—certainly not until after eleven o'clock!" So, I did have odd feelings about punk. During post-punk, as it were, Two Tone and them sort of things, we tried to redress the balance of that a little bit. We were more taken by the notions of The Buzzcocks and The Undertones rather than upper-class politicizing of the working class's plight in England. It concerned me just in its political application. Because of that punk never really gained full traction. It just became another fad. "Time to take the pins out of your ears now and wear your mom's clothes—it's time to be a new romantic!" It didn't get the social traction it might of because of that way it started. That was my feeling, which I think is a bit controversial.

JM: The song "White Riot" by The Clash was made in solidarity with Black people fighting oppression but was later used by white supremacists.

RED SAUNDERS (Rock Against Racism co-organizer): People misconstrued that. In the National Front newspaper called *Bulldog* they just took it and didn't have a fucking clue what The Clash were! There's a photograph of The Clash picketing with their placards outside the headquarters of the fascist National Front with Steel Pulse, the reggae band. That was the ultimate and before the big RAR Carnival. It was brilliant. This is the band that played, "White riot / I want a riot of my own." Jimmy Pursey and Sham 69 went on to use the song a lot and it got even more confusing because half of Jimmy Pursey's fans were British Movement and the NF, a bit like the Ku Klux Klan. They're skinheads and they supported Sham 69.

JON LANGFORD (The Mekons): I know what The Clash were trying to do with the song "White Riot." But it was the *way* that song was used. Politically it was quite extreme up in Leeds (1977). It was a long way from London and there was a very dark, longstanding core of racism and racist street politics with kids who identified themselves as Nazis. There were anti-Asian and anti–West Indian youth. With that song The Clash were pledging solidarity with West Indian youth around a specific historical event, the riots at the Notting Hill Carnival (West London, August 30, 1976) where police attacked West Indian youth. The Clash witnessed that and wrote the song "White Riot" saying that white youth should be doing the same thing. But by the time it got up to Leeds it had become an anthem for extreme right-wing kids.

As punk came up, these right-wing kids even had bands. People like Sid Vicious and Siouxsie and the Banshees were wearing swastikas in London to shock. Up in the north of England that became more of a call to action for some elements. And we were pinko-lefties and got very much the sharp end of that. We hated "White Riot" as a song and we wrote "Never Been in a Riot" because it was a description of what it was like to be a middle-class white kid. But having said that, by the time we'd written and recorded the song and started doing some gigs we ended up in loads of riots! Because our gigs became flashpoints for political violence.

CHRISTIAN PICCIOLINI (*White American Youth: My Descent into America's Most Violent Hate Movement—And How I Got Out*): The Clash was always my dirty little secret while I was in the (white supremacist) movement. They are my favorite band of all time. I loved them before I was recruited and I never gave them up, despite them being a leftist band. I knew they were leftists and I understood the song "White Riot" was not in support of white supremacy, rather it was an anti-racist song. I didn't let it bother me.

STEVEN BLUSH (*American Hardcore*): I was an exchange student during high school and went to England in 1978. I saw The Clash before they came to America. The whole thing was political. I saw Rock Against Racism. If you see the film *Rude Boy* when they do "White Riot" with Jimmy Pursey of Sham 69, I was right there. It was totally life-changing kind of stuff. I saw Gang of Four's first tour before the record came out. I came back to the suburbs of America and my friends were working on their cars, listening to Deep Purple.

JOE CORRÉ (Burn Punk London): Later on, punk played a major role in helping to fight racism. There was the whole Rock Against Racism with The Slits and those bands. I remember as a kid growing up in South London where previously I'd had to fight all the Black guys in the neighborhood because they hated punk rock. And suddenly they understood, we were on the same side! That was a really good moment for me because it made my life a hell of a lot easier. Certainly, punk was instrumental in bringing that united front against racism here in the UK.

ARI UP (The Slits): The Slits are multicultural. We're ageless. Many ages and many cultures, put it all together, throw it in one bucket, and open your mind to everything. Just be open-minded. People haven't fully learned this yet.

DAVE WAKELING (The English Beat): All the outcasts joined up together in England. Barbarella's Club in Birmingham was the only place where punks, rastas, and travelers—whatever they were called then—it was the only place you could go and everybody became friends. That huge bond between reggae and punk was, "Oh, we're in the same boat, aren't we?" That was good, even though the musical styles are quite different. They complemented each other in terms of social circumstances. Our idea of The Beat was to get elements of both types of music in the same three-minute song. We wanted to get the energy and vibrancy of punk and the soothing sway of the reggae. On a good day we managed it.

CHAPTER 15

JON KING (Gang of Four): A mounted cop smacked me across the mouth with a big truncheon at a demonstration against the British fascist movement—the British National Party—with their union jacks and all of that stuff. A bunch of hooligans went along shouting and all got clubbed down. It was a bit painful at the time and some people got quite badly hurt. But it's quite good to get through the other side of that and you get bragging rights.

ROCK AGAINST RACISM

RED SAUNDERS: We were Rock Against *Racism*. Racism was the heart of the campaign, but it was a cultural campaign. At its heart it was using culture to fight racism, which is unusual in the mainstream in this country. When Clapton let out his diatribe about Enoch Powell (August 1976), it was so shocking for this blues-god-legend to be bigging up the biggest racist in contemporary British society. A real white supremacist, old British empire colonialist. He's what we'd call here, back in the day, a kind of League of Empires Loyalist who had that real old attitude. For Clapton to be bigging him up was quite extraordinary.

It was the very beginnings of the punk movement. I wrote the letter that started RAR in the summer of '76 at a time when all these punk bands were forming. And at the same time the British reggae movement—as opposed to the Jamaican or Caribbean reggae movement—was moving to its own confidence and setting up its own bands rather than just importing Jamaican music to play at Jamaican Sound Systems. There was confidence among young British reggae artists. These two things—punk and reggae—coincided. There was a very good West Indian DJ called Don Letts. Don was playing reggae music in the early punk clubs and Don had a good relationship not so much with The Pistols but really with The Clash. He introduced all these bands. He was the real beginning of instigating this cultural thing that was about to explode by playing reggae music at the Roxy Club and these early punk get-togethers.

RED SAUNDERS: When we started RAR the key thing for us was to use music and culture in the fight against racism. To bring white and Black bands together on stage was the number-one thing. RAR had a very simple one-paragraph manifesto which basically said, "We want now music, we want rebel music. We want music that breaks down people's fear of one another." That was the key. We wanted to bring together Black and white bands to pioneer this idea, to break down this fear that was being played upon so successfully by the racist political party, which was called the National Front in the UK at that time. They'd have respectable people going around and knocking on doors, but then they'd have proper fascist street thugs who would attack Blacks, anti-racists, and socialist organizations and people selling left-wing newspapers. When the Front got the third-largest vote in London in 1976, it was terrifying. They got more votes than a party here called the Liberals, or the Liberal Democrats now. Suddenly you have this fascist organization getting over 150,000 votes in London. That mixed with Clapton is why I wrote the letter.

The letter that sparked Rock Against Racism was penned by Red Saunders et al. in 1976 and addressed to the UK music press:

> When I read about Eric Clapton's Birmingham concert when he urged support for Enoch Powell, I nearly puked. What's going on, Eric? You've got a touch of brain damage. So you're going to stand for MP and you think we're being colonized by black people. Come on . . . you've been taking too much of that *Daily Express* stuff, you know you can't handle it. Own up. Half your music is black. You're rock music's biggest colonist. You're a good musician but where would you be without the blues and R&B? You've got to fight the racist poison, otherwise you degenerate into the sewer with the rats and all the money men who ripped off rock culture with their chequebooks and plastic crap. Rock was and still can be a real progressive culture, not a package mail-order stick-on nightmare of mediocre garbage. We want to organise a rank-and-file movement against the racist poison in rock music—we urge support—all those interested please write to:
>
> ROCK AGAINST RACISM,
> Box M, 8 Cotton Gardens, London E2 8DN
>
> P. S. "Who shot the Sheriff," Eric? It sure as hell wasn't you!
>
> Signed: Peter Bruno, Angela Follett, Red Saunders, Jo Wreford, Dave Courts, Roger Huddle, Mike Stadler, et al.

RED SAUNDERS (RAR): The most extraordinary thing happened the other day. (May 2019) I had a parcel come through the post and I opened up this book that's just been published, *Letters that Changed the World*. In it is Karl Marx's letter to Abraham Lincoln congratulating him on the fight against slavery. Albert Einstein's argument with somebody. Letters by Paul Robeson and Mandela, Gandhi's letter to Galbraith. All these incredible letters and there on page fifty-nine is Red Saunders's et al. letter about Rock Against Racism. Letters that changed the world! Rock Against Racism changed so much in this country. What would've happened without RAR?

RED SAUNDERS (Rock Against Racism): When I look back, I understand now why RAR was successful. When I wrote the letter, it attracted a lot of friends who wrote in and said, "I'd like to join Rock Against Racism." It's kind of like making a big soup. After I'd written the letter and people responded, we set up a punky ad hoc committee and we used to meet in my big old studio in a wonderful part of London called Soho. The people who gravitated towards what we were doing were people in their late twenties and early thirties. I was in my thirties. They had all been influenced by hippie ideology: everything from Ginsberg to Dylan, The Lost Poets to Fela Kuti to African drummers and Zen Buddhism and fucking macrobiotic diets! We'd been through all of that stuff! We all loved all the great American hippie bands and had records of the Grateful Dead. At the same time, many of us had moved into radical left-wing politics and the Campaign for Nuclear Disarmament, what we called Ban the Bomb here, and radical economic campaigning, anti-imperialism, and against apartheid and Zimbabwe.

We were part of the underground and the anti-establishment so when it came to doing RAR, this tight little group of journalists, writers, agit-prop theater people, musicians, poets, agitators, academics, intellectuals were at the center of the start of RAR. It was no big deal to put on our first gig (RAR). We did the big carnival in Victoria Park with a hundred thousand people and it was half shambolic but half amazing (April 30, 1978). We had no money; we had nothing. We just had massive anti-racist energy. And sheer bravado and a background in these things I'm talking about. So, we were confident: "Fuck it, we'll do this big gig. Something will work out." We had the experience to take on the powers that be. That is the root of why RAR worked: we were prepared to bring our anti-racist energy onto the front boiler with our culture. And because we'd had a bit of experience with poetry readings in smoky rooms and industrial avant-garde music. Our theater group performed in occupied factories to workers on their lunch break. We performed in mental institutions. Just like the San Francisco groups who we got to know, like the Mexican grape pickers theater groups, who we met in France. It doesn't come out of nowhere; there had to be some kind of confidence to do this.

16

"EQUAL BUT DIFFERENT"
GENDER AND FEMINISM IN PUNK

Some people think little girls should be seen and not heard / But I think "Oh bondage, up yours!"

—"Oh Bondage Up Yours" by X-Ray Spex (1978)

You paid for dinner / She ate dessert / Those tender kisses they made you hurt / But no, no, no, means no!

—"No Means No" by Alice Bag (2016)

You're equal but different / it's obvious.

—"It's Obvious" by Au Pairs

GIRL IN A BAND

RIKKI VANDERPOL (Dying for It): I don't mind being called a woman singer or being described as a woman-fronted band. I'm proud to be a woman in punk rock. A lot of people have been fighting for equality and feminism within punk rock, and there's still so much to be done. We're in a time now because of the Trump administration and #MeToo with women speaking out about sexual assault (2018). It's a revolutionary time to be a woman in a punk band. I have to speak about feminism because there aren't many women in the scene. I want to be impactful.

CHAPTER 16

In San Diego I had a girl in her twenties come up to me, and she said it was the first show she'd ever been to and she was blown away to see a girl in a band! I thought that was really cool because I had that experience when I was thirteen. I bring as much feminism as I can to the scene and hope other women that have the platform are doing the same. I'm also fine if they're not because while we're fighting for women to be treated equally, not everyone has to be the stand-out feminist. I want it to be cool for women to be in the scene doing it the way she wants to do it.

When I was in the band Dance for Destruction, we played in Grass Valley (California) and I was wearing a dress. I wore skirts and dresses all the time. But this one time we were performing and a guy decided to stick his hand up my skirt and grab my pussy, basically. I was about eighteen at the time and my first reaction was, "I'm going to kick this guy in the fucking face!" But it happened mid-song and I was so shocked that I didn't do anything! Luckily, I had some friends in the crowd that saw what happened and they dragged this guy out and beat the shit out of him. It's still crazy for me to think, "Someone assaulted me while I was on stage." This guy thought it would be okay in a crowd full of people. That's the only time I had to deal with something that extreme.

MICHELLE CRUZ GONZALES (Spitboy): We want to put out our message: we are women singing about women's and other political issues and we want to be accessible to women. We'd go to Krishnacopy in Berkeley and make lyric sheets for every show. On tours we'd make a ton before we left and pass out lyric sheets so the message wasn't lost over the loud music. We played all-ages shows and tried to keep the door prices low.

JOHNETTE NAPOLITANO (Concrete Blonde): Punk was a free-for-all: grab something and play. It was great for girls because all hell was breaking loose. No one could tell you that you couldn't do it. You just did it. Rock and roll by default is androgynous; those labels don't apply like they do in the straight world. Bi boys? Bi girls? Hardcore biker dykes? Seems those lines are so blurry, I haven't noticed them in a while.

THE SLITS

> *Typical girls get upset too quickly . . . can't control themselves.*
>
> —"Typical Girls" by The Slits

ARI UP (The Slits): Women had a little window in punk to express themselves. It's sort of been shifted to something else; it's twisted and diluted and turned upside down. It's been perverted.

NADYA OSTROFF (The Slits / The Home Office): The whole thing about The Slits being women: they just got together with friends. They *were* the revolution! There were women who played music before The Slits, but they tended to be typecast into this ethereal, gentle goddess type playing acoustic guitar. There was Joan Jett and Suzi Quatro and great female musicians, but they just get written out. Even the riot grrrl movement got written out. Every time you think there's a push for women to be written as they appeared in history, they get written out.

JM: Tell me about The Slits and women in music. It can look like the rock and roll world has always been dominated by men and yet there's been a lot of important women.

JOHN LYDON (Sex Pistols / PiL): It was one of the most brilliant aspects of early punk. Girls could go on stage and be the equals of any man. It was most excellent to see girls just holding their own and, in many cases, be even better. And coming up with a complete wonderful world from a feminine point of view. Not *feminist*. The two things are very seriously different. It is like earning your wings rather than demanding them. Very excellent—loved those great girl bands. The Slits were fantastic. Poly Styrene and all of these wonderful people!

RECLAIM THE NIGHT

JON LANGFORD (The Mekons): A lot of our songs early on were quite chest beating. We had songs called "Fight the Cuts" and "Reclaim the Night" and all these left-wing slogans. (The Reclaim the Night movement in Leeds, England, began in 1977 to oppose violence against women.) We were very interested in employment issues, feminism, and anti-racist causes. We supported trade unions and firemen, who were on strike when the band first started, so we did a benefit for firemen. We went on to the coal mining issues. I'm not sure it was like that for everyone. It was just fun, drugs, and rock 'n' roll for a lot of bands probably. But for The Mekons these issues were important. Gang of Four definitely set about trying to create pop rock songs that were really exciting that embraced serious Marxist criticism of culture and society. It was a heavy time and ambitious. It was just the nature of being art students up in Leeds at the time, and the political climate in the country. It was inevitably a rebellious thing to be a punk rocker.

CHAPTER 16

ANDY GILL (Gang of Four): I found this little booklet that was from second-wave feminism written by men about how *not* to be sexist. The booklet was called "Why Theory?"—I nicked the song name from there. The nice thing about "What you think changes how you act"—it's such an obvious kind of thing to say, but I think it's quite big. In the context of the song, it gains momentum and meaning.

JM: I hear some of your lyrics pointing to a woman's perspective: "I Love a Man in a Uniform," "It's Her Factory," and "FMUSA." How important has feminism been for the band?

ANDY GILL: I think lots of women get quite irritated by a bunch of guys deciding to pontificate on their behalf. I'd be very distressed if anybody thought of us as prescribing ways that you *should* and *shouldn't* behave. "This is what you *should* do if you want to be a right-on guy." It is so much *not* about that. A lot of it is looking at the way we act ourselves. Why is it that we act in macho ways like dickheads in certain circumstances and other times you manage to transcend those things?

DAVE ALLEN (Gang of Four): The punk rock audience is very tribal and very male. The ability to bring feminism into the discussion lyrically was important. I always saw it as, *we have a lot of guys in our audience.* Some go to a rock concert to be stupid: spitting and fighting. Sort of what Andrew was just saying; guys are complete dicks. I think we're addressing that at least in a song like "It's Her Factory." I always had this idea that it put you in your place for a minute: "Have a think about that and then we'll get right back to you. Here's some music you can thrash around to." It was definitely a solid great idea to do it.

> *The family's head gives orders / In the end, what he says goes / This system's well-constructed / She owes him all she gets.*
>
> —"He'd Send in the Army" by Gang of Four

ANDY GILL: There was no politics to speak of in the first punk rock. The next bit came along when X-Ray Spex, Gang of Four, The Raincoats, and The Slits started to explore ideas. Obviously, there were things like Rock Against Racism in Britain, which was a huge movement. As you got into the beginning of the '80s, the country was very polarized politically and became more so. Something like Gang of Four was, in quite a cold, dispassionate way, trying to record what we saw around us, how economics played into that. We were very interested in talking about how things were *not* in a natural state of affairs. Hence the song "Naturals Not in It." We were interested in human constructs. That was key to us, which is sort of a feminist idea. It's where Marxism and feminism intersect: the understanding that the way we do things isn't because they were god-given or they're natural. They are constructs that we have built up over time, as civilizations do.

SUPER MASCULINE AND GENDER BALANCE

DARIUS KOSKI (Swingin' Utters): Punk is super masculine and tough guy. There's lots of bands that aren't introspective, like Black Flag. I love Black Flag. They're one of my all-time favorite punk bands. And they're pretty macho tough. Nothing wrong with that.

MITA SCHAMAL (Namenlos): Why were so few women in punk bands? Simply because we've been living in patriarchy for quite some time. Why are so few women in governments? Even at Woodstock there were fewer women on stage.

THURSTON MOORE (Sonic Youth): Punk rock has gone through phases of being gender imbalanced where it's like a boys' club. But then you have this whole resurgence of women in the scene creating riot grrrl. In New York City before riot grrrl, punk rock was completely gender balanced to the point you didn't even think about gender. The strongest players for me were the women on the scene: Debbie Harry, Patti Smith, Lydia Lunch. The same was true in the UK with The Slits: as strong as anything The Clash and The Pistols were doing. The Raincoats. I think it was a little problematic in the early '80s with hardcore and Black Flag, Minor Threat, and Dead Kennedys being at the center. It was like, where's the female voices?

LEFT MIDWAY THROUGH A (BLACK FLAG) SHOW

RON REYES (Black Flag): I firmly believe we could've been singing about unicorns, purple pussycats, and rocket ships from space and it wouldn't have mattered. They still would've gone agro. It just didn't resonate with me. So, I literally left midway through a show. We were up there playing our asses off and I see people punching each other out and girls that were getting hurt. I love having fun and I love the idea of going crazy and slam dancing—I love that! But there's a point where some people ruin it. There seemed to be a lot of that.

All of a sudden punk was very black and white. The politics, dogma, and the boxes and lines that were drawn became very black and white. A lot of fabulous

Lydia Lunch (Teenage Jesus & The Jerks). Photo: Beth B (1991)

eccentric things that those early bands were known for was lost. The poetry of X, for instance. A lot of it got trampled underfoot. quite literally. In punk we sort of did have *Lord of the Flies* with these little kids running the ship. What happens when you have a day care without any supervision? It's going to be bat shit fucking crazy!

JM: You were talking about anger and how women are generally taught to "point the knife inward" while men are taught to "point it outward." There were reports last year (2014) that the first women have graduated from the US Army Rangers School. Some people herald this as a step forward for women. I don't see it as a victory for feminism to have women in combat roles in the military.

LYDIA LUNCH (Teenage Jesus & The Jerks): The same with gays in the military. I thought they were smarter than that! The same with gay people wanting to be married. I understand that they want rights, but I thought they were smarter than that. Why would they want a false tradition like marriage and why should gays want to be in the military? It's a losing battle forever and you come out and you can't get a sandwich out of the VA. I don't think it's a good thing unless all women are armed, which is what I've promoted for years. I don't think it's a good step at all to promote a male ideal of homicidal colonization.

LISA FANCHER (Frontier Records): I don't think people were that super aware of me being a woman and label owner. I didn't have any amazing sexist experiences. I think I need to make one up because everyone wants me to have had one! I *will* say that at first The Circle Jerks said, "No *girl* is putting our record out!" But they obviously reversed themselves because I *did* put the record out!

CHRIS FRANTZ (Talking Heads): There were some pretty amazing women. Patti Smith, the high priestess of punk. Debbie (Harry) and Tina (Weymouth) and Chrissie Hynde. They weren't really punk, but The Runaways from Los Angeles. One of my favorites was The Slits with Ari Up and guitarist Viv Albertine. And Poly Styrene (X-Ray Spex). We played a few shows with The Adverts, who had a song called "Looking Through Gary Gilmour's Eyes," and they had a female bass player, Gaye Advert. Later in New York there were people like Lydia Lunch and out on the West Coast there was the band X with Exene (Cervenka).

JM: The Go-Go's website says, "Before the Go-Go's there were other all-female bands, but there was usually a seedy, cigar-chomping guy lurking just behind the curtain pulling the strings, like Phil Spector, Kim Fowley, Sonny Bono." How difficult was it to control what you were doing?

BELINDA CARLISLE (The Go-Go's / The Germs): It wasn't that difficult, to be honest. We started out as a girls' club—we had female roadies, female management. Kim Fowley would come to our shows and lurk in the background and we thought, "Ewww. Gross." For any man like that to come around us, we wouldn't have it! The Go-Go's as an entity is really sort of overwhelming and it's a force to be reckoned with! No man ever could come around and take control of the band because we would never have it! Only because we had a clear vision of what we were about. We weren't feminists, but we wanted to be true to ourselves, and back then it was all about not selling out. Of course, when The Go-Go's started being successful people said we were selling out. But from the beginning we were clear that we were a pop band. We just couldn't really play our instruments at the beginning! Our influences were The Clash and The Buzzcocks. We liked more melodic punk.

THE RUNAWAYS

LISA FANCHER (Frontier Records): I never worked with Kim (Fowley) professionally at all, but we hung out. Kim Fowley and Greg Shaw's dream was for a real all-female rock band. There was an ad in *Bomp* and they were trying to look for an all-girl rock band and they couldn't come up with anything. That's when Kim Fowley decided to create The Runaways himself. He really took a shine to me for some reason. I was there from its inception when the band started rehearsing. This was pre–Cherie Currie. This was with Micki Steele, who went on to be in The Bangles. I saw them play in all kinds of weird places and rehearsals. I wound up writing a cover story for *Bomp* about the whole Runaways debacle. A bit of it got used for their liner notes, which was pretty neat. I was in high school when that came out (1976) and I got The Runaways to play my high school, so that was pretty cool.

Kim (Fowley) and I had a friendly rivalry. I did some really funny interviews with him where we'd be on totally opposite sides of the fence screaming at each other through the whole thing! That man has no filters! I was a teenager living with my parents. It was '76 and I was like, "Kim, you can't call me at two o'clock in the morning because my parents think that means someone died!" And he'd go, "Uh-huh," and do it anyway. He just wanted to talk to somebody at two o'clock in the morning because he was awake. He got up that early and when the sun would come up, he would go to bed, like a vampire. I always got a kick out of him.

LISA FANCHER: Speaking of sexism, Micki Steele played bass and was the lead singer. But Mercury wouldn't sign The Runaways because they wanted a blonde to front the band. Kim (Fowley) kicked out Micki unceremoniously and told her to hit the road. And they got Cherie (Currie). She is like the most normal person on the entire planet! Joan (Jett) is the real thing, totally rocking, and Lita (Ford) is the real thing, a rocker chick with a Camaro, the whole bit. Cherie was just so normal, but she fit the bill. It was sort of like casting an actress to be the singer. It worked out okay. But The Runaways were as unauthentic as the Sex Pistols. It doesn't hurt my enjoyment of The Runaways.

RIOT GRRRL

SARA MARCUS (*Girls to the Front: The True Story of the Riot Grrrl Revolution*): Many people I interviewed for my book talked about the violence in the scene. The tough girls would not be scared away from that, but it was part and parcel of the masculine energy in hardcore especially in the late '80s and early '90s. Riot grrrl brought in equal parts feminism to punk rock, and punk rock to feminism. Riot grrrl became a way for young women to participate in punk scenes, as well as people who today would identify as nonbinary, although that wasn't an articulated part of the lens at that point.

SARA MARCUS (AKA Harlot Number One): The first band I was in was not an all-woman band. We practiced in the basement of our singer's house, a queer guy. He lent me his bass and he was connected with riot grrrl. He made me tapes of the bass lines and that's how I learned how to play bass. And the drummer taught me how to play drums. This was really central to the whole riot grrrl ethos: it can't just be guys on stage putting on shows, making zines, and taking pictures, although there were always more women taking the pictures than doing many other things. No one was going to give the seven-year-old girl the drum set back then. Now, hopefully people would. When my daughter is seven, if she wants a drum set you better believe she'll get one. I've already bought her three drums and she's one year old!

Certainly, there were already feminist ideas in punk music before riot grrrl. I was a feminist before I was a riot grrrl. I founded a feminist club at my high school two years before I ever made it to a riot grrrl meeting in DC. I was not connected to the punk scene. My first band was called AKA Harlot Number One. Then a friend from college and I formed a duo called Boys of Now. We were together about two years and toured with The Needs. That was our great achievement. Boys of Now is the band that once in a rare blue moon someone says, "I saw you play in 1999." It was a nice moment, a supportive, queercore moment in the Northeast and we had a wonderful time playing.

JM: Recently there's been new feminist movements including the #MeToo movement, Pussy Riot, women's marches, and the public calling out of men

CHAPTER 16

who have been violent towards women (2018). Would you say riot grrrl prefigured some of this?

SARA MARCUS: It feels very familiar to watch all of that. It's interesting how much a multiplier effect social media serves as. It's much easier to contact multiple people who had a similar experience to you now than it was in the '90s. This general impulse of banding together to hold abusers accountable felt very familiar to me from my time in riot grrrl.

JM: Your book is named after an experiment by riot grrrl bands to have women move to the front of concerts and men move back. Sometimes even good ideas can become dogmatic and I wonder if that happened in this case?

SARA MARCUS: I think it's really smart to move girls to the front of the audience. Kathleen Hanna would say that a lot of it for her and the band was a feeling of safety. Men were coming to Bikini Kill shows to start shit and stir up trouble and be aggressive. *Girls to the front* was a way to feel they had a protective zone right in front of the stage. I don't think I ever played a show where we did this, but I was many times an audience member where I was invited to be part of the girls who were going to the front. At many shows, maybe 10 or 20 percent of the audience would be girls. I came to punk through riot grrrl, but a lot of other girls might have gone with their guy friends. So, to get all the girls to be up front with each other is a way of helping people see their collective numbers and power. The idea is that you could have each other's back. As in any movement, there were excesses in riot grrrl, but I don't think asking girls to stand at the front of the show was remotely one of them.

STEWART EBERSOLE (*Barred for Life: How Black Flag's Iconic Logo Became Punk Rock's Secret Handshake*): Wow! What a mindfuck the first two years of Fugazi shows were! Going to a Fugazi show was like, "Five-dollar show? Great!" But it was like, "Alright, men stand in this line and women stand in that line. Now jump up and down in unison. If anybody moves in any other direction, I want everybody to point at them and say, 'You are stupid.'" You needed a rulebook to walk into a Fugazi show! They put restrictions on you and used a high school mentality to turn the crowd on you if you did something they didn't want—meanwhile telling you you're free to do whatever you want to do.

SPITBOY: WOMAN PLAYING MUSIC

JM: In your book you write, "Like the punk scene, punk record labels were run by men."

MICHELLE CRUZ GONZALES (*The Spitboy Rule: Tales of a Xicana in a Female Punk Band*): When you went to shows back then, the stereotype was that the woman was always there with her boyfriend. There were women at shows, especially at Gilman Street. I went to shows at The Mab and The Farm, but I started hanging around Gilman and found that safer. There were a lot of women who volunteered at Gilman and that was exciting! There weren't as many women in bands. We were a novelty act. It was like, "Wow! What's it like being a woman playing music?" "I don't know. I'm a woman and I play music. *This* is what's it like: people ask you what it's like!" [laugh]

Because we were all women, our first show was really well attended because people wanted to see if we could pull it off. A lot of people in the big bands from the East Bay and Bay Area were there for our first show in a warehouse. I remember hearing from people, "Yeah that was cool." But many of the men in the scene made it clear we were *not* going to get the same kind of acceptance that bands like Econochrist were going to get. I sensed right away it had to do with the fact that we weren't just a political band, we were a *feminist* band. That was hard on the ears for men. It threatened their position as kings of the scene. It forced them to look at the scene and women's issues in a way that they hadn't before. It was a threat.

As a band in the Bay Area, people speak fondly of Spitboy. People think we broke a lot of barriers. But at the time, when Econochrist played, all the scenesters would go. When Spitboy played I'd ask, "Are you going to come see Spitboy?" I'd hear, "Oh, we saw you guys play last month." Because of our feminism and it was in your face, people felt they were getting a lecture. But if Ben (Sizemore) from Econochrist was screaming about a political issue nobody felt they were getting a lecture! That was unfortunate and I don't think I've gotten over it completely.

MICHELLE CRUZ GONZALES: You can't talk about being a woman in a punk band in the '90s without talking about riot grrrl. Whether you were riot grrrl or positioned yourself otherwise. I wanted to situate Spitboy as *not* a riot grrrl band. That's one of the main things we are known for. That was uncomfortable for us to do. We skirted the question of whether we were a riot grrrl band for many months in interviews and finally we would get asked it so much that we had a conversation in the van and decided to say, "We're *not* a riot grrrl band."

At the DC show when we said that the boys do *not* have to stand in the back, that the men could stand anywhere they wanted, I very undiplomatically said, "We're not a riot grrrl band." It totally silenced the whole room. It was as if I'd kicked the statue of Jesus in the face. I thought, "I really blew it." In hindsight I could've been more diplomatic, but I don't regret saying it. We did wind up taking a lot of flack. The main reason we didn't want to be a riot grrrl band was that we didn't want to be called *girls*. Women and feminists in the 1990s in the Bay Area had decided that being called a girl was the worst. It assigned a hierarchical nature.

MICHELLE CRUZ GONZALES: We went on tour (Instant Girl) and took our friend Chris with us. On all of our other US tours, we did almost all the driving and didn't take men with us. That was one of our rules: no boyfriends on tour. If we got a flat tire, we changed the flat tire. Paula knew how to work on cars and she'd fix the van when it broke down. Only once or twice we had to take it to a shop because Paula would always fix it. We had this feminist attitude that we were going to do everything: drive, write the songs, load the equipment, change our own tires. For some reason we went on tour in winter and we were in snow and had to put chains on the car. We made Chris do it and none of us got out of the van! [laugh] This is the most incongruent thing we ever did! We waited in the warm van while Chris got under the van and put chains on. With no gloves! That was the worst feminist move ever. It's a little funny, but you can't always be perfect.

FIGHT LIKE A WOMAN

JENEDA BENALLY (Blackfire / Sihasin): Our new album *Fight like a Woman* is coming out on Earth Day (April 22, 2018). To "Fight like a Woman" is to fight with your heart. It goes back to our Indigenous concept of when you're making decisions, you're not making a decision for yourself. You're making a decision for the next seven generations and how it will impact them.

CLAYSON BENALLY (Blackfire / Sihasin): Think of Standing Rock or all of these different hotspots around the world that are the front line. When we were young, we'd go with our grandmother Roberta Blackgoat to a protest and being there at her side the guidance we received was, "Whatever your actions are going to be, it comes back to your people. Whatever you do out in this world is a direct reflection of your people. So, be wise about it." The concept of direct action or taking a stand is a spiritual battle. What we're up against is for our cultural survival.

ALEXANDER "SASHA" CHEPARUKHIN (Pussy Riot manager): I just got a text from Masha (Alyokhina) and she sent it from the plane (Moscow to Seattle). Masha says,

> Our project "Revolution" is a punk manifesto based on my book. Some political impotence *[sic]* assert that we have no voice and no choice. But we have a voice and we have a choice. We want to inspire people. We want new actions such as the Women's March. We want those who are silent not to be afraid to speak.

What we believe in, we will get it. Pussy Riot Theatre is a cultural revolution. Community is stronger than any government. To overcome nationalism, sexism, racism, fear and indifference we should riot together.

DENISE KAUFMAN (Ace of Cups): When I look at some of the punk women's bands, I'm like, "Yes! Go!" I love the wild, raw attitude of punk. I applaud it. We need to speak up now and let out anger, frustration, and wildness. The women of punk, Goddess bless them. When you think of Pussy Riot or some of the courageous women, it's one thing to be in San Francisco in a women's punk band, but to be in Russia criticizing the government! I have such a deep respect for these women who went to jail for what they sang. The music of the civil rights movement, of revolution, or the music from slavery that gave people courage in the darkest of days, I have such respect for people who have played their music in these circumstances where you could get crushed for just opening your mouth.

LOST IN THE FEMINIST MESSAGE

JOHN LYDON (Sex Pistols / PiL): Pussy Riot? There was a good idea; I knew their manager and had close connections with them, but it's all rather silly and a little bit fake. The things they were demonstrating against, it really annoyed me that they went into a Catholic Church in Russia screaming whatever it is they scream. They're against religion? Hello! In a country like that? [laugh] Religion is the *last* of your worries! You should be going somewhere where it really matters, not about your men in frocks and child molesters. That's somewhere down the line according to the bigger issues that Russia has with Putin. Misdirected is how I'd view them. But great it's women, isn't it? Tough good stuff, but kind of lost in the feminist message. There's a huge difference between feminism and feminists. Wish there wasn't.

The basic thing about human nature is that we're not all equal. Some of us are better at some things than others. You can't make these block bookings of "We're all equal." It doesn't make sense. Actually, it's anti-nature. When you start involving Marxist ideologies, you're going to get problems because you're not actually listening to what Karl Marx said. His was a wonderful world of theory, but as he openly declared in his writings, his theories are not to be slavishly adhered to. There's no flexibility in modern thinking with these kinds of things. It's even more appalling on the right, but they're locking themselves into these agendas and leading up to all manner of ferocity and combativeness that isn't answering any single question that regular people want about, "How can I make life better?" There's hatred in the background of all of these things, therefore they should be openly discussed and torn apart. If they have real value and can take open debate, then yippee! There might be something to learn there. But it's never openly debated. It's just thrown at you. It's infuriating.

I doubt whether I could do a university tour again because of the misinformation that's going on out there. There's an awful lot of hatred for differences of opinions. I'm very far removed from right wing and yet that's what I hear when I do those kinds of gigs, from people in the audience who have no knowledge at all of the years and years of work I've put into making clear what I think equality is.

JM: What are people saying . . .

JOHN LYDON: My world doesn't accept victimization. It accepts an understanding that some of us are better at some things than others. I don't want to see women have to suffer on a building site carrying heavy loads. That's not what a woman's brain is dedicated to. I don't want to see men pretending to be housewives. That's not what men are *supposed* to be doing. I don't want to see someone who has the capability of being a rocket scientist reducing himself to a garbage collector, and vice versa, because that's what society would find convenient. We're a very inconvenient species, the human race. And we're supposed to be. And our answers are in all of those confusions. But not by dogma. Is any of that clear?

JM: Yes. For clarity, in the case of a woman who *does* want to work on a construction site or a man who . . .

JOHN LYDON: Great! Go forth, young lady! [laugh] Have all the fun you can. But it's a tough world. I know because I worked on building sites when I was young; the bullying system is outrageous. Not to mention outright bloody dangerous. I doubt that that's a peculiarity to just British building sites. There's a serious power struggle to consider there. Believe me that most people that work on building sites do not believe in passive resistance. It's a physical world, that is. If you're a knowledgeable young girl and you know all that, well done, lady! One hundred percent get my backing. But I tell you, as a young man I found it very seriously challenging. Don't want to see people hurt where they don't need to be. And sometimes a physical situation requires a mental physicality. We can't all be scientists.

STOP VIOLENCE AGAINST WOMEN

KERRI O'KANE (*The Gits* film director): Home Alive was founded after Mia Zapata's murder (1993). Valerie Agnew, the drummer of Seven Year Bitch, and

Gretta Harley (Maxi Badd) and other people formed this nonprofit organization to stop violence against women. I embarked on this film after learning about Home Alive. I then learned about Mia's murder and couldn't believe they hadn't found the person who did it. The outpouring after Mia's murder was so incredible, it's hard to articulate. People came from everywhere. Nirvana, Joan Jett, and Pearl Jam were involved to help find the killer. The community decided not to collapse but to come together and form another collective, to find Mia's killer. After ten years, that's what happened, and they discovered it wasn't one of them. That's what the Seattle punk rock community was trying to accomplish and they succeeded. Joan Jett really did an amazing job by standing up and saying, "I'd like to play some songs with The Gits and raise some money to help find the killer." (Mia Zapata was the singer for The Gits and her killer was found March 25, 2004, twelve years after her murder.)

JM: "Blender" is a song on your album *Prom* where you're singing about privilege and lack of diversity among punk rockers: "In a sea of white faces / I heard the latest version of The Clash / How do we sing about the system / when we're a main offender?"

AMY RAY (Indigo Girls): In that song I was talking to myself as much as anything. And to my community of people who are actively questioning the system all the time and are part of the independent movement, on the Daemon (Records) and punk side of things, because Indigo Girls is such a different animal. I'm talking to myself as an Indigo Girl in that line. We had this big idea. Dischord, Northwest, Athens, all these movements talked a lot about breaking down barriers of race, class, and gender. And it just never happens. We just keep railing against this system that we think is too patriarchal and capitalist. But at the same time, we're beholden to it because we carry out those ideas in the demographics we appreciate. I don't know how to break those barriers down. I don't know if they can be and I don't even know if they should be. I'm just saying I don't know if you should force someone to listen to a certain kind of music just so your audience can be mixed. People should choose what they listen to. But you've got to ask yourself: How did it come about and how did it end up that way?

17

THE REVOLUTION IS PERSONAL
POLITICS WITH A SMALL "P"

The punk rock politics were the politics of the personal. The interdependent politics, the grassroots politics of, how do you treat each other?

—Exene Cervenka (X)

You cannot change anyone in the world / The only one you can change is yourself.

—"Ten Thousand Ways to Rebel and Fight" by SMZB

JM: It seems to me that self-transformation is a part of social revolution. How important is that to you?
CHRIS HANNAH (Propagandhi): For me, it is very important. Especially where I came from as a kid. I spent fourteen years being a very stupid person. I was sequestered from the realities of the world, living on military bases and reading statistics about different countries and how many tanks each country had. It was a very childish worldview. I think I was being weaned to be some sort of robot in the military.

The initial transformation, through finding bands like MDC, was pivotal in my life. I wouldn't credit punk rock from then on too much because I've found a lot of punk rock since then, especially in the past ten years, to be vacuous. It's meaningless to me, aesthetically. And often even when the politics are right on, it doesn't transform me! I would credit more interpersonal relationships as transforming me. A guy like me is going to be trying to evolve and get a little smarter until I'm dead. I've met people who are eighteen years old who blow me away! I think, "Well, this kid doesn't need to transform much anymore!" From year to year, I have to feel something more. I have to enhance what I know.

JM: What's your take on the relationship between changing yourself and the world?

DAVE WAKELING (The English Beat): It is symbiotic. You're just singing something to get it off your chest and then you find you've really moved people with it. You try and sing things that are really personal, but you try and express it in a way that is universal. You can really move people with it if you hit the nail on the head. Then you find, "I've got responsibility! What am I going to say next?" 'Cause they're really listening. That's really frightening! I wrote the first lot in the living room and I didn't expect anybody to hear it. In fact, I didn't *want* anybody to hear it! [laugh] I was doing it just so I wouldn't punch the wall!

JM: I hear in your music that you're addressing your own suffering and the suffering in the world around you at the same time.

DAVE WAKELING: Yeah, that's the idea, isn't it? I don't spend too much time praying for myself. I feel more comfortable sending prayers to other people. You do yourself at the end of it; you remember you're part of it as well. You're praying for the whole world and you think you're standing outside of it and forget that you're involved. When you pray for yourself it hits you the hardest. "Sorry, forgot!" You can sometimes get trapped in thinking that you're just your thoughts. It's another mistake.

The Buddha said that there was no evil, just ego. The ego makes you feel that you're separate and that's the first step toward being able to hurt someone else, because you view them as different or separate from you. I would've thought that about those photos from space, "Look at them lot, they're all one aren't they? [laugh] Whether they like it or not!" I've always felt that intuitively. You just do the best you can. If you fuck up, then that's what you were meant to learn. And don't beat yourself up. Someone else will do it if it's required. That's the worst bit of it, the constant self-denigrating thought.

JELLO BIAFRA (Dead Kennedys / Guantanamo School of Medicine): When I get up, I don't look in the mirror and see this great person who everybody should be patting on the head or bowing down to. I see a mound of work on my desk, all these songs that never got finished, and it would be *so* fucking cool if they ever got recorded! And all these other things I doubt I'll ever have time for. That's a good way to put the ego back in its cage! Or, put the ego back in its cobra basket!

WU WEI (SMZB): Personal liberation is first and foremost, but personal liberation must also be accompanied by self-discipline, although this is not easy to achieve.

To put it simply, there is no absolute freedom. This is the difference between humans and animals. Let me calm down first. Yes, for me, I can express my emotions through punk music. It is not meditation or martial arts. Understanding and knowing myself is also part of the content of thinking. Everyone is an individual, with their own ideas and way of life, and they should not interfere with others and should not be interfered with by others.

IAN MACKAYE (Minor Threat / Fugazi): I'm not a goal-oriented person. I celebrate the journey rather than the goal. My life is protest. That is what I do. It is not going to stop. I'm always going to be engaging in justice. I don't believe that if I don't reach a particular goal, then my actions were in vain or that I wasted my time. I don't get discouraged like that. I don't think of things as always getting resolved. Rather, what's in front of me is what I am doing. I actually don't think about it that much because it becomes a practice.

MARJANE SATRAPI (*Persepolis*): I try to be kinder to everyone I know. If I can be a better person, then maybe I can change something. We want the world to change, but none of us wants to change, really. The change has to come from us. But changing everything in a global way all together, I tried it and I don't think it works at all. We are imperfect human beings. With us being this imperfect, how can we make a perfect world?

STEVE SOTO (The Adolescents): One time after a show a guy said, "I don't have any friends, but when I listen to your records, I feel like that there's light at the end of the tunnel. Like I'm not alone." I think the message definitely got out there, that there's hope at the end of the day. It's more common with kids than people think. The generations before didn't talk about depression. For them to hear it from someone else, that they're not alone, is a positive thing.

> *What you think changes how you act.*
>
> —"Why Theory?" by Gang of Four

JON KING (Gang of Four): A lot of people think the opposite: that changing how you *act* changes what you *think*. [laugh] It's a funny thing! If you hit a little hammer on someone's knee, they will have a reflex. So much of what we do is reflex. I think there are situations where a lot of what happens is like white noise. And white noise is quite comforting because it fills everything up. You mentioned meditation. I've done that sort of thing over the years and it's interesting. At a certain point you can get a sense of emptiness. In moments of meditation, you're freed from the way you used to think. Karl Marx said the point is not to *describe* the world but to *change* it. That was a fantastically acute thing to say. It's almost banal to say, "What you think changes how you act," but it's quite hard to change what you think.

MOANA STROM (Stalin's War): Music is so powerful, especially to young people. When you're young you're listening to it all day. You hear every single word and hold on to all of it. If you can be a positive role model and sing about things that matter and are positive, then you can help form people's ideas. If you're talking about things like *spirituality* and *social change* rather than booze and drugs, it can be incredibly beneficial. The best way to help other people is to start by working on yourself and your own mind, developing wisdom. Then you can benefit others and do social change. But it all starts with you.

JM: I'm interested in the interconnection between social change and personal transformation. I have an idea that you're interested in that, too.

DICK LUCAS (Subhumans): Yeah. I would say that the latter leads to the former. Over a long period of time, gradually. So gradually you hardly notice it. Looking back at the '80s, the perfect example is vegetarianism. It was seen as something the hippies once did. For me and a lot of other people, punk rock came along and Crass and Conflict and other bands started singing about not eating meat and *we're all animals* and then we—the Subhumans and our friends, a lot of people—became vegetarian in theory and then in practice. There were certain things that you didn't give up for another six months, because you really

Dick Lucas shares the mic with a fan. (Santa Cruz, California; 2008). Photo: Matt Fitt

liked them. You had to overcome a lot of selfishness. It's an evolutionary way of thinking.

Suddenly there were very rare health food shops where you could buy veggie burgers and the more inspired of us went out and bought bags of lentils and figured out how to make our own. The whole thing developed rapidly for a lot of people because of anarcho-punk, vegetarian punk. And now vegetarian is a major-option diet choice. Not just because of the animal situation—them being killed or not being killed. But because it's more healthy. Meat stays in your guts for three or four days and there's only a certain amount of it that does you any good. The meat eaters say, "What about protein? You got to eat meat!" *Just eat nuts!* Have a bag of peanuts now and again. The conscience led to development of imagination of what one could eat. Some people went vegan, even further. It's an evolutionary development in human beings, with regards to their position on the planet. We're just another animal on the planet.

STRAIGHT EDGE

JM: Some punk rock is clear about political choices and personal actions. You decided not to take alcohol, drugs, or meat.
DAVE DICTOR (Multi Death Corporation): That is true. I found myself getting polluted by all of that. I've given up meat now for over thirty years. If you don't find yourself fitting in, or you're not liking what you're seeing, there is very much the temptation to overparty. And then you get to see that reality and where it's really getting you. Then you make a conscious decision to *not* overparty. In fact, let's *under*party. With that comes a clarity. For myself it has anyway. Then you start trying to find other things to fill up your life besides alcohol and drugs. A spirit-full nature is a nice thing to fill up yourself with. To fill a void that we all have: the hunger to survive and imagine something greater than what we're seeing.
JOHN STOCKBERGER (Sense Field): I was confused about the idea of punk as a revolution. I settled on it being a personal revolution. I wanted to live up to my ideals in the punk rock scene. When I was fifteen, I became vegetarian because I didn't want to eat things with eyes and I thought factory farming was wrong. I didn't go around trying to make other people do it. I thought it was enough that I was doing it. All I wanted out of punk rock and life in general was to be self-determining, not having anybody tell me what to do. Punk always had this socio-political aspect and was inherently nonreligious. The bands I was into—Subhumans and Minor Threat—were about being a conscious person living a

CHAPTER 17

life causing the least harm to others around you. That's what punk rock was really about.

IAN MACKAYE (Minor Threat / Fugazi): I would never think of it (straight edge) as renunciation whatsoever. I don't think of it as a lifestyle. People have said, "That's an interesting lifestyle." But that suggests somehow that it is an affectation. It is *not* an affectation. It is life! People are born naked and they are not born drinking alcohol. I do understand that, at least in theory, there are babies born with drug addictions because of their mothers' addictions. But I think we can agree that basically babies are born sober. They are born without all of the accoutrements of this society. From my point of view, it is really just the way we are. It is life. Everything we do beyond that is an additive. It wasn't like I was partying and then hit a wall; I just never drank or got high. I'm not trying to claim that I did things right; I'm just telling you the way I lived. I don't ever think about it as this incredible shift in my life or as a realization. It is just who I am.

In terms of the mental departure, the idea of getting high or drunk or just engaging in that kind of stuff—so much of that is tied into such a creepy economy that is so clearly preying on people's lack of self-confidence as well as their insecurities. Enormous companies dictate so many almost obscene cultural standards. The fact that people under twenty-one can't go see bands play is crazy to me! "*That* is how old you need to be to get into a show." Why? Because that's how old you have to be to buy alcohol. But if bands are playing there, why do you have to be twenty-one to see those bands? It's because these laws have been fashioned around the alcohol industry.

MARK ANDERSEN (Positive Force DC cofounder): Addiction is something that impacts many of us directly through ourselves or the ones we love. I'm acquainted with addiction and I always want to be honest about how this is still a process for me. It comes back to *revolution is a process*. It's a state of becoming. So is the spiritual life. When it stops, then you're in trouble. For those of us who want a revolution that is more than some material thing but is also personally significant and spiritually powerful, we're trying to figure out how we got here, what in the world we're supposed to do while we're here and what it all means. We want to do something that is real or else it just feels like a waste.

ADAM NIGH (Too Bad Eugene): When I was in high school discovering punk rock, what really got me going was particularly 7 Seconds and their message, "Have a positive youth and not be like what our parents are telling us we're like," which is a bunch of alcoholics addicted to drugs. Let's pick ourselves up! Minor Threat, Youth Brigade, and this whole, "We're *not* going to be what the stereotypes say we are." It started with a love of self and the idea of trying to oppose things that are self-destructive. But in my experience the straight edge movement was a bit too prideful to accomplish much positive. I wasn't straight edge when I wrote "Morning Song." In general, it's this idea of getting to a place where you can live in a meaningful way. You want to eliminate things that keep you from that and drugs and alcohol are things that can do that. But more what I had in mind was my own life and being too busy. Simplify. Don't say "yes" to everybody that asks you for your time because that will rob you of your own life. It was *stop and smell the roses every once in a while.*

JM: About your song "Through with This," you've said, "It's just being free from accumulated garbage, whether it's emotional or physical." Tell me about the journey of freeing yourself from what is not essential.

JOHNETTE NAPOLITANO (Concrete Blonde): It's something you don't realize until you have all this crap, stuff you haven't seen in years. It just becomes karmic baggage. But for a nation of people that are supposed to be so free, we sure burden ourselves with a lot of obligations and pressures we really don't need. Then, typically the things we own start owning us. We're less mobile, not traveling, not discovering the world around us, caught in a cycle of working to maintain the things we have. We have more than most people on the planet and it's never enough.

MIKE NESS (Social Distortion): A friend told me that pain is good and *extreme* pain is *extremely* good. To understand that, you have to realize that for most people pain usually brings us closer to our God and therefore makes us stronger in the long run. At a certain point I was able to take life's experiences and turn them into positive. When Dennis (Darnell) died, the first thing I thought was: "We need to stop the band." It only took a couple days of reflection to realize that he and I started this band. This is our dream. Rather than quitting I was able to turn it around. I had a new purpose. I thought, "We need to continue in honor of him. (Darnell was guitarist and cofounder of Social Distortion from 1979 until he died suddenly in 2000.)

SINGING IS NOT ENJOYABLE

DAVID THOMAS (Rocket from the Tombs / Pere Ubu): To me, singing is not enjoyable. I don't like doing it. I would like to quit as soon as I can. But I can't quit until I get it right. As soon as I get it right, I would quit. "I am out of here!" I am not that keen on it. It hurts. It's hard and I would rather do something else.

JM: If you're not enjoying music making . . .

CHAPTER 17

DAVID THOMAS: Well, I have *never* enjoyed it. It's not an enjoyable thing to me. It is sometimes a hard concept for people to grasp. I don't really go into it very much because people say to me, "Well, why don't you do what you *want* to do?" Well, I *am* doing what I want to do, but what I want to do is to get it right and then quit. The only thing that drives me is an overwhelming sense of failure. Again, sometimes it's hard for people to grasp that you do something because you are not good at it. [laugh] If I get good at it, I will stop. I had no intention of going into music. I had no particular mindset for going into music. But I did it and I realized that I could get much better at it and that I wasn't good enough at it. I was stubborn enough to not want to quit before I got good at it. That was thirty-something years ago.

JM: Music has offered you something like a challenge to keep you growing towards a perfection or completion?

DAVID THOMAS: I suppose. You're putting it into terms that I don't really identify with. I think in very specifically limited personal terms. Like, *I am no good at it and I am not going to stop until I am good at it.* That is not fishing for compliments. I know how good I am. I know that I am extremely good and that I do things that other people would not even dare to dream of. But that doesn't matter because every time I do something, all I see is what's wrong with it. That is probably why I try to get better. You're coming from a far more principled or esoteric angle where you interpret things in certain ways. I am not necessarily disagreeing with you. I'm just telling you that I have never thought about that sort of stuff. I had no natural voice and ability and was tone deaf. Yeah! That is a good clue to not go any further.

Timing is a very important part of how I construct a vocal line. I'm a great admirer of Frank Sinatra from the '50s. His timing in those two particular albums is the most amazing thing you've ever heard in your life. You hear it and think, "He is never going to finish this phrase! He can't possibly." You know, the next section, the next measure is coming up too fast. Pull out Frank, pull out! But then Frank just slides through it! Rhythm is clearly a major component of this issue.

JM: I hear in some of your lyrics ideas that address suffering. Personal suffering and collective suffering. I'm curious what you think about suffering.

DAVID THOMAS: It is best not to! [laugh] It *is* better if you don't! Go on with your question.

JM: I like that answer, though.

DAVID THOMAS: Well, that is the most obvious answer there is. You'd be a fool to like suffering. But we live in times where there is a lot of it. My pain isn't anywhere near the same pain as some starving, dying child somewhere in Africa or Asia. It's a different sort of pain. But I don't think you can get away without talking about pain.

JM: It's ironic but tragic that some ways people try to get away from suffering cause more suffering.

DAVID THOMAS: That's the general human condition. Whatever you try to solve you usually end up screwing up more. That is pretty standard stuff at this point.

JM: I came across a recording of John Cage reading his diaries. It's titled *Change the World: You'll Only Make Things Worse*.

DAVID THOMAS: Yeah, I'd endorse that one. That's one of the reasons my bands don't deal with world issues. World issues are not as important as human issues or the struggle of the individual to fit into the world or to find a separate peace. If we (Pere Ubu) have any sort of social message, that's generally it: how you come to an arrangement with the world and other corollaries. In the end, we are all individuals. Separate islands. Art is the attempt to reach out beyond the prison of words, pictures, and sign language. I love music the most of any kind of art. When people say, "Would you ever want to do anything else?" and I say, "No!" it's because I'm at the peak of the pyramid as far as art goes. Writers are little ants, way down the slopes of the pyramid. Painters are teenier little ants. Music works with the same elements that human consciousness works with. You try to achieve some kind of communion with other human beings at a deep level. And that level has to be beyond words because words are images and concepts. Human beings are a weird combination of physicality and spirituality, as music is.

RHYTHM OF FREEDOM

RAMSEY KANAAN (Political Asylum / AK Press / PM Press): I don't view it that way at all (punk as a revolutionary movement). Punk is a genre of music. No more, no less. What defines punk, as opposed to folk, reggae, jazz, or classical music, is not the instinct for freedom. All music contains within it an instinct for freedom, a *rhythm* of freedom. Music is one of those wonderful things like words and ideas, which ought to be unfettered, like the broad river of life which we both drink from and we also contribute back to.

> *International cabaret performers since 1977, still rocking it hard and hilarious.*
>
> —The Dickies website (2022)

CHAPTER 17

JM: Some people think punk has tried to be a revolutionary force.
STAN LEE (The Dickies): I don't know. We've never been into that. We don't do it for the statement. Let politicians do that! [laugh] We're just in it for the fun! Something makes us laugh, we write it down and make a song out of it. I like looking at things on the light side. There's enough negativity going on for everybody! I've always been against that heavy thing, all those bands in England: "No future! Parents suck! Hittin' the dole and it's all fucked." We never played it that way. We were more like, "Where's the water slide? Where's Bob's Big Boy? Who's got a swimming pool?"

PUNK IS FUNNY!

> *He is the light and new king to be / So get out of my way and don't fuck with me.*
>
> —"Jesus Is Love" by Tartar Control (Hardcore Mormon band that features a robot on bass and drums)

STEVEN LEE BEEBER (*The Heebie-Jeebies at CBGB's*): Punk is funny! Early punk is very funny. A lot of rock wasn't funny. The Beatles were funny, but they were a peculiar kind of funny—cheeky. Aside from that, not lots of jokes. Lenny Bruce was one of the big role models for a lot of these guys. I call him the patron saint of punk.

For a good laugh at punk rock, check out the 2010 appearance of fictional band Crisis of Conformity on *Saturday Night Live*, with Fred Armisen (SNL), Dave Grohl (Nirvana), Ashton Kutcher (producer and host of practical joke MTV series *Punk'd*), and Bill Hader (SNL). The skit has the band playing at a wedding, performing a song called "Fistfight in the Parking Lot." Due to popular appeal, the song was later released as a seven-inch single by Drag City Records (2011). And if you like that, watch music videos from Tartar Control, a comedic hardcore punk band from Salt Lake City that pokes very dark fun at religion. Songs like "Jesus Is Love" and "My God's Cock" feature Robert on vocals, Sean on guitar, and their robot providing bass and drums. Then there's Weird Al Yankovic's cover of "Beat on the Brat" by the Ramones, included in the 2018 Dr. Demento double album *Covered in Punk*. Surely metal/punk band Arnocorps (distributed by Jell Biafra's Alternative Tentacles label) falls solidly into the humor punk category; their lyrics and stage act are inspired by the action movies of actor-turned-politician Arnold Schwarzenegger. The band speaks to their audiences with Austrian accents.

JM: Dead Kennedys is one of the standout band names in punk rock. I remember on one of your early spoken word albums you're talking about new bands asking for advice on choosing a name. John Wayne on Acid was a good one!

JELLO BIAFRA (Dead Kennedys / Guantanamo School of Medicine): I just can't shut that faucet off, can I? There are pages and pages of them that didn't even get on *No More Cocoons*. Nobody has called their band The Rodney King Halloween Mask. Or Lactating Pentagram or Cocaine Unicorn. The lists go on and on, which makes it all the more absurd that we keep getting stuck with band names like Minus the Bear or Suddenly Tammie or Taking Back Sunday. It's very frustrating.

JM: Guantanamo School of Medicine is a pretty good runner up to Dead Kennedys.

JELLO BIAFRA: That was a tough one because a lot of these names I just mentioned—like Osama McDonald or Jean Benet Milosevich—or calling your band Free Drugs and watching what happens when you put up posters all over town with that on it! But you can't do that if you're going to put your own name at the top of the band. I knew I had to do that in order to get anybody to give us the level of gigs we deserved. Otherwise, if it was Guantanamo School of Medicine alone, we might still be playing for thirty people once in a while in the Bay Area.

JM: I spoke with Brad Logan from Leftöver Crack—that's a pretty hilarious name.

JELLO BIAFRA: Oh, yeah. That's one of my favorite band names in years. The whole purpose of the *Fresh Fruit* poster at the time was: *The Stations of the Crass* album had come out (1979) and people were beginning to realize how much great art you could make with album covers and the packaging if you just got rid of putting your own ugly face on the cover! The Crass stuff folded out into posters—that was really cool. I thought, "Okay, we gotta do something, too. . . . What if Crass was funny?" So, I began working on the *Fresh Fruit* poster and stayed up all night, well into the next day, and Winston (Smith) came over and added a few more things and voilà! Off it went!

Jello Biafra's sense of humor has often been raw and sardonic in spoken word monologues and songs like "I Kill Children" and "Kill the Poor." His current (2022) biography on the Alternative Tentacles website says Biafra (Eric Boucher) was "born and raised in Boulder, CO six blocks from the JonBenet Ramsey murder site. So far, he has not been named as a suspect." This reference has more meaning if you know that Biafra was once actually accused by police

CHAPTER 17

of similar crimes and has generally being targeted by state/corporate powers, including the PMRC (Parents Music Resource Center), established by Tipper Gore in 1985. San Francisco and Los Angeles Police broke down Biafra's door and confiscated artwork from the Dead Kennedys *Frankenchrist* album. During the April 15, 1986, raid police found old milk cartons with photos of missing children that were part of a refrigerator collage in Biafra's kitchen. Police interrogated the punk singer, "Do you know where these kids are?"

JELLO BIAFRA (Dead Kennedys): When freak was a badge of honor and the way to rebel was long hair, degenerate looks, and weed, and there was heavier music than a lot of people liked, me and my friends would go in the back bedroom, start passing joints around, listening to Krautrock or the better side of Prog Rock, and we're all tripping out. And then they'd all start looking at my art wall and crisscrossing different pictures in their minds and they couldn't help but laugh and the brain spin would begin! Even though you couldn't quite put it into words. That's the way I make my collages to this day. I have either the same skills or same vision as Winston Smith. Mine are a little random with more text.

POLITICS ARE PERSONAL

EXENE CERVENKA (X): The punk rock politics were the politics of the personal. The interdependent, grassroots politics of, *how do you treat each other?* How do you treat people that need help? How many benefits can you play? How many bands can you help give a leg up to? That was the politics of punk. It was sharing in the victories of everybody, whether it was political, economic, or artistic victories. It was a collective. That was how it was political. Of course, some bands are more overtly political, like the Dead Kennedys.

We have a song called "The New World" and there's line in it about a person that is homeless and it's election day and they say, "It was better before they voted for what's his name." What's really good about that is the way it stays current. It wasn't "better before we voted for Ronald Reagan." It's *what's his name.* And it's always going to be what's his name. Or what's *her* name. We expressed ourselves in a more poetic version of the political. And there were a lot of gender politics in what we were doing.

CLEM BURKE (Blondie): It's a weird thing, politics and music. Music is a great platform to get the word out about anything you believe in your heart. I don't like reactionary ideas, but everyone has the right to voice their opinion, whether they're a plumber or a rock and roll star. Politics in Blondie—it's obvious we're to the left, to say the least. But we don't necessarily have to get on a soap box about it. It's how you conduct yourself.

CRIS KIRKWOOD (Meat Puppets): The politicism that we bring to the rock world, if any, is playing the music we want. We're not going to be so overt as to say, "This is how we think you should vote," or, "You should overthrow the government." I think people *should* overthrow the government and burn the world down, but definitely in that other direction is more the influence that we've had. It's this way of looking at music and of viewing the world. Not being so sure of yourself and what you think about what's right and wrong. We want to be a little more open-minded about things.

STEVEN BLUSH (author of *American Hardcore*): New York hardcore has kept hardcore alive all of these years and that's not political. Cro-Mags, Agnostic Front, Murphy's Law, Sick of It All. It's about brotherhood and fraternity. A lot of these folks come from broken homes and they found their place and community. It's very strong. But it's not political. It's a revolution of the body, not a revolution of the mind.

SARA MARCUS (*Girls to the Front: The True Story of the Riot Grrrl Revolution*): It's very hard to pursue the work of changing any part of the world from a space of feeling isolated and unsupported. Building communities that can home us can be a really important element in a larger attempt to effect greater systems. It's not always easy. . . . That's an understatement! It's almost *never* easy. It was Archimedes who said, "I can move the world with a lever if you show me where to place it." You hear a lot about self-care these days because it's a long haul. I want to challenge the idea that there's necessarily an opposition between trying to calm one's mind and trying to produce more justice in the world.

BRAD WARNER (*Hardcore Zen* / Zero Defects): When we were punk rockers the whole Nicaragua thing was going on and that was a big deal (Iran-Contra Scandal, 1985–1990). Many of us wanted to freeze nukes. We were all fired up about stopping all this suffering we saw, but we were just causing all kinds of misery for ourselves. We were living in really squalid conditions. And not just because we were poor, but because we were too lazy to clean up after ourselves! There's nothing wrong with doing good deeds to feed the poor and house the homeless. It is really good. The problem is when we start to divide up life into the worthwhile causes and the things that don't really matter, the things that we can just let slide. In Buddhism you don't let anything slide.

LISA FANCHER (Frontier Records): I hate to say it, but in LA I don't know if we had any big revolutionary message in terms of workers unite or overthrow the government. Not in a place with a climate like ours and the income. Our politics were more of a personal politics. It was okay to be a certain way and do whatever you want, as opposed to English bands like Crass, people with collectives. We never had anything like that.

I would say it was more like DIY. Everyone can play and start your own club and put out your own records. I can't really comment on how it goes now. There is a huge punk scene—there's punks everywhere! You go down on Melrose (Hollywood) and there's millions of kids. I don't think they all think the same way about anything. It's splintered and fractioned. There was a two-day punk and metal grrrl festival called "Smash the Sausage" with all-girl bands. Then you have bands that are absolutely huge, like Green Day. Are they really punk? I guess so.

JOHN LYDON (Sex Pistols / PiL): In England what we viewed as punk was very, very different from anything out of America when we first started. Early English punk was absolutely related to the society we were facing and dealing with. Hence, what we did and the changes we made in the world were because of that, because we were dealing honestly with our immediate surroundings. I don't think anything like that came out of New York, really.

STEWART EBERSOLE (*Barred for Life*): I always found bands that talked the most about unity and political change never did anything outside. "I'm in a band—I'm trying to get people interested!" Well, what did you do after that? Not just sing songs about it. There's always been that issue with punk. Can I involve myself in something radical and *not* go home afterwards and say, "I'm a sellout." I may go to a political meeting, but when I get home, I don't want the neighbor's dog shitting in my yard, their trees blowing leaves into my yard. Getting older is rough. You start to become your parents!

CHRIS HANNAH (Propagandhi): People should think about self-reliance. Do what you can to organize yourselves. Because things are going to come to a point where we're all going to have to take care of ourselves. Things are fucking going down the toilet and we are on the edge of a near extinction and people are going to have to know how to take care of themselves cooperatively.

DAVID J (Bauhaus): What we're going through is a very necessary part of our evolution. There is a real truthful resonance in something that my friend Alan Moore said (*V for Vendetta*). He compares this time as going through an evolutionary quantum leap. It's rather like water beginning to boil and changing its nature. As water turns into steam, we will change into something else that will probably be almost unrecognizable to us: a different form of this race. There is something about that vision that rings true. It also fits into the laws of acceleration and major discoveries speeding up. It's like we're heading very fast towards something very big. And I think, "Bring it on!"

C. J. RAMONE (Ramones): We've blown up the world enough and killed enough people to understand that violence and hatred just breeds more of it. We've been in that cycle ever since we stood up and walked straight. I'm focused on trying to break that cycle. I'm not talking about a utopia. There's no grand beautiful shining day when we all live in peace. But there can be a day when we learn that we don't have to kill everything and everyone around us for the world to be safe and for people to have what they need. Violence goes way back. Politics is part of that cycle of violence because the ending for politics is always violence. "We'll talk up to a point and then we'll just kill the hell out of you!" I'm not a big fan of politics. We're never going to work it out if we just keep using the same systems. That's my anti-politics speech!

JM: I like your anti-politics speech. It resonates with me. Politics is a corrupt system that relies on threatening or using violence.

C. J. RAMONE: The thing that gets us further down the evolutionary road is that we figure out how to bring about change in a way where we're not killing everybody and the environment and everything else. *That's* real change. That's a type of change that we haven't seen yet. We've had a couple of peaceful revolutions that are notable, but until everyone is thinking that way, that we can change things without killing, it's going to take some time.

BELIEVE IN YOURSELF

MIKE MUIR (Suicidal Tendencies): People always say they want everyone else to change. No one wants to make the change in themselves. People refuse to see their own weaknesses and mistakes. The hippies said we should all sit around and smoke pot and that's going to change everything. They didn't really change things. You can't change people's hearts unless they're moved. You can make music, you can talk to people, and it may go in their ear but it doesn't go in their brain if they don't feel it in their heart. With Suicidal, and my albums as Cyco Miko, I say you can be crazy enough to believe in yourself. They don't teach you to believe in yourself at schools. If you don't believe in yourself, nobody will!

18

THE REVOLUTION WILL BE COMMODIFIED

I don't know if anyone today talks about the concept of selling out. I don't think it even exists. I think it's because that has already happened.

—Pat MacDonald (Timbuk 3)

I'm always for individuality. I'm not for mass consumption. If I wanted to join an army, well I'd pick one with a better uniform!

—John Lydon (Sex Pistols / PiL)

One paradox of all revolutionary art is what might be called the *punk paradox*. Radical music, writing, painting, filmmaking, and other creative acts of liberation can inspire us to notice our collaboration with social/political systems that are unjust and unhealthy. Ideally this recognition ignites direct actions toward liberation. Yet those very same revolutionary songs, ideas, and images are often commodified and co-opted by the very institutions that promote the opposite of freedom: conformity and control.

Rage Against the Machine's Tom Morello protested to the US government after discovering his music was being blasted to augment torture at Guantanamo Prison. And Joe Strummer cried when he discovered "Rock the Casbah" had been written on US bombs being readied to drop on people in Iraq. Punk rock has also been widely co-opted for use in TV commercials, films, and video games. Indeed, the revolution was being commodified long before punk came

CHAPTER 18

along. Rock 'n' roll soundtracks for corporate TV ads had its beginning with a 1987 Nike commercial that used The Beatles's song "Revolution."

Advertising agencies have produced television commercials that use music from bands like the Ramones (Peloton Exercise Bikes, PS4, Cadillac, Diet Pepsi, GoPro, Google), Blondie (K-Mart), The Buzzcocks (Toyota), Gang of Four (Xbox), and The Smiths (Nissan). The Minutemen sold thirty seconds of "Love Dance" for an automobile commercial (Volvo) and the fee was given to bandmember D. Boon's father, who had emphysema.[1] Iggy Pop's music has been used to sell shoes (Nike), car insurance (Swift Cover), and cruises (Royal Caribbean International). Black Flag sold their classic song "Rise Above" for use in a skate punk video game called "Tony Hawk's American Wasteland," released in 2005. The in-game soundtrack has sixty-three songs including music by Circle Jerks, Green Day, Seven Seconds, Bad Religion, and Dead Kennedys. Joan Jett's "Real Wild Child" was in a sleek Hyundai commercial released June 9, 2014, by the Innocean USA ad agency. And the 1965 song "Demolición" by Los Saicos from Peru was used in a 2015 TV commercial for cat food.

When The Buzzcocks song "What Do I Get?" was used in a 2016 McDonald's commercial, former Smiths vocalist Morrissey expressed surprise about that band supporting meat-eating and a fast food chain infamous for environmentally destructive practices.[2] A few years later Morrissey would himself be called out: "Morrissey is anti-immigrant and backs a white nationalist political party."[3]

Around the world, punk rock has supported revolutionary movements and inspired young people to engage in activism, study anarchism, feed the hungry, embrace vegetarian and drug-free lifestyles, learn hidden political histories, and create independent bands, record labels, performance venues, communal living spaces, and infoshops. Moving forward with the punk revolution, each band and person determines how they want to balance money, marketing, and messages with their personal and political values. Here's how one punk singer describes this double-edged punk paradox:

> Probably some bands that start out authentic end up selling out. It's probably better for a person to not get famous. But on the other hand, if you do become well-known, then a lot more people are exposed to what you're trying to get across and that can be a good thing. You're trying to balance these things: getting your message out and making sure you're not breaking your ideals to get the message out there. —Yishai Romanoff (Moshiach Oi!)

THE REVOLUTION WILL BE COMMODIFIED

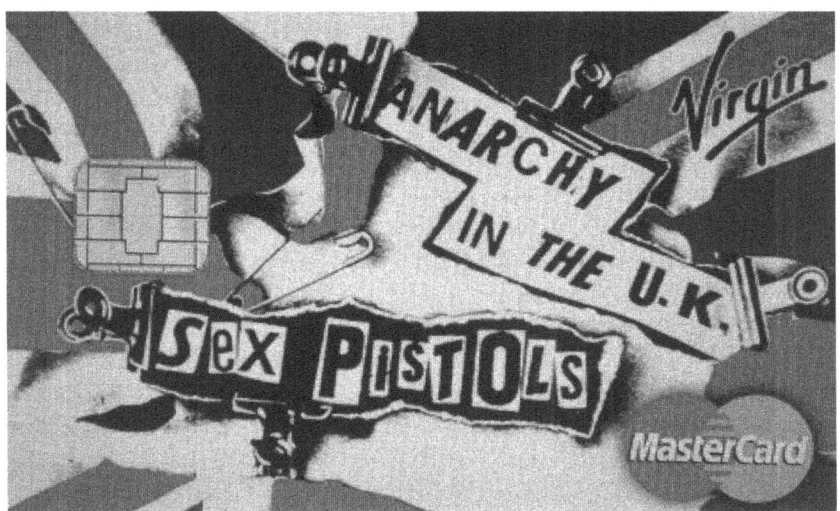

Anarchy gets commodified. Public Domain

New York–based cultural critic Stuart Ewen summed it up in his 1988 study: "As punk became marketable style, it became its opposite."[4] Another conclusive perspective was offered by Dave and Stewart Wise in 1978: "All rebellion expressed in terms of art merely ends up as the new academy. Punk and reggae are merely the latest recruits to enter the new academy."[5] And rock wordsmith Charles Shaar Murray wrote in *NME*, July 9, 1977: "We have a new kind of rock star now, and—like all other new kinds of star—it arose out of an attempt to break down the star system. . . . Punk/new wave is literally forced into being more dishonest than any previous rock 'n' roll epoch. They must be poverty-stricken but necessarily rich. They ride in Rolls Royces and wear bin liners."

AUTOMATICALLY COMMODIFIED

JELLO BIAFRA (Dead Kennedys / Guantanamo School of Medicine): Commodification is something that was bound to happen. Even the first time Dead Kennedys went to New York and lost our shirts as an unknown band in 1979, I noticed how the music industry worked and how even underground artists fought and functioned. I thought, "Yeah, this is the octopus that strip mines the rest of the country, repackages it, and sells it back to us at twice the price." And it's inevitable that this is going to happen—maybe not to some of us—but to some people whose music we liked because their music is so goddamned good!

CHAPTER 18

When I heard "Amoeba" by The Adolescents, I thought, "In the world as it should be, this would be all over the radio right now, in addition to 'My Sharona.'" But of course, it wasn't! It was no surprise to me that at some point this stuff was going to click. Whether anyone likes it or not, Green Day, Rancid, Offspring, and even NOFX got as big as they did because they were good at what they do. There is genuine talent there, and I don't begrudge them that. But then, of course, all the pressure comes back down on people like Green Day to try and figure out who they are and how to live their lives. And handle parenthood at the same time.

JELLO BIAFRA: Inevitably punk was going to catch on and anything that catches on at that level is automatically commodified. Suddenly there's all those Hot Topic stores and what do you know? There's Dead Kennedys T-shirts! If they really want to put Dead Kennedys in Walmart, then no Tipper Gore stickers! No restriction on the content or changing the back of an album cover so there aren't any fetuses on it like Nirvana did with *In Utero* to get it into Walmart. But totally on our terms, where somebody in a smaller town who has no other way of stumbling into our music has their mind blown. And Dead Kennedys becomes a kind of gateway drug, as they obviously were to you. It's like the martial arts principle of using the enemy's strength against them. But I don't think that applies to putting Dead Kennedys in TV commercials—that really fucking sucked!

I was already reeling from hearing the opening chords of "Search & Destroy" from Iggy's *Raw Power* album in a Nike commercial! (1996) That just turned my stomach and I thought, "There's a lesson here. Every artist needs to decide how they want to handle that." I won't tell another artist on Alternative Tentacles how to handle that. I will tell them my feelings about it, but I'm not going to try and block them and get heavy handed. But in the case of my music, my songs, my bands—fuck no!

JELLO BIAFRA: This brings us back to "Holiday in Cambodia" being put in a Levi's commercial. I never thought that hell would come to my house! Why would they want us in the first place? [laugh] I was vehemently opposed. Klaus said, "It's Levi's. It's a good company." I said, "But Klaus, they just laid off six thousand people in Texas! At the same time giving a fifty-million-dollar golden parachute to one executive. We should not be supporting this company!" It's like the audience at a Bob Seger show, some of whom booed when he sang "Like a Rock" because it had become the all-too-tiresome jingle for Chevy Trucks. I don't want anybody to be that sick of hearing any Dead Kennedys song, especially my favorite Dead Kennedys song of all—"Holiday in Cambodia." To put "Holiday in Cambodia" or any Dead Kennedys song in a corporate

TV commercial is like spray-painting the McDonald's logo on the Mona Lisa! In my case I have to say fuck no!

JM: I've heard that Dead Kennedys were in negotiations to sell "Holiday in Cambodia" for a Levi's TV commercial and has sold songs for use in films like *Neighbors* and *Class*.

EAST BAY RAY: Let me clarify something: there was not a negotiation. Levi's contacted us to use the song in a commercial, and I was the one that turned them down. The reason this got resurrected is that a year later we discovered Biafra, who was running our record label Alternative Tentacles, skimmed $70,000 from us. We went to court, and he refused to pay it and ultimately, he lost. He said we sued him because we wanted the commercial, and that's a total myth. I was the one that turned down that commercial. It was turned down a full year before we discovered what happened at Alternative Tentacles.

EAST BAY RAY (Dead Kennedys): Yes, we do movies and video games. *Selling out is when you change your music in order to get a bigger audience.* From the Dead Kennedys viewpoint, back in the day we were in VHS snowboard videos and video games. It was a way for new people to hear our music because we weren't played on the radio. Right now, we're talking to someone who wants to use our song "Soup Is Good Food" in a video game. This is great because that's a political song. (*Watch Dogs 2*, 2016)

JM: Why didn't you want your music in the Levi's commercial?

EAST BAY RAY: We have *never* done a commercial. Hello! We don't sell products. What aren't you getting? We've never done a commercial for a product. Are you equating being in a video game soundtrack as the same as doing a commercial?

JM: I'm asking where you draw the line of where Dead Kennedys music will go.

EAST BAY RAY: There was an offer where they wanted to use a (DKs) T-shirt in a movie, which happens a lot. It was for a scene where some young kid was murdering his grandmother. We said, "No." People misunderstand Dead Kennedys; they think we're like Sid Vicious. It would be like someone wanting to use our song "Kill the Poor" while showing some psychopath killing poor people. They don't get the irony. If it's ultraviolence or homophobic, we don't do it.[6]

JELLO BIAFRA: Yes, Alternative Tentacles owed Dead Kennedys money. When we discovered the problem, we paid them in full. And then they sued anyway, claiming a long-term conspiracy, which was complete horseshit. Then Dead Kennedys got yanked away from Alternative Tentacles and has been mistreated in some pretty awful ways ever since. Not the least of which is all these fake reunion shows where my picture keeps turning up in the ad. Dead Kennedys was never meant to be Fraudcore.

CHAPTER 18

It was a perfect storm and a terrible mistake on Alternative Tentacles' part, which means it was my fault, and I'm sincerely sorry. I've said that many times. But it was never my intention to rip off my brothers. Never. It was only about $1,500 per person per year. But it was still a mistake that had to be rectified. But they made a bigger, much more vicious mistake. Was revenge one of the real motives for the Levi's commercial? You bet it was!

Klaus also said, "Well, why don't you go to the press and say we donated the money to charity and then we'll donate 10 percent?" After already having my knees smashed at Gilman Street for being a "sellout" (May 7, 1994), the last thing I wanted was to be forced into prostitution and catch all of the bullets for something I didn't even agree with!

I LOVE A MAN IN A UNIFORM

ANDY GILL (Gang of Four): The US military were going to use "I Love a Man in a Uniform" on their TV commercial for joining the army. Jon King has said he wouldn't have let that happen. I would've whole-heartedly embraced it. The song is about the army and the motivation and thought processes of people in the army. I'm not personally critical of anybody who's in the military. It's another job. If it had been used in the American military commercial, that would be the perfect outcome as far as I'm concerned. Because at the end of the day it doesn't really have much of an effect on whether the American military is going to have enough soldiers next year. But it would be added power to the meaning of the song. But some clever sergeant must have pointed out to the general that perhaps the song was being slightly sarcastic.

JON KING (Gang of Four): We would never, ever have sold "Uniform" to the US military. Our music publisher had an initial approach that we would've declined, but it never went further. I would have vetoed any use had it ever gone that far. A stupid approach was made to our music publishers that died at birth, and no offer was ever made. I would have said no. I always imagine the uncomfortable moment when some officer realized "Uniform" was doing great in gay clubs, and realized what the song was about.

MILES COPELAND (I.R.S. Records): In the case of Gang of Four, if they had licensed their song to the military, that would have basically thrown a monkey wrench into their whole rap. Because how can you be anti-establishment if you've allowed your song to be used by the military?

ANDY GILL (Gang of Four): There's certainly nothing problematic in terms of, "Oh, I'm supporting the capitalist system." Look, Gang of Four. Who did we sign to in the very first instance? The very first record was done with a little indie (Fast Records), but then we signed to EMI. Not only were they a massive corporation, but they also produced arms. We didn't want to be stuck in an indie niche; we wanted to mix it up in the real world. The commentary in the UK press was a bit like the question you've put to me: "Why didn't you sign to Rough Trade? Why did you sign to this major? It's not only a major, but Thorn EMI manufactured armaments as well." And the answer was: the album is called *Entertainment!* It makes sense when it's in the racks next to big commercial pop stuff. It makes much less sense, and is much less powerful, when it's ghettoized in a corner and labeled avant-garde.

It's quite hard to make a buck in the music industry these days. Bands and artists have to sustain themselves. With the collapse of the music industry, people will tell you how you can make money from ringtones or that the live market is booming and that's replacing the loss of record sales. None of that is really true. Basically, except for the highest paid 5 percent of musicians, everyone else is struggling. We've done gigs sponsored by Tequila manufacturers. We've accepted the money gladly.

JON KING: We've never made a penny from our recordings outside of the United States. Not one cent from the recorded music. In the United States we licensed it to Warner's. For the rest of the world, we're still signed to the evil EMI Corporation. The United States has the most progressive law in the world about giving musicians the right to get their work back after thirty-five years. It doesn't exist anywhere else in the world because their deals are all in perpetuity. In perpetuity is quite a long time! We recorded the EP *Damaged Goods* for about one hundred bucks and it was an indie hit. It sold 60,000 plus copies. We never got paid.

JM: I'm guessing there are corporations or institutions that you wouldn't agree to have Gang of Four music connected to. What if the World Bank wanted to use "Capital (It Fails Us Now)" for a video? Or if "Armalite Rifle" were used by a weapons manufacturer?

DAVE ALLEN (Gang of Four): Those two examples are quite interesting. Obviously, we wouldn't allow a weapons manufacturer to use one of our songs. That's pretty straightforward. We wouldn't allow political parties to use one of our songs. The World Bank using "Capital (It Fails Us Now)" would be the ultimate irony and we would embrace that whole-heartedly. Just listen to the lyrics; what we're saying is very anti-capital. You're bringing up examples that I can't imagine ever happening. We're open to our music ending up in more movies as long as the movies aren't super violent, sexist, or overtly political in the wrong direction.

CHAPTER 18

ANDY GILL (Gang of Four): "Naturals Not in It" was used by Xbox in a global advert. The first line is, "The problem of leisure / what to do for pleasure?" How much more appropriate would that be for mindlessly playing games on Xbox? Jon (King) was very influenced by the situationist movement and commodification generally. You will hear that a lot in the lyrics. Commodification defines people in general, much more now than it did twenty-five years ago.

DAVE ALLEN: What better than to have "Natural's Not in It" on television? I don't think having it in the commercial is against anything we've been known for throughout the years. The same song was in the film *Marie Antoinette* (2006) as the title track. Sofia Coppola mentioned in an interview that she was fixated on that song when she was writing *Marie Antoinette* and the lyrics resonated with her and led her to build a soundtrack around this sort of flawed woman. In Sophia's mind everything added up to the title of the song, "Natural's Not in It." She presented the glossy veneer of life that Marie Antoinette was living in, so separate from what was happening outside her doors. And how that led to the revolution.

If Gang of Four had turned down an offer from Microsoft you never would have heard about it. We're not the sort of band that would get front-page news if we told Microsoft to go screw themselves. As a matter of fact, you've never heard about the corporations we've turned down in the past. We were getting to a point in our career where I had three kids going through college—it's expensive! If it's considered selling out because I actually get a bit of a payday to help my kids get through college while exposing a larger audience to our music, then so be it.

DICK LUCAS (Subhumans): Xbox got in touch with Southern Records in London, who basically financed Bluurg Records and Crass Records, and asked if they could use "Subvert City" for an Xbox game. I was thinking, "This is weird," because none of us do the Xbox thing. We thought, "Does this mean we're going to get two million dollars each for copyright?" We asked and they said, "No. You're going to get about a hundred dollars between you." And they wanted the right to change the song in any way they like. We said, "Forget it," immediately!

THE REVOLUTION *WILL* BE TELEVISED

The Ramones song "Do You Remember Rock and Roll Radio?" was featured in a 2014 Cadillac commercial. In the thirty-second spot actor Robert Ratinoff says, "Amazon started in a garage. Hewlett Packard and Disney both started in garages. . . . the Ramones started in a garage. My point? You never know what kind of greatness can come out of an American garage." While many remember the Ramones as not being overtly political, the diverse movement they helped birth—punk rock—has often stood for a way of life that's clearly in opposition to the Hewlett Packards and Amazons of the world.

JM: In your book you describe seeing a TV commercial with a song by the Ramones. You write that "punk has changed so much that it alienated the original punks."

STEVEN LEE BEEBER (*The Heebie-Jeebies at CBGB's: A Secret History of Jewish Punk*): A great song like "Blitzkreig Bop" being used in a commercial to sell (Diet Pepsi, 2005) is complicated. The Beatles' song "Revolution" was in a Nike commercial years ago when Michael Jackson owned all The Beatles' songs. I was upset. It just turns your song into something else! With that said, it's nice to see the Ramones finally get some compensation for what they do. At the same time, having punk rock music and messages in TV commercials is not so great. It's that idea that the revolution will not be televised. But if the revolution is in a Nissan Pathfinder commercial, then the message is being co-opted.

JM: How have you avoided commodification of your music?

GLENN BRANCA (Theoretical Girls): Nobody wanted to fucking sign me! [laugh] Pretty simple. I think the word got out pretty fast that I was not, shall we say, easy to work with. I wasn't a young kid when I moved to New York. I was about twenty-eight, and I'd been around the block a few times. They don't want to sign somebody who knows what the hell's going on. They want to sign young kids who are willing to sign really bad contracts. If they had gotten to me when I was twenty, maybe I would've been stupid enough to sign such a contract. They want to own you and steal every penny they can from you.

GREG GRAFFIN (Bad Religion): Bad Religion has always been very blunt: if we'd been offered a major label deal, we would've taken it when we were kids. We started Epitaph because there were no major labels interested in us. Brett (Gurewitz) was passionate about it, and he turned into a great record man. I wouldn't call Epitaph a commercial company, but he also makes no bones about the fact that he's in business to make money.

I think there's a romanticism attached to that, and usually the romanticism is espoused most vociferously by people who haven't sold many records. "Yeah, man. We wanna be unpopular!" Even when I was sixteen years old, I could see through that bullshit! If you want to be unpopular just throw a party every night in your garage. But if you're really passionate about songwriting, it seems to me your goal should be to write something that everyone in the world is going to embrace.

CHAPTER 18

It was really cool in the very early days to say, "The Eagles are corporate, so I hate The Eagles." I personally didn't care how commercial some band was as long as it was good! There are guys saying, "It's so shocking that the Ramones are selling their songs for commercials!" Why is it not shocking that "this is forty years going and people are still singing their songs!" There must be something to it. I'm sorry there are no Mekons songs being sung today. But that doesn't mean that The Mekons had more credibility. It just means they didn't write a song that was as popular as "Hey Ho Let's Go."

JM: I recently realized the Mekons song "Where Were You?" was used in a TV commercial. It's a thirty-year celebration of the brand Acura, and there's footage of twenty-first-century factory workers assembling cars and we hear the narrator say, "When you're young, you do crazy things. You do wild things." He even says, "When you're young you ignore hierarchy and empower anarchy."

JON LANGFORD (The Mekons): An advertising company wanted to use the song and said it was going to be just an online thing for internal promotion. It was all very vague. It was the original band, so we got in touch with everyone and I expected everyone to say, "No. Fuck that." And that's not the way it turned out. Everybody was like, "Well, what's the point? The song is thirty-eight years old so maybe we'll just go with it." Then it came back that they wanted to use it for a major commercial for Acura. And it was going to be on during the Olympics and the NBA finals. So, I got back in touch with everyone and said, "What about that?" With the Mekons, no one has made any money out of the whole thing for all those years. We thought we might as well have the money and use it to support struggling artists.

CHRISTIAN ASPLUND ("Sacred Music and The Punk Ethic"): I remember when I first saw a Nike commercial that used the song "The Revolution Will Not Be Televised" (1995). You imagine these ad men who come together, maybe from a punk rock background, trying to use cultural references to bring associations to their audience. It's insidious that a lot of people with very antimaterialist views and goals ended up joining the corporate world and view their previous life as a fun lark. But we saw that happen with the hippie generation, who became conservative and more corporate than anything we've ever seen.

FEEL LIKE YOU'VE BEEN RIPPED OFF?

"Do I buy Country Life Butter because it's British?" asks John Lydon in the 2008 TV advert for a British butter company. In the ad, Lydon is also comically chased by cows across a green pasture. The *Guardian* newspaper reported,

THE REVOLUTION WILL BE COMMODIFIED

"The Country Life advert cashes in on Lydon's standing as a British icon, albeit of the nihilistic variety."[7] This was twenty-five years after Lydon sang, "Big business is very wise," in the 1983 Public Image Limited song "This Is Not a Love Song." And just thirty years after he posed this question to the very last audience to see a live performance of the original, short-lived Sex Pistols at Winterland in San Francisco in 1978: "Do you feel like you've been ripped off?" Lydon's butter commercial was created by the Grey London agency, which itself is owned by WPP, whose website boasts of being among the top-ten advertising agencies in the world with offices in over eighty-three countries.

JM: You've been in TV ads for things like butter. I think you haven't used any Pistols or PiL music in commercials but put yourself in the ads to make money to produce albums.

JOHN LYDON (Sex Pistols / PiL): Yep! Hilariously so! And under a great deal of self-analysis about whether this is the right or wrong thing to do. Ultimately it was the right thing to do because they gave me a free hand. Like, "Here's the script, John. We expect you to ignore it!" [laugh] Oh, yippee! I could introduce a sense of humor. I loved early English advertising on the TV. When we first got a TV back in the '60s, British TV adverts would always have a sense of fun. They'd be putting themselves down in a very sly, comedic way. That was what I was trying to reintroduce. Rather than deadpan, aim it at the young and hope they're submissive. And the product being butter of all things! Well, hello, the reality is that I eat butter!

And if they're going to give me enough money to reform Public Image and get me out of the quagmire that I found myself in with the record companies, then yippee! And that's exactly what happened. I put every single penny into getting Public Image back together again. I could start rehearsals and put money against outstanding debt. And all I had to do was eat butter! And I've got to tell ya, I wouldn't be the fat man I am today without that free butter! [laugh] And I laugh at that, but it's kind of true! And I don't see that as a bad thing. And in the long run it wasn't because, oddly enough, by 87 percent the British dairy industry was improved. Just on those commercials! Those are bizarre figures, mate. When I release records and promote them, I don't have the money for TV advertisements. In music, less is best. A massive audience is a massive problem.

HIPPIES TURNED INTO CORPORATIONS

JOHN LYDON (Sex Pistols / PiL): A lot of damage was done in the late '60s in the hippie movement. Young people hooked into that: "Yeah, man. I just don't

CHAPTER 18

care." Well, you *have* to care because them same hippies turned into Virgin Records and then I had to deal with corporate hippies! Which was: *meet the new boss, same as the old boss*. They're there to make money and if you understand that, that's fine, then you can deal with it. But the fakism of it all is what upsets me!

> Ultimately, though, Western punk has got soft and largely apolitical thanks to us living in one of the freest countries in the world. Punk in America and Britain is John Lydon selling computer games and Green Day filling stadiums. But if you think punk—the spirit of punk—is dead, go to South America, go to Russia, go to Eastern Europe and see what the young punk fans there have to say about it.[8]

FUTURE'S SO BRIGHT

MILES COPELAND (I.R.S. Records): When Ray-Ban called up and said, "We want to use 'Future's So Bright, I Gotta Wear Shades'" and they're gonna offer a million dollars, I thought I'd be a hero! So, I said, "Sure, we'll do it." I called up Pat MacDonald (Timbuk 3) and said, "Great news. I've got you half a million dollars." Because our deal was that we split everything 50/50. I said, "You can go buy a house!" He said, "No, Miles. Don't do it. Don't give the rights away." Pat was so married to the idea that if you let a song go for whatever reason, it's wrong.

PAT MACDONALD (Timbuk 3): I think Miles did definitely see the irony in "The Future's So Bright, I Gotta Wear Shades." The song is about nuclear war. But I think at the same time, it might have been some kind of sport for him to see if there was no such thing as a band with political integrity. That every band had a price. Sometimes I entertained the thought that he might be playing a little game of, *what's their price?*

MILES COPELAND (I.R.S. Records): Up until the Sting "Desert Rose" song (1999) was used in a Jaguar commercial the rule in the music business had been that a new act, or an act with a current record, does *not* give its music to a commercial. That's tantamount to selling out. There had been songs in Levi's commercials, but they were old songs. Nobody had ever used a commercial as part of the marketing strategy to sell a current record. But I recognized the fact that if the product is cool, why not? If it had been a Tampax commercial or deodorant, it might have not worked. But the Jaguar car for Sting was really cool. From that point on you started seeing bands saying, "If Sting can do it then it must be okay." That Sting commercial actually lowered the age group of Jaguar buyers from sixty-five to forty-five and saved Jaguar Cars. Sting can proudly say, "I saved Jaguar Cars."

DON REDONDO (JFA): If I saw a really cool commercial and it was kids skateboarding with "Hey, Ho, Let's Go!" I'd be like, "Cool! The Ramones! Look, they're on a commercial!" But the other side of me sees a Jaguar ad with "London Calling" and I know Joe Strummer is rolling over in his grave! Advertising Jaguar with "London Calling" has nothing to do with what that song was written about and they damn well know it!

CLASH BECAME THE ESTABLISHMENT

MICHELLE CRUZ GONZALES (Spitboy): I'm glad The Clash "sold out." Spitboy's aim was not to be on a major label and be virtuoso musicians. We were a message band and everything else was secondary. I've always been uncomfortable with using the term "sellout," the s-word. I don't think we would've had the opportunity; no one was going to put Spitboy on a major label. We were way too political and in your face. I'm glad The Clash "sold out." I live in a really small town and if The Clash hadn't put out *Combat Rock* and been played on the radio I maybe would've never become as political as I am.

MILES COPELAND (I.R.S. Records): The reality is that most people formed a rock and roll band and pretty soon they began to think about how much money they could get. They'd make a record deal and, "How big was the advance?" But at the beginning, what was exciting was the fact that you could do it without having years of study at university before you could be a musician. Politics came into it, but I think it was more of, "Let's be anti-establishment" as a way to get attention.

Everything changed because we were successful. And that's part of what happens to a successful business; we ended up being the establishment. As Joe Strummer once said to me, "One day we're going to be the establishment." He recognized the fact that you can be antiestablishment at the beginning, but once you gain success, you're the establishment. That's what happened to I.R.S. Records; we became a corporation like everybody else. We had to pay the rent, pay taxes, and we had to give bonuses at Christmas time.

ANTONINO D'AMBROSIO (*Let Fury Have the Hour: Joe Strummer, Punk and the Movement that Shook the World*): In the film I made, director John Sayles addresses this very vexing contradiction: if you're really serious about making art that speaks to as many people as possible, you have to figure out how to make the system work for yourself without letting the system use you. That's

CHAPTER 18

the big obstacle for a lot of artists who get popular on a major label, like The Clash. Rage Against the Machine is a good example. As long as this economic system remains in place it's very difficult to remove yourself from that. Like John Sayles said, "Don't let the system use you. Figure out how to use the system."

CHRIS FRANTZ (Talking Heads): We were no Michael Jackson, but we were having enough commercial success that we could continue. We were alternative before there was alternative. We were trying things that were challenging, but not so challenging like Captain Beefheart that you never have any success. We loved Captain Beefheart, but we wanted to have more success than that!

CLEM BURKE (Blondie): Blondie had a lot of success back in the day, so we're able to still have an audience. We could play a festival with underground bands and then go and play a festival with Kelly Clarkson. We walk that line between commercial and underground.

NAUGHTY OR NICE?

On December 9, 2018, Hyundai released a Christmas-themed ad that plays on that perennial Santa Claus judgment, "Have you been naughty or nice?" The commercial features a back-and-forth soundtrack with two versions of "Winter Wonderland" that wrestle playfully with each other. "The ad cleverly contrasts Sihasin's 'Naughty' version with a 'Nice' big jazz band version of the same song recorded by vocal legend Tony Bennett to show the versatility of Hyundai's sedans and SUVs," says a note from Hyundai accompanying the thirty-second spot posted on YouTube. The band was also quoted, "We are excited to further open the doors for Native American artists."

JENEDA BENALLY (Blackfire / Sihasin): We actually politicized "Winter Wonderland" so we were more than excited that that song was going to get out there. We changed "Eskimo" to "Inuit." And at the end of the song we say, "Don't eat that yellow snow." That's a reference to the fact that we sued the federal government to protect the holy San Francisco Peaks. I was so excited thinking we'd be able to get that message out there. Yes! You can stand up against the federal government, although we weren't successful in our lawsuit and that was heartbreaking. In fact, that's the whole story about how we became Sihasin after Blackfire. For me, it is useful to get punk and politics out there. At first, I'll admit, I gave this ad a lot of thought. I realize we're all using fossil fuels, and we're all addicted to it. I don't like the concept of money to rule one's world. But the fact is that we have to find different ways to be sustainable.

CLAYSON BENALLY (Blackfire / Sihasin): There's that struggle of not wanting to sell out if something is corporate, and the reality is that we're living in an era where you're bombarded with media that is dictating who we are. If our story is not represented out there, then we're not part of that discussion. So how do we put ourselves into that discussion? How do we make sure that we have a seat at the table? It's ensuring our voice is heard. If that is by *any means necessary* and taking it to the front lines and if that front line is a car commercial? Hell yeah! That's an opportunity for people to potentially learn about an Indigenous Navajo band that has views that might be contrary to yours, but at least now we have some sort of voice.

CONSUMING PRODUCT

MARJANE SATRAPI (*Persepolis*): Everything that begins as a good thing, very quickly it becomes a consuming product. It's so sad. In Paris, where I live, all these bourgeois women nowadays have pins and leather jackets and they have a feeling that the rebellion is at its height. In reality they are bourgeois. Everything has become a product. The first time I heard Iggy Pop I was fourteen and he was singing about the A Bomb: "Search and Destroy." This is the music for today. But who listens to that now? They all prefer to listen to Ed Sheeran and look like Mark Zuckerberg. They all think they're rebellious, but they're all polite. To rebel you need to be not polite. You need to irritate people. Most of the time with good things, people know the value of it twenty or thirty years after because at the time it comes, it irritates people.

FERN FIELD (director *The Day My Kid Went Punk*, 1987 ABC Afterschool Special): In those early days, punks wanted to create a community where you could feel a part of something. That was very real. What social media has done is more mercenary. We've been very good at creating mindless consumers. It's more than ever about money and influencers. It's a different world. I'm not sure what kids today consider success or being accepted. It seems that looking like everybody else is the norm now. There are so many messages out there that I'm not sure what's going on. A lot of what was groundbreaking has now entered into the collective consciousness.

JUSTIN SANE (Anti-Flag): I'm proud to say that I was on the cover of the *Wall Street Journal*! [laugh] I never could've imagined that this band that played punk rock basement shows the first five years of our existence, that I would one day be on the front page of the *Wall Street Journal*! It was a good laugh. Our band has been approached by major labels for about four or five years. We've never said we would not work with a major label. We have found there are ways we can manipulate the corporate media to talk about the issues we care about. We do not want to be exclusive in who we work with when it comes to working for greater change. Working with Congressman McDermott to limit military recruitment at schools just makes sense because he's on the same page as us. There are not a lot of people in government who are willing to ally themselves with a group of punk rockers! It's not necessarily the politically savvy thing to do! (In 2006 Anti-Flag and McDermott opposed a section of the No Child Left Behind Act giving US military recruiters access to school records, including student contact information.)

THURSTON MOORE (Sonic Youth): I always thought most of the main players of punk rock—be it Joe Strummer or John Lydon—always viewed themselves as being very proud of being working class and not expressing any desire to get into a situation of luxury. The idea was to have a modicum of happiness and pay your rent. That was an incredible model to have instead of the pompous ultra-wealthy rock star. It got a little distorted by the end of the '80s. All of a sudden there was a new model when Nirvana became as massive as anybody and they sort of joined these ranks almost unwittingly. It was problematic for them as people, but I think they learned how to deal with it. Two out of three of them did. Kurt (Cobain) took his life for reasons that we'll never really know.

SARA MARCUS (*Girls to the Front: The True Story of the Riot Grrrl Revolution*): I'm not a person who is going to be only putting out my work through DIY and noncommercial venues. I'm also not a person who's going to dismiss somebody else's work for doing that. We could say the powers that be are allowing this to come through for a certain reason, because it lets essential economic and other unjust organizations remain intact. But at the same time, something actually liberatory does get through. Is that always going to be the case if there's a punk song in a car commercial? I wouldn't make that case about every instance. But overall, something can get through.

HARDY FOX (The Residents): The Residents were done with punk stylistically by the time that word existed. However, we saw money-making potential in it and we rereleased "Satisfaction" due to the fact that the style had become popular. We sold an awful lot of them. That single was coming from exactly the punk place; it was a creation of frustration. But there was no reason to do it twice. Once it was done, it was done.

JM: Was there pressure from audiences or record companies to define your sound more clearly?

JAMES WILLIAMSON (Iggy & The Stooges): Record companies for sure. You can't blame them. They're in the business of making money and we weren't a money-making proposition! I don't regret any of it because I think the music holds up pretty well. It sounds relatively contemporary. But they didn't know what to do with us! Never did. We remained anti-establishment. To this day the Rock and Roll Hall of Fame: seven times the band has been up for that and seven times they won't vote us in. It's almost a sign of pride at this point. (Iggy & The Stooges were finally inducted in the Rock and Roll Hall of Fame in 2010 by Billie Joe Armstrong of Green Day.)

CORPORATE AMERICA GOT INTO IT

JD PINKUS (Butthole Surfers): Punk rock was the first time that corporations—people who had no interest in music—started investing in it because they saw how many copies had sold. That's when corporate America got into it. Nowadays it's totally different; the only way anyone can make money off a major would be if you sold your soul for a whole umbrella deal. They'd have a piece of you in everything: merchandise, recordings. Big pockets.

JOSEPH OJO TAYLOR (Undercover): Punk rock showed up and it had its two years in the spotlight and then it got co-opted by pop culture. And because it's a rather extreme subculture with violence and an anti-establishment mindset—like we saw with the hippies at the end of the 1960s—it couldn't last long. Having said that, there have been important musical developments that have come from punk like Elvis Costello's idea that he considers himself a punk at heart, but he wants to be more melodic. There is always going to be a revolutionary voice.

CHRISTIAN ASPLUND ("Sacred Music and The Punk Ethic"): How much has punk rock permeated our lives? That has a very dark answer because I think the conservative movement and Fox News now borrow so much from punk rock. This *in-your-face* breaking down of social norms. The reason people were doing that in the punk period was because it was asymmetrical warfare. It was a way of communicating when you didn't have a place at the table. The sad thing is that this style of expression and using profanity in music is now sort of de rigueur for a lot of popular music. But we have a president who uses profanity all the time! (Trump, 2018) This is a perverted version of the punk ethos.

STEVE IGNORANT (Crass): The Poison Girls did a song, "Everybody's Got Their Price. Up Yours." I'll go to that. There's no way on earth that one of those corporations is going to use a fucking Crass song to promote their shite. That's not punk rock. That's commercialism. I remember hearing a story about the Chumbawambas and they'd been getting a lot of stink because they'd signed to EMI. They were in Italy and FIAT got in touch with them, "Can we use one of

CHAPTER 18

your songs to do this car ad?" And Chumbawambas went, "Well, how much are you going to give us?" FIAT went, "Blah, blah." So, the Chumbas went to the nearest anarchy center and said, "Look, FIAT wants to use our song for an advert. If we do it and give you the money, do you think it's okay?" And the anarchists went, "Yeah, fucking hell. Uh huh!" Brilliant! *That* I can get. But the rest of it, I don't. I'm a bit dismayed. I'm being very polite.

IT BECAME A FASCIST THING

D. J. BONEBRAKE (X): Everyone had their own idea of what punk was. It wasn't just this one thing. Sometimes they would try and enforce it: "You can't wear anything other than black." Or, "Your hair has to be this length!" It became a fascist thing. I thought punk was just the opposite. That's one reason I liked X. We said, "We do what *we* want to do! You can't tell us we can't do a slow song. We can do 'Adult Books.' Fuck You!"

JM: Don Bonebrake told me, "The Go-Go's were smart because they said, 'We're not punk rock.'" There was this idea that if you're punk then you shouldn't sound good or be successful.

BELINDA CARLISLE (The Go-Go's / The Germs): Right. Exactly. I remember going to The Canterbury for rehearsal in 1979 and saying, "We're going to be famous rock stars one day!" When you go into music you have to have dreams of being on stage and being a big success! There's nothing wrong with making money and nothing shameful about being popular. It was because we didn't know how to play our instruments in the very beginning that things sounded a certain way! But our music was always very melodic. We always said our influences were from where we grew up, Southern California. That would be The Beach Boys and The Mamas & The Papas. But also, The Clash and The Buzzcocks. We came out of the punk scene and when we started becoming proficient on our instruments people started saying, "The Go-Go's are sellouts." Especially when *Beauty and the Beat* (1981) came out and sold millions, then we were completely ostracized by the punk scene. In retrospect, we always stayed true to ourselves. We were ambitious of course. To do what we did there had to be a certain amount of ambition and there's nothing wrong with ambition.

LYDIA LUNCH (Teenage Jesus & The Jerks): Punk got caught in conformity. There are a lot of bands that are stuck with that title (punk rock) just because they were around at that period. I don't think Wire is a punk rock band. I loved Wire. Nor was Joy Division or The Birthday Party. Nor were a lot of bands that get slandered by that title just because they happened at the same time and had some visual affectation that related.

JOHN LYDON (Sex Pistols / PiL): I've gone from being championed as King of Punk to outright animosity because I wouldn't follow the new manifesto! For god's sake—it was *against* rules! Not adhering rigidly to be ridiculous and stupid and cliché. There we have it—the studded leather jacket brigade—wow! They're still hanging around! The art of the individual was ignored. I'm always for individuality. I'm not for mass consumption. Or mass copying. I don't want to fit in, in that way. If I wanted to join an army, well I'd pick one with a better uniform!

STEVE IGNORANT (Crass): That unwritten punk rule book must be fifty thousand pages long by now! It's got to be bigger than the Bible! I've broken just about every rule in it. [laugh] I found that ridiculous—to be a punk you had to wear a certain uniform? No! The whole idea of punk was to be individual. Punk rock isn't a stylized singing. It's not wearing right brittle Creepers, as we used to call them, or wearing eighteen-hole Dr. Martens or a leather jacket with studs in it. It's deeper than that. Punk rock is an emotion. It's a lifestyle. If you're really there, you don't wear it, you *are* it. Same goes for anarchism as well. The minute people start putting down rules and regulations, that's the end of it.

KID CONGO POWERS (The Gun Club / The Cramps / Pink Monkey Birds): Punk rock was also quite separatist. Punk rockers didn't want to be part of the rest of the world and the people I knew were a subculture within a subculture. Also, at the time my queerness was not a political issue for me. I had John Savage write the introduction of my book (*A New Kind of Kick*, 2022) and he mentions there was a ready-made acceptance to take in gay liberation, but the punks rejected it. They were saying, "We're our own thing. We're separate from the rest of the world. Fuck you!" Punks wanted to be confrontational and different from what was going on. Music was boring and there was overblown prog rock. And hard rock was so macho and sexist. Punk rock was really perfect for a group of budding teens.

By the time I was in The Gun Club that was already 1979, late in punk, and things were changing. The Gun Club had to contend with a punk scene that was not very free. Hollywood still had a very free-thinking scene, but as we played out of town, the hardcore scene was already budding. For me, it was like, "Oh, those silly kids." I was already an old hag of twenty-one and wondered, "What are these kids thinking?" After playing several hardcore shows to people having their backs to the stage, I thought, "Okay, kids being kids." I didn't begrudge them, but it seemed to be coming from a real anger, as opposed to a disappointment or an anarchistic reconstruction. I didn't see any reconstruction. I saw a lot of tearing down and not a lot of building in the scene at large. I'm not talking

CHAPTER 18

about the artists, because there was some great art coming out of that, and really strange and interesting hardcore bands like The Middle Class. I actually really liked The Circle Jerks at the time. There was stuff going on. But it was not for me and I knew I had to leave that.

By the time I got in The Cramps in 1980, I was definitely over the hill and I was onto my own thing and I left that hardcore scene to do what they were going to do. I was ready to make the music I wanted to make and hopefully follow an original path. I started to learn that I wanted to connect with people, as opposed to being separate from people. That whole separatist notion was not for me. I wanted to connect with other people, and becoming a musician changed my view of what punk rock was and that pushing people away was not incredibly constructive.

WE'RE DESPERATE

JM: There's a scene in *The Decline of Western Civilization* where we hear Exene talk about the song "We're Desperate." She says, "Someday people are going to pay five dollars to see us play and they're going to say, 'They're not desperate!'" Now there's an exhibit honoring your band called "X: Forty Years of Punk in Los Angeles" at the Grammy Museum in LA (October–March 2018). You probably didn't expect X to last forty years.

D. J. BONEBRAKE (X): I didn't think *I* would last that long! [laugh] I feel lucky to be alive, you know? When you reach my age of sixty-two (2018), by then you've lost people. The scene we were in was wild and crazy. We were all living for the moment. Exene was talking about something very real about "five dollars." We would charge *three* dollars. It was such a small scene and if you charged three dollars people complained! I have these Xeroxes of our guest lists from the Whisky a Go Go with 125 people! [laugh] And it only holds three hundred! So, if you don't let in everyone from the guest list and charge them five dollars, people used to say, "Sellout!" Like you shouldn't make a living!

LENNY KAYE (Patti Smith Band): Everybody likes to have things classified, to file it away, to see it in simplicity rather than complexity. It's like punk rock. That word "punk" covers a lot of different types of bands, from power-pop groups to extreme hardcore bands, but everyone likes a good pigeonhole. I'm a bird that likes to be free, myself.

JELLO BIAFRA (Dead Kennedys): I ran into one person who was in one of the more militant anarcho-punk hardcore bands in the Bay Area, and one of the best and most influential. And he'd become a stockbroker! He saw the look on my face and said, "I couldn't take it anymore, man." To me there's got to be a better way: have a moral code that you can live with. Even if you're going to catch shit from some of your more-radical-than-thou peers.

BRAD LOGAN (Leftöver Crack): The bottom line is—do whatever you want to do and don't let anybody else put a label on you. Put a label on yourself, if you want. I know that for me the most fun, interesting, and inspiring music I see are bands where there are fucking ten or twenty people there. It's always been that way. Some of these bands have gone on to be huge and that's great and they're absorbed by other people. But it's like, *the fucking revolution will not be televised*. These things are born out of poverty and frustration. Not necessarily monetary poverty, but *spiritual poverty*. That bankruptcy is what motivates a lot of this stuff. It's boredom, which is a byproduct of that.

BURN PUNK LONDON
JOE CORRÉ AND EXTINCTION REBELLION

In the mid-1970s punk rock was blossoming in London, England, after musicians, artists, and producers traveled across the pond to CBGBs in New York City to check out bands like the Ramones, Television, Iggy & The Stooges, Blondie, The Dictators, and Patti Smith Group. The aggressive music, fashion, and politics of punk rock thumbed its nose at the status quo and back in London the political establishment fought back. On November 10, 1977, the *Guardian* newspaper reported that record shop managers in England were being charged with violating an 1889 Indecent Advertisement Act and 1824 Vagrancy Act after they displayed a new album in their shop windows: *Never Mind the Bullocks—Here's the Sex Pistols*, released on October 28, 1977. The *Guardian* article, "Punk Record Is a Load of Legal Trouble," also said, "Mr. Al Clarke, press officer for Virgin Records, said, 'The LP was released 11 days ago. It brought in £250,000 before it was even released and went straight to number one in the charts.'"

Forty years later, the same forces that attempted to destroy punk rock robustly celebrated "Anarchy in the UK" with an official series of music, film, and lecture programs in 2016 called "Punk London." The August 14, 2016, *New York Times* outlined concerts and events planned for Punk London in an article titled "Hey Ho, It's Old: England Embraces Punk Rock 40 Years Later." It also highlighted a protest against the commodification of punk by Joe Corré, the son of Vivienne Westwood and Sex Pistols manager Malcolm McLaren: "The anniversary of that summer is being celebrated in Punk London, a citywide, yearlong series of exhibitions, talks and concerts supported by the mayor's office and the National Lottery. Proving, perhaps, that punk's rebellious spirit

Cash from Chaos. Contributed: Joe Corré

hasn't yet receded into rock's history books, this institutional endorsement of an anti-establishment movement has drawn skepticism, a little bit of ridicule and even some mild acts of resistance. . . . In March, Joe Corré, the son of the fashion designer Vivienne Westwood and the Sex Pistols manager, Malcolm McLaren, vowed to burn 5 million pounds, or about $6.46 million, worth of punk memorabilia to protest what he saw as the co-opting of the movement."

On November 26, 2016, Corré floated on the Thames on a barge and burned a pile of Sex Pistols T-shirts, records, forty-year-old handmade Sid Vicious dolls, and other memorabilia while a drummer accompanied the media event. On land, Vivienne Westwood read an Extinction Rebellion statement from the back of a red double decker bus including, "By 2100 there will only be one billion people left. It's started already. We'll all be migrants, all trying to get to the green parts." (In March 2022 a wedding dress with graffiti designed by Vivienne Westwood was worn by Stella Moris as she married imprisoned WikiLeaks founder Julian Assange during a ceremony in front of London's Belmarsh prison.)

> *As much as anything, punk was a rallying call for direct action. Whether forming a band, starting a record label or making your own clothes, punk provided the momentum for a generation of creative democracy, and that spirit remains arguably the movement's most important legacy.*
>
> —Punk London website (2016)

Meanwhile Virgin Money, a subsidiary of Virgin Records, released a Sex Pistols credit card. In a 2015 promotional video, Virgin Records president Richard Branson recalls being at the 100 Club in London for a Sex Pistols concert: "Everybody was jumping up and down and going absolutely mad. . . . I'd never come across such energy." In the video Branson places "Anarchy in the UK" on his office turntable and pretends to pogo and spit. He also reminds us that early in his career he signed the Sex Pistols to Virgin Records in May 1977 after the band was dropped by EMI and A&M Records. "A company is just a group of people," continues Branson in the video. "At Virgin Records we love to challenge the established way of doing things. . . . I can't think of anything more appropriate than Virgin Money adopting the Sex Pistols on their credit card."

CHAPTER 19

MCDONALD'S GOING PUNK

JOE CORRÉ ("Burn Punk London"): What you're seeing are the ideas of punk being used by marketing machines. Now you have McDonald's going punk! They've got the McVicious Peri Peri Chicken Wrap, using a Buzzcocks track and Jamie Reid artwork ("What Do I Get" by The Buzzcocks, 2016 McDonald's TV ad). You've got Louis Vuitton doing bondage trousers and using the front of my parents' shop—Seditionary—as the backdrop for their fashion show. And by the way, do you know what Louis Vuitton does at the end of the season when they haven't sold everything from their collections? They send it back to Paris and they burn it all! These are the kind of people that are using punk as a marketing ploy.[1]

You can now get a punk credit card from Virgin Money, 19 percent APR with "Never Mind the Bullocks" or "Anarchy in the UK" on the front. You can buy Punk Beer. It's all become a bit of a joke and very meaningless. For me, the idea with the fire is I'm going to stick two fingers up to that and burn it! Because it doesn't mean anything anymore. It's become conformity in another uniform. That's what I'm trying to say with burning it.

JOE CORRÉ: With this burning event we're seeking to draw parallels between what we call the No Future Generation of the 1970s, where you had a lot of young people who *really* had no future and nothing to look forward to. And they used punk rock to give them confidence in their own creativity to create their own way out of the no future situation. This eventually gave birth to thousands of designers, creative people, filmmakers, and musicians. That is the most positive legacy of punk rock: it was used by people to create their own way out of a no future situation.

If you look at the younger generation today and ask the question about what their future is, we're now living in a city, here in London, where people are facing social cleansing because nobody can afford to live here anymore and their homes are being eyed up as valuable assets. They're being pushed out because they can't afford them. You've got students coming out of university so riddled with debt that they're only taking courses in subjects where they're going to get some kind of corporate job that will enable them to pay off their debt. The solutions that we need in this city and in the world are not going to be found by creating more bankers.

Then there's climate change and all the horrors that come with that, including the migration crisis, breathing down our necks. So, really the parallels couldn't be stronger. In some ways what I'm saying is punk is dead. It doesn't mean anything anymore. It's just another kind of uniform for conformity. What

On Nov. 26, 2016, Malcolm McClaren's son, Joe Corré, burned $6.46 million worth of original Sex Pistols memorabilia, including this Sid Vicious doll, to protest the commodification of punk. Contributed: Joe Corré

CHAPTER 19

we need is a different kind of punk. First of all, we need to properly kill this one off. Punk is now being used by the establishment. I struggle to understand what they're actually celebrating here! Those are the reasons behind what I'm trying to do.

PUNK TOURIST ATTRACTION POSTCARD

JM: I view punk rock as a potentially revolutionary movement for living free. It seems that any movement with potential eventually gets commodified by the establishment. It also seems that living free is a process and requires a continual rebirthing. It's not static.

JOE CORRÉ: Yeah. Let's be honest—right back in the early '80s punk was already used here in the UK by the establishment to show the rest of the world how tolerant, open, and democratic we are as a society. Because we *allow* these punk rockers to put pins through the Queen's nose! We don't mind them jumping around and making a mess. In a way, those guts were ripped out of the movement a long time ago.

When you talk about punk being a revolution, it started out very much like that. A lot of people were drawn to those ideas and they jumped up and down and drank the beer and did the pogo to whichever band they were into. But after that, they didn't really have much to offer. They didn't have many solutions. Yes, a lot of people drew a lot of benefit personally from having the confidence that punk gave them to go out into the world and do some pretty amazing things. As I said, that is the most positive legacy from punk.

But the whole spirit of what punk was about *originally* got lost quite quickly. Even by the late '70s and definitely early '80s it was kind of over and punk had already become a kind of tourist attraction postcard. You know if you come to London, you can buy the postcard of the guards of Buckingham Palace? You can also buy the postcard of the punk with the Mohican haircut. That's all right. If you're going to commoditize something and make it into a pose because the meaning of it has entirely disappeared, then fine. Just like the Beefeaters of the Tower of London. But then you should give these guys an allowance for the uniform and they should be employed to entertain the tourists.

JOE CORRÉ: But if you're going to turn around and start talking about how meaningful this thing was as a movement and start being nostalgic, punk was never meant to be nostalgic. It had an urgency about it. It wasn't about looking back and taking a trip down memory lane. But if you're going to take a trip down memory lane, then you should really talk about some of the home truths: it was despised by the establishment and they did everything in their power to try and crush it. So, for them to be supporting it forty years later, and all of these old punks to be going along, pulling their exhibitions together and taking part in it? It's like they're all holding their hands out for a bowl of gruel. Just like Oliver Twist saying, "Please sir, can I have some more?" That was never the spirit of punk!

I've been a bit surprised by some of the reactions I've had from people who just don't get it at all and think by me taking this action I'm some sort of spoiled rich kid who's throwing his toys out the pram and I should give it to charity or it should be put in a museum. That's the way to castrate any kind of bullocks that it had left. But that's where we are. Punk went on and created a lot of separate movements. The skate kids in the US think they're punks. And maybe *they are* in some kind of way. I don't really know. It spawned all kinds of little groups of people that felt that they were being outsiders or nonconformists in one way or another. But in reality, they're all conforming. And the solutions that this world needs today in order to survive are not going to come from conformity.

JOE CORRÉ: Do I care if Johnny Rotten sold himself to the butter industry to promote butter? Do I care that Iggy Pop sells car insurance? Do I care that the Sex Pistols sell credit cards? Not really. It don't really bother me. I'd just rather we have an honest conversation that this stuff is now meaningless. And if it's meaningless, don't try to pretend that it's got some importance. What does it matter that these things are going to be burned and destroyed? I'm interested in what kind of phoenix can rise from the ashes.

Most people are interested in this thing I'm doing because of its value of five million pounds. If you ask them, "What value does this T-shirt have? What does it represent? What value does this poster or record have?" They don't know because they don't really have value to them. It only means something to people who were either there at the time and have some nostalgic memory of what those things were supposed to mean, or it's something that's been lost along the way and makes up a vague picture of an idea of nonconformity that doesn't really exist anymore. It's just another sort of pose, really. It's a pose without any kind of intention.

COMMERCIALIZATION OF PUNK

JELLO BIAFRA (Dead Kennedys / Guantanamo School of Medicine): I heard about it (Burn Punk London) and to me it's just a thoughtless, selfish action of a spoiled rich kid. If he really wanted to have any kind of protest value, why didn't

CHAPTER 19

he sell it all off and donate the five million pounds to a deserving charity? People in Puerto Rico, Haiti, Houston, and the Florida Keys—they could use that help right now, but instead the guy burned it all up! It's something you'd only be so thoughtless about if you were brought up sheltered by excess wealth.

MARK REEDER (Die Unbekannten / *B Movie: Lust & Sound in West Berlin 1979 -1989*): Pathetic. Attention grabber. Some of the artifacts he (Joe Corré) destroyed could be considered public domain. I'm fairly certain his father would not have approved of this action, no matter what the headlines. A fact that is often overlooked is that punk band number one—the Sex Pistols—were initially signed to EMI, a very major record label, in 1976. McLaren was all for the commercialization of punk. He told me so himself. He wanted to tip the scales. Otherwise, he wouldn't have signed to EMI. And that's probably why he went to the *Sun Newspaper* in the first place, to use this daily rag to reach millions of their readers. I was one of them. Once it became a topic of conversation and bands started selling out huge venues, traveling the world, and hitting the charts, it was obviously a very commercial enterprise.

ANDY GILL (Gang of Four): Malcolm McLaren got everyone hyped up about it. Getting the Sex Pistols onto an early evening TV show where they'd all swear—"That's going to set the nation alight!" That was clever PR.

CLEM BURKE (Blondie): It doesn't make any sense to me. He's trying to make a Dada-esque statement I suppose. A nihilistic statement. But what a waste of something that could've been used for the good. Knowing the Pistols, as I do, certainly Lydon was a wild card, and he still is a wild card. But the other three just wanted to be pop stars. They invented a new way to become a pop star. Stylistically they were influenced by what came before. They loved Bowie and T-Rex. Steve Jones loved all kinds of heavy metal.

DICK LUCAS (Subhumans): I heard about it (Burn Punk London) a few months back. I got the idea: return the Sex Pistols and what they initially meant back to a state where they meant it—on fire! They turned the nature of success on its head, but then the ball rolled full circle and Mr. Lydon did a TV ad for butter. Bye, Johnny! Joe Corré is a McLaren, so proving it's neither nature nor nurture that makes us. It's attention. And he seems to be after as much as possible. Do what you want, mate. Don't expect the attention you think you deserve though!

CHRIS FRANTZ (Talking Heads): That was pretty wild that he burned Sex Pistols memorabilia. He also designs some great lady's underwear! Did you know that? To me that's more fun than burning punk rock stuff.

PUNK IS IN THE BRAIN

JM: If part of the revolution is going to address capitalism and we recognize that capitalism is a big part of the problem, then it's absurd to have punk become a product of consumer culture.

JOE CORRÉ (Burn Punk London): Yes. I remember the Vogue Met Ball in New York did a punk thing a couple of years ago and it was interesting to see these people arrive down the red carpet and see what they had to say. Anna Wintour showed up in this floral pink dress in that boring '60s style that she always wears and they asked her, "What are you wearing? What's so punk about it?" And she said, "Paul Simonon from The Clash told me the color of punk is pink, so I'm wearing pink tonight." I thought, "This is just hilarious!"[2]

JOE CORRÉ: I'm in a strange position here because I don't want to come across as being the oldest punk in town. And to be honest with you, am I really that interested in punk? Not anymore. I was interested in it forty years ago. I think there are huge problems in the world and it's time that people started considering those. You can go around your life saying you're punk and go to see all these bands and buy their records and wear their leather jackets and get the uniform haircut and wear the uniform trousers and you're just a conformist like everyone else. That's not punk to me.

Punk is in the brain. It's not in terms of what you wear, of what bands you're into. I'm not even sure punk rock has anything to do with music. Punk rock is an attitude: you're awake and you're not going to take this shit and you're going to do something about it! Buying a pair of Louis Vuitton bondage trousers doesn't add to that. It doesn't take you in that direction. The only thing that will take you in that direction is your own creativity. You don't create things in a vacuum. Ideas come from other ideas and from immersing yourself in some kind of culture. That means feeding your brain and understanding what position you have in the world and what you can do about it.

All that a punk rock attitude does is gives you the confidence in yourself to say, "I don't care if I make a fool of myself. I don't care that I can't play the guitar, I'm going to create a band anyway." Just by that action alone, by having the confidence to get up on stage and make a fool of yourself, that confidence doesn't leave you. Next time you have to do it, it's so much easier. That's the way you start on a road to really find out something and not listen to the propaganda.

CHAPTER 19

PRIVATIZATION OF PUNK ROCK

JOE CORRÉ: Oscar Wilde famously said, "People know the price of everything and the value of nothing." That's very indicative of where we are now. Everything has become for sale. Everything seems to have a price. As a kid, I grew up in the 1970s right through the Margaret Thatcher era and beyond, through Tony Blair. I have witnessed the privatization and sell-off of practically every asset this country ever owned, from water to the electric to the telephone, school playing fields, the post office, everything! Last year they tried to sell the National Parks. They wanted to sell the fucking Lake District because they didn't want to pay anymore for a visitor's center!

What it comes down to this year (2016) is the privatization of punk rock. This is just another commodity. The establishment is now going to own it because the British Museum is going to have a whole section on punk rock. The British Library, Museum of London, and the British Fashion Council are going to support it. All these designer brands are going to make it a trend again and Louis Vuitton are going to do their catwalk show and McDonald's has discovered that they're going to be able to sell to this demographic. So, they're *privatizing ideas* now! It's not just about privatizing *assets*. And punk rock was never meant to be privatized. That freedom of the mind, you can't buy it and you can't sell it! It's not for sale. You either have it or you don't. If you don't have it, then by opening your mind to some of those ideas, you might get some. And it would do you the world of good.

JM: Years ago, private ownership of entities like factories and workplaces seemed like a left alternative to government ownership and control. But now privatization means corporate control by a minority who are often protected by government.

JOE CORRÉ: Of course. We've seen it as the trickle-up theory and not the trickle-down theory. Now there's the top 1 percent of the population controlling the other 99 percent. And everyone going along with it, buying their hamburgers and Louis Vuitton. It seems very obvious to me. I'm very surprised to see so many people just go along with it. It's forty years later so I guess a lot of those people at the time were probably getting high and having a good time. You know, living in a squat and joining a band. Got some fame, lost it all, became NA, and now what have they got? Well, all they've got are some memories. Some keep trying to drum up a bit of interest in themselves in order to sell themselves. But not everyone. There's still a lot of people with principles out there.

20

HOW REVOLUTIONARY HAS PUNK ROCK BEEN?

If you're going to go for a source for deep political thought, a rock and roll band probably is not your best choice.

—Klaus Flouride (Dead Kennedys)

Punk had that potential for a real uprising. It didn't occur because we didn't ally ourselves to any other cause, and in any social revolution you certainly must do that.

—Penny Rimbaud (Crass)

The presumption that music can change the world is a bit of a utopian myth. But I think what music can change is individuals.

—East Bay Ray (Dead Kennedys)

CRAZY HOPES THAT WE'D CHANGE THE WORLD

JM: Many punk rock folks hoped their music might effect positive change. How revolutionary has punk been?
DON REDONDO (Jodie Foster's Army): I don't think in a mass hippie *We're going to change the world* way. But certainly, there are people that have written songs that illustrate issues. Songs like "Kill the Poor" or "California Über Alles" or

CHAPTER 20

songs we've written. You just find something that's so stupid that you write a song about it to call attention to it. You don't really expect people to march in the streets about it, but you feel like you did your part—"This is really stupid and if I write a really sarcastic song about this, maybe someone is going to get how stupid it is!"

BRIAN BRANNON (JFA): I was a little younger—still am—than Don when I joined the band. So, I was a little more idealistic. I probably had these crazy hopes that we'd change the world. JFA did have some commentary on stuff going on, but we were also a skate band. The '80s was kind of a crazy time politically with the trickle-down theory that still seems to be with us. And we hoped to somehow help change that. But the other thing was skateboarding. When we first started, we were even lower than punkers, which was pretty low on the social scale. All the skate parks had closed down and we were outcasted. I remember thinking, "Maybe someday there'll be skate parks everywhere again." And now there are!

JM: For many people there was a lot of idealism and vision for what punk rock might do in the world to make revolutionary, positive change. How do you think that's played out?

KLAUS FLOURIDE (Dead Kennedys): Obviously fairly poorly. We're still singing about a lot of the same stuff. But also keep in mind that I'm a firm believer, and we state at our shows, that if you're going to go for a source for deep political thought, a rock and roll band probably is not your best choice. We didn't try to come up with answers as much as questions. We tried to show absurdities and get people to think for themselves. We wanted people to do their own looking into things. That was our system. We didn't tell people, "This is how you have to think."

How successful that was and how successful punk has been in changing the world, I don't know. The Beatles and Bob Dylan revolutionized the world a lot in the '60s, but I think a lot of that would've happened possibly with or without The Beatles and Bob Dylan. Just as much with people like Eldridge Cleaver. There are lots of voices outside of rock and roll and music that shape culture.

Did we serve our purpose? Did we reach our goal? No, I don't think so. At least, it fell short of what everybody was hoping. There are a few more people that maybe think a little more than if we hadn't had the punk spirit, movement, and attitude. But it's frustrating. It seems like there is no silver bullet to get people to think. You just have to keep encouraging. We had a song even about the Red Brigade that we never recorded. It was one of our very first songs. It was called "Kidnap" and was inspired by the Red Brigade. We were writing about things like that, too. Both ends of it: the Red Brigade and Pol Pot and all the crazy people out there that run the world.

HOW REVOLUTIONARY HAS PUNK ROCK BEEN?

JELLO BIAFRA (Dead Kennedys): When you're talking about culture and politics—I have never considered punk a movement. Movements are political. Movements have an eye on the prize. What was the prize for the so-called punk movement? More punk? I think that has succeeded a little too well! But punk was really inspiring, maybe lifesaving in my case. It's a rebel culture that inspired people to jump in and join movements, some of which even sprang from punk people bringing up the issues first. But *culture* and *movement* are two different things. One often inspires the other. In either direction.

JONATHAN RICHMAN (Jonathan Richman and the Modern Lovers): What punk movement? It was just a bunch of guys playing in rock bars. That "movement" was created by the press. There was no movement. Not here in the States at least, I don't know about overseas. I never had anything to do with punk rock. I saw some when my band toured England in the mid-70s. But I never had anything to do with it. I never thought I played it. I started out painting and the music came when I heard The Velvet Underground. As soon as I heard the beginning chords of the song "Heroin," that's what I thought was beautiful.

PENELOPE HOUSTON (The Avengers): When the Sex Pistols came to the US, we realized that punk rock coming out of England had a different social impetus than it did here. In the US the kind of bands that influenced us—Patti Smith, the Ramones, Blondie, Jonathan Richman and the Modern Lovers, the bands that were around before '77—were more a cultural revolution than political or social. In England it seemed because of their society and a certain amount of economic hardship there, the things that influenced punk and its coming to be were different than what influenced the people who were the forebearers of punk in the US.

DAVE ALLEN (Gang of Four): Punk rock was very conservative and more about fashion. Punk was quickly co-opted by culture, rather like the Seattle grunge scene. On the surface these things may look like they're political, but ultimately, they're not revolutionary at all. In fact, there hasn't been a lot of revolutionary rock music that we could point to that's had a massive effect. I think punk over the years just got mainstreamed. If you look at Green Day for instance, they just chucked it all away. Great! Massive commercial success with three chords!

I've never seen punk rock as, "Wow, we really kicked down some doors and got things done!" It didn't really happen. That's probably true of a lot of popular movements. If there isn't a cultural force that has cultural leaders, then it obviously makes sense that The Clash moved to America and became a big rock band. It's not very different than U2 capitalizing on large audiences. Forgive me if I sound a little down on this, but today I find rock music totally boring. There is nothing that I can point to that excites me. So, we lost the battle. Thirty-four

CHAPTER 20

years later (2011) I can look back and say, "What did we do? Not a lot." Thank god people still like *Entertainment!* and *Solid Gold*. But I don't know what that means. I'm pretty removed from thinking of rock music as a cultural force.

DAVE DICTOR (MDC): Punk, for all its rebellion, can be very sexually conservative. Or just as conservative as many parts of the classic rock world.

PENNY RIMBAUD (Crass): Punk had that potential for a real uprising. It didn't occur because we didn't ally ourselves to any other cause, and in any social revolution you certainly must do that. At the time, ironically, there were plenty of people one might have allied with but were probably all feeling the same: that the moment we ally with them, we create a different identity. One with which we can't take responsibility.

My conundrum is allying—working—with others. Crass was an experience where, as long as we were carrying the same banner, we got on wonderfully. In the seven years that we all lived and worked together and had this common core, we were like lovers. The moment that common cause was gone, everything went up in the air and there was a huge division and conflict between us. Because we hadn't been looking at our own inner and deeper resonances during the seven years we were working on this external cause. And we lost whatever our*selves* is. We'd even lost the inquiry into it, so it was a dangerous experiment.

RAY MANZAREK (The Doors / X): Punk has *not* been effective in changing society! From the perspective of my seventy-plus years, *nothing* is effective in changing society. The only thing that it's effective in doing is changing *you*. That's how *you* change society. *You* change! You embrace a new ethic, a new way of doing things. An act of enlightenment. That's the way you change society. I don't think you can change society with music. [pause] But so what? That's not our job! Our job is to set up a spiritual vibration that allows people to transcend their daily lives and to lose themselves in a Dionysian frenzy on a Friday and Saturday night without the tubes. And come Monday, go back to your school and go to your job and do a damn good job. You're a responsible citizen with Dionysus waiting in the background for a chance to come out again.

JM: Has punk been a revolutionary force in relieving suffering and stopping injustices? Do you think your musical expression has affected people in that way?

GLENN BRANCA (Theoretical Girls): No. I just want to get to the people who can hear it. When I grew up in Harrisburg, Pennsylvania, in the '50s and '60s, I didn't know there was a whole other world out there. It was only when I moved to Boston and lived in London for a little while and then moved to New York, I found this whole other world that existed! Part of what I simply want to do is to be an example. I want to say to people, "You're not alone. You're not the only one who thinks like this. You're not the only one who feels like this." That's important. We've got to find the people who are willing to change, who are looking for something else, and have the curiosity and interest to think about change.

As far as taking actual political action, that's not the way I think. One thing I like about Obama is that he talks a lot about education. I think education is the single most important thing that we need to do in the entire world. When people are creating computers that can be sold or given away very cheaply to Africa and other third world areas, that to me is the single most important thing we can do: disseminate education and information. Intelligence is not limited to race or class, as we all know. We want to get to the most intelligent people that we can possibly get to, if we want to see real change in the world.

The truth is—I hate to say it—I don't think there are very many of us. But we've got to get all of us who are there and that's where the change is really going to come. I think it's what the people who want to keep control of the world, and who want to use and take advantage of all of us, are trying to hold down. They don't want us to be educated and know what's going on.

JD PINKUS (Butthole Surfers): We went up to see Scream play at Rock Against Reagan in DC (1983). It wasn't much about politics for me. I really liked the stuff that made me laugh. I liked The Angry Samoans and Circle Jerks. I don't like being preached at and I don't like the political or religious stuff. We had our moshpits when we were kids and we liked to get our energy out. But The Butthole Surfers were definitely not political.

THURSTON MOORE (Sonic Youth): I'm a New York kid. I always thought punk rock was preternaturally political, especially when it was creating an independent means outside of the mainstream music industry. But that isn't how it initially started. Initially when you started having voices like Patti Smith coming out, she was from the city and it was very urban. It was the first time there was this person who had all this energy for people our age—I'm fifty-six—in '76 and '77 that was not dealing with escapism such as the hippie ideal of going to the country and getting away from society and living in this separate world like Crosby, Stills, Nash & Young, James Taylor, or Joni Mitchell. Even though they were millions-selling artists who had lots of money and Hollywood homes, their album covers showed them on little rowboats out on the lake with their dog or sitting on the porch. Fabulous shots of them living this hippie ideal while they were actually living on the Sunset Strip.

MILES COPELAND (I.R.S. Records): There was a lot of political talk around the early punk days. But really what was happening was this whole new generation of acts that were coming out, they were popping up everywhere. Bands

CHAPTER 20

were getting excited that they didn't have to be great musicians in order to form a group. The beauty of the punk movement was that it was sort of free. The entry was easy. It attracted a wild selection of people who didn't feel restricted because they only knew three chords. The fact that they knew one chord, they could form a group. The drummer in Lords of the New Church couldn't play drums the day before he joined the group. A lot of them felt that they needed to talk politics. But that really wasn't the driving force as far as I was concerned.

When I had conversations with The Clash, they seemed to be pretty bright and understanding of what was really going on. But I didn't think a lot of their manager (Bernie Rhodes), who seemed to think it was all about politics. I think there were a lot of things about England at that time where people were objecting to Margaret Thatcher. But I was kind of a fan of Margaret Thatcher. I knew that England had its problems. The punks really said a lot of things that were political, but I don't think they really were that much.

STEVEN LEE BEEBER (*The Heebie-Jeebies at CBGB's*): Bernard Rhodes was another Jewish manager who went off on his own to work with The Clash. It was Rhodes's idea to get them writing political songs. He suggested that to Joe Strummer and Strummer immediately said, "Yeah, great idea. Why don't we do that?" Bernie Rhodes came from a really lefty tradition, too. A lot of the Jews were left on the political spectrum.

JM: You were a part of The Stooges, Iggy Pop's band. It was a vital musical force at that time. Tell me about playing with The Stooges and how you felt to be playing that music.

JAMES WILLIAMSON (Iggy & The Stooges): First, I have to make a slight correction. I don't think that it was all that vital or important at that time. It seems to have become more vital and important lately than it was in those days.

JM: Some realms of music have tried to contribute to positive change in the world through lyrics and activism. How do you think that's played out?

JAMES WILLIAMSON: Better than it did in those days. I don't know of anybody within the punk rock genre that actually has done this, but lots of artists have. Guys like Bono who use their stardom to leverage social programs. He's awesome. I think it's wonderful and I wish there was a lot more of that. Unfortunately, most people in the entertainment business are in it for themselves.

STEVE IGNORANT (Crass): Punk has been incredibly productive. If you can call it music; some of it is. Punk has been incredibly strong in making people think for theirselves. I don't think that's what it particularly set out to do. I don't think the Sex Pistols got together and thought, "We'll make the music and people will start thinking for theirselves." It just happened. In the same way that Crass did.

HOW REVOLUTIONARY HAS PUNK ROCK BEEN?

We didn't set out with the idea of, "Okay, we'll write these songs and make this music—if you can call it that—and people will start thinking for theirselves." We just wrote about what we saw around us, and what we felt, and did it as honestly as we could. And that's the difference when you're talking about punk rock, because if it's talking about social stuff, punk is the most honest genre of music that I've ever come across.

MIKE NESS (Social Distortion): There we were, this revolution that was against the status quo. We definitely changed things on a music and fashion level. There was a quote I remember hearing that punk was about getting off your ass and doing something! Instead of standing on the fringes of society and complaining. That's my interpretation of it.

MARK REEDER (The Frantic Elevators / Die Unbekannten): I think punk rock was very revolutionary. It was political from the outset. It was meant to make a statement and it did. It completely changed the fabric of the UK music scene and the lifestyles of so many people. It gave many young people a vocation and signaled a way out of the boredom that most young school leavers were feeling at the time. Everyone was frustrated regarding the lack of prospects for their future. I felt very lucky because I had a job working in an advertising agency in Manchester (UK) at that time and also a part-time weekend job in the small Virgin Record shop. Fact is, though, by the mid-1970s most people had no prospects and no jobs, there were constant strikes, factories appeared to be closing everywhere. The traditional jobs in the local textile and steel industries that families had held for generations since the Industrial Revolution were suddenly evaporating and being outsourced. The situation for the future looked very bleak. Out of this boredom the idea of punk was born.

BILLY BRAGG: The ideals of punk were always about self-empowerment. About not waiting for someone to come and ask you to make a record, write a book, design a poster, or put on a gig. For you to go out and do it yourself. The idea of punk rock is imbedded in late twentieth-century rock and roll, a period when people believed that rock and roll could change the world. It was our social media. It was the only medium available if you were working class. If you had something to say about the world, the only way you were going to get a platform was if you learned to play guitar, wrote songs, and did gigs.

What punk rock tried to do, quite successfully, was to take empathy and share it. The very currency of music is empathy. All music is making you feel an emotion. Whether it's about somebody else's situation or something you can't quite articulate. Punk rock understood that you could harness that empathy if you mixed it with activism, and then you created solidarity. Real political solidarity in the real world. And that's the revolutionary idea of punk rock.

CHAPTER 20

Punk rock had to articulate everything that young people felt because young people were marginalized by mainstream media. Now if you're nineteen and you're angry at the world, you've got loads of ways to express that. Music no longer has that vanguard role in youth culture. But it still does have a power and that power is the power of solidarity, to make you feel that you're not alone.

KEITH MORRIS (Black Flag / Circle Jerks / Off!): All I know is that all punk did was it broke down a barrier. It was a little bit more all-encompassing. That kid standing out there watching a bunch of guys jump around making a bunch of noise said, "If those guys can do it, I can do it, too." That's pretty much what punk rock was.

JAY BENTLEY (Bad Religion): I was *that kid* when I watched Keith singing in Black Flag.

KEITH MORRIS: When we were doing Black Flag, we weren't thinking about all of this stuff that was going to happen. We just wanted to get through that show! We just wanted to have fun. Whatever happened after that was kind of out of our control.

JM: I've often thought of punk rock as part of a much larger revolutionary movement that would bring down capitalism and deal with racism, sexism, and classism. Now I'm fifty-five years old and a little disappointed that the revolution hasn't gotten a little farther along.

RED SAUNDERS (Rock Against Racism): You're fifty-five? I'm seventy-three and even more disappointed! But I keep plugging away because my life and activity in politics have taught me that activism is the key to everything. That's the burning hope. Here in London, we have incredible young people on the streets every day, campaigning against climate change. We have these huge demonstrations called Extinction Rebellion.

JELLO BIAFRA (Dead Kennedys / Guantanamo School of Medicine): I was part of a big and very tense Earth First! march on the company logging town of Fortuna, California, where some of the leaders were really frightened of what might happen to them. I, of course, naïvely wasn't. Because I'd already been through the LAPD beating up our own fans in California in front of the Whisky a Go Go. But I felt like a fish out of water, wanting to support the cause but, my god, I'm surrounded by all of these new agey people and Deadheads! But then I noticed that some of those very people had fading-skull-with-Mohawk tattoos on their arms! It was just how they evolved in their own time.

Once the *Frankenchrist* obscenity charges hit and, in their own weird way, vaulted me on to the college lecture circuit as a so-called expert on censorship—where I gave my spoken word performances, instead—a lot of people who brought

HOW REVOLUTIONARY HAS PUNK ROCK BEEN?

Poster for Rock Against Racism / Anti-Nazi League march and concert in London co-organized by Red Saunders including Tom Robinson Band, Steel Pulse, The Clash, and X-Ray Spex (April 30, 1978).

me in were campus political activist groups and it opened my mind to the fact that, "Hey, not everybody who is political or an activist or conscious, let alone revolutionary, likes punk rock." Some people have said, "I used to read *Maximum Rocknroll* when I was a teenager, but then I outgrew it." That was a little cause to be taken aback. It was weird how many people asked me, "What do you think of The Cocteau Twins?" I go, "I've never listened to them! [laugh] I'm not sure why I need to!" Others were Tracy Chapman fans and hip-hop people of course.

EAST BAY RAY (Dead Kennedys): My view has changed from when we started. My view is more bottom up than top down. The presumption that music can change the world is a bit of a utopian myth. But I think what music can change is *individuals*. What I hope for is that how you treat your fellow workers, how you treat your family and friends—that's where politics starts. When you improve your own game with the people around you, then maybe they'll improve it and it'll spread from the bottom up. I don't think there is going to be some revolution. Musicians use the emotional side of the brain, which is not conscious and articulate. Most musicians feel these things but don't know how to talk about them. So, musicians tend not to be good politicians at all. I mean politicians in the good sense, like Martin Luther King Jr.

CHAPTER 20

A current example is Bernie Sanders (2016). He's talking about socialism. And he's having an uphill battle, considering what people have been fed for the last decades. But it's good. He's been trying to change people's minds and it looks like he has changed people's minds, because he's slowly rising in the polls. That's politics in the good sense. He's speaking rationally about issues and getting people to change their minds. But what it's going to take is a lot more than him. It's going to take people to make a better world. What we have is a half-socialist, half-capitalist society anyway. People don't realize that. What it's going to take is you treating people better and those people treating their friends, family, and people they meet in a store better. That's getting more and more difficult because the resources are running out.

DAVE ALLEN (Gang of Four): "Guerrilla war struggle is the new entertainment." When we originally wrote and performed that song ("5.45") in 1979 there was a sense that you could bring these subjects to the fore and people would be upset. And that some shift would happen by presenting the idea that guerrilla warfare is on the news as a form of entertainment! Whereas now, it doesn't even get ten seconds! The news in America is amazing on your local channels—"And now here's some news from Iraq," and it's some crap and then straight to, "Today, the Mariners won their baseball game." It's not *even* entertainment any longer. It's just going on as if the general public here has got no influence politically. They are totally off the map. It's not *even* entertainment. I'm not sure that still holds out. Do you have an opinion on that? (To Andy Gill.)

ANDY GILL (Gang of Four): That song is quite cool and, in many ways, it feels more like it was written about now (2005). When that song was written the Soviet Union was apparently doing well and was very powerful (1979). Now it very much *is* about guerrilla war struggle, with covert operations rather than superpowers standing off against each other. One of the things about that song is that it is a bit odd musically.

JM: Some punk rock has been explicit in criticizing and noncollaborating with government, militarism, and nationalism.

LENNY KAYE (Patti Smith Band): And some punk rock has not. Look at the skinhead followers—Oi! music is often used politically. With Patti (Smith) we have a political position and it's kind of like we are into a "hearts and minds" thing, but we also realize music operates in a world that is kind of beyond this world. The things that music really wakes up within you are not political; they're emotional. If you're tapping into the basic emotions of sad, happy, whatever, it's hard to make a point for that. You know, saying which side is wrong in some border war. The fact is that music is a powerful force for all of that. It's part of the great dialogues of our time.

Hopefully we'll get it *more* right. But it doesn't seem like it. Especially when you see that all these horrors that the twentieth century had, the twenty-first century is not going to escape. The eighteenth, nineteenth centuries as well—all of these are characterized by great wars, pestilences, horrible suffering for large portions of the population, and I think we'd be naïve to think that that's what it's going to be, because it isn't. But on the other hand, maybe we can grab a moment of peace and go to a nice rock bar in the middle of Santa Cruz called The Catalyst and have a really great time. And for one moment forget that the world is at odds with each other and just appreciate the togetherness of being in the same room listening to some loud music.

A TEMPLATE FOR THE FUTURE

EXENE CERVENKA (X): I think punk was greatly successful in a lot of ways: culturally, artistically, and politically. And it's a great template for the future. That's why punk rock is still so popular and has never gone away.

STEVEN LEE BEEBER (*The Heebee-Jeebies at CBGB's*): How successful were the punks? They were not remotely successful and yet immensely successful. What I mean by that is in their day they created a lot of press and a lot of attention and yet most of them were broke. Most of them didn't go far and their music didn't go far. But where it did go—it's almost a cliché now, but—when The Velvet Underground or the Ramones would go to towns and play little clubs and ten people would show up, the story is that out of those ten people, five would start a band. Even though the audience was very small at the beginning, it grew and grew. It never went away.

RAMSEY KANAAN (Political Asylum / AK Press / PM Press): You said that every generation has its revolutionary music. I think that unfortunately is *not* the case. Punk has provided a gateway into radical politics for many people today, but they're listening to bands that broke up before they were born. I find that heartening on the one hand and on the other to be kind of bizarre. Crass broke up in 1984 and there's people now being politicized by that band. I guess it's no more odd than people being inspired by Peter Kropotkin and Emma Goldman.

I don't view punk that way at all (as a revolutionary freedom movement). Punk is a genre of music. No more, no less. Because what defines punk, as opposed to folk, reggae, jazz, or classical, is not the instinct for freedom. All music contains within it an instinct for freedom, or rhythm of freedom, shall we say. Music is one of those wonderful things, like words and ideas, which can and ought to be unfettered, like the broad river of life which we both drink from and we also contribute back to.

As far as punk rock is concerned, it's a particular genre of music. We would say that a band is a punk band because of the music they're playing, not because of their visions of freedom or their desire for a better world. There are all kinds of punk bands that are very reactionary who have desires for all kinds of horrible worlds: Dead Kennedys put out a seven-inch called "Nazi Punks Fuck Off." Punk is not this wonderful panacea as a freedom movement. I think quite the opposite. Punk is a particular style of music. Because I happen to like punk rock, I'm going to look for and accentuate the positive aspects of that musical genre.

JM: Do you think punk rock must be political?

MITA SCHAMAL (Namenlos): No, not at all. And it isn't. I myself played in a punk band after Namenlos, which was very poetic even if it had political fragments. Ton Steine Scherben (Clay Stone Shards) have made many wonderful love songs. I'm sure Patti's lyrics were also more poetic. The question is: How do you define politics? I can structure my day in such a way that I adhere to, or exceed, my own laws. I may punish or reward myself for it. Everything is political. Or almost everything. Who is above or below while having sex can be political, right? Taken this way, all songs are political. Even the *Four Seasons* of Vivaldi can be played as a political statement. Or if I record screaming children's voices and explode them like a bomb into a dumb, clunky debate on principles in the Bundestag about allowing motorway tolls or a few more tanks to Saudi Arabia. It doesn't take the punk music direction to make political music. There are so many good lyrics in German rap, for example, which can give as much power as punk.

Pressure always creates back pressure, whether it's called punk or rap or gospel, blues, rock, whatever. Perhaps all the housework is something of an inhalation, followed by the exhalation in a whole new form. I would be in favor of silence. Or laughing yoga. That we all don't take ourselves so seriously anymore because humanity certainly doesn't. I would also find a weeping, howling concert exciting. It's actually very sad that it seems that the species of man will not achieve a revolution that frees itself from its own addiction to power, displacement, and destruction. I'm sorry for the animals that will go down with us, but they're sure to come back in some form, even if we don't. With or without punk.

21

WHERE IS THE REVOLUTION NOW?

When did punk rock become so safe?

—"Rock for Sustainable Capitalism" by Propagandhi (2005)

If knowledge is power then where's the revolution?

—"Fear and Confusion" by Subhumans (2019)

Where are today's punk bands singing about social and political issues? How important is it to reflect on the devastation left behind by recent wars upon Iraq and Afghanistan, the longest war in US history? Are there songs that bring attention to drone warfare in Pakistan, Yemen, and Somalia conducted by US soldiers sitting in leather chairs in air-conditioned rooms in Nevada? Are there lyrics about the US government killing people suspected of terrorism without trial, including American citizens? Are there punks screaming with anger and frustration about police murders and mass citizen shootings? Worldwide spying by the NSA? Who's singing about Chelsea Manning and who remembers Edward Snowden, still hiding out somewhere in Russia? And Julian Assange being dragged from London's Ecuadorian Embassy in 2019 after five years there? Did bands sing out when it was discovered that the United States had secret torture sites at Bagram Air Base in Afghanistan, Abu Ghraib Prison in Iraq, and the Chicago Police Department's Homan Square facility? We face an overwhelming number of issues, including growing homeless encampments across the United States, a widening worldwide wealth gap, and the continuing COVID-19 pandemic. There's plenty to be singing about.

While many punk musicians have always dedicated their music to destroying authoritarian culture and building a more equitable and peaceful world,

CHAPTER 21

some punks become sparked into revolutionary lyrics by particular events. Milo Aukerman wanted to affect the results of the US presidential elections of 2020, so a month before elections he released a three-song ukulele-based EP of "protest songs" that couldn't wait for the next album by his band The Descendants.

> *#MAGA / What a fucking joke / For we the people / It's not too late!*
>
> —"Hindsight 2020" by RebUke (Milo Aukerman, The Descendants)

Aukerman's press release explained, "I've spent most of my punk rock life avoiding the temptation to write political songs; it always seemed like politics is the obvious go-to subject of punk and thus not of interest to me. Unfortunately, after the 2016 U.S. Presidential election I find myself virtually unable to write songs about anything else."

While former US President Donald Trump was lambasted by some punk bands about his jingoist, racist, and sexist postures, other punk artists have made it clear that the issues we face have long, complex histories. Songs from 2015 by long-lasting post-punk band Killing Joke include "New Cold War" and "War on Freedom," which hits everything from media monopolies to police militarization and RFID chip surveillance. The 2017 song "Everything Now" by Arcade Fire is a robust criticism of our current culture that's technology addicted, overconsumed, attention deficited, instantly gratified, and overwhelmed by choices. Earlier in 2017 Depeche Mode released their most political song to date, "Where's the Revolution?" and The Downtown Boys released the song "A Wall" referring to Trump's plan to build a border wall between the United States and Mexico. Hip-hop and blues artists also honed in on the Donald: on "This Land" (2019) Gary Clark Jr. sings, "Right in the middle of Trump country, I told you, 'There goes the neighborhood.'" And Chuck D of Public Enemy sings, "Vote this joke out or die trying" on "State of the Union STFU" (2020).

> *You've been pissed on for too long, your rights abused, your views refused.*
>
> —"Where's the Revolution?" by Depeche Mode (2017)

"The Kids Are Alt-Right" by Bad Religion (2018) has a music video that features an animated Donald Trump chasing a shotgun hanging from a string.[1]

More recently, Houston band Lenin linked the past to the present on their 2020 album *Fuck It Part 1—Times Have Been Worse:*

> *The lazy liberals punch above their weight / still relying on Cold War Russian hate / I'm a media man who understands our scheme / of our brands-based democratic corporatocracy.*
>
> —"Donald Trump's America" by Lenin (2020)

In 2023 Anti-Flag released their thirteenth studio album, *Lies They Tell Our Children*, which they announced was, ". . . spawned out of a compulsive need to not just comment on the dystopian corporate wasteland we all face but to trace it back to the origin of this fate; the political policies, laws, cultural shifts, and lineage of injustice that have lead us to the world we live in today."

> *Poison the rivers, slaughter the cows / Build up the prisons, burn forests down / Food to the landfill, patent the seeds / They waste your labor, and your dignity / They want to use you up, and steal your soul.*
>
> —Work & Struggle by Anti-Flag (2023)

HISTORY CHANGES

Since the 1969 police murders of Black Panthers Fred Hampton and Mark Clark in Chicago and the 1991 police beating of Rodney King in Los Angeles, the issue of police brutality has been an American discussion that comes and goes, between wars and economic recessions. But after May 25, 2020, there were worldwide protests calling to "defund" or "abolish" the police. That day, Minneapolis police choked George Floyd for nine minutes as he told them he couldn't breathe, until he died. As white European cultures continue to grapple with how to take responsibility for the recent history of brutality, slavery, and genocide, punk (and other musicians) push along the discussion to make changes in the present.

Andy Gill of Gang of Four told me, "History changes." Indeed, as our vantage point extends and we know more, even our view of the past shifts. Our understanding of the present, and how we got here, also transforms. Ultimately, most of history was recorded by those who controlled culture at the time, and they highlighted themselves and diminished the voices of the "other" or "outsider."

CHAPTER 21

Electrocuting my nerves, I don't trust you today / Police baton on my ribs, I'm singing with blood today.

—"RAGE" by Pussy Riot (2020)

The press release for Pussy Riot's 2020 song "RAGE" explained their urgency to get the song out:

> "RAGE" was filmed in February 2020 and originally it was to be released with Pussy Riot's debut studio album *RAGE* later that year. The recent wave of political repressions led to a decision to release the video sooner and dedicate it to all political prisoners in Russia. It's Pussy Riot's only weapon against the authoritarian oppressive regime—art. By sharing this video as well, you help us to stand against Putin.

The Downtown Boys describe their music as "a bilingual, political sax punk party." Their first full-length LP—*Full Communism*—was released in 2015. Their press release says,

> *Full Communism* is full of songs about smashing the prison-industrial complex, racism, queerphobia, capitalism, fascism, boredom, and all things people tell us that try to close our minds, eyes, and heart. The record comes directly out of our current critical moment in the struggle for justice being fought in the US and throughout the world.

The Downtown Boys's video for their song "Wave of History" informs us, "Many modern finance corporations got their start profiting off the slave trade," including Wachovia, AIG, Aetna, and JP Morgan. "And they continue to profit off that capital today." The video continues by quoting Angela Davis on prison abolition and adds, "So far in 2015, the number of people killed by cops averages to three people every day." The video ends with "Black Lives Matter" and the image of arms holding a placard, "You Can't Stop This Revolution." The Downtown Boys's rendition of "L'Internationale" was featured in the 2020 film *Miss Marx* directed by Susanna Nicchiarelli about Karl's wife Eleanor and her fight against sexism. Their 2017 album *Cost of Living* featured the song "A Wall" about the militarized border between the United States and Mexico.

STEVEN BLUSH (*American Hardcore: A Tribal History*): Do I feel that bands today are political enough? (2020) Obviously, it's not political enough because you'd hear people horrified by it, if it was! You'd hear Fox News going nuts over a Millions of Dead Cops kind of band. Or Dead Kennedys. Their heads would explode! I don't see any political music. Ten years ago Neil Young said, "I'm tired of sitting around waiting for the next radical music to happen, so I have to do it myself." I think that's unfortunately what we're seeing now. Public Enemy is cool, but they probably have more cache for you and I than they do young Black kids. I'm waiting. There's lyrics here and there, but they take on easy targets. That's not revolution. That's like revolution incorporated.

JM: The Mekons have a 1989 song, "Empire of the Senses," that is a criticism of state surveillance. How important is it that bands sing about political themes these days? (2016)

JON LANGFORD (The Mekons): More so than ever. I think it's really important. I'm sure some people are quite happy not doing it and don't feel there's a role for musicians there. The kind of lineage that we link ourselves to is a folk tradition and that goes way back before contemporary media. It's a way of telling stories and addressing things happening in the world that affect people's lives. We're programmed to do that now, really. It would be very hard for us to think about making an album that *didn't* address what's going on. We don't necessarily address it directly; sometimes it's fairly oblique.

BRAD LOGAN (Leftöver Crack): Where we come from is mostly bands doing that (political songs). We do a mainstream version of crust punk. In the underground of punk in New York City, Los Angeles, and San Francisco—that's very much the norm. Does it surprise me that more people aren't doing it? I wouldn't say I'm surprised. We also put those themes in a black-humor-type setting, to have fun with it. I really like that aspect of Leftöver Crack because I don't see a lot of people doing that: taking elements of crust and black metal and anarchism and putting a humorous twist on it. It's typically serious, the bands that sing about political ideas, not that there's any problem with that.

JOHN LYDON (Sex Pistols / PiL): Most people find it very difficult to deal with what is going on out there (2019). Since becoming an American (2013) you're not spoiled for choice, are you? Between Republican and Democrat! I really dislike both lots so much. The lies, tomfoolery. They just assume either Marxist or right-wing philosophy so quickly without questioning it and then throw it out as if we're all supposed to stand in line and follow. Unfortunately, as those politicians are well aware, that is what people tend to do. There is not enough media out there to challenge what we assume to be correct. There should be a daily political program that questions every single aspect of the lies they are propagating. There is extremist CNN or extremist Fox. I'd like to see politics ridiculed in a really appropriate way.

STEVE IGNORANT (Crass / Slice of Life): I'm surprised that younger bands aren't being more vocal about what's going on. But it's been forty years. I'm sixty-one (2019). I'm an old bloke now! What the fuck do I know about what young people think? You've got all this technology and social media so I don't know

CHAPTER 21

whether that's had an effect on them. Whether they feel it's too rude or they're afraid of offending someone. But part of growing up is that you offend people. You don't do it on purpose, if you know what I mean.

With the new songs I do with Slice of Life I tend to put in references to, for example, presidents or prime ministers. They're in there, but you have to read between the lines. I'm still angry, but at the age of sixty-one, it's not for me to write "Owe Us a Living" again. It's for younger people to do. I'm sure there are bands doing it. You just don't hear of it. Maybe.

JELLO BIAFRA (Dead Kennedys / Guantanamo School of Medicine): People ask, "Why isn't there more political music now?" It's always there. You just have to look for it for crying out loud! When people were running around saying, "Green Day getting popular ruined the whole punk scene"—that's *not* true! If you don't like what happened with Green Day—don't listen to them! Turn it off. If you hate MTV, turn off the fucking TV! Gilman Street is still there; go out and see some *new* bands! Find some new bands you like and support the underground and you'll be digging it like you always have.

You're not going to like all political music. Not anybody from one side of the Feminista scene has a single good thing to say about Peaches. Personally, I think Peaches is pretty awesome and anybody who accuses her of not being her own-style feminist, she would be quite good at ripping your head off. There has always been really political hip-hop even if it's been graphically violent storytelling about what people go through where they're living, in the most violent ghettoes in this country. And there's political folk music. And now—like it or not—there is a lot of politically conscious metal, too. No small part because a lot of young metal fans have been harassed by small town and bigger city cops just as relentlessly as hip-hop and punk fans. It's always there and you just have to look for it. In the digital age, you don't have to look very far, do you?

EAST BAY RAY: With the Dead Kennedys we have a song called "Bleed for Me" which is about war for oil, which is totally applicable today. Our singer Skip McSkipster changes the words a bit to reflect the new situation. Some other songs unfortunately still apply and we update the lyrics to reflect the current times.

RAMSEY KANAAN (Political Asylum / AK Press / PM Press): Punk is, in a sense, bigger than it has ever been. I'm sure there are punk bands that sing about current politics and the global situation. Dead Kennedys or The Clash were always a tiny minority in punk. I loved the Ramones, but you didn't learn about politics from the Ramones or X or Black Flag. Black Flag sang about alienation and being pissed off, particularly at the cops. But you wouldn't have learned anything about geopolitics from Black Flag.

WHERE IS THE REVOLUTION NOW?

Bands like MDC were the exception, who were popular and had explicit political lyrics. Most bands, including punk bands, are not that explicit politically. When Crass was around they were hugely influential and they sold hundreds of thousands of records in the UK and across the world, but they were not on the scale of The Clash and Dead Kennedys. I saw Crass several times and there were never more than four or five hundred people in the audience. They were on a completely different level. In one sense the presumption behind that question is unfair: that there used to be loads of political bands opening our eyes to what's going on in the world and now there isn't.

DAVE ALLEN (Gang of Four): There's *not* a lot of bands going on about political ideas now. I'm not really surprised. What was a real shock for Gang of Four when we first toured the United States was just how conservative students were (1980). If you played tours in Europe you could feel the tension in the air about

Album by Subhumans, Crisis Point *(2019).* Contributed: Dick Lucas

society and politics and what was going on. And then we'd come over here and play universities in America and it's just a show. "Here we're just enjoying ourselves." Now that I've lived here for a long time, I realize what a conservative society America really is. That might account for it. "How are we going to get on MTV if we're going on about Abu Ghraib?" It's a shame, but it makes sense if you look at the broader landscape of politics and culture in America. I've lived in America for twenty-five years and I've learned that everything seems to fall into the center. The complacency kind of wears you down.

ANGRY, POETIC, AND SPECIFIC

JM: There seems to be a lot of material to sing about now: torture, constant war, for-profit prisons, drone assassinations. Why do you think so few bands are singing about all of it?

DICK LUCAS (Subhumans): Someone asked me this in another interview. I quoted a couple of English bands who are along the same political lines as we are—more so, in fact. They are actually naming the times, events, and politicians involved. Great. I tend to feel that if you name politicians (in songs) once *they're* out of power, the song goes out of date. So, we haven't got any songs about Thatcher. We've got songs about consumer culture and the rise of capitalism. Our songs are broadly speaking anarchic, but they are not so precise as to be losing the point a few years down the line. But there are bands that are more specific about certain taxes and laws that have come down recently. They're on the ball. They're average age is twenty-two. It makes me very happy to see these bands coming through.

JM: Who are the political bands?

DICK LUCAS: The Autonomads. And an alter-ego reggae dub band called the Black Star Dub Collective from Manchester. Another band called Global Parasites from North Wales. Very musical, not so thrashy. They mix a bit of reggae, ska, and punk rock; it's very dynamic music. And they're angry, poetic, and specific. They haven't got any filler songs. It's very inspiring to see people about half my age and still as angry. And they *should* be because it's now a lot worse than it was when Thatcher and Reagan were in. A *lot* worse.

We are absolutely under the surveillance thing and the whole world has gone to globalized consumerism. It's destroying Indigenous cultures across the planet. It's destroying the *planet* across the planet. It's going to get to the point where the planet no longer has the nutrients within it to grow more food to feed an ever-rising population. I read recently we've got about seventy-five years before the whole human race will just die off. Or starve to death or just bomb itself in an ever-increasing amount of wars over the scarcity of water and food. Forget the oil; that's going to run out anyway. But when the food and water start running out then you've got real trouble. Then you've got real riots and everything's going to go feral.

JM: Do you see a downturn now in the political-ness of punk?

DICK LUCAS: I'm not looking for a downturn so I'm not seeing one. In a general sense, things are roughly the same as they were. Roughly. When we come to the States things here are roughly how they've always been. The pocket of really political punk rock is a very small percentage of the overall. Especially since the early '90s with the rise of the Green Day and Bad Religion resurgence of punk rock. The politics became very watered down, if it was there in the first place. But there's a DIY undercurrent going out beyond all the stuff that gets in the press over here that still exists. The fact that it's not noticed as widely doesn't diminish its power once you discover it. There's still a lot of angry young men about.

Back in England in the '80s when the anarcho-punk thing was broadening, a lot of kids were getting into the message that Crass was sending out, even if they didn't get the message and thought it was about wearing black clothes all the time. A lot of people, like ourselves, got into it. Built on it and got very inspired by it. A lot of those people are still out there. Not so much in bands but doing things like teaching. Doctors. I know ex-punk rockers who are now doing the most amazing things; they're doing it in a different way. They're not educating kids the way I was educated. They're doing it on a more, "What are you good at? Concentrate on *that*." They're offering cheaper education to poorer kids. It's just brilliant. These people were deeply involved with punk rock in one way or another, being in bands or helping us set up shows and benefit gigs, and they're now teaching or nursing. It's awesome.

There are punk rockers out there that don't look anything like punk rockers anymore, but they're retaining the idealism that was sparked up by punk rock. If I hadn't been sparked up by punk rock, I would've ended up a librarian. Reading is good for a while, but being surrounded by books is not the option to choose if you want to meet people and jump about and make a lot of noise!

HUGO BURNHAM (Gang of Four): I teach at college. What disappoints me now is that I don't see anyone being as dissatisfied or pissed off with the status quo as we were. Everything has been commodified. When I was growing up you couldn't get bananas all year round! You can now. There is nothing to complain about, it seems. My students are far less politicized and aware than my generation was when we were in our early twenties, late teens. There were plenty of people who didn't give a fuck then either, but now it just seems there's universally dazed contentment. If they're pissed off it's because they can't get the Beemer that's as good as their friend's Beemer.

JM: Some of the lyrics of Gang of Four have to do with commodification, exploitation, and suffering that happens from people feeling alienated from each other and sensing that they're inside of systems and institutions that aren't meeting their needs. I see some of Gang of Four lyrics pointing to liberation from that and some sense of self-awareness . . .

HUGO BURNHAM: Not *some* sense! Ah! You can break it down very simply: *You must take responsibility for your own situation, for your own actions!* This is what I teach. It's critical thinking instead of just rote memorization of facts or what you see on TV as the options: "Here, you can be this or this." Rather more, "Don't be satisfied with that which is offered." You have to do it yourself. Find it within, or from without, yourself. Do not just accept the surface of what is there! You have to analyze things critically yourself to come up with your own answers and take responsibility for doing something noisy and annoying and fun. That is what you're supposed to do when you're a teenager. You're supposed to piss your parents off! I'm probably stealing this from Pete Townshend, but whether its hip-hop, punk, or whatever, rock and roll is really *the soundtrack to kill your parents to.* I, figuratively speaking of course, highly endorse that. Even though we are the parents now.

JAY BENTLEY (Bad Religion): All I can say is I notice what you notice, but it's none of my business to tell other bands what to talk about. What I do know—something that Keith (Morris) said—is you don't think anyone will ever hear what you have to say. But you're going to scream it at the top of your lungs! And it's not going to have any impact because you're just a meaningless flea on the butt of the world. But now, bands seem to have some management lawyer or artist label rep up their ass telling them, "Don't get into any trouble! Don't pull a Dixie Chicks! Don't speak your mind. You'll lose your fan base if you tell people what you really think." Well, fuck them! Go ahead and do your thing. People aren't going to be Keith (Morris). People aren't going to speak their mind and say, "This is bullshit! Think for yourself," because that doesn't sell records.

When you said there's a lot of different variants of punk; no there's not! There's a lot of different variants of *music.* In my mind, when you can get up there and say exactly what you feel, that's punk. We had a discussion when we were fifteen and we said, "There's already a lot of bands out there saying, 'Fuck the cops,' so let's *not* be a band that says, 'Fuck the cops.'"

WHERE IS THE REVOLUTION NOW?

THURSTON MOORE (Sonic Youth): You're right—I wish there was some major punk rock outcry. Why isn't there? There's a certain exhaustion of protest that exists in our culture. After 9/11 when people went out in droves to make a stand against the Bush government going into Afghanistan and Iraq, it was completely ineffective towards their decisions. It's this whole "ignore it and it will go away" power that is figured out now. The '60s will never happen again. Protest has been decoded by the war players and they realize that it's ineffectual to their moves. It's a different landscape now.

> *It was the tail end of the 90s punk scene, where activism and anarchist politics were still prevalent. In a couple of years, Homeland Security would strike fear into the hearts of punk protestors after 9/11. After that, the scene forever changed and became more complacent. Really, it was the perfect time for our songs like "Baby, I'm an Anarchist" to connect with people.*
>
> —Laura Jane Grace of Against Me![2]

ROB FISH (108): At a show we played a couple months ago there was a kid saying how every cop in this world is inherently evil and if something happened to them then they deserve it. I agree with the idea of Gandhi that you dissemble the negative, but there has to be a sense of architecture and governing. I don't believe in this spiritual utopia where everybody is so advanced that they're always helping the person next to them, they never take advantage of people. That's just not a realistic thing.

In the punk rock scene, the shows I've played lately (2007), I've thought there is really no sense of political, social, or spiritual context to it. If you go to a show it's all about stage diving and scene unity and, "What group are you aligned with?" And not as much give-and-take about spiritual or political topics. In the late '80s, in the hardcore scene, everyone was straight edge or vegetarian. That really defined everything about it. A few years later in the early '90s there started to be a lot more ideas around politics and social issues and the whole spirituality thing came to the forefront. I think it's cyclical and I think it'll come around.

JM: How important is it that bands are singing about social and political issues for you?

CECI BASTIDA (Tijuana No!): As a teenager, I used to think people in bands should talk about socio-political issues in their music. But people express art in their own way, and it doesn't have to be political. It can be whatever you want. That is what's great about art and music. It provides other ways of being involved

CHAPTER 21

with these social issues. I know many people that make music that don't talk about anything political, but they're active in their own personal lives, participating in events that benefit certain groups or donating time with different organizations that are doing great work.

PROPHETS OF RAGE

> *Prophets of Rage is the right band, saying the right shit, at this very critical moment.*
>
> —Director Michael Moore in *Rolling Stone*[3]

Prophets of Rage formed in May 2016 for a breath of fresh revolutionary rhythms with the amazing lineup of Chuck D (Public Enemy), Tom Morello (Rage Against the Machine), and B-Real (Cypress Hill). The video for their song "Unfuck the World" was directed by radical filmmaker Michael Moore, who was booed during his anti-war speech at the 2003 Academy Awards as he won best documentary feature for *Bowling for Columbine*. In the video for the song "Prophets of Rage" there's a T-shirt and banner parodying Donald Trump's 2016 presidential campaign slogan: "Make America *Rage* Again." Some of the first concerts by Prophets of Rage were for inmates at Norco Penitentiary in California, residents of Skid Row in Los Angeles, and protestors at the 2016 Republican National Convention. "Prophets of Rage represent a dying breed: a dedicated protest act from a previous era at a time when pop music is not exactly known for its revolutionary spirit."[4]

> *The world is not going to change itself. That's up to you.*
>
> —Text at end of video for "Unfuck the World" by Prophets of Rage

TOM MORELLO (Rage Against the Machine / Prophets of Rage): My twin passions were political activism and rock 'n' roll, and they didn't really come together until I was in Rage Against the Machine. Prior to being in Rage, I worked for US Senator Alan Cranston as his scheduling secretary. Alan Cranston was a very progressive member of the Senate, but my views were considerably to the left. At the time I was playing in another band (Lock Up) that had put out one record on Geffen. It was a much more commercial endeavor and every kind of music industry shafting that can happen, did happen, to that band. When we were finally dropped from our label, I vowed that I would never again play another note of music that I didn't believe in from my heart.

And the next batch of music that I was a part of writing was the first Rage Against the Machine record. That was really a synthesis of our political ideals and the music that we felt the most passionate about. In 1991 it stood in stark contrast to everything else. There wasn't anything else remotely like it. It was a multi-ethnic band that combined genres—rock, metal, and hip-hop—with revolutionary neo-Marxist politics. That wasn't exactly a recipe for getting on commercial radio at the time. But we just believed in it. I think it was that belief and commitment that helped it translate to a broader audience and bring the politics and the music together in a way that was very natural and compelling for us, as members of the band.

Where's the revolution? Many punk musicians and activists are disappointed we're not further along in creating a new society. Our generation grew up hearing that World War II had been the war to end all wars and that humanity was on a journey toward more justice, enhanced civil rights, gender equality, environmental harmony, and peaceful co-existence. Not long before punk exploded Buckminster Fuller coined the phrase "Spaceship Earth" in 1967, pointing to the need to replace earth's oppressive political systems based on colonization, violence, and war with sustainable, ecological, collaborative systems. While some of the earliest punk musicians born in the 1950s and '60s were empowered by the modern mantra "Save the Planet," now in 2022 the phrase takes on more of a desperate, bitter translation: "The ship is going down. Start baling."

The next revolutionary music styles probably won't sound or look like punk rock, but will combine diverse elements. Hip-hop, rap, blues, jazz, and classical music are rich with experiments filled with socio-political ideas and inspirations. The seeds of punk rock ethics have been planted in surprising places, like the philosophy of Solar Punk currently growing within technology industries. Meanwhile, Afro-Futurism envisions radical shifts in social-political realms to respond to the climate crisis and other issues.[5]

Looking further outside of punk rock, there are great examples of current socio-political music. Laurie Anderson's 2015 "Habeas Corpus" performance piece featured live video of Mohammed El Gharani speaking about the seven and a half years he was held at the US Guantanamo Bay prison and tortured following 9/11, without any proof he committed a crime. Jazz composer and trumpeter Wadada Leo Smith continually addresses socio-political issues on albums like *Occupy the World* (2013) and 2019's *Rosa Parks: Pure Love, An Oratorio of Seven Songs*. The year 2019 brought the first new album in twenty

CHAPTER 21

years from The Specials and has feminist/humanist songs like "10 Commandments" and "Vote for Me."

David Rovics's 2021 album *Rebel Songs* continues decades of his punk-infused political folk music. The 2021 album *G_d's Pee at State's End* from Canadian chamber rock ensemble Godspeed You! Black Emperor exhibits a rare optimism about social revolution with songs like "Government Came" and "Our Side Has to Win." And *Breaking the Thermometer* by Haitian American musician Leyla McCalla (2022) documents the history of radical Radio Haiti and the political assassination of journalist Jean Dominique in 2000.

"The Virus" by Canadian band Halluci Nation (2016) features Saul Williams and samples of American Indian Movement activist/musician John Trudell. The song title refers to the genocide of Native Americans: "We are not a conquered people." The intense video for the 2018 song "This Is America" by Childish Gambino (Danny Glover) is a disturbing reflection on gun violence and racism. It won four Grammy awards, including song of the year, and inspired political analysis from the *New York Times* and NPR.[6] The 2021 Afrobeat album *Stop the Hate* by Femi Kuti is full of political songs like "As We Struggle Everyday" and "You Can't Fight Corruption with Corruption." On "The American Negro" (2021) Adrian Younge sings, "Black people, listen to your own music / As soul is the connection to our ancestors / A language of tonal tensions / Teaching an audience it was never intended for."

During a May 15, 2016, concert in North Carolina by Against Me! transgender singer Laura Jane Grace burned their birth certificate on stage as a protest against state law HB2, requiring transgender people to use bathrooms that correspond with the biological sex on their birth certificate.[7] Later in 2016, on November 26, Malcolm McLaren's son Joe Corré held a public bonfire on a barge on London's Thames River to protest the commodification of punk rock. Hand-crafted, forty-year-old Sex Pistols T-shirts and original vinyl melted away while a drummer pounded out a simple rhythm.

JIM LINDBERG (Pennywise): While there's the Ramones's idea of sniffing glue and "Sheena is a Punk Rocker" and the whole fashion of punk rock, through the late '80s and '90s a lot of people from the punk scene were actually the people keeping the flame alive for the peace movement, keeping environmental issues at the forefront. A lot of very progressive ideas have been kept alive in the punk rock community. Now so many people are getting it, that we have to be concerned about the environment, human rights, and nonviolence. That groundswell is growing. That's going to be contagious. I definitely have hope for the future and

Laura Jane Grace (Against Me!) burns their birth certificate on stage (May 15, 2016) to protest law requiring transgender people use bathrooms that correspond with the sex on their birth certificate. Photo: Kathryn Wymer

CHAPTER 21

the next generation to be able to pull us out from the dogmas that we've been stuck under for a long time.

The voices within *Punk Revolution!* point to hurdles to watch out for on the path of revolution: commodification from inside or outside a movement/scene, homogeneity of style, internal conflicts that go unresolved, and the human propensity for violence and authority. One useful insight is that living free is not a static experience achieved once and then remaining forever. Freedom is alive and invigorated when it's re-created from moment to moment, day to day, and generation to generation. So, where's the revolution? It may be at an underground punk show right now. Or maybe it's right outside your window. Where's the revolution?

NOTES

INTRODUCTION

1. Rick Riordan, *The Trials of Apollo: The Dark Prophecy* (Disney-Hyperion, 2017), 253.
2. Punk Scholars Network, https://www.punkscholarsnetwork.com/.
3. The Punk Rock Museum, https://www.thepunkrockmuseum.com/.
4. Manjir Samanta-Laughton, *Punk Science: Inside the Mind of God* (Iff Books, 2006).
5. "Anarchy in the UK: Sex Pistols' Denmark Street Home Given Listed Status," *The Telegraph*, March 22, 2016.

CHAPTER 1

1. Mark Woodlief, "No WTO Combo's Live Album Revisits Battle in Seattle," MTV.com, May 18, 2000.
2. Laurence Lotlikoff, "Beware: Uncle Sam Can't Count," *Forbes Magazine*, January 9, 2019.

CHAPTER 4

1. "87 Concert Was a Genesis of East German Rebellion," Deutsche Welle, July 4, 2007.
2. Andy Greene, "Flashback: David Bowie Sings 'Heroes' at the Berlin Wall," *Rolling Stone*, June 9, 2016.

3. Kalina Oroschakoff, "Archive Immortalizes East German Punk Rock Scene," Reuters, July 20, 2011.
4. "The Cold War Broadcast That Gave East German Dissidents a Voice," NPR, November 4, 2014.
5. Chris Bowlby, "Rocking the Stasi," BBC World Service, Berlin, July 1, 2017.

CHAPTER 5

1. Gil Kaufman, "Joey Ramone Rocks the Reservation," MTV News, October 22, 1996.

CHAPTER 7

1. Jon Ginoli, *Deflowered: My Life in Pansy Division—The Inside Story of the First Openly Gay Pop-Punk Band* (Jersey City, NJ: Cleis Press, 2009), 28.
2. Ibid.

CHAPTER 9

1. "Western Europe: The Peace Movement After Initial INF Deployment," sanitized copy released by the CIA on January 27, 2011.
2. See the 2018 documentary *Rumble: The Indians Who Rocked the World* directed by Catherine Bainbridge.
3. "Business as Usual? Arms Sales of Top 100 Arms Companies Continue to Grow Amid Pandemic," Stockholm International Peace Research Institute, December 2, 2021, https://www.sipri.org/media/press-release/2021/business-usual-arms-sales-sipri-top-100-arms-companies-continue-grow-amid-pandemic.
4. "Drones Killed All Hope," TMZ, September 26, 2013.
5. Matt Patches, "Shepard Fairey on the Future of Political Art," *Esquire*, May 28, 2015.

CHAPTER 10

1. See Norman Solomon, *War Made Easy* (Hoboken, NJ: Wiley, 2005).

NOTES

CHAPTER 11

1. TV ads using Hendrix's music: Pepsi vs. Coke with "Purple Haze" in 2004, "All Along the Watchtower" for Chanel perfume in 2015, and "Purple Haze" for Citi Visa Credit Card in 2014.
2. "The Vandals at PB Volunteer, Baghdad, Iraq 2004," https://www.youtube.com/watch?v=TKwUor_nb2U.
3. "The Vandals Play for U.S. Troops in Iraq (Sadr City)—Nice Army Moshpit," https://www.youtube.com/watch?v=H-UOz0e0dEk&lc=UggO-UFM3tz3T3gCoAEC.
4. Jason Bracelin, "Musicians Take Sides," Alternet, September 15, 2004. Escalante described as "Bush Backer."
5. Jan Critchfield, "Punk Rockers 'Vandals' Perform for Troops in Iraq," *US Department of Defense News*, January 1, 2005.

CHAPTER 12

1. Greg Palast, "The Election Was Stolen—Here's How," Gregpalast.com, November 11, 2016.
2. Steph Harmon, "Amanda Palmer: 'Donald Trump is going to make punk rock great again,'" *The Guardian*, December 26, 2016.
3. Eric R. Danton, "Where Is All the Protest Music of the Trump Era?" *Paste*, July 19, 2017.
4. "Ivanka Trump Reveals 'Punk Phase' When She Liked Nirvana," BBC News, October 18, 2017.
5. Audie Cornish, "Donald Glover's 'This Is America' Holds Ugly Truths to Be Self-Evident," NPR, May 7, 2018.
6. "'The Kids Are Alt-Right' Delivers Bad Religion's Signature Brand of Socially Conscious and Sardonic Punk," Epitaph Records website, June 20, 2018.

CHAPTER 18

1. "Ad Benefits Minutemen Guitarists Dad," MTV News, March 9, 2000.
2. "Morrissey Berates Buzzcocks Over Song Usage in McDonald's Ad," *Rolling Stone*, June 17, 2016.
3. Randall Roberts, "Morrissey Is Anti-Immigrant and Backs a White Nationalist Political Party: Why Don't Fans Care?" *Los Angeles Times*, October 24, 2019.
4. Stuart Ewen, *All Consuming Images: The Politics of Style in Contemporary Culture* (New York: Basic Books, 1990), 253.
5. Dave Wise and Stewart Wise, "The End of Music," in *What Is Situationism: A Reader*, edited by Stewart Home (Chico, CA: AK Press, 1996).

NOTES

6. Dead Kennedys music has appeared in many films, including *Green Room* (2015), *I Melt With You* (2012), *The Social Network* (2010), *The Manchurian Candidate* (2004), *SLC Punk* (1998), and the 2007 zombie flick *Planet Terror*.

7. Mark Sweney, "Sex Pistols Singer John Lydon Flies the Flag for Butter in TV Ad," *The Guardian*, October 1, 2008.

8. Ben Meyers, "Punk's Not Dead—It Just Emigrated," *The Guardian*, September 8, 2008.

CHAPTER 19

1. Jenna Amatulli, "Burberry Burned Millions of Dollars Worth of Unsold Stock," *Huffington Post*, July 19, 2018.

2. Nickas, Bob, "Never Mind the Bollocks, Here's Anna Wintour," *VICE*, August 1, 2013.

CHAPTER 21

1. "'The Kids Are Alt-Right' Delivers Bad Religion's Signature Brand of Socially Conscious and Sardonic Punk," Epitaph Records website, June 20, 2018.

2. Laura Jane Grace, *Tranny: Confessions of Punk Rock's Most Infamous Anarchist Sellout* (New York: Hachette Book Group, 2016), 34.

3. Elias Leight, "Prophets of Rage Prep Debut Album, Release Firey, Michael Moore-Directed Video," *Rolling Stone*, June 1, 2017.

4. Joe Coscarelli, "Prophets of Rage Bring Their Anger to the Republican Convention," *New York Times*, July 20, 2016.

5. Nicola K. Smith, "What Is Solarpunk and Can It Help Save the Planet?" BBC News, August 3, 2021.

6. Audie Cornish, "Donald Glover's 'This Is America' Holds Ugly Truths to Be Self-Evident," NPR, May 7, 2018.

7. Jayme Deerwester, "Transgender Singer Laura Jane Grace Burns Birth Certificate Onstage in N.C.," *USA Today*, May 17, 2016.

LIST OF INTERVIEWS

Allen, Dave (Gang of Four)—In-person and phone interviews, 2003 and 2014
Alyokhina, Masha (Pussy Riot / *Riot Days*)—Skype interview, 2017
Andersen, Mark (Positive Force DC / *Dance of Days*)—Phone and Zoom interviews, 2010 and 2022
Anderson, Laurie ("Oh Superman")—Phone interview, 2015
Asplund, Christian ("Sacred Music and The Punk Ethic")—Phone interview, 2017
Beeber, Steven Lee (*The Heebie-Jeebies at CBGB's: A Secret History of Jewish Punk*)—Phone interview, 2010
Bestida, Ceci (Tijuana No!)—Zoom interview, 2022
Benally, Clayson (Blackfire / Sihasin)—Phone interview, 2017
Benally, Jeneda (Blackfire / Sihasin)—Phone interview, 2017
Benally, Klee (Blackfire)—Phone interview, 2020
Bentley, Jay (Bad Religion)—In-person interviews, 2000, 2003, and 2011
Berger, Ishay (Useless ID)—Phone interview, 2016
Biafra, Jello (Dead Kennedys / Guantanamo School of Medicine)—Phone interview, 2017
Blount, Jake (*The New Faith*)—Zoom interview, 2022
Blush, Steven (*American Hardcore: A Tribal History*)—Phone interview, 2020
Bonebrake, D. J. (X)—Phone interview, 2018
Bragg, Billy—Zoom interview, 2020
Branca, Glenn (Theoretical Girls)—Phone interview, 2009
Brannon, Brian (Jodie Foster's Army)—In-person interview, 2017
Burke, Clem (Blondie)—Zoom interview, 2020
Burnham, Hugo (Gang of Four)—In-person and phone interview, 2003 and 2014
Cappo, Ray (Shelter / Youth of Today)—Phone interview, 2007

LIST OF INTERVIEWS

Carlisle, Belinda (The Go-Go's / The Germs / Black Randy & The Metrosquad)—Phone interview, 2017

Case, Peter (The Nerves / The Plimsouls)—Phone interview, 2008

Cervenka, Exene (X)—Phone interview, 2008

Cheparukhin, Alexander "Sasha" (Pussy Riot manager)—Phone interview, 2017

Chomsky, Noam (Bad Religion / "Manufacturing Consent")—Phone interview, 2005

Clements, Joe (Fury 66 / The Deathless)—In-person interview, 2017

Colver, Edward (punk photographer)—In-person interview, 2013

Cooper, Justin (Revelation Records)—In-person interview, 2007

Copeland III, Miles (I.R.S. Records, The Police manager, father established CIA)—Phone interview, 2021

Corré, Joe (Burn Punk London)—Phone interview, 2016

Critchfield, Jan (Department of Defense journalist)—Email interview, 2019

Cruz Gonzales, Michelle (*The Spitboy Rule: Tales of a Xicana in a Female Punk Band*)—Zoom interview, 2009

D, Chuck (Public Enemy / Prophets of Rage)—In-person interview, 2007

D'Ambrosio, Antonino (*Let Fury Have the Hour: Joe Strummer, Punk, and the Movement that Shook the World*)—Phone interview, 2007

Dictor, Dave (Millions of Dead Cops / Multi-Death Corporations)—Phone interview, 2006

Dinsmore, Clifford (Bl'ast)—In-person interview, 2015

Doe, John (X)—Phone interviews, 2008 and 2009

Ebersole, Stewart (*Barred for Life*)—Phone interview, 2013

Elfman, Danny (Oingo Boingo)—Phone interview, 2019

Fancher, Lisa (Frontier Records)—Phone interview, 2010

Field Brooks, Fern (*The Day My Kid Went Punk* director)—Phone interview, 2019

Fish, Rob (108)—Phone interview, 2007

Fowley, Kim (The Runaways producer)—Phone interview, 2010

Fox, Hardy (The Residents)—In-person interview, 2010

Frantz, Chris (Talking Heads / Tom Tom Club)—Phone interview, 2020

Freeman, Chris (Pansy Division)—Phone interview, 2009

Fujiwara, Hide (Ultra Bidé)—In-person interview, 2013 (Live on Free Radio Santa Cruz)

Garcia, Camille Rose (The Real Minx)—Phone interview, 2007

Gibson, William (Cyberpunk author, *Neuromancer*)—Phone interview, 2008

Gill, Andy (Gang of Four)—In-person and phone interviews, 2003, 2015, 2016, and 2017

Ginoli, Jon (Pansy Division / *Deflowered: My Life in Pansy Division*)—Phone interview, 2009

Goodstein, Scott (Punk Voter)—In-person interview, 2007

Graffin, Greg (Bad Religion)—In-person and phone interviews, 2000, 2003, 2006, 2015, and 2016

Gregory, Glenn (Heaven 17 / Musical Vomit)—Zoom interview, 2022

LIST OF INTERVIEWS

Grisham, Jack (TSOL)—In-person interview, 2007
Hannah, Chris (Propagandhi)—In-person and phone interviews, 2006 and 2013
Harron, Mary (*I Shot Andy Warhol* director)—Phone interview, 2012
Hern, Matt (*Everywhere All the Time: A New Deschooling Reader*)—Phone interview, 2011
Hosler, Mark (Negativland)—Phone interview, 2020 (Live on KZSC)
H. R. Human Rights (Bad Brains)—In-person interview, 2010
Houston, Penelope (The Avengers)—Phone interview, 2010
Ignorant, Steve (Crass / Slice of Life)—Phone interview, 2019
J, David (Bauhaus)—Phone interview, 2003
Jarboe (Swans)—Phone interview, 2019
Jarecke, Kenneth (photographer, "Just Another War")—Phone interview, 2017
Jones, Preston (co-author with Greg Graffin, *Is Belief in God Good, Bad or Irrelevant?*)—Phone interview, 2010
Kanaan, Ramsey (AK Press / PM Press / Political Asylum)—Phone interview, 2015
Kaufman, Denise (Ace of Cups)—Phone interview, 2019 (Live on KZSC)
Kaye, Lenny (Patti Smith Group)—In-person interview, 2009
King, Jon (Gang of Four)—Phone and Zoom interviews, 2015, 2021, and 2022
Kirkwood, Cris (Meat Puppets)—Phone interview, 2009 (Live on Free Radio Santa Cruz)
Knight, Michael Muhammad (*The Taqwacores*)—Email interview, 2016
Koski, Darius (Swingin' Utters)—Phone interview, 2008
Kuhn, Gabriel (*Sober for the Revolution: Hardcore Punk, Straight Edge and Radical Politics* / lefttwothree.org)—Phone interview, 2013
Langford, Jon (The Mekons)—Phone interview, 2016
Lasn, Kalle (*Adbusters* publisher)—Phone interview, 2016
Lee, Stan (The Dickies)—In-person interview, 2010
Lester, David (Mecca Normal / Horde of Two)—Zoom interview, 2021
Levine, Noah (*Dharma Punx* / The Deathless)—In-person and phone interviews, 2003, 2011, and 2018
Lindberg, Jim (Pennywise / "Punk Rock Dad: No Rules Just Real Life")—Phone interview, 2007
Lisher, Greg (Camper Van Beethoven / Monks of Doom) Phone interview, 2020
Logan, Brad (Leftöver Crack / Rats in the Wall / Adolescents)—In-person interview, 2016
Lucas, Dick (Subhumans / Citizenfish)—In-person interviews, 2008 and 2015
Lunch, Lydia (Teenage Jesus & The Jerks / Big Sexy Noise)—Phone interview, 2015
Lydon, John (Sex Pistols / Public Image Limited)—Phone interview, 2019
MacDonald, Pat (Timbuk 3)—Phone interview, 2021
MacKaye, Ian (Minor Threat / Fugazi / Embrace / Positive Force DC)—Phone interview, 2006 (Live on Free Radio Santa Cruz)
Manzarek, Ray (The Doors / X)—Phone interview, 2013

LIST OF INTERVIEWS

Marcus, Sara (*Girls to The Front: The True Story of the Riot Grrrl Revolution* / AKA Harlot Number One)—Phone interview, 2018

Marić Goran "Max" (Bjesove)—Snail mail interview, 2008

McHenry, Keith (Food Not Bombs cofounder)—In-person interview, 2018 (Live on Free Radio Santa Cruz)

Moore, Thurston (Sonic Youth)—Phone interview, 2014

Morello, Tom (Rage Against the Machine / Prophets of Rage)—Phone interview, 2003

Morris, Keith (Black Flag / Circle Jerks / Off!)—In-person interview, 2016

Muir, Mike (Suicidal Tendencies) Phone interview, 2014

Napolitano, Johnette (Concrete Blonde)—Email interview, 2007

Nawrocki, Norman (Rhythm Activism)—Phone interview, 2012 (Live on Free Radio Santa Cruz)

Ness, Mike (Social Distortion)—Phone interview, 2008

Nigh, Adam (Craig's Brother / Too Bad Eugene)—Phone interview, 2010

Numan, Gary (Tubeway Army)—Zoom interview, 2021

O'Kane, Kerri (*The Gits* film director)—Zoom interview, 2011

Ostroff, Nadya (The Slits / The Home Office)—In-person interview, 2007

Ott, Jeff (Fifteen)—Phone interview, 2018

Peligro, D. H. (Dead Kennedys)—Phone interview, 2011

Picciolini, Christian (White American Youth / *White American Youth: My Descent into America's Most Violent Hate Movement—And How I Got Out*)—Phone interview, 2017

Pinkus, JD (Butthole Surfers)—Phone interview, 2019 (Live on Free Radio Santa Cruz)

Powers, Kid Congo (The Gun Club / The Cramps / Nick Cave & The Bad Seeds / Pink Monkey Birds)—Zoom interview, 2022

Pundik, Jordan (New Found Glory)—Phone interview, 2014

Ramone, C. J. (Ramones)—Phone interview, 2018

Rankin, Russ (Good Riddance)—In-person and phone interviews, 2006 (Live at Free Radio Santa Cruz) and 2020

Ray, Amy (Indigo Girls / Daemon Records)—In-person and phone interviews, 2003 and 2015

Ray, East Bay (Dead Kennedys)—Phone interview, 2016

Redondo, Don (Jodie Foster's Army)—In-person interview, 2017

Reed, Tait (Junk Sick Dawn / Noise Clinic)—In-person, 2013 (Live on Free Radio Santa Cruz)

Reeder, Mark (The Frantic Elevators / Die Unbekannten / *B Movie: Lust and Sound in West Berlin 1979–1989*)—Email interview, 2018

Reyes, Ron (Black Flag / Piggy)—In-person interview, 2015

Richman, Jonathan (Modern Lovers)—In-person interview, 2008

Rimbaud, Penny (Crass)—Zoom interviews, 2020 and 2021

LIST OF INTERVIEWS

Rollins, Henry (Black Flag / Rollins Band)—Email and phone interviews, 2007 and 2018 (*Rollins's interviews are not included in* Punk Revolution! *Available only online at KZSC.org/blog*)

Romanoff, Yishai (Moshiach Oi!)—Email interview, 2014

Sane, Justin (Anti-Flag)—Phone interview, 2010

Satrapi, Marjane (*Persepolis*)—FaceTime interview, 2019

Saunders, Red (Rock Against Racism)—Zoom interview, 2020

Schamal, Mita (Namenlos)—Email interview, 2019

Soto, Steve (The Adolescents)—Phone interview, 2008

Spheeris, Penelope (*The Decline of Western Civilization / Suburbia / Wayne's World*)—Phone interview, 2007

Spooner, James (Afro-Punk / *The High Desert: Black. Punk. Nowhere*)—Phone interview, 2009

Stockberger, John (Sense Field)—Phone interview, 2017

Strom, Moana (Stalin's War)—Phone interview, 2007

Talen, Reverend Billy (The Church of Stop Shopping)—Phone interview, 2010 (Live on Free Radio Santa Cruz)

Taylor, Joseph Ojo (Undercover)—Phone interview, 2015

Thomas, David (Rocket from the Tombs / Pere Ubu)—Phone interview, 2006

Thu Win, Kyaw (Rebel Riot)—Email interview, 2018

Up, Ari (The Slits)—In-person interview, 2007

Vanderpol, Rikki (Dying for It)—Phone interview, 2018

Wakeling, Dave (The English Beat)—In-person interview, 2007

Warner, Brad (*Hardcore Zen* / Zero Defects)—In-person interview, 2007 (Live on Free Radio Santa Cruz)

Wei, Wu (SMZB)—Email interview, 2021

Wickersham, Jonny (Social Distortion)—Phone interview, 2011

Williamson, James (Iggy & The Stooges)—In-person and phone interviews, 2007 and 2013

INDEX

Page references for photographs are italicized.

"5.45" (Gang of Four), 134–35
9/11 attacks, 147, 152–54
20/20 Vision (Anti-Flag), 184, 317
108, 143
"1945" (Social Distortion), 6

ABBA, 214
"ACIYHAB" benefit single, 2
activism: Animal People Alliance, 15–16; "Band Aid" charity group, 8–9; Food Not Bombs, xii, 13–15, 35; Live Aid Concerts, 8–9; political responsibility and, 4; Positive Force DC, xiii, 3, 111–24, 148; prisons, 16–17; Punk Voter, 11–14; West Memphis Three Support Fund, 16
ACT UP (Aids Coalition to Unleash Power), 96, 106
Adbusters, 20
addiction, 260
The Adolescents, 28, 274
Afrika Bambaataa, 126
Afro-Futurism, 327
Afro-Punk (film), 225–26, *225*

AIDS crisis, 96
Albert, Michael, 217
album art, 265
alcoholism, 212–13
Alekan, Henri, 67
Allen, Dave: on anarchism, 205; on the commodification of punk, 277–78; on feminism, 242; "5.45," 134–35; on politics, 321–22; on punk as a revolutionary movement, 305–6, 312
Alternative Tentacles Records, 2, 105–6, 275–76
All the Power: Revolution Without Illusion (Andersen), 112
alt-right, 177
Alyokhina, Masha (Maria), xiii, 38–44, 197
"America Fuck Yeah," 165–66, 168–69
American Hardcore (film), 133–34
American Idiot (Green Day), xii, 4, 184
American Indian Smithsonian Institute, 75
Ammiano, Tom, 10
"Amoeba" (The Adolescents), 274

INDEX

anarchism, 93, 190–207
The Anarchists (Horowitz), 206
"Anarchy in the UK" (Sex Pistols), 4–5, *273*
Andersen, Mark, *117*; on activism, 3; activism and, xiii; on addiction, 260; *All the Power: Revolution Without Illusion*, 112; on anarchism, 205–6; *Dance of Days: Two Decades of Punk in the Nation's Capital*, 112; Positive Force and, 111–24; on situationism, 199
Anderson, Laurie, 24, 327
Anger Is an Energy (Lydon), 179
Animal People Alliance, 15–16
anti-capitalism, 210–11
Antifa, 177
Anti-Flag: *20/20 Vision*, 184, 317; activism of, 148; *Beyond Barricades: The Story of Anti-Flag* (film), 121; "Die for the Government," 148; "The Fight of Our Lives" video, 119, 120–21; Morello and, 160; *Newsweek Magazine* article, 159; Occupy movements and, 2
anti-politics, 269
apartheid, 116
Appropriation (Klee Benally), 70
"Arab Music Goes West" project, 159
Arab Spring, xv
Arcade Fire, 316
Armisen, Fred, 264
Armstrong, Billy Joe, 4
Arnocorps, 264–65
art: originality and, 25–26; as a reflection of society's problems, 5
Asplund, Christian, 280, 287
Assange, Julian, xiv
The Audacity of Hype (Biafra and the Guantanamo School of Medicine), 138
Aukerman, Milo, 316

authority, 203–4
The Autonomads, 322
Avail, 14
The Avengers, 97, 101
"Average Men" (Pansy Division), 106
"Axis of Justice" project, 148

Bad Brains, 14, 113, 229
Bad Religion, 148, 184, 316
Bag, Alice, 88
Balkans, 45
"Band Aid" charity group, 8–9
band names, 265
Basque musicians, 89
Bastida, Ceci, 82–94, *90*
"Battle of Seattle," xiii, 2
Beckett, Samuel, 136
Become the Media (Biafra), xiii
Beeber, Steven Lee: on the commodification of punk, 279; on the DIY movement, 27; on humor, 264; on Kristal, 26; on Rhodes, 308; on the success of punk, 313; on zombies, 212
Belarus Free Theater, 41–42
Benally, Berta, 70, 77
Benally, Clayson, 70–79, 205, 233, 250, 285
Benally, Jeneda, 70–76, 79, 204–5, 250, 284
Benally, Jones, 70, 77
Benally, Klee, xiii, 70, 81
Bentley, Jay, 155–57, 310, 324
Berger, Ishay, 167
Berlin Wall, 52–53, 56
Bestida, Ceci, 325–26
Beyond Barricades: The Story of Anti-Flag (film), 121
BFBS (British Forces Broadcasting Service), 55
BIA (Bureau of Indian Affairs), 72

INDEX

Biafra, Jello, *175*; on anarchism, 195; *The Audacity of Hype*, 138; "Battle of Seattle" and, xiii, 2; *Become the Media*, xiii; on Burn Punk London, 299–300; on the commodification of punk, 273–74; on the DIY movement, 29–30; on ego, 256; on entertaining US troops, 168; The Guantanamo School of Medicine, 138, 175–78; humor, 265–66; Iraq Veterans Against the War, 161–62; on moral codes, 290–91; "Nazi Trumps Fuck Off," 176–77; Pansy Division and, 105–6; on political responsibility, 4; on politics, 175–78, 320; on punk as a revolutionary movement, 305, 310–11; on racism, 229; San Francisco mayoral race, 2; on social consciousness, 108–9; on socialism, 218–19; travel to Israel, 47–49; on voting, 10; "We Occupy" (D.O.A), 2; WTO protests and, 119–20

Bjesove, 44–45

Black Bloc, 119

Blackfire, xiii, 70–79, *74*

Black Lives Matter, 2, 176, 318

"Blender" (Amy Ray), 253

Blondie, xi

Blount, Jake, 24–25

Blues Masses, 56–57, 61

Blush, Steven, 7–8, 133–34, 235, 267, 318–19

B Movie: Lust and Sound in West Berlin 1979–1989 (film), 54

Boehlke, Michael, 53

Bomp Records, 21

Bondi, Vic, 133

Bonebrake, D. J., 196, 288, 290

The Boomtown Rats, 8–9

"Borders" (MIA), 181

border walls: Berlin Wall, 52–53, 56, 89; Mexico-USA, 86, 89, 183, 185, 318; Reeder on, 185

"Born in the USA" (Springsteen), 169

"Born to Die" (MDC), 185

Bowie, David, 52, 55–56, 97

Boys of Now, 247

Bragg, Billy, 148, 309–10

Branca, Glenn: on anarchism, 207; on changing the world, 144; on the commodification of punk, 279; death of, xii; on punk as a revolutionary movement, 306–7; on situationism, 199

Brannan, Justin, 10

Brannon, Brian, 187, 304

Branson, Richard, 295

The Brat, 88

Breaking the Thermometer (McCalla), 328

Breski, Jürgen, 53

"A Brief History of Punk Rock in the Cold War" (essay), 134

Broadway, xii

Brujeria, 181

Buddhism, xv

Build Them to Break, 181

Bureau of Indian Affairs (BIA), 72

Burke, Clem, 34, 266–67, 284, 300

Burnham, Hugo, 205, 323–24

Burn Punk London, xv, 293–302, *297*

Bush, George H. W., *114*, 147

Bush, George W., 147

Buzzcocks, 272

"By What Right, America?" (Rhythm Activism), 142

Cage, John, 263

capitalism, 122, 210–11

Cappo, Ray, 142, 201

Carlisle, Belinda, 15–16, 73, 245–46, 288

cartoons, xii

Case, Peter, 19–21, 136, 220–21, 228

Cash, Johnny, 6

343

INDEX

Cave, Nick, 66
CBGB, 26
censorship, 5
Central Intelligence Agency (CIA), 125, 131–32
Cervenka, Exene, 149; on anarchism, 191; on politics, 150–51, 207, 266; on the success of punk, 313
Cheparukhin, Alexander "Sasha," 40–44, 187–88, 250–51
Chicano heritage, 229–30
Childish Gambino, 328
China, 50
China White, 28–29
Chomsky, Noam, 148–50, 181, 190
Christian Church, 57, 61
Christianity, 123–24
Chuck D, 139–40, 214, 316
Chumbawamba, 287–88
churches, 56–57, 61
Circle Jerks, 28
Clapton, Eric, 236–37
Clark, Gary, Jr., 316
Clark, Mark, xii
Clark, Tori, 159
Clarke, Al, 293
The Clash: *Combat Rock*, 283; *London Calling*, 8, 128; O'Rourke and, 10; politics and, 6–8, 92; *Sandinista*, 6–7; "selling out," 283; "White Man in Hammersmith Palais," 8; "White Riot," 234–35
class struggle, 210–11
Clements, Joe, 205
climate change, 82, 163
Cobb, David, 13
Cody, Robert Tree, 77
COINTELPRO, 75, 126
Colbert, Stephen, 10
Cold War, 125
"Colorado" (Fifteen), 9
Colver, Edward, 21, 127, 130

Combat Rock (The Clash), 283
commodification of punk, xv
Complicit (Gang of Four), 181–83
Concert for Berlin, 52
conformity, 289
Cooked Tandem, 21
Copeland, Miles III: career of, 131–32, 158–60; on the commodification of punk, 276, 282, 283; on punk as a revolutionary movement, 307–8; on Sting, 217–18
Coppola, Sophia, 278
corporate globalization, 162–63
corporations, 215–16, 281–82
Corré, Joe, xiv, 235, 293–302, *294, 297*
Costello, Elvis, 102
Country Life Butter advert, 280–81
COVID-19 pandemic, xiii, 2, 80–81, 120–21
The Cramps, 66, 133, 290
Cranston, Alan, 326
Crash, Darby, 73
Crass, *145*; activism and, xiii; album art, 265; history of, 323; Kanaan on, 198; nuclear war and, 128–29; politics and, 195–96; "They've Got a Bomb," 128
Crawford, Scott, 9
Crime, 97
Crisis Point (Subhumans), xi
Critchfield, Jan, 169–71
Crosscheck program, 178
Cruz, Ted, 10
Currie, Cherie, 246–47

Daemon Records, 34
D'Ambrosio, Antonino, 6–7, 128, 218, 283–84
Dance of Days: Two Decades of Punk in the Nation's Capital (Andersen), 112
Darnell, Dennis, 261
DDR (Deutsche Demokratische Republik), 53

INDEX

Dead Kennedys, *175*; "Holiday in Cambodia," 1, 274–75; name of, 5; politics and, 7; Rock Against Reagan show, 115
democracy, 13
"Demolicion" (Los Seicos), 85, 88
Depeche Mode, 183, 316
depression, 257
Dial House, xiii
The Dickies, 29
Dictor, Dave: activism of, xiii; on anarchism, 192–93; "Born to Die" (MDC), 185; on clarity, 259; on the DIY movement, 23; *P.E.A.C.E.* compilation album, 2; on racism, 228; on Rock Against Reagan, 134; on sexuality, 107–8, 306
"Die for the Government" (Anti-Flag), 148
Die Haut, 66
Die Toten Hosen (The Dead Trousers), 57–63, *59*
Die Unbekannten (The Unknown), 54, 57
Die Vision, 62
Diggles, Steve, xiv
The Dils, 97
Diné, 79
Dinsmore, Clifford, 127, 201
Dischord Records, 116, 124
disco, 104–5
DIY movement: CBGB and, 26; concerts and, 33; creative control and, 27; "do it together" and, 23; evolution of, xv; filmmaking and, 30; Food Not Bombs, 35; idea of, 19, 21; major labels and, 29; means of production and, 27–29, 33–34; publishing and, 32–33; record labels and, 19–20; reggae and, 26–27; role of, 24
D.O.A, 2
"Do as I Say" (Gang of Four), 148

Doctors Without Borders, xiii
Doe, John, 196–97
"Donald Trump's America" (Lenin), 317
The Downtown Boys, 183, 318
"Do You Remember Rock and Roll Radio?" (The Ramones), 278–79
Drag City Records, 264
drinking, 100
drones, 137–38
Dury, Ian, xii
Dylan, Bob, 200

East Bay Ray: on climate change, 163; on the commodification of punk, 275; on corporations, 215–16; on political responsibility, 4; on politics, 320; on punk as a revolutionary movement, 311–12
Ebersole, Stewart, 248, 268
Echols, Damien, 16
Edmonds, Lu, *194*
ego, 256
Eisenhower, Dwight D., 135
Ejército Zapatista de Liberación Nacional (EZLN), 87
elections, 10
Elfman, Danny, 217
Ellsberg, Daniel, 125
EMI, 135, 277, 300
The English Beat, 192
Entertainment! (Gang of Four), 199
Epitaph, 279
equality, 252
Escalante, Joe, 167–68
The Eurythmics, 52
Evennett, David, xiv
"Everybody's Got Their Price. Up Yours." (The Poison Girls), 287
"Everything Now" (Arcade Fire), 183, 316
Ewen, Stuart, 273
Exit Through the Gift Shop (film), 137

345

INDEX

experimentation, 24–25, 31–32
EZLN (Ejército Zapatista de Liberación Nacional), 87

Factory Records, 54
Fairey, Shepard, 137–38
Fancher, Lisa, 15–16, 27–29, 227, 245–47, 267–68
"Fascist Groove Thang" (Heaven 17), 128
fashion designers, xiv, 295
Fat Mike, 11–14, 148
Fat Wreck Chords, 11–12
FBI, 75–76, 126
feminism, 239–40, 242
Field, Fern, 285
Fifteen, 9, 14–15
"The Fight of Our Lives" (Anti-Flag), 119, 120–21
filmmaking, 30, 67
Fire Party, 116
The First Rule of Punk (Perez), xii
Firth, Scott, *194*
Fish, Rob, 143, 325
Fisk, Matt, 166
Flipper, 97
Flores, Erwin, 85
Flouride, Klaus, 12–13, 191–92, 204, 218–19, 304
Food Not Bombs, xiii, 13–15, 35
"Food Not Bombs" (Fifteen), 14–15
food security, 80
Foucault, Michel, 200
Fowley, Kim, 203, 227–28, 245–46
Fox, Hardy, 286
Franti, Michael, 14
The Frantic Elevators, 54
Frantz, Chris, 227, 245, 284, 300
Freaks (film), 78
freedom, 23, 40, 46
Freeman, Chris, 30, 98, 100, *101*, 102–5
free press, 13

Freire, Paulo, 124
Frontier Records, 28–29
"Fuck Donald Trump" (YG), 181
Fugazi: live shows, xiii, 14, 117–18, 248; Punk Percussion Protest, 148; Strummer on, 124
Fujiwara, Hide,' 129, 202
Full Communism (The Downtown Boys), 318
Fuller, Buckminster, 327

G-7 Welcoming Committee Records, 216–17
Gabriel, Peter, 43
Gang of Four: "5.45," 134–35; *Complicit*, 181–83; "In the Ditch," 127; "Do as I Say," 148; *Entertainment!* 199; "I Love a Man in a Uniform," 130, 276; "Naturals Not in It," 278
Garcia, Camille Rose, 7, 197, 215
Garrett, Peter, 9
gay issues: ACT UP (Aids Coalition to Unleash Power), 96, 106; AIDS crisis, 96–98; Freeman on, 102–4; humor and, 98; identity and, 97, 104–5, 289; "I Love a Man in a Uniform," 276; military service, 245; politics and, 100, 108–9; sexuality, 107–8
G_d's Pee AT STATE'S END (Godspeed You Black Emperor), 328
The Gears, 25–26
Geldof, Bob, 8–9
gender balance, 243
Genesis, 52
German Democratic Republic (GDR), 53, 55
The Germs, 73
Gibson, William, 25
Gill, Andy: "5.45," 135; on the commodification of punk, 276–78; *Complicit*, 181–83; death of, xii; on

INDEX

feminism, 242–43; on history, 317; on McLaren, 300; on situationism, 199
Ginoli, Jon, 95–96, 99–101, *101*, 104–7
The Girl Who Kicked the Hornet's Nest (film), xii
The Gits, 30, 252–53
glam rock, 97
Global Parasites, 322
global warming, 82, 163
Glover, Donald, 328
Godsmack, 168
Godspeed You Black Emperor, 328
The Go-Go's, 245–46, 288
Goldman, Emma, 123
Gonzales, Michelle Cruz, 240, 249–50, 283
Good Charlotte, 112
Good Riddance, 13–14
Goodstein, Scott, 11–12
Gore, Tipper, 5
Grace, Laura Jane, 325, 328, *329*
Graffin, Greg: on the commodification of punk, 279–80; on the future, 190–91; *Population Wars*, 140; *Punk Paradox*, xi; on success, 211; on war, 143–44
graffiti, xiv
Great Replacement theory, 94
Green Day: activism of, 184; *American Idiot*, xii, 4, 184; musical play, xii; success of, 30, 102–3, 274
Greenwald, Robert, 12
Gregory, Glenn, 31, 128
Grimace Records, xiii, 2
Grisham, Jack, 10–11, 16–17, 140–41, 207, 214
Grohl, Dave, 115, 264
Ground Zero, 154
grunge bands, 29–30
Guantanamo School of Medicine, 138, 175–78
Guardian newspaper, 293
Gulf War, 147–51

The Gun Club, 66, 289
gun violence, 9

Hader, Bill, 264
Hallelujah the Hills, 180
Halluci Nation, 328
Hampton, Fred, xii
Hanna, Kathleen, 248
Hannah, Chris: on participatory economics, 216–17; on privilege, 228; on self-reliance, 268; on self-transformation, 153–54, 255–56; on violence, 138
harmony, 204–5
Harron, Mary, 32
Harvey, Mick, 66
Haw, Brian, 155
Headon, Topper, 7
Heaven 17, 128
Hedges, Chris, 138
Helmet, 109
Hendrix, Jimi, 129–30, 227
Hern, Matt, 33
The High Desert: Black. Punk. Nowhere (Spooner), xi
hippie movement, 281–82
history, 6, 317
"Holiday in Cambodia" (Dead Kennedys), 1, 274–75
Holstrom, John, 32
Home Alive, 252
Horowitz, Irving, 206
Hosler, Mark, 30–31, 211–12
Houston, Penelope, 97, 193, 228, 305
H. R., 229, *231*
Hucknall, Mick, 54
humor, 98–100, 264–66, 281
Hüsker Dü, 29
Hussein, Saddam, 131–32
Hype (film), 30
Hyundai, 284

INDEX

identity, 203
"I Don't Like Mondays" (The Boomtown Rats), 8–9
"If the Nuremberg Laws Were Applied" (Chomsky), 181
Ignorant, Steve, 195–96, 287, 289, 308–9, 319–20
"I Love a Man in a Uniform" (Gang of Four), 130, 276
The Independents, 70
Ingraham, Greg, 101
Interior, Lux, xii
"In the Ditch" (Gang of Four), 127
Iran, 45–47
Iraq Veterans Against the War, 168
Iraq war, 117–18, 157–58
I.R.S. Records, 131–32, 283
ISIS, 163
Islam, 47, 231–32
Israel, 47–49
Italian anarchists, 191–92

J, David, 268
Jaguar commercials, 282–83
Jarboe, 31–32
Jarecke, Kenneth, *149*, 150–51
jazz, 226
Jello Biafra & The Guantanamo School of Medicine, 175–78
Jesus Was Gay (Rhythm Activism), 109
JFA, 176, 304
Jones, Mick, 6, 92
Jones, Preston, 141
journalism, 4
Joy Division, 54
Just Another War (Cervenka), *149*, 150–51
justice, 153–54

Kanaan, Ramsey: on changing the world, 142; on the DIY movement, 23; on politics, 198, 320–21; on punk as a revolutionary movement, 263, 313–14; on success, 214–15; on the threat of nuclear war, 129
Kaufman, Denise, 251
Kaye, Lenny, 204, 228, 290, 312–13
Keithley, Joey "Shithead," 9–10
Kennedy, Robert, xii
"The Kids Are Alt-Right" (Bad Religion), 184, 316
Killing Joke, 316
King, Jon, *220*; on action, 257–58; on the business of war, 137; on capitalism, 219, 221; on the commodification of punk, 276–77; on Hendrix, 130; on military service, 162; on protesting, 236; on situationism, 199–200; on the threat of nuclear war, 127
King, Martin Luther, Jr., xii, 124
Kirkwood, Cris, 267
KISS, 105
Knight, Michael Muhammad, 46–47, 231–32
Kobach, Kris, 178
The Kominas, 46
Koski, Darius, 243
Kristal, Hilly, 26
Kropotkin, Peter, 82, 197
KROQ, 21, 203
Kuhn, Gabriel, 24, 202–3
Kutcher, Ashton, 264
Kuti, Femi, 328

L7, 109
Laibach, 44, 165–67
Lange, Fredrik, 56
Langford, Jon, 213–14, 234–35, 241, 280, 319
Lasn, Kalle, 21
Las Vegas Punk Rock Museum, xii
Lee, Stan, 98, 195, 264
Leftöver Crack, 265

INDEX

Lenin, 317
Lennon, John, 144
Lester, David, 193
"Let's All Make a Bomb" (Heaven 17), 128
Letters that Changed the World, 237–38
Letts, Don, 236
Levine, Noah, 228
Levi's, 274–75
LGBTQ+ issues: ACT UP (Aids Coalition to Unleash Power), 96, 106; AIDS crisis, 96–98; Freeman on, 102–4; humor and, 98; identity and, 97, 104–5, 289; "I Love a Man in a Uniform," 276; military service, 245; politics and, 100, 108–9; sexuality, 107–8
Liberation Day (film), 44
Lindberg, Jim, 143, 203–4, 328–30
Lisher, Greg, 25–26
Live Aid Concerts, 8–9
Logan, Brad, 12, 265, 291, 319
London Calling (The Clash), 8, 128
Los Illegals, 89
Los Seicos, 85, 88
Louis Vuitton, 296
Lucas, Dick, *258*; on anarchism, 201–2; on Burn Punk London, 300; on the business of war, 137; on the commodification of punk, 278; on freedom, 154–55; on personal transformation, 258–59; on political bands, 322–23; on religion, 139; on the threat of nuclear war, 127
Lunch, Lydia, *244*; on the business of war, 135–36; on conformity, 288–89; on feminism, 245; on the power of words, 5; on violence, 143
Lycett, Kevin, 214
Lydon, John, *194*; on anarchism, 193–95; anarchism and, 93; *Anger Is an Energy*, 179; on the business of war, 136; on conformity, 289; on corporations, 281–82; Country Life Butter advert, 280–81; on equality, 252; graffiti, xiv; on politics, 7, 185–86, 319; on the power of words, 4–5; Powers on, 186–87; on punk as a revolutionary movement, 268; *Rotten: No Irish, No Blacks, No Dogs*, 179; support of Pussy Riot, 44, 251; on surveillance, 179; on technology, 179–80; on women in music, 241; "World Destruction," 126

MacDonald, Pat, 132–33, 183, 282
MacKaye, Ian, *117*; on the 9/11 attacks, 152; on goals, 257; on the Iraq war, 157; Punk Percussion Protest, 117, 148; Rock Against Racism (RAR), 113; on straight edge, 260
M.A.D. (Mutually Assured Destruction), 127
major labels. *See* record labels:
Malcolm X, xii–xiii, xiii
Manzarek, Ray, 121–22, 306
March for Women's Lives, 12
Marcus, Sara, 32–33, 247–48, 267, 286
Marić, Goran "Max," 45
Marines, 171–74
The Masque, 196
mass shootings, 9
McCalla, Leyla, 328
McCartney, Paul, 43, 77
McDermott, Jim, 286
McDonald's, 296
McHenry, Keith, 13–15, 35
McLaren, Malcolm, xiv, 295, 300
McNeil, Legs, 32
MDC, 115, 185
media consolidation, 162
Media Zona, 41
Meese, Edwin, III, 115
The Mekons, 280

INDEX

Melnick, Monte, 172–73
The Melvins, 176
Mexico-USA border wall, 86, 89, 183, 185, 318
MFS, 65
MIA, 181
Midnight Oil, 9
militaryfreezone.org, 159
military-industrial complex, 135
military service, 159–60, 245, 276
"A Million Miles Away" (The Plimsouls), 19–21
The Minutemen, 272
Mizrahi, Sylvain, xii
Moore, Alan, 268
Moore, Thurston, 3, 243, 286, 307, 325
More Fun in the New World (Doe), 171
Morello, Tom: activism of, 91, 162–63, 271; Anti-Flag and, 160; "Axis of Justice" project, 148; career of, 326–27; Occupy movements and, xiii, 2
Moris, Stella, xiv
Morris, Keith, 310, 324
Morrissey, 93, 272
Moss, Neil, 54
MTV News, 2, 69
Mullen, Brendan, 196
murals, 190
Murray, Charles Shaar, 272
The Mutants, 97
Mutual Aid: A Factor in Evolution (Kropotkin), 82
Mutual Aid Disaster Relief, 2
Mutually Assured Destruction (M.A.D.), 127
Myanmar, 49
My Buddha Is Punk (film), 70–71

Namenlos, 65–66
Napolitano, Johnette, 240, 261
National Front, 236–37

"Naturals Not in It" (Gang of Four), 278
Navajo people, 69–79
Nawrocki, Norman, 34, 109, 142–43, 206
"Nazi Trumps Fuck Off" (Jello Biafra and the Guantanamo School of Medicine), 176–77
Ness, Mike, 30, 261, 309
Neue Slowenische Kunst (NSK), 44
Never Mind the Bullocks—Here's the Sex Pistols (The Sex Pistols), 293
"A New Burma" exhibition, xiii
Newsweek Magazine, 159
New World Order: War #1. (Bad Religion and Chomsky), 148
New York Times, xiv
Nick Cave and The Bad Seeds, 66
Nigh, Adam, 202, 260–61
nihilism, 191
Nike commercials, 272, 274, 279, 280
Nirvana, 29–30, 109
Niter, Mike, 127
Nixon, Richard, 9, 126
No Child Left Behind Act (2001), 159–60
"No Future" meme, 21, 45–46, 296
NOFX, 148
noise protests, 116
nonviolence, 140
"Nothing Rhymes with Orange" (Build Them to Break), 181
No WTO Combo, 2
nuclear war, 126–27
Numan, Gary, 31
The Nuns, 97

Obama, Barack, 12–13, 137–38
Occupants (Rollins), 171
Occupy movements, xiii, xv, 2, 122
The Offs, 97
The Offspring, 28
Oingo Boingo, 217

INDEX

O'Kane, Kerri, 30, 252–53
One Nation Under (Blackfire), 78–79
"Only a Lad" (Oingo Boingo), 217
opportunity, 211–12
O'Rourke, Beto, 10
Ostpunk!—Too Much Future (film), 53, 70
Ostroff, Nadya, 241
Ott, Jeff, 13–15
The Outnumbered, 99

Pakistan, 47
Palast, Greg, 178
Palmer, Amanda, 180
pandemic, xiii, 2, 80–81, 120–21
Pansy Division, 95–107, *101*
Pansy Division: Life in a Gay Punk Rock Band (film), 102
Parecon (participatory economics) model, 216–17
Parents Music Resource Center (PMRC), 5, 266
patriarchy, 243
P.E.A.C.E. compilation album, 2
Pearl Jam, 109
Peel, John, 55
Peligro, D. H., xii, 108, 229
Peltier, Leonard, 75
Pence, Mike, 178
Perez, Celia C., xii
Persepolis (Satrapi), xii
personal transformation, 255–59
Picciolini, Christian, 235
Pickering, Amy, 116
Pierce, Jeffrey Lee, 229
Pink Floyd, 103
Pinkus, J. D., 287, 307
Piper, Adrian, 91
Planlos, 53, 58–59
Platt, Chuck, 213
The Plimsouls, 19–21
The Plugz, 88

PMRC (Parents Music Resource Center), 5, 266
poetry, 4
The Poison Girls, 287
Poison Idea, 109
political responsibility, 4
politics: The Clash and, 6–8, 100; Pansy Division and, 100; personal, 100, 266–69. *See also* activism
Pop, Iggy, 73
The Pop Group, 3
Population Wars (Graffin), 140
pornography, 5
Positive Force DC, xiii, 3, 111–24, 148
Positive Force: More Than a Witness: 30 Years of Punk Politics in Action (film), 112
Powell, Enoch, 236–37
Powers, Kid Congo: on Berlin, 66–67; Chicano heritage of, 229–30; on conformity, 289–90; on Copeland, 133; on identity, 97–98; on Lydon, 186–87; *Some New Kind of Kick*, xi
Pray, Doug, 30
Prerokbe Ognja (*Predictions of Fire*) (film), 44
"The Price of Oil" (Bragg), 148
"The Prisoner" (television show), 180
prisons, 16–17, 39
privacy, 179
privatization, 302
privilege, 226–27
Propagandhi, 109, 228
Prophets of Rage, 176, 326–27
protests: Arab Spring, xv; "Battle of Seattle," xiii, 2; Burn Punk London, xv, 293–302, *297*; current state of, 325; importance of, 154–55; Occupy movements, xiii, xv, 2, 122; punk percussion protests, *114*, 115–18, 148; Rock Against Racism (RAR), 113, 236–37, *311*; Rock Against

351

INDEX

Reagan, 113–15, 133, 307; Vietnam War, 9
Pundik, Jordan, 5–6
"Punk for Ukraine" compilations, xiii
Punk in Africa (film), 70
"Punk in Translation" podcast series, 85
Punk London, 293–302
Punk Magazine, 32
punk paradox, 271–72
Punk Paradox (Graffin), xi
punk percussion protests, *114*, 115–18, 148
"Punk Prayer" (Pussy Riot), 38, 42–44
Punk Scholars Network, xii
Punk Science: Inside the Mind of God (Samanta-Laughton), xii
Punk Voter, 11–14
Pursey, Jimmie, 234
Pussy Riot, xiii, 38–44, *38*, 251, 318
Putin, Vladimir, 188

racism, 224–38
"Radio Glasnost," 53
Rage Against the Machine, 91
"RAGE" (Pussy Riot), 318
Ramone, C. J.: on the 9/11 attacks, 154; antipolitics speech, 269; Blackfire and, 70, 76–78; military service of, 171–74; on politics, 7; on the threat of nuclear war, 129; on war, 139
Ramone, Joey, xii, 69–70, 77, 78
The Ramones: "Do You Remember Rock and Roll Radio?" 278–79; history of, 76–78, 88; humor and, 98; influence of, 97, 103–4; members of, 171–74; Sex Pistols and, 79
Rankin, Russ, 13–14, 205, 212–13, 228
Ray, Amy, 33–34, 206, 253
Reagan, Ronald, 96, 112, 126
Rebel Riot, xiii, 2, 49
Rebel Songs (Rovics), 328
Reclaim the Night movement, 241

record labels: Alternative Tentacles Records, 2, 105–6, 275–76; Bomp Records, 21; capitalism and, 213–14; Cooked Tandem, 21; Daemon Records, 34; Dischord Records, 116, 124; DIY movement and, 19–20, 29; Drag City Records, 264; EMI, 135, 277, 300; Epitaph, 279; Factory Records, 54; Fat Wreck Chords, 11–12; Frontier Records, 28–29; G-7 Welcoming Committee Records, 216–17; Grimace Records, xiii, 2; I.R.S. Records, 131–32, 283; MFS, 65; R Radical Records, 2; Virgin Records, 293, 295
Redondo, Don, 187, 303–4
Reed, Lou, xii
Reed, Tait, 23
Reeder, Mark: on border walls, 185; on Burn Punk London, 300; East Berlin concerts, 54–65, 66, 89; on punk as a revolutionary movement, 309
refugees, 40
reggae, 3, 8, 26–27, 227, 234–36
religion, 57, 61, 231–32
Relocation Act (1974), 72
The Residents, 286
Revenge of the Mekons (film), 214
"Revolution" (Pussy Riot), 41–42
Reyes, Ron, 243–45
RFID chips, 5
Rhodes, Bernie, 308
Rhythm Activism, 109, 142
Richman, Jonathan, 30, 305
Rimbaud, Penny, 129, 144–45, 183, 196, 306
Rimmer, Dave, 56
Riordan, Rick, xii
riot grrrls, 32–33, 247–48, 249–50
"Rise" (PiL), 179
Ritter, Scott, 12
Roberts, Eric, 17

INDEX

Robinson, Randall, 116
Rock Against Bush, 12, 148, 160
Rock Against Racism (RAR), 113, 236–37, *311*
Rock Against Reagan, 113–15, 133, 307
Rock the Reservation (Hoodíítsa') concert, 69–70
Rollins, Henry, 91, 148, 167–71, *170*
Romanoff, Yishai, 272
Rotten, Johnny. *See* Lydon, John; *Rotten: No Irish, No Blacks, No Dogs* (Lydon), 179
Rovics, David, 328
Rowe, Martin, 220
R Radical Records, 2
"Rumble" (Wray), 129
Rumsfeld, Donald, 159
The Runaways, 245–47
Runaway Train (film), 17
Russia, 38–44, 187–88

Samanta-Laughton, Manjir, xii
Sanders, Bernie, 312
Sandinista (The Clash), 6–7
Sane, Justin, 148, 159–61, 211, 221, 285–86
Satrapi, Marjane, xii, 45–47, 215, 257, 285
Saturday Night Live, 264
Saunders, Red, 26–27, 234, 236–37, 310
Savage, John, 289
Sayles, John, 283–84
Schamal, Mita, 65–66, 243, 314
Schwenkow, Peter, 52
science fiction, 25
The Screamers, 97
self-harm, 73
self-reliance, 268
self-transformation, 255–59
sexism, 242
Sex Pistols: "Anarchy in the UK," 4–5, *273*; Burn Punk London, 293–302, *297*; history of, xiv; *Never Mind the Bullocks—Here's the Sex Pistols*, 293; The Ramones and, 79; success of, 300; Virgin Records and, 295
sexuality, 107–8
Sham 69, 234
Shea, Christopher D., xiv
"She Is Beyond Good and Evil" (The Pop Group), 3
Shelter Island Studio, 79
"Shock and Awe My Ass" tour, 148
Sid Vicious doll, *197*
Sihasin, 70, 284–85
Silence Is a Weapon (Blackfire), 70
Sit Down and Shut Up (Warner), 158
situationism, 199–200
ska, 8
The Slits, 240–41
smallpox, 80
"Smells Like Teen Spirit" (Nirvana), 123
Smith, Bruce, *194*
Smith, Mark E., xii
Smith, Patti, 2, 44, 97–98, 105
Smith, Wadada Leo, 327
The Smiths, 93
SMZB, 50
Snyder, Tom, 6
SO36, 52, 54
social change, 258–59
Social Distortion, 6
socialism, 218–19, 312
Solar Punk, 327
"Somebody's Looking at You" (The Boomtown Rats), 8–9
Some New Kind of Kick (Powers), xi
Something Better Change (film), 9
Soto, Steve, 257
sound system movement, 26–27
Soupstock concert, 14
The Specials, 184, 328
Spheeris, Penelope, 21
Spight, Ralph, 176

INDEX

spiritual journeys, 3
Spitboy, 249
Spooner, James, xi, 224–27
Springsteen, Bruce, 55, 169
Steele, Micki, 246
Sting, 217–18, 282–83
Stockberger, John, 259–60
Stop the Hate (Kuti), 328
straight edge, 259–61
Strom, Moana, 258
Strummer, Joe: on the DIY movement, 23; Iraq war and, 158, 271; on punk, 124; on success, 7; Wakeling on, 233
Styrene, Poly, xii
Subhumans, xi, *321*
suffering, 262–63
surveillance: Blackfire and, 75; in China, 50; drones, 137–38; Lunch on, 5; Lydon on, 179; religion and, 232
symptoms of want, 212–13

TÃ¡ala Hooghan Infoshop, 81
Talen, Reverend Billy, 211
Talking Heads, 134
Taqwacore, 232
The Taqwacores (Knight), 46
Tartar Control, 264
Taylor, Joseph Ojo, 287
Team America, 165–66, 168–69
technology, 179–80
Temple, Julian, 158
terrorism, 152–57
theme songs, xii
Thetic, Pat, 159
"They've Got a Bomb" (Crass), 128
"This Is America" (Childish Gambino), 328
Thomas, David, 261–63
Thompson, Jack, 5
Throwing Stuff, 2
Thu Win, Kyaw, *22*; activism of, xiii, 14–15, 49; on the DIY movement, 23

Tijuana No! 82–94
Time Zone, 126
Tolokonnikova, Nadya, 41
Tolstoy, Leo, 197
torture, 91
TransAfrica, 116
Trump, Donald, 40, 93, 176, 181, 184–85
Trump, Ivanka, 181–82
TSOL, 28–29
Tubeway Army, 31
TV cartoons, xii

Uncovered (film), 12
Underground Action Alliance, 160
The Unsustainable Sessions (Benally), 81
Up, Ari, xii, 235, 241
uranium mines, 80
Ure, Midge, 8–9
Useless ID, 47–49, *48*
USO tours, 167–71, 174
utopia, 201

The Vandals, 91, 165–67
Vanderpol, Rikki, 239–40
Vedder, Eddie, 16
Vega, Arturo, 88, 92
vegetarianism, 258–59
Velvet Underground, 25
Vietnam War, 9, 130
vinyl, 28
violence: causes of, 5; Chinese government and, 50; justice and, 153–54; vs. nonviolence, 140–41; self-harm, 73
Virgin Records, 293, 295
"The Virus" (Halluci Nation), 328
"Viva Presidente Trump!" (Brujeria), 181
Voight, Jon, 17
voting, 9–14, 160, 178

INDEX

Wakeling, Dave: on capitalism, 221; on identity, 109–10; on politics, 192; on self-transformation, 256; on violence, 139; on the working class, 233–35
"A Wall" (The Downtown Boys), 183
Walsh, Ryan, 180–81
War Is a Force that Gives Us Meaning (Hedges), 138
Warner, Brad, 19, 158, 195, 267
Warped Tour, 12
Watts, Alan, xv
weapons of mass destruction, 156
We Are Family Senior Outreach Network, 112, 120–21
We Come in Peace (D.O.A.), 2
Weller, Paul, 233–34
Wenders, Wim, 66–67
"We Occupy" (D.O.A), 2
West Memphis Three Support Fund, 16
Westwood, Vivienne, xiv, 295
"What Would Jello Do?" 177
"Where's the Revolution" (Depeche Mode), 183, 316
"Where Were You?" (The Mekons), 280
"White Man in Hammersmith Palais" (The Clash), 8
"White Riot" (The Clash), 234–35
white supremacism, 224–38
Wild, Chuck, 96–97
Wilde, Oscar, 302
Williamson, James, 207, 286–87, 308

Wilson, Thom, 28–29
Wilson, Trevor, 61
Wings of Desire (film), 66
Wintour, Anna, 301
The Wisdom of Insecurity (Watts), xv
Wise, Dave and Stewart, 272
working class, 233–34
"World Destruction" (Time Zone), 126
Wray, Link, 129
WTO protests, 119–20
Wu Wei, 50, 256–57

X, 97, 290
Xbox, 278

Yankovic, Weird Al, 264
YG, 181
Yippie movement, 113
Yohannan, Tim, 218
Young Center for Immigrant Children's Rights, 90

Zahra, Ehad, 46
Zapata, Mia, 252–53
Zapatista Liberation Army, 87
Zappa, Frank, 10
Zero Defects, 195
zines, 32–33
Zinn, Howard, 160
zombies, 212
Zona Prava, 41

ABOUT THE AUTHOR

JOHN MALKIN is a musician, activist, filmmaker, photographer, and radio/print journalist. His journalism focuses on social and personal liberation, music, and creating cultures free from authoritarian systems like police, prisons, and war. His previous books are *Sounds of Freedom: Musicians on Social Change & Spirituality* (Parallax Press, 2005) and *The Only Alternative: Christian Nonviolent Peacemakers in America* (Wipf & Stock, 2008, co-authored with Alan Nelson). His interviews/writings have been published widely, including in *Punk Planet, Z Magazine, In These Times, Ode, Spirituality & Health, Shambhala Sun, Tricycle, The Sun, The Santa Cruz Sentinel, The Monterey Herald, The San Jose Mercury, Film International,* and *Sojourners*. He produced and hosted a weekly interview-based radio program on Free Radio Santa Cruz for twenty years called *The Great Leap Forward* (1997–2017). His current radio program—*Transformation Highway*—is broadcast on Thursdays at noon PST on KZSC 88.1 FM / kzsc.org. He has produced six albums of original music and has performed percussion and piano for thirty years. He lives in Santa Cruz, California, with his wife and son.

www.ingramcontent.com/pod-product-compliance
Ingram Content Group UK Ltd.
Pitfield, Milton Keynes, MK11 3LW, UK
UKHW022129220326
469203UK00008B/127